JOHAN & AUGUSTA ZIRPEL

Folgten Ihren Träumen

(Followed Their Dreams)

By

Mona C. Zirpel

I am not responsible for any missing names in families
which chose to not submit any information or updates.

AuthorHouse™ LLC
1663 Liberty Drive
Bloomington, IN 47403
www.authorhouse.com
Phone: 1-800-839-8640

Published by AuthorHouse   09/22/2014

ISBN: 978-1-4969-3688-2 (sc)
ISBN: 978-1-4969-3687-5 (e)

Library of Congress Control Number: 2014916465

Preface

I started my research into my husband's great grandfather, Johan Zirpel back in 1999 or 2000. I would like to dedicate the printing of this family history to Erwin Karl Zirpel, who graciously and eagerly assisted me with the use of his paper records, which he had been keeping for a number of years. Erwin encouraged me to continue the research, put it into a book and most of all not to quit. At some point before Erwin died I had made a promise to him to finish it.

Therefore I have worked a number of years expanding on his information. I have researched backwards to locate as many documents as I could on family members. Documents such as land records, ship manifests, as well as census images to validate and extend the list of names given to me by Erwin. I have been researching and gathering as much information on every branch of the family to give a broader picture in words of their lives.

I would like to acknowledge a thankful appreciation to everyone of the family members who were generous enough to give of their time assisting me with a large variety of updates and correction to the family records. Also anyone who generously share copies of their old family photos for the book.

I do apologize if there are any incorrect spelling of names or places. There were some differences among several types of documents used. If there are any mistakes it was not intentional. A large amount of the information was merely verbally passed along several generation with any mean of validating it.

I am not responsible for any missing family names in some generations in several branches. There were several families which chose not to submit any information or updates.

Mona C. Zirpel

TABLE OF CONTENTS

CHAPTER FIVE

CHAPTER SIX

CHAPTER SEVEN

CHAPTER TEN

CHAPTER ELEVEN

CHAPTER 1

History of The ZIRPEL Surname

"Zirpel" a distinguished surname has been traced back to the province of Brandenburg, which we now identify as the birthplace of our modern Germany. Historically it would have been known as Brandenburg-Prussia.[1]

The surname "Zirpel" first appeared in the medieval time; in addition it was identified with the great and social and economic development in Prussia from the 13th century. One of the prominent families of the region were the bearers of the family surname "Zirpel".[2]

The surname "Zirpel" went through a number of changes in the spelling or pronunciation throughout its history. The addition of a phrase at the beginning or end of the root name, particularly for German names, became a quite common indicator of a person's character, place of origin, or their religious beliefs. During the middle ages, very few people could read or write, so scribes would often record a name simply by how its sounded. Therefore there a number of variations recorded of the surname "Zirpel". They are Zirpel, Zerbst, or Serbtik, to name a few.

During the period of changes, the family surname "Zirpel" moved into Prussia, which has been established as the primary origin of the family surname. The name flourished in this region for several centuries throughout the early middle ages. Later, from the mid 16th century, the family surname migrated to other parts of the continent as the family members had pursued their interests in the military, the religious setting, or in politics. With planned marriages the families gained both in social and economic status, and they were also intermarried with knights and chevaliers. Later the families achieved the distinction of being elevated to the ranks of nobility such as barons. During this period in Prussia there had been very notable members of the family with family surname of "Zirpel".[3] Areas of German settlements in America included Pennsylvania, Texas, New York, Illinois, California, Ohio, and the Dakota Territory. In Canada, German settlements centered around Ontario and the Prairies. The settlers bearing the family surname "Zirpel" traveled to the new world and established themselves along the eastern seaboard of the United States and Canada in the 18th and 19th centuries. In our modern period, members of the families with the surname "Zirpel" have achieved prominence through their contribution to society, such as those notable personalities whose Social, cultural, and professional accomplishments have been known on both sides of the Atlantic.

Research has determined the Coat of Arms below to be most ancient recording for the family surname "Zirpel".[4]

A Brief History of Prussia

Albrecht the Bear, created margrave in 1184, he battled the Slavic tribe of the Wenden as he drove the borders of his region eastwards, then naming it Brandenburg. In 1323, the members of the Bavarian house became the rulers of this area until the Emperor with the Hohenzollern house of Nuremberg replaced them. The Hohenzollerns, a great ruling dynasty, made Berlin their capital in 1486 and they introduced the Reformation in 1539.[5]

In the area that we now recognize as Prussia in the extreme earlier day was occupied by the Baltic and Slavic people. The modern day Poles in the west were descendants of the Slavic people, while the Baltic people would have been directly related to the Lithuanians in the east.

In the area that was later known as Silesia, the Pagan German tribes or the Prussians marched their way into the area. There was farm land, also plenty of iron, copper, and coal for mining. In later years factories would be created in this area.

A large portion of Silesian people were Roman Catholic with a very small segment Protestant by the nineteenth century. With a combination of German and Polish people, in the western and central regions virtually spoke a German language, while everyone in the eastern regions of Silesia or Upper Silesia spoke a Polish language.

Skilled workers and craftsmen based Prussia's strength on the government's promotion of the settlement of its agricultural and industrial regions. Prussia's liberal government made it a safe place for political and religious refugees, which included the Salzburg Protestants fleeing from the Catholic Austria and the French Huguenots and Colonists from Holland and Flanders. The greatest King was Frederick II, whose region reform of the civil service, the cultivation of the land, and encouragement of the industrial development made Prussia the unifying force behind the German empire. The Prussian army became the most feared and respected military force in Europe, a model of skill and efficiency, which at one time successfully fought the French, Austrians, and Russians all at the one time.[6]

Frederick's successors were not as skilled in the field of diplomacy and government. And following their defeat by Napoleon, Prussia was divided in half. When the Congress of Vienna in 1815 gave the rich territories of Rhineland and of Westphalia to Prussia. The recovery of Prussian strength was due to Bismarck, who triumphed over Austria and Denmark.[7]

After the Napoleonic War between 1796 and 1815, many of the German immigrants wanted freedom from all the military involvement and the political domination that were being place upon them, so they came to America.

In Prussia the people began losing many of their physical occupations to the automation in the manufacturing of goods. The congestion in the cities forced many of the Germans back into the rural areas.

Before World War I, most of the German people who left the country, they were searching for more freedoms as well as a better life.

By 1871, Germany was united under Prussia, after which Kaiser Wilhelm I was crowned Emperor of the German Empire at Versailles. After the Great War Prussia became a state of the Weimar Republic, only to be incorporated into the German Democratic Republic in 1952, already giving its lands east of Oder River to Poland.[8]

There were a substantial number of people who left the German states, because of the inheritance laws. The "Primogeniture Law" said that only the eldest son in a family could inherit the property when his father died. Women were not allowed to own or control any property in the German States. The "Entail Law" made it illegal for a son to divide any of his newly acquired property with his younger siblings after his father's death. Around the 1870's, in Prussia it was required that all able-bodied males serve in the military. It was not uncommon for the family to lose their home and property, if that male refused.

In the German States taxation had increases

substantially which placed a financial strain onto the people. As the population increased, the land was progressively more restricted, if any was available the cost was extremely high. So the younger siblings began moving to America during the decades of 1860's, 1870's and 1880's. There were many who immigrated into Minnesota as well as the Dakota Territory.

A good number of German population left the country, because the ethic cleansing after the Conference at Potsdam in 1945. When the German people left the country, they were forbidden to take any personal items, such as their passports, birth certificates, family photos, or any other family collectibles. Without a doubt many of the direct descendants lost track of their ancestor's families back in Poland, the Soviet Union and also the German States.

Johan Zirpel's parents, John & Johanna (Simonsek) Zirpel*

Johan Zirpel's parents were John Zirpel and Johanna Simonsek. It is believed that John Zirpel married Johanna Simonsek in Germany, no records of a date or location have been found. Together John and Johanna had at least 13 children according to information printed in a obituary on Thursday, February 4, 1937, in the "*The Parkston Advance*" Parkston, SD. According to the obituary, there were six sons and seven daughters. There have been no records found for the names of Johan Zirpel's siblings. There have been no records found for any locations of where Johan's parents or siblings were born or died. There is no knowledge of where any of the family members might be buried. It is believed Johan Zirpel was the only child to leave Germany.[9]

The Early Years in Prussia for Johan Zirpel*

Johan Zirpel, one of six sons of John and Johanna (Simonsek) Zirpel was born on November 2, 1858 in Steindorf, Kr. Ohlau, Schlesien, Prussia. The historical Schlesien in Prussia would have been located in our modern-day Poland.

Johan's parents, John and Joanna Zirpel at some later date took him to Minken, Germany to be baptized; and he was also later confirmed into the Lutheran faith by Rev. Winker.[10] While Johan lived in Germany he attended school, and he was able to speak both German and English according to Census German and English according to Census records located in America.

At fifteen Johan began working as a apprentice to the "Tischer Handwerk" or "Joiners trade". German to English translation (TischlerHandwerk Tischler, der; -s, - Handwerker, der Holz bes.zu Möbeln ver-, bearbeitet: der T.hobelt ein Brett; den Beruf eines Tishlers erlernen dazu Bau-, Kunst-, Mödell-, Modell- Sar-tischler Joiner;-s) or (the craftsman who works on wood part. The occupation of a joiner learn in addition construction, piece of furniture, model and coffin joiner.)

For any number of reasons only known to Johan, he made the decision and left his parents and family in Prussia and acquire his passage on the ship named Bohemia. It is not known whether Johan purchased a second class, or steerage ticket. Most individuals leaving Prussia in this time period usually could only afford a steerage ticket. Average cost of a second class ticket to across the Atlantic could cost as much as $143, while a steerage ticket average between $25 and $35 as the going rate for adults traveling from Prussia. The rates for adults traveling with their children were at half-price. It is presumed that Johan probably traveled in steerage. If so the conditions probably were not very clean, with very little heat, and overly crowded. Around April 23rd of 1882 Johan boarded the Ship and he left from Hamburg.

"Bohemia Steamship years of service was from 1881 until 1898. It had several alias names: Pompeji in 1898 and Pompei 1899. The Bohemia was originally built by A. & J. Inglis, Ltd. Glasgow, Scotland as the BENGORE HEAD for that Ulster steamship company. The dimensions were 351 feet x 41 feet with 3,441 tonnage. The ship had two masts rigged with sails and one funnel with an iron hull. It had compound engines with asingle-screw and ran about 11-12 knots. Originally it had accommodations for 100 people in First Class and addition 1,200 people in steerage.[11]

"On September 30, 1881, she was sold to the Hamburg-American Shipping Line and she was renamed the Bohemia. The Bohemia left Hamburg on her maiden voyage to New York on October 30, 1881. She started her last voyage be-

tween Hamburg and New York on April 2, 1897. In 1898, she was sold to the Sloman Line of Hamburg, and renamed POMEJI. She made three voyages from Hamburg to New York before being sold to Laurello SA, Genoa in 1900 after which it was renamed POMPEI. She was scrapped in 1905 in Spezia, Italy."[12]

According to a copy of the ship manifest for the Bohemia, Johan had left Steindorf, Prussia as a workman. On the same manifest was his future wife, Augusta Sperlich, her parents, brothers and sisters, who had all left Grob Dobern, Prussia. It is not known whether or not Johan knew Augusta prior to the voyage, but they may have gotten acquainted during their trip to America.

Johan Zirpel arrived into New York on Monday, May 8, 1882.

Castle Garden opened as an immigrant landing depot on August 3, 1855. The creation of Castle Garden, the official immigrant processing center in the nation signal a change in American immigration policy.

Johan was likely processed through Castle Garden as it was, the official immigrant processing center in New York at that time.

Johan's Journey Into The Dakota Territory*

Johan began his journey from New York down across the central part of United States over into the Dakota Territory. He may have purchased a train ticket for a portion of the way and went the remainder of the trip by horse, as there are no records showing his manner of travel.

Based upon a copy of the Naturalization Record 1st Papers, Davison County, South Dakota, Volume 229, page 187 document on May 16, 1882 in the Territory of Dakota County of Davison, in the Second Judicial District Johan personally appeared before the Clerk of District Court and made an oath that he was born in Germany on or before the year of 1858, that he had emigrated to the United States and landed in New York on or about the month of May 1882 and his intention was to become a CITIZEN OF THE UNITED STATES, and wanted to renounce forever all alliance and fidelity to any foreign Prince, Potentate, State, and particularly William, the Emperor of Germany and he would support the Constitution and Government of the

3

United States. He made this oath before AMC Metcalf.[13]

The Early Life in Berlin Township In The Dakota Territory*

The property that Johan chose to homestead on was located in what would be later organized and named Berlin Township. According to Mrs. William Zangle most of the early settlers in Berlin Township came from Silesia and Flensburg, Germany.[14] In 1880, many of those first immigrants settled into a community, then known as Plainview; which was located two miles north and one and one half miles east of the property in Johan built his shanty on. There was a great amount attention directed towards the German immigrants that were living in Berlin Township between 1882 and 1919. Around 1919 Berlin Township was renamed, known today as Washington Township. The tracking down of early documents was rather confusing until it was noted of the renaming of the Township. So many of Johan's early documents have reference to Berlin Township with later reference to Washington Township.

"Everything Teutonic had been eliminated: German books, German dishes and especially the *damned Hun language,* as was viciously referred to so often.[15] "The Council of Defense, in it, Ordinance No. 13, actually banned any German telephone conversations, as well as the use of the German language in any of the churches, schools, and any other public gathering place. Their neighbors actually spied on each other and those who were caught breaking the law had to pay a really stiff fine, which went into the Red Cross Coffers."[16]

Brief History of St. John's Lutheran Church

Along with improving his land and building his permanent home, Johan Zirpel was very much involved the beginning of the St. John's Lutheran congregation locate near Dimock and Hillside. The St. John's Lutheran Church actually began in 1880, with a group of immigrants from Silesia, Germany who had settled in the Dakota territory. Most of those settlers were very thankful that they had homes and a way of making a living in

their new country; and they expressed a need for a pastor to serve them as well as a house to worship God.

St. John's Lutheran Church was originally located in the area which was known as Plainview, which was about three miles west of its present location. "In November of 1882, Pastor Fred Holter answered the call to come and serve. The congregation was organized on the 3rd of January during the meeting. Fifteen members signed the charter: They were Gottfried Rother, Gottlieb Maskus, Wilhelm Maskus, Daniel Tschirley, Paul Tschirley, Johan Bialas, Gottlieb Weinert, Traugott Goldammer, Carl Goldammer, Gottlieb Sperlich, Gottlieb Pietz, Heinrich Baars, Johan Zirpel and Gustav Lepinsky."[17] Pastor Bishoff ordained Fred Holter at a member's home on April 15, 1883; and he continued to serve the congregation for two years. Pastor Holter took a government claim on one hundred and sixty acres of land for only $3 late in the spring of 1883. He then gave the congregation ten acres of the land for their church yard, which has remained to this day. During the summer he had a shanty built measuring twelve feet by twelve feet; where he lived with his horse during the winter. Later another addition, fourteen feet by twenty–two feet, was built to serve as a parsonage. However, it also served as the place of worship for nearly nine years; because of the drought and crop failures.

Parsonage (on the left side). The 14' x 22' addition (on the right side) served as the first place of worship for the St. John's Lutheran congregation. [1]

When the congregation outgrew the parsonage, they purchased the Methodist Church located about five miles south of Hillside for $400 in the year of 1892. Later in the fall on frozen ground the members volunteered a lot of hard work.

The congregation voted to build a new brick church in the summer of 1929. Descendants of Johan believe that he may have had some influence with this decision to build the church with brick, as he had built a two brick homes by this time.

The new brick church for St. John's Lutheran Congregation was dedicated on October 12 and 13, 1930. [2]

Marriage of Johan Zirpel and Anna Augusta Sperlich*

Anna Augusta Sperlich Zirpel [3]

Anna Augusta Sperlich, daughter of Gottlieb Johan and Susanna Sperlich, was born on April 20, 1868 in Grob Dobern, Brieg, Schlesien, Germany. She came to America with her parents in 1882.

Johan Zirpel, son of John and Johanna Zirpel and Anna Augusta Sperlich, daughter Gottlieb Johan and Susanna Sperlich, were married on June 24, 1883 in Douglas County by Pastor George A. Bishoff according to church records. It was the first marriage in the settlement for this church. Gottlieb Wenzel and Gottlieb Maskus were the witnesses. However, in both of their obituaries it said Rev. Fred. Holter married them.

Johan and Anna Augusta Zirpel had twelve children: Anna Emile, Robert Hermann, Johann Gottlieb, Bertha Auguste, Emma Katharina, Bertha Rosina, Emma Bertha, Wilhelm Otto, Gottfried Johan, Elisabeth Augusta, Edward Richard, and Bertha Rosina Zirpel between 1884 and 1904.

They had two sets of twins, one set of twins grew up and married, while the other set died as babies. Two other children also died, but seven children in all grew up, married, and had families. They all had children adding to the descendants of Johan and Ann Augusta Zirpel.

CHAPTER 2

Brief History of The Sperlich Families[18]

Anna Augusta's Parents, Gottlieb Johan Sperlich & Susanna Pietz

Gottlieb Johan Sperlich [5]

Gottlieb Johan Sperlich was born on September 26, 1836 in Groß Döbern, Kreis Brieg, Schlesien. Gottlieb married Susanna Pietz, the daughter of Gottfried and Anna Rosina (Nowak) Pietz.

Susanna was born on February 23, 1850 in Rosenhain, Ohlau, Schlesien and she died on Pietz. April 15, 1888 in Douglas County, South Dakota. There are no known pictures of Susanna Sperlich. When he lived in Schlesien, Gottlieb had been a horticulturist. So he brought a large variety of trees as well as flowers when he decided to come to America.

On Sunday, April 23, 1883, Gottlieb, and his wife, Susanna and seven of their children: Anna Augusta, Anna Louise, Anna Rosina, Karl Wilhelm, Anna Marie, Carl Julius, and Anna Pauline boarded the ship "Bohemia". After only fifteen days at sea the Gottlieb Sperlich family landed in New York, on Monday, May 8, 1882. After the processing in the port the family continued by train and arrived in Mitchell in the Dakota Territory on Saturday, May 13, 1882.

Gottlieb filed for a Homestead claim of Two Quarters of land located three miles south of Flensburg in Douglas County in the Dakota Territory. The homestead was located just east of Johan Zirpel's property in Berlin or now known as Washington Township. Around May 26, 1882, he built a small sod house 18' x 30' according to his homestead testimony of claimant papers. Along with his farming, Gottlieb also grew a large orchard. Four additional children: twins: Johanna Louise and Emma Bertha, Johann Gottlieb and Karoline Martha, were born to Gottlieb and Susanna Sperlich in the Dakota Territory.

Gottlieb became a naturalized citizen of the United States on September 20, 1887.

Unfortunately, Susanna had a runaway with a horse and buggy, during which she had been thrown from the buggy. Somehow the buggy whip pierced her in the chest, causing her sudden death on April 15, 1888, according to the story that has been told.

The Gottlieb Sperlich summer kitchen was their sod house [6]

GOTTLIEB JOHANN SPERLICH FAMILY Back Row: Karoline Martha Storm, Carl Julius Sperlich, Anna Pauline Metzger, Johanna Louise Metzger, Anna Augusta "Baer or Bär" Titze, Karl Wilhelm Sperlich, and Emma Bertha Kreth. Front row: Anna Rosina Frahm, Anna Louise Titze, Anna Augusta Zirpel, and Anna Marie Kramer. [7]

After Susanna's death, Gottlieb returned to Groß Döbern, Brieg, Schlesien for his second wife in 1889, Johanna Rosina (Baer or Bär), who had been married before. They return to the United States leaving Hamburg on March 7, 1889 and arrived in New York on March 25, 1889 on the ship "Polynesia".

Gottlieb Johan Sperlich & Johanna Rosina Baer

Johanna Rosina (Baer or Bär) was born on May 21, 1845 in Grob Döbern, Brieg, Schlesien and she died on April 8, 1937 in Douglas County, S.D. Gottlieb married Johanna on April 23, 1889 at St. John's Lutheran Church.

They had no additional children, however, it has been said that Gottlieb"adopted" her daughter, Anna Augusta Baer or Bär.

Gottlieb return to Germany when he was 68 years old for a visit. He came back to America on May 25, 1905.

Gottlieb and Johanna Rosina Sperlich, April 23, 1889 [8]

Gottlieb Johann Sperlich's Headstone, located in St. John's Lutheran Church Cemetery, in Douglas County, South Dakota [9]

Gottlieb Sperlich died on September 29, 1906, and he was buried at the St. John's Lutheran Cemetery.

Upon his death Gottlieb had left the farm to his daughter, Karoline Martha Storm, according to his will.

Anna Louise Sperlich & Gottlieb John Titze & Their Children

Anna Louise Sperlich Titze [10]

Anna Louise Sperlich, the second daughter of Gottlieb and Susanna Sperlich was born on November 17, 1869 in Groß Döbern, Kreis Brieg, Schlesien. She married Gottlieb John Titze on May 18, 1885 at the St. John's Lutheran Church located in Douglas County, South Dakota Anna Louise died on March 3, 1953 in Mt. Vernon, Davison County, South Dakota and she was buried at the St. John's Lutheran Cemetery.

Gottlieb John Titze was born on February 16, 1859 in Neuvorwerk, Schlesien. He died on January 20, 1930 in Parkston, in Hutchinson County, South Dakota and he is buried with his wife at St. John's Lutheran Cemetery.

Gottlieb John and Anna Louise Titze had thirteen children and twelve of them grew into adulthood: Paul Otto "Herman, Emma Louise, Friedrich Wilhelm "Bill", Anna Emilie, Amelia Anna, Anna Martha, Anna Bertha, Bertha Anna, Paul "Otto" Carl, John Gottlieb, Martha Minnie, Alfred "Albert", and Paul "Ehrich" Titze.

Gottlieb Titze owned one hundred and sixty acres of property located in southeast quarter of section 20 in Berlin or Washington Township in Douglas County, South Dakota.[19]

He owned an additional three hundred and twenty acres of property located in the southwest and southeast quarters of section 17 in Berlin or Washington Township in Douglas

County, South Dakota.[20]

As of January 21st in 1920, Gottlieb and Anna Louise Titze were still living on their homestead property according to Mrs. Carl Bertram, the Census Enumerator of the 1920 United States Census with seven of their twelve children: Anna, Bertha, Otto, John, Minnie, Albert and Erich.[21]

Anna Rosina Sperlich & Wilhelm H. Jurgensen, & 2nd Husband, Wilhelm Claus Emil Frahm & Their Children

Anna Rosina Sperlich Jurgensen-Frahm [11]

Anna Rosina Sperlich, the third daughter of Gottlieb and Susanna Sperlich was born on Jan. 28, 1872 in Groß Döbern, Kreis Brieg, Schlesien.

She was confirmed in the year of 1885 at the St. John's Lutheran Church.

On July 17, 1889, she married Wilhelm H. Jurgensen at the St. John's Lutheran Church in Douglas County, South Dakota.

Wilhelm H. Jurgensen was born in Schleswig -Holstein on December 22, 1854. He died on March 10, 1901 in Sioux City, in Woodbury County, Iowa. And his burial was the St. John's Lutheran Cemetery.

Wilhelm H. and Anna Rosina Jurgensen had five children before Wilhelm's death: Martha Wilhelmina, Wilhelmina Marie, Anna Catharina, Friedrich Wilhelm "William", and Johann Heinrich Jurgensen.

Wilhelm Jurgensen owned three hundred and twenty acres of property located in the southwest and southeast of quarters of section 33 in Baker Township in Davison County, South Dakota.[22]

Wilhelm H. and Anna Rosina Jurgensen lived in Davison County, South Dakota when their children were born and after the year of 1897 the family may have moved or went for a visit to Iowa where Wilhelm died.

Anna Rosina Jurgensen and her children must have moved back to South Dakota.

Later in the year after the death of her first husband, Anna Rosina Jurgensen married Wilhelm Claus Emil Frahm on August 16, 1901 at the St. John's Lutheran Church in Douglas County, South Dakota.

Wilhelm Claus Emil Frahm was born on August 16, 1866 in Borby Schleswig-Holstein, Germany. He died On February 2, 1939 in Mt. Vernon, Davison County, South Dakota and he was buried at Hillside Cemetery in Douglas County by his wife.

Wilhelm Frahm owned one hundred and sixty acres of property located in southeast quarter of section 35 of Mt. Vernon Township in Davison County, South Dakota.[22]

On the United States Census on April 20th of 1910, Wilhelm and Anna Rosina were living in Mt. Vernon in Davison County, South Dakota, according to the Census Enumerator, George W. Lawrence.[24] There were four from Anna Rosina's first marriage: Martha, Anna, Wilhelm, and Johann Jurgensen as well as four of her children with her second husband: Lillie, Erich, Ehrhart, and Charlotte Frahm on the same census report.

Anna Rosina Frahm died on September 15, 1921 in Mt. Vernon in Davison County, South Dakota and she was buried at the Hillside Cemetery.

After Anna Rosina death in 1921, Wilhelm remained in Mt. Vernon, Davison County, South Dakota on April 2, 1930, Census Enumerator, E. O. M. Ewen recorded him on the 1930 United States Census with three of his children: Erich, Charlotte, and Ulrich Frahm.[25]

Wilhelm Claus Emil and Anna Rosina Frahm had six children: Lillie Louisa Amelia, Erich Ewald, Ehrhart Wilhelm, Charlotte Susanna, Ella Hulda Pauline and Ulrich Otto "Pete" Frahm.

Karl Wilhelm Sperlich & Wilhelmina Albertine Storm, & 2nd Wife, Augusta Neugebauer & Their Children

The oldest son of Gottlieb and Susanna Sperlich, Karl Wilhelm "William" Sperlich was born on October 15, 1873 in Groß Döbern, Kreis Brieg, Schlesien.

In 1888, he was confirmed at the St. John's Lutheran Church in Douglas County, South Dakota.

He married Wilhelmina Albertine "Minnie"

Karl Wilhelm Sperlich [12]

Storm on April 12, 1898 at the St. John's Lutheran Church.

Wilhelmina Albertine Storm was born on November 8, 1877 in Dargislaff Pommern. She died on June 3, 1907 in Douglas County, South Dakota and she was in St. John's Lutheran Cemetery.

In section 35 of Berlin township in Douglas County, South Dakota, Karl Wilhelm Sperlich owned one hundred and sixty acres of property located in southeast quarter.[26]

Karl Wilhelm and Wilhelmina Albertine Sperlich had four children before Wilhelmina's death: Anna Louise, Otto Friedrich, Wilhelm Theodor and Arthur Alwin.

Karl Wilhelm Sperlich married Augusta Neugebauer on January 27, 1908, at the St. John's Lutheran Church.

Augusta Neugebauer was born on July 26, 1879, Peisterwitz Schlesien. She died on November 20, 1955 and she was buried at the St. John's Lutheran Cemetery.

Karl Wilhelm and Augusta Sperlich had seven more children: Helena Wilhelmina, Martha Wilhelmina, Gertrude Emma, Johann Gottlieb, Hilda Leona, Regina Eldora and Herbert Arnold Sperlich.

On April 16, 1910 Karl Wilhelm Sperlich and his wife, Augusta were recorded by Census Enumerator, Walter L. Koehn for the 1910 United States Census in Berlin Township in Douglas County, South Dakota with six children: Anna, Otto, Willie, Arthur and Helena.[27]

There were nine children: Anna, Otto, Willie, Arthur, Helena, Martha, Gertrude, John, and Hilda recorded with their parents, Karl Wilhelm and Augusta Sperlich on January 19, 1920 in Washington Township, Douglas County, South Dakota by

Census Enumerator, Mrs. Carl Bertram.[28]

Still living in Washington Township in Douglas County, South Dakota Census Enumerator, Mrs. Ida Bertram recorded Karl Wilhelm Sperlich and his wife, Augusta and six children: Willie, Gertrude, John, Hilda, Regina, and Herbert on April 23, 1930 on the 1930 United States Census.[29]

Karl Wilhelm Sperlich died on October 4, 1962 and he was buried with his wives.

Anna Marie Sperlich & Ernest Gottfried Hoffmann, & Their Children & 2nd Husband, Johan Kramer

Anna Marie Sperlich Hoffman-Kramer[13]

The fourth daughter of Gottlieb and Susanna Sperlich, Anna Marie Sperlich was born in Groß Döbern, Kreis Brieg, Schlesien on March 18, 1876.

She was confirmed at the St. John's Lutheran Church in Douglas County, South Dakota.

Anna Marie Sperlich married Ernest Gottfried Hoffmann on May 27, 1892 at the St. John's Lutheran Church.

Ernest Gottfried Hoffmann was born on June 26, 1852 in Prussia. Ernest Gottfried died on May 5, 1913 in Hutchinson County, South Dakota and he was buried in the St. John's Lutheran Cemetery.

Ernest Gottfried and Anna Marie Hoffmann had twelve children: Carl "Hermann", Carl "Wilhelm", Wilhelmina E., Bertha Louise, Otto Fredrich, Fred Edward "Fritz", Emil Karl, Alfred Bernhardt, Johann Gottfried "John", Martha Ann Marie, Amanda L., and Leonhard Ehrich Hoffman.

The family of Ernest and Annie Marie Hoffman lived in Douglas County, South Dakota until November of 1910, and sometime before Jan-

uary 1914 the family moved to Parkston in Liberty Township of Hutchinson County, South Dakota.

Sometime after Ernest's death, Ann Marie Hoffmann married Johann "John" Kramer on January 1, 1922 at the St. John's Lutheran Church.

Johann Kramer was born in Glückstal Russia about 1871. Johann died on June 8, 1946 in Parkston, Hutchinson County, South Dakota.

Anna Marie Kramer died on January 25, 1950 in Dimock, Hutchinson County, South Dakota. and she was buried in the St. John's Lutheran Cemetery.

Carl Julius Sperlich & Augusta Moke and their Children

Carl Julius Sperlich [14]

The second son of Gottlieb and Susanna Sperlich, Carl Julius Sperlich was born on July 31, 1877 in Groß Döbern, Kreis Brieg, Schlesien. He was confirmed in the St. John's Lutheran Church in Douglas County, South Dakota.

Carl Julius married Augusta on May 22, 1901, at the St. John's Lutheran Church. Augusta Moke was born in Gruentanna Schlesien, on June 27, 1883. Augusta Moke died on October 15, 1969 in Blue Earth, Faribault County, MN., and her burial was in St. John's Lutheran Cemetery with her husband.

Carl Julius Sperlich died on June 10, 1932 in Dimock, Hutchinson County, South Dakota, and he was at the St. John's Lutheran Cemetery.

Carl Julius and Augusta Sperlich had ten children: Karl Hermann, Ernest Louis, Bertha Elma, Alvin Julius Bernhardt, Emil Gottlieb "Mike", Karl Herbert, Elsa Susanna "Elsie", Mina Augusta, Edwin Elmer, and Norma Lorraine Sperlich.

Carl Julius Sperlich owned one hundred and sixty acres of property located in northwest quarter of section 21 in Berlin or Washington Township in Douglas County, South Dakota.[30]

On April 27, 1910, Carl Julius Sperlich and his wife, August was recorded by the Census Enumerator, Walter Koehn in Berlin Township in Douglas County, South Dakota with 5 children: Herman, Ernest, Bertha, Alvin and Emil.[31]

Carl Julius Sperlich and his wife, Augusta were recorded by the 1920 United States Census Enumerator, Floy Z. Bowers in Union Township in Davison County, South Dakota on February 17, 1920 with eight children: Herman, Ernest, Bertha, Alvin, Emil, Karl, Elsie and Minnie.[32]

J. S. Muller, the 1930 United States Census Enumerator recorded Carl Julius and Augusta Sperlich on April 24, 1930 in Cross Plains Township in Hutchinson County, South Dakota with six children: Emil, Carl, Elsie, Minnie, Edwin, and Norma.[33]

Anna Pauline Sperlich & Herman Karl "Carl" Metzger & Their Children & 2nd Husband, Reinhold Metzger

Anna Pauline Sperlich Metzger [15]

The fifth daughter of Gottlieb and Susanna Sperlich, Anna Pauline was born on April 8, 1880 in Groß Döbern, Kreis Brieg, Schlesien.

She was confirm at the St. John's Lutheran Church in Douglas County, South Dakota Anna Pauline married Herman Karl "Carl" Metzger on February 14, 1900 at John's Lutheran Church.

Herman Karl "Carl" Metzger was born on May 13, 1877 in Limburg, Germany. Herman died on April 29, 1915 in Davison County, South Dakota and he was buried in the St. John's Lutheran Cemetery.

Herman Karl and Anna Pauline had six children of eight who grew into adulthood: Hermann, Hildegard Martha, Arthur Hermann Gottlieb,

Harry Herman, Helen Pauline, Raymond Henry, Freda Emma, and Martin Otto.

Herman Metzger owned one hundred and sixty acres of property located in southeast quarter of section 28 in Baker Township in Davison County, South Dakota.[34]

Herman Metzger and his wife, Anna Pauline were recorded by the 1900 United States Census Enumerator, James C. Earl on June 16, 1900 in Baker Township in Davison County, South Dakota living with his brother, Gottlieb Metzger.[35]

Herman and Anna Pauline Metzger with their five children: Hildegard, Arthur, Harry, Helen and Raymond were living in Baker Township of Davison County, South Dakota according to the Census Enumerator, Guy W. Cook on April 28, 1910.[36]

Floy Z. Bowers, 1920 United States Census Enumerator recorded Pauline Metzger with five of children: Harry, Helen, Henry, Freda and Martin living in Baker Township of Davison County, South Dakota on March 7, 1920.[37] Pauline was listed as a widower.

After the death of Hermann, Anna Pauline married Reinhold Metzger on May 22, 1921 at the St. John's Lutheran Church. They had no additional children. Reinhold Metzger was born in Limburg, Germany on March 6, 1874. Reinhold died on December 30, 1936 in Davison County, South Dakota, and he was buried at the Metzger Cemetery in Metzgerville, Davison County, South Dakota.

Anna Pauline Metzger died on November 19, 1974 in Parkston, Hutchinson County, South Dakota, she was buried in the St. John's Lutheran Cemetery with her first husband.

Johanna Louise Sperlich & Gottlieb Johann Metzger & Their Children

Johanna Louise, the sixth daughter of Gottlieb and Susanna Sperlich, was the first daughter, to be born in Douglas County, a twin, in the Dakota Territory, on November 25, 1882. Johanna Louise was confirmed in 1897 at St. John's Lutheran Church. Johanna Louise married Gottlieb Johann Metzger on April 14, 1901 at the St. John's Lutheran Church.

Gottlieb Johann Metzger was born in Limburg Schlesien on October 13, 1875. He died on December 1, 1938 in Douglas County, S.D. and

Johanna Louise Sperlich Metzger[16]

Emma Bertha Sperlich Burmeister-Kreth [17]

and he was buried at St. John's Lutheran Cemetery.

Gottlieb Johann and Johanna Louise Metzger had eight children: Adela Louise, Martha Grace, Minnie Anna, Louise Rose, Edwin Gottlieb, Herbert Hermann, Floyd Raymond, Melvin Irvin Metzger.

In Baker Township in Davison County, South Dakota, Gottlieb Metzger owned one hundred and sixty acres of property located in northwest quarter of section 33 and also owned one hundred and sixty acres of property located in southwest quarter of section 28.[38]

Guy W. Cook, 1910 United States Census Enumerator recorded Gottlieb Metzger with his wife, Johanna Louise living in Baker Township in Davison County, South Dakota with four of their children: Della, Grace, Minnie, and Louise Rose on April 28, 1910.[39]

On April 27, 1930 Census Enumerator, E. O. M. Ewen recorded Gottlieb and Johanna Louise Metzger with five of their children: Minnie, Edwin, Herbert, Floyd, and Melvin living in the Mount Vernon Township in Davison County, South Dakota.[40]

Johanna Louise Metzger died on December 6, 1966 in Mitchell, Davison County, South Dakota and she was buried with her husband.

Emma Bertha Sperlich & Otto Burmeister & 2nd Husband, Ernest Karl Henry Kreth & Their Children

Emma Bertha, the seventh daughter of Gottlieb and Susanna Sperlich, was the second daughter, a twin to Johanna Louise, to be born in Douglas County in the Dakota Territory, on November 25, 1882. Emma Bertha was confirmed

in 1897 at St. John's Lutheran Church.

Emma Bertha Sperlich married Otto Burmeister on April 14, 1901 at the St. John's Lutheran Church in Douglas County, South Dakota.

Otto Burmeister was born on January 7, 1872 in Berlin, Marathon County, WI. He died on December 3, 1911 in Baker Township in Davison County, South Dakota.

Otto owned one hundred and sixty acres of property located in northwest quarter of section 34 in Baker Township, Davison County, South Dakota.[41]

Otto and Emma Bertha Burmeister had five children: Johann Hermann Leonardt, Alma Alvina Louise, Alvina Emma Martha, Edwin Otto Bernhardt and Ewald Wilhelm Harry.

Emma Bertha Burmeister married Ernest Karl Henry Kreth on January 22, 1913 at the St. John's Lutheran Church in Douglas County.

Ernest Karl Henry Kreth was born on January 13, 1884 in Alfeldt, Germany. He died on October 29, 1980 in Parkston, Hutchinson County, South Dakota and he was buried at the St. John's Lutheran Cemetery.

Ernest Kreth owned one hundred and fifty-nine acres of property located in north-west quarter of section 11 in Baker Township, Davison County, South Dakota.[42]

Ernest and Emma Bertha Kreth had six additional children: Erna Hildegard, Bernard Heinrich, Ernest Karl Jr., Gladys, Luvern August Norbert, and Valindy Emma.

Johann Gottlieb Sperlich

The 3rd son of Gottlieb and Susanna Sperlich, Johann Gottlieb Sperlich was the first son to be born in Douglas County in the Dakota Territory on October 4, 1884. Unfortunately, Johann

Gottlieb was the first child to die as a baby on October 4, 1884. He is buried at St. John's Lutheran Cemetery.

Karoline Martha Sperlich & Gustav Albert Julius Storm & Their Children

Karoline Martha Sperlich Storm[18]

The last daughter of Gottlieb and Susanna Sperlich, Karoline Martha Sperlich was born in Douglas County in the Dakota Territory, on June 20, 1887.

She was baptized on July 3, 1887 at the St. John's Lutheran Church and she was confirmed in 1901. Karoline died on June 30, 1961 in Parkston in Hutchison County, South Dakota and she was buried in St. John's Lutheran Cemetery.

Karoline Martha married Gustav Albert Julius Storm on October 17, 1905 at the St. John's Lutheran Church in Douglas County, South Dakota.

Karoline had received two hundred and forty acres of property after her father's death according to his will, located in the south and east quarters of section 34 in Berlin Township later known as Washington Township in Douglas County, South Dakota.[43]

Gustav Albert Julius Storm was born on December 7, 1880 in Dargislaff, Pommern. Gustav died on July 16, 1961 in Parkston in Hutchison County, South Dakota and he was buried in St. John's Lutheran Cemetery with his wife.

Gustav and Karoline Storm had eleven children: Agnes Louise, Albert Emil, Sophie Minna, Bertha Emma, Otto Herman, Erna Margareta, Gerhard Emil, Arthur H., Leonard Ehrich, Lawrence Arnold, and Doris Agnes.

On January 19, 1920, the 1920 United States Census Enumerator, Mrs. Carl Bertram recorded Gustav and Karoline Storm with seven of their children: Agnes, Albert, Sophie, Bertha, Otto,

Erna, and Gerhard as well as Karoline's mother, Rosina Sperlich living the Washington Township in Douglas County, South Dakota.[44]

Gustav and Karoline Storm were recorded by the 1930 United States Census Enumerator, Mrs. Ida Bertram on April 16, 1930 with eight children: Sophia, Bertha, Otto, Erna, Gerhard, Leonard, Lawrence, and Doris, as well as mother-in-law, Johanna Rosina Sperlich still living in Washington Township in Douglas County, South Dakota.[45]

Anna Augusta (Bär) Sperlich & Wilhelm Titze & Their Children

Anna Augusta Baer Titze [19]

The daughter of Johanna Rosina (Baer or Bär) Sperlich, Anna Augusta (Baer or Bär) Sperlich was born on June 11, 1883 in Groß Döbern, Brieg, Schlesien. Anna Augusta died on March 25, 1969 in Corsica in Douglas County, South Dakota and she was buried at the St. John's Lutheran Cemetery.

Anna Augusta (Baer or Bär) Sperlich married Wilhelm Titze on February 11, 1990 at the St. John's Lutheran Church in Douglas County, South Dakota.

Wilhelm Titze was born in January of 1872 in Schlesien, Germany. He died on March 19, 1948 in Hutchinson County, South Dakota and he was buried in the St. John Lutheran Cemetery with his wife.

Wilhelm and Anna Augusta Titze had eleven children: Bertha Hedwig, Elsie Louise, Emil William, Minna Amelia, Alma Martha, Pauline Louise, Martha Anna, Edward Alvin, Wilhelm Gustav, Leonard Oskar, and Mabel Rosina Christina.

On June 2, 1900, Wilhelm and Anna Augusta Titze were living in Lincoln Township in

13

Douglas County, South Dakota according the 1900 United States Census Enumerator, William Pfifer.[46]

The family had moved to Baker Township in Davison County, South Dakota according to the 1910 United States Census Enumerator, Guy. W. Cook on April 28, 1910. Wilhelm and Anna Augusta and four of their children: Bertha Hedwig, Elsie Louise, Emil William, and Minna Amelia were recorded.[47]

Wilhelm and Anna Augusta, were recorded in Baker Township in Davison County, South Dakota according to the 1920 United States Census Enumerator, Floy Z. Bowers on March 17, 1920 with nine of their children: Elsie Louise, Emil William, Minna Amelia, Alma Martha, Pauline Louise, Martha Anna, Edward Alvin, Wilhelm Gustav and Leonard Oskar.[48]

In Baker Township, Davison County, South Dakota the 1930 United States Census Enumerator, Frances Dahl, recorded Wilhelm and Anna Augusta with seven children: Emil William, Pauline Louise, Martha Anna, Edward Alvin, Wilhelm Gustav, Leonard Oskar and Mabel Rosina Cristina on April 5, 1930.[49]

CHAPTER 3

Johan & Anna Augusta Zirpel

Created Their New Life*

Johan Zirpel located some property in Douglas County, in accordance with Homestead Act approved on May 20th of 1862. He applied for 160 acres of land located in the South West quarter of Section 34, in Township one hundred North of Range sixty-two, West of the Fifth Principal Meridian in the originally named Berlin Township, later renamed Washington Township in Yankton Dakota Territory Land Office the application No. 8429. A land document with Certificate number 4661 stated that Johan Zirpel and his heirs were assigned forever, subject to any vested and accrued water rights for mining, agricultural, manufacturing, or other purposes.

Johan was required to build a home, drill a well and cultivate the land for a time of at least five years. During this five-year length of time Johan was required to have continuous residency on the land before receiving ownership. His neighbors to the west in Berlin Township were Ernest Bertram who had one hundred and sixty acres and to the east Karoline M. Storm who had two hundred and forty acres and Herman Bialas had property to the north of his according to the Berlin Township Map from the 1909 Atlas for Douglas County, South Dakota.

Johan and Augusta began their dreams and life together with their home they built up together on the homestead property.

Since there were no trees on the prairie of the Dakota Territory, Johan probably built a sod house as the first home for him and Augusta.

No pictures have ever been located, however, descendants have mentioned that Johan and Augusta did have a sod home.

At the Land Office Yankton Dakota Territory, as required by law Johan made a final payment of four dollars to cover the examination fee. The payment was made on August 26, 1887. Johann gave his payment to F. M. Ziebach, receiver at land office. The receipt was later filed on September 12, 1887 at 1 PM and recorded in book 3, on page 40, by Kel. Foster, the Register of Deeds.[50]

Johan later received a copy of the Land Patent Certificate Number 4661, which said that Johan Zirpel had complete ownership of the said property.[51] The document had a signature for the President, Grover Cleveland, with the signature of M. McKean, Secretary. It was recorded by Robt, W. Ross, Recorder for the General Land Office on September 22, 1888. The document was later filed in the, State of South Dakota, Douglas County by H. Henderson, Register of Deeds on November 11, 1911, at 9 AM and recorded in Book 4, on page 71 of Patent Records.[52]

Possibly in April of 1887, Johan applied for additional land under the Timber Culture Act of 1873. The application No. 4225 was for Lots numbered One and Two, and the South half of the North East Quarter of Section Four in Township Ninety-nine North of range Sixty-Two West of Fifth Principal Meridian in South Dakota, containing one hundred and Sixty-one acres and Twenty hundreds of an acre.

During the next five years, Johan and Augusta were required to plant trees on 40 acres of their land. The trees planted was based on a mistaken belief that if trees were planted on the land it would help produce rainfall. However in reality it did not, but did provide future shade and a wind block for their home and livestock.

During the next five years, Johan and Augusta were required to plant trees on 40 acres of their land. The trees planted was based on a mistaken belief that if trees were planted on the land it with produced rainfall. However in reality it did not, but did provide future shade and a wind block for their home.

After fulfilling the requirements of the Timber Culture Act, Johan received his Timber Culture Certificate No. 1071, a signature for the President, Benjamin Harrison with the signature of M. McKean, Secretary. It was recorded by D. P. Roberts, Recorder for the General Land Office on April 16, 1892 in Volume 8 on page 438.[53] The document was later filed in the, State of South Dakota, Douglas County by Leo J. Baumgartner, Register of Deeds on August 3, 1892, and recorded in Book 2, page 66 of Patent Records.[54]

Between June of 1883 and May of 1897, John and Anna Augusta Zirpel built up their home and family. Johan and Anna Augusta Zirpel had ten children. There were seven girls and three boys added the family. Unfortunately a son and a daughter died young, as well as one set of twins daughters who died shortly after their birth. This gave them six living children.

Johan and Anna Augusta Zirpel's home approximately 1897 after over 10 years of work. [19]

Robert Hermann, Anna Augusta, Anna Emilie, and Johan Zirpel taken around 1900. [20]

Birth of Anna Emilie Zirpel*

Anna Emilie Zirpel, the oldest child of Johan and Augusta Zirpel was born on Monday, October 6, 1884 in Dimock, Hutchinson County, in the Dakota Territory later known as, South Dakota.

The family had Anna Emilie baptized on Sunday, October 26, 1884, at St. John's Lutheran Church, located in Douglas County, and her sponsors were Gottlieb Pietz, Daniel Mode or Kiok, and Gottlieb Sperlich. According to church records at St. John's Lutheran Church, Anna Emilie was confirmed in 1899.

George Julius Heidner & His Family*

George Julius Heidner, the oldest son of Conrad Edward Heidner and his wife, Hannah Klehn Heidner, was born on Tuesday, March 11, 1884 in Green Valley, Shawano County, Wisconsin.

Conrad Edward and Hannah Heidner were recorded on the 1880 United States Federal Census in their home in Green Valley, Shawano County, Wisconsin. Conrad was listed as a farmer with his parents being born in Prussia.[55]

They moved their family from Wisconsin to

16

Lincoln Township, Douglas County in Douglas County sometime before January of 1889.

George Julius Heidner appeared on the 1900 United States Federal Census in Lincoln Township, Douglas County, South Dakota with his parents, Conrad and Hannah, and two brothers: Arthur Benjamin and Nelson Edward; and two sisters: Lillian Rosalie and Rosadie Georgina.[56]

Anna Emilie Zirpel & George Julius Heidner Marriage & Family*

Anna Emilie appeared on the 1900 United States Federal Census with her parents, Johan and Augusta Zirpel on June 21, 1900 in Berlin Township, now known as Washington Township, Douglas County, South Dakota. Her other siblings were Robert Hermann, Emma Bertha, Wilhelm Otto, twins: Gottfried Johann and Elisabeth Augusta, and Edward Richard. Johann was listed as a farmer. The document was recorded by Henry Ruff, Census Enumerator on June 21, 1900.[57]

Johan and Augusta Zirpel's daughter, Anna Emilie was married to George Julius Heidner, son of Conrad Edward and Hannah Heidner, on Friday, October 10, 1902 in Armour, Douglas County, South Dakota. There is no known picture of their wedding.

George and Anna Heidner were blessed with four daughters: Emma Emilie, Emilie Verla, Gertrude Louise, and Bertha Emma Heidner.

The Birth of Emma Emilie Heidner*

Emma Emilie, the first daughter of George and Anna Heidner was born on Wednesday, July 15, 1908, in Douglas County, South Dakota. Unfortunately, Emma only lived six days as she died on Tuesday, July 21, 1908. She was baptized on the day of her death at the St. Peter's Lutheran Church, near Armour in Douglas County, South Dakota. She was buried on Wednesday, July 22, 1908 in the St. Peter's Lutheran Church cemetery located in Armour.

On April 28, 1910, Anna Emilie appeared with her husband, George Julius on the 1910 United States Federal Census living in Lincoln Township of Douglas County, South Dakota.

Tombstone for Emma Emilie Heidner located at the St. Peters Lutheran Church Cemetery Near Armour, South Dakota [21]

The Birth of Emilia Verla & Gertrude Louise Heidner*

George and Anna Heidner's twin daughters: Emilie Verla and Gertrude Louise were born on Monday, May 30, 1910 in Douglas County, South Dakota.

Both Emilie Verla and Gertrude Louise were baptized on Monday, May 30, 1910 at the St. Peter's Lutheran Church near Armour in Douglas County, South Dakota. Both girls died on Wednesday, June 1, 1910 in Douglas County, South Dakota. Emilie and Gertrude were buried near their sister, Emma in the St. Peters Cemetery.

Tombstone for Emilie Verla and Gertrude Louise Heidner located at the St. Peters Lutheran Church Cemetery near Armour, South Dakota [22]

The Birth of Bertha Emma Heidner & Death of Anna Emile Heidner*

The fourth daughter of George and Anna Heidner, Bertha Emma was born on Thursday, April 26, 1912 the Douglas County, South Dakota. She was baptized on Saturday, April 28, 1912, at the St. Peter's Lutheran Church near Armour, Douglas County, South Dakota. Bertha's nickname was "Little Bertha" according to relatives.

Anna Emilie Heidner died on Saturday, June 12, 1912 in Dimock in Hutchinson County, South Dakota from complications after giving birth to Bertha. She was buried near her daughters, Emma, Emilie, and Gertrude in the St. Peters Lutheran Church Cemetery near Armour.

Tombstone for Anna Emile and George Julius Heidner located at the St. Peters Lutheran Church Cemetery near Armour, South Dakota [23]

George Julius Heidner & Hulda A. Doering Marriage *

On August 20, 1918 George J. Heidner married his second wife, Hulda A. Doering. According to the Kiecker Family Tree on Ancestry.com her parents were Ledwig Doering and Christina Hillie and her birth was in 1898 in North Dakota.

On September 12, 1918 in Douglas County, South Dakota, George Julius Heidner registered for the World War I draft. According to a copy of the draft registration document George had another wife named Hulda.[58] George was listed as a farmer on the document recorded by William Bertram.

George Julius and his wife, Hulda were recorded on the 1920 United States Federal Census by the Census Enumerator, Mrs. Carl Bertram on January 12, 1920 living in Lincoln Township in Douglas County, South Dakota. George owned his own farm. Hulda was recorded as being 22 years old and she was born in North Dakota.[59]

There are no records of Hulda's death. There have been no divorce records for Hulda and George Heidner.

George Julius Heidner & Amalia Gladys Pauline Wermeister Marriage *

Amalia Gladys Pauline was born on December 12, 1906, in Wall Lake, Sac County, Iowa. She was baptized on January 2, 1907.

According to South Dakota marriage records, George Julius Heidner married Amalia Gladys Pauline Wermeister on the 22nd of December in 1928, in Mitchell, Davison County, South Dakota by Clergyman, Alfred O. Storsick.[60]

George and his wife, Gladys and daughter Bertha appeared on the 1930 United States Federal Census on April 7, 1930 still living in Lincoln Township in Douglas County, South Dakota, according to the Census Enumerator, Mrs. Ida Bertram.[61] George was still working as a farmer.

According to the United States City Directories, George Heidner had moved to Parkston sometime after 1935 , and continued to live at 609 W. Walnut St., Parkston, South Dakota until 1967.

On April 26, 1940 according to the Census Enumerator, Lawrence Amend, for the 1940 United States Census George J. Heidner and his wife, Gladys were still living in the same house since 1935. George listed at the age of 55, while Gladys was only 33 years old. George had worked 80 hours between March 24th through March 30th, as a grain farmer. The census also said that both George and Gladys had only went up to the eight grade in school.[62]

George Heidner died on December 26, 1967. in Parkston in Hutchinson County, South Dakota at the age of 83 years. He was buried in the St. Peters Lutheran Church cemetery near Armour, Douglas County.

In his obituary, George's favorite hobby was playing the violin and he gave lessons during his younger years. His third wife, Gladys continued to live at their address in Parkston until the time of her death on September 21, 2003 at the age of 96.

Amalia Gladys Pauline Heidner was buried on September 26, 2003, also in the St. Peters Lutheran Church Cemetery by Armour in Douglas County, South Dakota.

Bertha Emma Heidner & John G. Moege Marriage *

Bertha Emma Heidner appeared on the 1920 United States Federal Census on January 3, 1920 with her grandparents, Conrad Edward and Hannah Heidner in Lincoln Township, Douglas County, South Dakota.[63]

Bertha Emma Heidner, the daughter of George Julius and Anna Emilie Heidner married her first husband, John Gottlieb Moege, the son of Gottlieb Moege and Elisabeth Grabola on November 22, 1933 in Mitchell, Davison County, South Dakota by Clergyman, Alfred O. Storsick according to South Dakota Marriage records.[64]

John Gottlieb Moege was born on February 22, 1898, in Berlin Township, Douglas County, South Dakota. He was baptized February 24, 1898, in the Immanuel Lutheran Church in Douglas County, South Dakota. He died on July 10, 1954 in Hutchinson County, South Dakota and was buried at the Immanuel Lutheran Church Cemetery in Douglas County, South Dakota.

Bertha's marriage to John ended in divorce.

Bertha Emma Moege & Raymond L. Wurm Marriage *

Bertha Emma Moege married Raymond Lewis Wurm on March 11, 1953 in Alexandria, Hanson County, South Dakota. No records are found on how the marriage ended.

Raymond Lewis Wurm was born on November 8, 1890 and Laverne, Rock County, Minnesota. He died on February 26, 1978 in Mitchell, South Dakota. No records were found for where he is buried.

Bertha Emma Wurm & Cecil E. Bainbridge Marriage *

Cecil E. Bainbridge was born on May 24, 1914 in South Dakota.

Cecil Bainbridge appeared on the 1920 United States Census on February 6, 1920 in Tobin Township, Davison County, South Dakota with his parents: Zachariah and Lydia C. Bainbridge, brothers: Edell C., Gordon L., and sisters: Josephine M., Pauline L. and Louise F. Bainbridge recorded by Census Enumerator, Michael J. Boyul.[65]

On April 16, 1930, Cecil was recorded on the 1930 United States Census still living with his parents and siblings in Tobin Township, Davison County, South Dakota according to Census enumerator, Mrs. L. Van Metre.[66]

Bertha Emma Heidner Wurm married her third husband, Cecil E. Bainbridge on November 18, 1983.

Cecil E. Bainbridge died on February 16, 1990 in Mitchell, Davison County, South Dakota at the age of 75. It is not known where he is buried.

Bertha Emma Bainbridge died on July 19, 1992 in Mitchell, Davison County, South Dakota. The location of where she is buried is unknown.

Bertha Emma & Cecil E. Bainbridge 1983-1990 [30]

CHAPTER 4

Birth of
Robert Hermann Zirpel*

On Saturday, October 23, 1886, Robert Hermann, the oldest son of Johan and Augusta Zirpel was born in Douglas County of the Dakota Territory later known as South Dakota.

He was baptized on Sunday, November 7, 1886 at the St. John's Lutheran Church in Douglas County. His sponsors or God parents were Gottlieb Pietz, Daniel Rade, Anna Titze, and Friedrick Baden according to the St. John's Lutheran Church records.

Robert Hermann Zirpel appeared with his parents, Johan and Augusta on the 1900 United States Census in Berlin Township, now known as Washington Township, Douglas County, South Dakota. The other siblings list on the census report were Anna Emilie, Emma Bertha, Wilhelm Otto, twins: Gottfried Johann and Elisabeth Augusta, Edward Richard and Bertha Rosina Zirpel. His father, Johan was listed in general farming and owning his farm. According the census report the farm had a mortgage against it. Information was recorded on June 21, 1900 by Census Enumerator, Henry Ruff.[57]

He was confirmed on March 23, 1902 at the St. John Lutheran Church in Douglas County, with his parents, Johan and Augusta and his brothers and sisters according to the St. John's Lutheran Church records.

On April 28, 1910, Robert Hermann appeared on the 1910 United States Census living single as the head of the household employed as a farmer in Lincoln Township, Douglas County, South Dakota at the age of 23.[58]

Robert Hermann Zirpel &
Bertha R. Riecke Marriage*

Robert Hermann Zirpel, the oldest son of Johan and August Zirpel married Bertha Rosina Riecke, the daughter of Peter George Riecke and Anna Catherine Shottinger Riecke, on Thursday, November 7, 1912 at the St. John's Lutheran Church in Douglas County and Pastor P. Teckenburg, performed the wedding ceremony.

Bertha wore a black wedding dress during their wedding ceremony, which for the time

Wedding photo of Robert Herman Zirpel and Bertha Rosina Riecke, November 7, 1912 [25]

period in the country was not so unusual.

A great-granddaughter, Kimberly Danner, daughter of Rodger and Janet Danner, said that Bertha Rosina Riecke's mother, Anna had passed earlier in the year on January 12, 1912 of the same year that Bertha and Robert were to be married.

According to Kimberly, it was the common practice according to her father, Rodger if there was a marriage within the year, the bride would wear black because of morning the death of their parent or family member. Kimberly didn't think that it was a religious belief, just something done out of respect for the parent.

Kimberly still has possession of her great-grandmother's wedding dress, which she had restored. She said that it is very fragile, but she still has it.

During the next seventeen years Robert Herman and Bertha Rosina Zirpel had six children: Alvina Anna Augusta, Martha Bertha, Alma Emma, Herman Walter, Anita Margaret and Violet Bernice Zirpel. Their daughters grew up and had families of their own, while their only son lived for only two years.

Bertha Rosina Riecke
& Her Family*

Bertha Rosina Riecke's great-parents were Johann Frederich Riecke and Juliana D. Jorgenson. Her great-grandfather was born on March 7,

Riecke Homestead taken the summer of 1892. There is the sod house with a team of oxen on a walking cultivator. In front of the new house with horses are Anna Catherine and Peter George Riecke, the grandparents. In front of picture seated are great-grandparents Juliana and John Frederich Riecke, standing is Bertha Rosina, seated on lap of Juliana is Margaret, standing by John Frederich are George Peter, William F. and John Fredrick Riecke.[26]

1822 on Hanover, Germany and died on May 26, 1907 at the age of 85 years. Her great-grandmother was born on March 26, 1828 in Germany and died on Feb 18, 1911. The information for the great-grandparents came from a 2nd great grandson, Maylon Ray Schuh's wife, Bonita Marie Schuh.

Bertha's parents were Peter George Riecke and Anna Catherine Shottinger. Bertha Rosina Riecke was born on May 9, 1888 in South Dakota.

Her father, Peter George was born on February 1, 1853 in Hiede, Schleswig-Holstein, Germany and he died on March 24, 1918 in Corsica, Douglas County, South Dakota.

Her mother, Anna Catherine Shottinger was born on October 7, 1853 in Schleswig Holstein, Germany and she died on January 12, 1912 in Corsica, Douglas County, South Dakota.

Peter George Riecke became a citizen of the United States by declaring a oath before, Henry Wulff, the Clerk of the County Court of Cook County, in the State of Illinois on February 7, 1883 according to Bonita Schuh.

The picture of the homestead above was located in Douglas County, South Dakota.

Peter George Riecke and his wife, Anna were recorded in the 1900 United States Census on June 9, 1900, by Census Enumerator, Henry Ruff

living in Valley Township, Douglas County, South Dakota.[69]

They had been married 18 years. Six of their seven children were also register on this census: John Fredrick age 16, William F. age 15, George Peter age 13, Bertha Rosina age 12, Margaret age 10, and Carl August age 8.

According to the census report John Fredrick and William F. Riecke were born in the state of Illinois, while the remaining Riecke children were born in South Dakota. Peter George's parents, Johann Frederich age 78 and his wife, Juliana D. age 71 were also recorded on this census.

The Peter George Riecke family was recorded living in Garfield Township in Douglas County, South Dakota on May 10, 1910 by the Census Enumerator, Bert E. Fenenga.[70] There only four of their children living with them. They were George Peter age 22, Carl August, age 19, Bertha Rosina age 21 and Margaret Riecke age 20. Peter Riecke and his wife, Anna, were both age 57. The couple had been married 27 years at the time of the census recording.

On January 7, 1920, Peter George and his wife, Anna were recorded on the 1920 United States Census by Mrs. Carl Bertram living in Lincoln Township in Douglas County, South Dakota.[71]

21

Peter George Riecke Family. Back Row: George Peter, John Fredrick, William F., Bertha Rosina Riecke. Front row: Carl August, Peter George and Anna Catherine (Shottinger) Riecke and Marget Küinke. [27]

According to family records kept by Bonita Schuh, Peter George Riecke died on March 24, 1918 and his wife, Anna died on January 12, 1912. Both were buried in Corsica, Douglas County, South Dakota.

The Birth of
Alvina Anna Augusta Zirpel*

Alvina Anna Augusta Zirpel, the oldest daughter of Robert Hermann and Bertha Rosina Zirpel was born on Sunday, September 28, 1913 in Douglas County, South Dakota. Woodrow Wilson was the President of the United States the year Alvina was born.

She was baptized in the St. John's Lutheran Church on November 19, 1913. Her sponsors or God parents were George Riecke, Emma Riecke, and Elisabeth Zirpel according to the St. John's Lutheran Church records.

Alvina Anna Augusta was confirmed on May 8, 1928 in the St. John's Lutheran Church, Douglas County, South Dakota.

The Birth of
Martha Bertha Zirpel*

The second daughter of Robert Hermann and Bertha Rosina Zirpel, Martha Bertha was born on Saturday, October 28, 1914.

She was baptized on November 23, 1914 in the St. John's Lutheran Church in Douglas Coun-

ty, South Dakota. Her sponsors or God parents were Emma Riecke, Margareta Kiemke, and Wilhelm Zirpel according to the St. John's Lutheran Church records.

Martha Bertha was confirmed on May 8, 1928 in the St. John's Lutheran Church in Douglas County, South Dakota.

The Birth of
Alma Emma Elisabeth Zirpel*

Alma Emma Elisabeth Zirpel was born on Thursday, October 8, 1920, the third daughter of Robert Hermann and Bertha Rosina Zirpel.

She was baptized on an unknown date at the St. John's Lutheran Church in Douglas County, South Dakota.

Alma Emma Elisabeth was confirmed on April 14, 1935 in the St. John Lutheran Church in Douglas County, South Dakota.

The Effects of World War I
On Robert Hermann Zirpel *

With the start of World War I in 1914, Robert Hermann had to register a draft registration card when the United States joined the side of the Triple Entente in 1917.

Woodrow Wilson, was the President of the United States and the young men were required by law to for the draft in World War I.

According to the Draft Registration Card recorded for Robert Hermann Zirpel by William Bertram in Douglas County, South Dakota on January 5, 1917 or 1918, Robert was married with 2 children and farmer for himself.[72]

He was described as being short in height with a medium built. He had blue eyes and brown hair according to a copy of the draft registration document.

The family was recorded on the 1920 United States Census on January 7, 1920 by Census Enumerator, Mrs. Carl Bertram owning their home in Lincoln Township in Douglas County, South Dakota. Robert Hermann was 33 years old and his wife, Bertha Rosina was 30 years old. On the report were two daughters: Alvina Ann Augusta 6 years old and Martha Bertha 5 years old.[73]

The Birth of Hermann Walter Zirpel*

The only son of Robert Hermann and Bertha Rosina Zirpel, Hermann Walter was born on Tuesday, April 17, 1923 in Douglas County, South Dakota.

He was baptized on May 6, 1923 at the St. John's Lutheran Church. His sponsors or God parents were Edward Zirpel, Oscar Gerlach and Margareta Kiemke according to the St. John's Lutheran Church records.

Unfortunately, Herman Walter Zirpel at the age of only 2 years died on Friday, November 13, 1925 in Davison County, South Dakota. There were no records found for the cause of his death.

Tombstone for Herman Walter Zirpel located at the St. John's Lutheran Church Cemetery in Douglas County, South Dakota[28]

He was buried on Friday, November 17, 1925 in the St. John's Lutheran Church Cemetery in Douglas County, South Dakota with his parents, Robert Hermann and Bertha Rosina as well as his sisters: Alvina Anna Augusta, Martha Bertha and Alma Zirpel as well as his grandparents, Johan and Anna Augusta Zirpel.

The Birth of Anita Margaret Zirpel*

The fifth daughter of Robert Hermann and Bertha Rosina Zirpel, Anita Margaret was born on Tuesday, March 24, 1925.

There is no record located for her baptism, but it is assumed that she was baptized at the St. John's Lutheran Church in Douglas County, South Dakota with the rest of her sisters.

Anita was confirmed on May 1, 1939 at the St. John's Lutheran Church in Douglas County, South Dakota.

Daughters of Robert Herman and Bertha Rosina Zirpel taken about 1932-1935. Back Row: Alma Emma Elisabeth and Martha Bertha. Front Row: Violet Bernice and Anita Margaret Zirpel. [29]

The Birth of Violet Bernice Zirpel*

Violet Bernice, the last daughter for Robert Hermann and Bertha Rosina Zirpel was born on Sunday, November 24, 1929 in Douglas County, South Dakota.

She was baptized at the St. John's Lutheran Church on a unknown date.

Violet Bernice was confirmed on April 18, 1943 at the St. John's Lutheran Church in Douglas County, South Dakota.

Robert & Bertha Zirpel - The Later Years*

Robert Hermann and Bertha Rosina were recorded on the 1930 United States Census by Mrs. Ida Bertram, living in Lincoln Township in Douglas County, South Dakota on April 9-10, 1930. Robert Hermann was about 43 years old working as a farmer and his wife, Bertha Rosina was about 41 years old. Their children were also recorded on the census. Alvina Anna Augusta was age 16, Martha Bertha was age 15, Alma Emma was age 9, Anita Margaret was age 5 and Violet Bernice about 4 months old.[74]

Bertha Rosina and Robert Hermann Zirpel [30]

Robert Hermann Zirpel Family taken about 1937.
Standing are Alma Emma Elisabeth, Anita Margaret, Martha Bertha, Alvina Anna Augusta Zirpel.
Sitting are Robert Hermann, Violet Bernice and Bertha Rosina Zirpel. [31]

24

Robert and Bertha Zirpel's daughters with their husbands. Standing in the Back: Raymond G. Solomon Semmler, Robert L. Danner, Raymond F. Bittiker, Donovan E. Anderson, and Herman J. Sprecher. Standing in the front: Violet B. Semmler, Anita M. Danner, Alma E. Bittiker, Martha B. Anderson, and Alvina A. A. Sprecher.[32]

On April 26, 1940, Robert Hermann and Bertha Rosina were still living in Lincoln Township in Douglas County, South Dakota according to the 1940 United State Census taken by the Census Enumerator, Lawrence Amend. Robert still averaged 70 hours a week working as grain farmer. Anita Margaret was about age 15 and Violet Bernice was about 10. Both Anita and Violet were attending school while living with their parents.[66]

After all the girls were married and had families of their own, Roberta and Bertha moved to Sioux Falls, South Dakota around 1959.

Robert Hermann Zirpel died in a Sioux Falls Hospital in Sioux Falls, Minnehaha County, South Dakota on May 22, 1965.

At the time of Robert's death, he had been living with his wife, Bertha, at 713 S. Blaine, Sioux Falls, South Dakota.

Last rites for Robert Zirpel were held on May 24 at the Grace Lutheran Church in Sioux Falls, with Rev. Kenneth J. Helgesen officiating. He was buried in Hills of Rest Memorial Park.

He was survived by his widow, Bertha and their five daughters: Alvina Winterton of Brandon, South Dakota; Martha Anderson of Sioux Falls; Alma Bittiker of Hawthorne, California; Anita Danner of Anderson, California; and Violet Semmler of Sioux Falls, South Dakota.

He was preceded in death by a son, Herman Walter Zirpel, and by two sisters.

Pallbearers were Walter Robert Zirpel, Norbert Johan Zirpel, Waldmar Gotthelf Zirpel, Peter Riecke, George Riecke, and Walter Hermann Gerlach.

According to Karel Janis Amend, daughter of Darwin Alvine Winterton and Alice Irene Olsen, she said that she was already in college before her father married Alvina. However, she said that she remember Robert as a dear sweet man who enjoyed staying out at the farm and with his family, especially his grandchildren. She said that she could picture Robert sitting in a chair out in the yard in the sun smoking his pipe.

Sometime before 1959, Bertha was in a nursing home and not able to communicate very well. She was also bed ridden as long as Karel Amend could remember after her father married Alvina.

Bertha Rosina Zirpel, the wife of Robert Hermann Zirpel died on May 17, 1968 in Sioux Falls, Minnehaha County, South Dakota.

The last rites for Bertha Rosina Zirpel were held at the Grace Lutheran Church in Sioux Falls, South Dakota with the Rev. Kenneth J. Helgesen officiating.

Her burial was in Hill of Rest Memorial Park in Sioux Falls, South Dakota by her husband, Robert Hermann Zirpel.

She was survived by five daughters: Alvina Winterton of Brandon, South Dakota; Martha Anderson of Sioux Falls, South Dakota; Alma Bittiker of Hawthorne, California; Anita Danner and Violet Semmler of Sioux Falls, South Dakota; as well as 34 grandchildren and 10 great grandchildren.

Pallbearers were Martin Riecke, Albert Riecke, Martin Wilhelm Zirpel, Elmer Gottfried Zirpel and Lawrence Bialas.

Alvina Anna A. Zirpel & Herman J. Sprecher Marriage & Family*

On December 3, 1937, Alvina Anna Augusta Zirpel, daughter of Robert Hermann and Bertha Rosina Riecke Zirpel married Herman J. Sprecher, son of Fredrich G. Sprecher and Helen Doering at the St. John's Lutheran Church in Douglas County, South Dakota. According to the marriage certificate, Rev. P. Tecklenburg performed the marriage ceremony. At the time of their marriage Herman had been a resident of Ethan in Davison County, South Dakota. Alvina was a resident of Parkston in Douglas County, South Dakota, however, Parkston is in Hutchinson County.

Herman J. Sprecher was born on July 5, 1915 in South Dakota and he was christened in Helena, Lewis and Clark County, Montana.

Herman J. Sprecher appeared with his parents, Helen and Fredrich G. Sprecher on the 1930 United States Census on April 15, 1930 in Lake Flat Township, Pennington County, South Dakota according to the Census Enumerator, Fred N. Leavis.[76]

He died on August 24, 1989 in Sioux Falls, Minnehaha County, South Dakota. Herman was buried in the Hills of Rest Memorial Park in Sioux Falls, Minnehaha County, South Dakota.

Herman J. and Alvina Anna Augusta had four children: Beverly Jean, Jerald, James Richard, and Harlan Sprecher.

The family lived at 323 N. Minnesota Ave in Sioux Falls, South Dakota between 1942 until 1948, while Herman worked as a laborer according to U.S. Directories.

Around 1950 the family moved to 416 West Bailey in Sioux Falls, South Dakota. Herman worked as a steelworker.

Their marriage ended in divorce sometime before August of 1959.

Alvina Anna A. Sprecher & Darwin Alvine Winterton Marriage & Family*

Darwin Alvine Winterton was born on November 23, 1910 in Humboldt County in Iowa. He was also christened in Humboldt County, Iowa, date is not known.

As a child, Darwin moved with his parents to a farm in Lincoln county near Shindler, South Dakota. As a young man he farmed in Minnehaha County near Sioux Falls, South Dakota.

Darwin was united in marriage to Alice Irene Olsen in Brandon, South Dakota on May 5, 1936. The couple farmed near Canova, South Dakota. In 1940 the family moved to a farm near Brandon. His first wife, Alice died on January 2, 1954.

Darwin Alvine and Alice Winterton had four children: Karel Janis, Judith Ann, Darrell Wesley, and Donna Rae Winterton.

Alvina Anna Augusta Sprecher, daughter of Robert Herman and Bertha Rosina Zirpel married Darwin Alvine Winterton, son of Gunder Winterton and Marie Lerdahl on August 21, 1959 in Luverne in Rock County, Minnesota.

Darwin and Alvina lived on the farm near Brandon for awhile. Darwin began working at The Farmer's Union Warehouse in 1965 and he later retired in 1975 after ten years of service. They moved into Sioux Falls, South Dakota.

Alvina Anna Augusta died on June 13, 1985 in Garretson, Minnehaha County, South Dakota and she was buried in the Split Rock Lutheran Cemetery, Brandon, Minnehaha County, South Dakota.

According to Karel Amend, Darwin's daughter, Darwin and Alvina enjoyed many years together. They had traveled to Sanger Fests in the United States and to Norway, Germany, and Japan visiting family. She said that her father, Darwin was held in high esteem by Alvina's children, and Alvina was also well regarded by Darwin's children. At the time they were married only Beverly and Karel were not living at home. Of the remaining six children, five were teenagers. Despite the challenges this situation may have presented, the marriage flourished until Alzheimer's and ill health made some difficulties. Their legacy continues in the friendly relationships enjoyed by all their children.

Darwin had been a member of the East Side Lutheran Church, the Minnehaha Mandskor, Norse Glee Club & Son of Norway. He loved his Lord, family, friends, farm, Norwegian heritage and music, especially singing. He also enjoyed dancing, bowling, and playing horseshoes.

Darwin A. Winterton of 3901 S. Marion Road, Sioux Falls, South Dakota died Monday 3, 2006 at the age of 95 years, 4 months, and 10 days old.

His funeral was held at the East Side Lutheran Church in Sioux Falls, South Dakota with Rev. Olaf Roynesdal officiating. He was buried in the Split Rock Lutheran Cemetery in Brandon, South Dakota.

The Family of Darwin Alvine & Alvina Anna Augusta Winterton December of 1981. Back row: Darrell Wesley Winterton, Karel Janis Amend, Donna Rae Devries, Beverly Jean Pittman, and Jerald Sprecher. Middle Row: Darwin Alvine Winterton, and Alvina Anna Augusta Winterton, Front Row: Judith Ann Winterton, James Richard Sprecher, and Harlan Sprecher. [33]

Beverly Jean Sprecher & Elmer E. Biteler Marriage & Family*

Beverly Jean Sprecher, daughter of Herman J. Sprecher and Alvina Anna Augusta Zirpel, was born on March 2, 1929 in Douglas County, South Dakota.

She was christened on March 26, 1939 at the St. John's Lutheran Church in Douglas County, South Dakota.

Elmer E. Biteler, son of Homer and Mae Biteler was born on March 7, 1937 and he was christened in Flandreau, Moody County, South Dakota.

On April 12, 1940 the Census Enumerator, Hazel B. Kaubone for the 1940 United States census recorded Elmer Biteler three years old living on North Wind Street with his parents, Homer and Mae Biteler and one sister, Emery five years old in Flandreau, Moody County, South Dakota. [77]

Beverly Jean Sprecher married Elmer E. Biteler, son of Homer Biteler and Mae on July 13, 1958 in Sioux Falls in Minnehaha County, South Dakota.

Elmer and Beverly Jean Biteler had four children: Steven Eugene, Vicki, Roxann, and Philip Biteler. Their marriage ended in a divorce.

Steven Eugene Biteler, son of Elmer and Beverly Biteler was born on April 19, 1959 in Sioux Falls, Minnehaha County, South Dakota.

Vicki Biteler, daughter of Elmer and Beverly Jean Biteler was born on August 5, 1961 in Brookings, Brookings County, South Dakota.

Roxann Biteler, daughter of Elmer and Beverly Biteler was born on October 19, 1965 in Lincoln, Lancaster County, Nebraska. She was also christened in Lincoln, Lancaster County, Nebraska.

Phillip Biteler, son of Elmer and Beverly Biteler was born on February 5, 1970 in Lincoln, Lancaster County, Nebraska and he was christened in Lincoln, Lancaster County, Nebraska.

Steven Eugene Biteler & Teresa Marriage *

Steven Eugene Biteler married Teresa in October of 1978. Their marriage ended in divorce in 1979.

Steven Eugene Biteler & Pam Marriage & Family*

Steven Biteler married Pam on December of 1980. They had two children: Michael J. and Steven Christopher Biteler. Their marriage ended in divorce in May of 1986.

Michael J. Biteler was born on October 4, 1977. Pam adopted him.

Steven Christopher Biteler was born on June 12, 1982.

Steven Eugene Biteler & Kelly S. Marriage *

Steve Eugene Biteler married Kelly S. on August 27, 1988.

Vicki Biteler & Jeffrey Smalley Marriage & Family*

Vicki Biteler married Jeffrey Smalley on October 17, 1980.

They had one child: Jason Smalley. Their marriage ended in divorce in 1987.

Jason Smalley was born on March 11, 1981.

Vicki Smalley & Chester Streeter Marriage *

Vicki Smalley married Chester Streeter on October 14, 2007.

Roxann Biteler & Dan Taylor Marriage & Family*

Roxann Biteler married Dan Taylor on November 5, 1988.

Dan Taylor was born on September 10, 1959 and was christened on May 31, 2008.

Dan and Roxann Taylor had four children: Amber, Aaron David, Jamie Lynn and Jessica Nicole.

Amber Taylor was born on March 12. 1990.

Aaron David Taylor was born on June 8, 1991.

Jamie Lynn Taylor was born on December 4, 1992.

Jessica Nicole Taylor was born on December 31, 1998.

Phillip Biteler & Louisa A. Parfay Marriage & Family*

Philip Biteler married Louisa A. Parfay on July 22, 1995 in Sioux Falls, Minnehaha County, South Dakota.

Louisa A. Parfay was born on September 8, 1974.

Philip and Louisa Biteler had four children: Brielle Christina, Jamin Philip, Brekken Dean and Josie Ann Biteler.

Brielle Christina Biteler was born on July 29, 2003. Brielle was adopted.

Jamin Philip Biteler was born on November 8, 2005. Jamin was adopted.

Brekken Dean Biteler was born on November 14, 2008.

Josie Ann Biteler was born on November 2, 2009.

Beverly Jean Biteler & Richard Floyd Pittman Marriage & Family*

Richard Floyd Pittman, son of Floyd Winston and Adeline Mabel Gintant, was born on November 1939 in Nobles County, Minnesota and he was also christened in Nobles County, Minnesota.

Richard Pittman was recorded as 5 months old on the 1940 United State Census on April 5, 1940, by the Census Enumerator, Hanna R. McCall. His father, Floyd Winston Pittman was about 24 years old and he was born in Illinois. And his mother, Adeline Pittman was about 25 years old and she was born in Minnesota.

His father was a farmer according to the census and living in Hersey Township in Nobles County, Minnesota. Also on the report a sister, Dorothy was five years old.[78]

Beverly Jean Biteler married Richard Floyd Pittman, son of Floyd Pittman and Adeline on March 29, 1986 in the St. John's Lutheran Church in Sioux Falls, Minnehaha County, South Dakota.

Jerald Sprecher & Helen D. Rasmussen Marriage & Family*

Jerald Sprecher, son of Herman J. Sprecher and Alvina Anna Augusta Zirpel, was born on March 28, 1943 in Douglas County, South Dakota.

He was christened in the St. John's Lutheran Church in Douglas County, South Dakota.

Jerald Sprecher married Helen D. Rasmussen, daughter of Albert Rasmussen and Elsie Eggert on November 5, 1967 in the St. John Lutheran in Howard, Minor County, South Dakota.

Helen D. Rasmussen was born on November 17, 1945 and she was christened in Minor County, South Dakota.

Jerald and Helen D. Sprecher had two children: Teresa and Angela Kaye Sprecher.

Teresa Sprecher was born on October 3, 1971 in Lake County, South Dakota. She was christened on November 7, 1971 in Minor County, South Dakota.

Angela Kaye Sprecher was born on July 8, 1976 in Kingsbury County, South Dakota. She was christened in Miner County, South Dakota.

Teresa Sprecher & Cortney French Marriage & Family*

Teresa Sprecher married Cortney French in 1990.

They had a child: Tyler Paul French. The marriage ended in divorce.

Tyler Paul French was born on January 30, 1989.

Teresa French & Lowell Gerry Marriage & Family*

Teresa French married Lowell Gerry on February 14, 1997 in Madison, Lake County, South Dakota.

Lowell Gerry was born on July 22, 1967.

Lowell and Teresa Gerry had three children: Elijah Lee, Maddie Sheila, and Zoey Teresa Gerry.

Elijah Lee Gerry was born on December 15, 1998.

Maddie Sheila Gerry was born on September 9, 2000.

Zoey Teresa Gerry was born on December 28, 2004.

Angela Kaye Sprecher & Jason B. Bishop Marriage & Family*

Angela Kaye Sprecher married Jason B. Bishop on June 7, 1997 in Howard, Miner County, South Dakota.

Jason B. Bishop was born on April 5, 1976.

Jason and Angela Bishop had two children: Micala and Alexis.

Micala Bishop was born on March 9, 1998.

Alexis Bishop was born on November 25, 2001.

James Richard Sprecher & Setsuko Aiko Nakama Marriage & Family*

James Richard Sprecher, son of Herman J. Sprecher and Alvina Anna Augusta Zirpel, was born on November 4, 1945 in South Dakota.

He was christened on December 16, 1945 in St. John's Lutheran Church in Douglas County, South Dakota.

James Richard Sprecher married Setsuko Aiko Nakama on May 31, 1948 in Okinawa, Japan.

Setsuko Aiko Nakama was born on May 31, 1943 in Okinawa, Japan.

James Richard and Setsuko Aiko Sprecher had two children: James Darwin and Sakura A. Sprecher.

James Darwin Sprecher was born on March 9, 1976 in Okinawa, Japan.

Sakura A. Sprecher was born on January 16, 1979 in Okinawa, Japan.

James Darwin Sprecher & Yuki Marriage *

James Darwin Sprecher married Yuki on December 14, 2005.

Sakura A. Sprecher & Matthew Mauer Marriage & Family*

Sakura A. Sprecher married Matthew Mauer on May 29, 2004.

Matthew and Sakura A. Mauer had one child: Eli Matthew Mauer.

Eli Matthew Mauer was born on March 22, 2007 in Coon Rapids, Anoka County, Minnesota.

Harlan Sprecher*

Harlan Sprecher, son of Herman J. Sprecher and Alvina Anna Augusta Zirpel, was born on January 14, 1953 in Sioux Falls, South Dakota.

He was christened in St. John Lutheran Church in Douglas County, South Dakota.

Martha Bertha Zirpel & Donovan Eldon Anderson Marriage & Family*

On November 5, 1939, Martha Bertha Zirpel, daughter of Robert Hermann and Bertha Rosina Riecke Zirpel, married Donovan Eldon Anderson, son of Hendrick Anderson and Helen at the St. John's Lutheran Church in Douglas County, South Dakota.[79] According to the marriage certificate they were married by Rev. P. Teckenburg, a Lutheran Minister.

Donovan was registered living in Lynd, Lyon County, Minnesota while Martha was registered living in Parkston, Hutchinson County, South Dakota.

Donovan Eldon Anderson was born on April 13, 1914 in Minneapolis, Hennepin County, Minnesota.

He was christened in Minneapolis, Hennepin County, Minnesota.

He died on January 22, 1994 in Colorado Springs, El Paso County, Colorado at the age of 79 years old. He was buried on January 25, 1994 in the St. John's Lutheran Church Cemetery.

Donovan Anderson was recorded on the 1920 United States Census living with his parents, Hendrick and Helen Anderson in Dunn County, North Dakota by Census Enumerator, John F.. Rooney between February 9-21, 1920.[80]

According to the 1930 United States Census taken by the Census Enumerator, Mrs. Ela Narland on April 2, 1930, Donovan and his parents, Hendrick and Helen Anderson had moved from North Dakota to Lincoln, Hamilton County, Iowa.[81]

On the 1940 United States Census, between April 11-15, 1940 Donovan and Martha Anderson were recorded living in their home in Lake Marshall, Lyon County, Minnesota according to the Census Enumerator, John T. Baker. Donovan spent as much as 60 hours a week working as a farmer.[82]

Donovan and Martha Anderson had five children: Sylvia Martha, Wendell Gene, Gary Lee, Duane Eldon, and David Hendrick Anderson.

Martha Bertha Anderson died on October 19, 2007 in Aurora, Arapahoe County, Colorado at the age of 92 years.

She was buried on November 10, 2007 in the St. John's Lutheran Church Cemetery in Douglas County, South Dakota.

Sylvia Martha Anderson & Carl Drake Iverson Marriage & Family*

Sylvia Martha Anderson was born on October 1, 1940 in Douglas County, South Dakota.

She was christened in the St. John's Lutheran Church in Douglas County, South Dakota.

Sylvia Martha Anderson married Carl Drake

Iverson, son of Wallace Iverson and Opal Drake, on April 2, 1961 in Sioux Falls, Minnehaha County, South Dakota.

Carl Drake Iverson was born on November 7, 1941 in Pope County, Minnesota.

Carl and Sylvia Iverson had two children: Cory Dean and Julie Lynn Iverson.

Cory Dean Iverson was born on August 9, 1961 and he was christened in Minnesota.

Julie Lynn Iverson was born on March 16, 1964.

Cory Dean Iverson & Cynthia Rae McBride Marriage & Family*

Cory Dean Iverson married Cynthia Rae McBride on May 8, 1982. Cynthia Rae McBride was born on January 5, 1963.

Cory Dean and Cynthia Iverson had two children: Courtney Rae and Kyle Drake Iverson.

Courtney Rae Iverson was born on May 20, 1984.

Kyle Drake Iverson was born on March 23, 1987.

Julie Lynn Iverson & Scott Charles Hurlbert Marriage *

Julie Lynn Iverson married Scott Charles Hurlbert on October 19, 1982.

Scott Charles Hurlbert was born in January of 1962.

Wendell Gene Anderson & Betty Jean Perkins Marriage & Family*

Wendell Gene Anderson was born on January 2, 1943 in Lion County, Iowa. Wendell Gene Anderson married Betty Jean Perkins on June 22, 1963 in Sioux Falls, Minnehaha County, South Dakota.

Betty Jean Perkins was born on March 28, 1945.

Wendell Gene and Betty Jean Anderson had two children: Connie Michelle and Bonnie Kay Anderson.

Connie Michelle Anderson was born on May 7, 1965.

Bonnie Kay Anderson was born on August 22, 1968.

Connie Michelle Anderson & Ibrahim Sleiman Marriage & Family*

Connie Michelle Anderson married Ibrahim Sleiman on December 2, 1985.

Ibrahim Sleiman was born in about 1963.

Ibrahim and Connie Michelle Sleiman had one child: Susie Sleiman.

Susie Sleiman was born on June 19, 1996.

Bonnie Kay Anderson & Paul Duffy Marriage *

Bonnie Kay Anderson married Paul Duffy on July 24, 1993.

Gary Lee Anderson & Shirley Wisniewski Marriage & Family*

Gary Lee Anderson was born on April 9, 1944 in Lyon County, Minnesota and he was christened in Lyon County, Minnesota.

Gary Lee Anderson married Shirley Wisniewski on February 4, 1967 in Sioux Falls, Minnehaha County, South Dakota.

Shirley Wisniewski was born on December 14, 1949.

Gary Lee and Shirley Anderson had two children: Lisa Ann and Donavan Charles Anderson.

Lisa Ann Anderson was born May 17, 1968.

Donavan Charles Anderson was born on August 2, 1970.

Lisa Ann Anderson & Kevin Dale McPherson Marriage & Family*

Lisa Ann Anderson married Kevin Dale McPherson on September 4, 1999 in the First Presbyterian Church in Rapid City, Pennington County, South Dakota.

Kevin Dale McPherson was born on April 1, 1959.

Kevin Dale and Lisa Ann McPherson had one child: Danika McPerson.

Danika McPherson was born on April 18, 1989.

Donavan Charles Anderson & Christine Bennett Marriage & Family*

Donavan Charles Anderson married Christine Bennett on April 10, 2004. Christine Bennett was born on April 22, 1972.

Donavan Charles and Christine Anderson had four children: Justin, Ryan, Griffin and Austin Anderson.

Justin Anderson was born on April 9, 1992.

Ryan Anderson was born on August 1, 1997.

Griffin Anderson was born on February 25, 2000.

Austin Anderson was born on November 15, 2001.

Duane Eldon Anderson & Nancy Jean Westerland Marriage & Family*

Duane Eldon Anderson was born on November 12, 1950 in Lyon County, Minnesota and he was christened in Lyon County, Minnesota.

Duane Eldon Anderson married Nancy Jean Westerland on February 6, 1972.

Nancy Jean Westerland was born on September 22, 1952.

Duane Eldon and Nancy Anderson had two children: Daniel Eric and Kelly Michelle Anderson. Their marriage ended in divorce on August 15, 1997.

Daniel Eric Anderson was born on May 31, 1978.

Kelly Michelle Anderson was born on December 28, 1985.

Daniel Eric Anderson & Christina Fritzen Marriage *

Daniel Eric Anderson married Christina Fritzen on August 24, 2003.

Christina Fritzen was born on March 17, 1978.

Duane Eldon Anderson & Charlotte Marie Diekmann Marriage & Family*

Duane Eldon Anderson married Charlotte Marie Diekmann on July 4, 2005.

Charlotte Marie Diekmann was born on March 4, 1950.

Duane Eldon and Charlotte Marie Anderson had one child: Christine Joan Anderson.

Christine Joan Anderson was born on December 24, 1979.

David Hendrick Anderson & Mary Rose Fisher Marriage & Family*

David Hendrick Anderson was born on February 3, 1952 in Lyon County, Minnesota and he was christened in Lyon County, Minnesota.

David Hendrick Anderson married Mary Rose Fisher on November 10, 1974.

Mary Rose Fisher was born on June 11, 1955.

David Hendrick and Mary Rose Anderson had four children: Jennifer Marie, James Donovan, Janelle Lynn and Jacklyn Ranee Anderson. The marriage ended in divorce on March 30, 1987.

Jennifer Marie Anderson was born on August 11, 1976.

James Donovan Anderson was born on April 28, 1978.

Janelle Lynn Anderson was born on April 11, 1980.

Jacklyn Ranee Anderson was born on August 26, 1982.

Jennifer Marie Anderson & Christopher Robin Rother Marriage & Family*

Jennifer Marie Anderson married Christopher Robin Rother on August 31, 1998.

Christopher Robin Rother was born on February 26, 1976.

Christopher and Jennifer Rother had two children: Pacey Robert and Christopher David Rother. Their marriage ended in divorce.

Pacey Robert Rother was born on November 29, 1999.

Christopher David Rother was born on September 20, 2003.

Jennifer Marie Rother & Jason Gehn Roe Marriage & Family*

Jennifer Marie Rother married Jason Gehn Roe on July 21, 2006.

Jason Gehn Roe was born on August 5, 1971.

Alma Emma E. Zirpel & Raymond F. Bittiker Marriage & Family*

Raymond F. Bittiker, son of Joseph Fredolin Bittiker and Bertha May Burright, was born on April 2, 1916 in Broken Arrow, Tulsa County, Oklahoma.

He died on March 8, 2005 in Horseshoe Bend, Boise County, Idaho and his burial was in Boise County, Idaho.

Between January 17-19, 1920, Raymond F. Bittiker was three years and eight months old and recorded living with his parents, Joseph and his wife, Bertha, by the Census Enumerator, G. L. Kemersine, Washington in Doniphan County, Kansas on the 1920 United States Census.[83]

The report said that his father, Joseph was born in Missouri and was about fifty-seven years old. Joseph worked as a farmer laborer. The report said his mother, Bertha was born in Kansas and was about thirty-five years old. On the report Raymond had five sisters and a brother also recorded: Daisy M. age seventeen years old, Mary L. age fifteen years old, Lehman J. age thirteen years old, Dora B. age eleven years old, Agnes J. age five years and one month old, and Margaret P. age one year and nine months old.

After the death of Joseph in 1924, the family was recorded on the 1930 United States Census living in Lafayette, Clinton County, Missouri on April 5, 1930 by the Census Enumerator, William F. Naffty.[84] Raymond's mother, Bertha was working as a housekeeper in the home of George L. Coy. Raymond was fourteen years old and his sister, Margaret was eleven years old.

On February 22, 1940 Alma Emma Elisabeth Zirpel, daughter of Robert Hermann and Bertha Rosina Riecke Zirpel, married Raymond F. Bittiker, son of Joseph Fredolin Bittiker and Bertha May Burright, in the St. John's Lutheran Church in Douglas County, South Dakota.

Raymond and Alma Bittiker had their home in Wathena, Doniphan County, Kansas according to the 1940 United States Census.[85] On the report Raymond was working as a laborer in a Nursery and he was twenty-four years old. His wife, Alma was nineteen years old.

Raymond F. and Alma Emma Bittiker had two children: Janet Rae and Dennis Robert Bittiker.

Janet Rae Bittiker & William Christopher Wamsley Marriage & Family*

Janet Rae Bittiker was born on April 30, 1943 in Hawthorne, Los Angles County, California and she was christened in 1977.

Janet Rae Bittiker married William Christo-

32

Robert Hermann and Bertha Rosina Zirpel Family around 1947. Back Row: Raymond Gideon Solomon Semmler, Robert L. Danner, Raymond F. Bittiker, Donovan Eldon Anderson, and Herman J. Sprecher. Middle Row: Robert Hermann Zirpel, Violet Bernice Semmler, Rodger Danner, Anita Margaret Danner, Alma Emma Elisabeth Bittiker, Martha Bertha Anderson, Alvina Anna Augusta Sprecher, James Richard Sprecher, and Bertha Rosina Zirpel. Front Row: Gary Lee Anderson, Janet Rae Bittiker, Sylvia Martha Anderson, Beverly Jean Sprecher, Wendell Gene Anderson, Jerald Sprecher. [34]

pher Wamsley on March 31, 1962 in Los Angles, Los Angles County, California. Their marriage ended in divorce in June of 1977 according the California Divorce Index, 1966-1984.

William Christopher Wamsley was born on August 11, 1939.

William and Janet Wamsley had three children: Charles Craig, Steven Robert, and Lorraine Elizabeth Wamsley.

Charles Craig Wamsley was born n October 10, 1962 in Los Angles, Los Angles County, California.

Steven Robert Wamsley was born on October 26, 1967 in Los Angles, Los Angles County, California.

Lorraine Elizabeth Wamsley was born on October 3, 1968 in Los Angles, Los Angles County, California.

Lorraine Elizabeth Wamsley & Bryan Dejong Marriage & Family*

Lorraine Elizabeth Wamsley married Bryan

Lorraine Elizabeth Wamsley married Bryan Dejong on November 21, 1992 in Clark County, Nevada.

Bryan Dejong was born on September 2, 1965 in Los Angles, Los Angles County, California

Bryan and Lorraine Dejong have one child: Chloe Joy Dejong.

Chloe Joy Dejong was born on February 18, 1993 in Los Angles, Los Angles County, California.

Dennis Robert Bittiker & Marsha A. Tuskey Marriage & Family*

Dennis Robert Bittiker was born on June 15, 1948 in Los Angles, Los Angles, California.

Dennis Robert Bittiker married Marsha A. Tuskey on February 22, 1970 in Los Angles, Los Angles County, California. Marsha A. Tuskey was born on March 8, 1951.

Dennis and Marsha had three children: Amber Ray, Tahnee Elizabeth and David Robert

Bittiker.

Amber Ray Bittiker was born on July 23, 1972 in Los Angles, Los Angles County, California.

Tahnee Elizabeth Bittiker was born on May 24, 1976 in Los Angles, Los Angles County, California.

David Robert Bittiker was born on December 11, 1977 in Los Angles, Los Angles County, California.

Robert L. Danner & His Family*

Robert L. Danner, son of Carl C. Danner and Inez A. was born on May 25, 1923 in North Carolina.

Robert L. Danner and his family was recorded on the 1930 United States Census living in Winston-Salem in Forsyth County, North Carolina on April 18, 1930 by the Census Enumerator, Alta E. Mikey.[86] His father, Carl C. was twenty-nine years, his birthplace was North Carolina and he worked as machine operator in a tobacco factory. His mother, Inez A. was twenty-seven years old and her birthplace was in Tennessee. There were four children recorded: William C. age 9 years old, Robert L. age 6 years old, Charles H. age 3 years 10 months old, and James E. age 1 year and 2 months old.

On April 12, 1940, the family was living in Ogburn-East and Northeast Winston-Salem in Forsyth County, North Carolina on the 1940 United States Census according to the Census Enumerator, Raymond W. Burke.[87] Their home was located on Mains Mill Road. Carl C. still worked as machine attendant in a tobacco factory for about 28 hours a week. William C worked as a gas station attendant for about 60 hours a week. All of the four boys: William C., Robert L., Charles H. and James E. were still living with their parents.

Anita Margaret Zirpel & Robert L. Danner Marriage & Family*

Anita Margaret Zirpel, daughter of Robert Hermann and Bertha Rosina Riecke Zirpel, married Robert L. Danner, son of Carl C. Danner and Inez A. on September 15, 1945 in the First Lutheran Church in Inglewood, Los Angles County, California.

Robert L. and Anita Margaret Danner
shorty after they were married[35]

According to Kim Danner, a granddaughter, Anita and Robert were such a beautiful couple. She said that they had only known each other for about month before they got married. She said that she heard the story that her grandfather knew he was going to marry her the first time be laid eyes on her. Robert and his brother had been home on leave from the service and they both "tied one on" and were sneaking back into the home late that night. Robert had found Grandma (Anita Zirpel) sleeping in grandpa's bed, as she had been friends of one of his family, not sure who. So he first seen her grandmother in his own bed and then told his brother, in a drunken stupor, that he was going to marry that girl. Both families weren't too happy about their marriage and really didn't think it would last. However, Kim said that they had been married for 56 years.

Robert L. and Anita Margaret Danner had three children: Rodger, Robert C. and Carol L. Danner.

Rodger Danner was born on January 7, 1947 in St. Joseph, Buchanan County, Missouri.

Robert C. Danner was born on July 2, 1948 in Parkston, Hutchinson County, South Dakota.

Carol L. Danner was born on August 7, 1956 in Shasta County, California.

Rodger Danner & Janet Lanning Marriage & Family*

Rodger Danner married Janet Lanning, daughter of Harry Lanning and Thalia Juanita Locke, on November 9, 1968 in Mentor Lake

County, Iowa.

Janet Lanning was born on January 21, 1947 in Painesville, Lake County, Ohio.

Rodger and Janet Danner had three children: Kimberly D. Jeffery, Michael.

Kimberly D. Danner was born on September 7, 1969 in Shasta County, California.

Jeffrey Danner was born on March 1, 1972 in Painesville, Lake County, Ohio.

Michael Danner was born on June 21, 1974 in Portsmouth, Scioto County, Ohio.

Rodger currently owns the Bible passed down to him from his mother, Anita Danner. The bible was originally owned by Hermann Robert Zirpel, Anita Margaret Danner's father.

The Title Page of the Bible which was originally owned by Herman Robert Zirpel written in old German Style text.
English Translation is:
The Bible
Old Testament and the New Testament
After the German Translation
Dr. Martin Luther's
With 240 Pictures After Julius von Karlsällt, Dr. Jäger, F. Daerbeck, U. Rethel, J von Zürich u.a.
Printed in Germany
Chicago, Illinois
Wartburg Publishing House [36]

Robert C. Danner & Mary Ann Molley Marriage & Family*

Robert C. Danner married Mary Ann Molloy on August 31, 1970 in California.

Mary Ann Molloy was born on December 8, 1950.

Robert and Mary Ann Danner had two children: Robert E. and Mary Alice Danner.

Robert E. Danner was born on July 29, 1973 in Merced County, California.

Mary Alice Danner was born on March 11, 1975 in Merced County, California.

Carol L. Danner & Richard Julian Kraft Marriage & Family*

Carol L. Danner married Richard Julian Kraft on September 7, 1974 in Shasta County, California. The marriage ended in divorce.

Carol L. Kraft married Robert Campbell.

Robert and Carol Campbell had two children: Jamie Elsie and Hollee Anita.

Jamie Elsie Campbell was born on December 23, 1987 in Shasta County, California.

Hollee Anita Campbell was born on December 17, 1990 in Shasta County, California.

Anita Margaret & Robert L. Danner - The Later Years*

Anita Margaret Danner died on February 14, 2003 in Cottonwood, Shasta County, California at the age of 77 years old. Anita was cremated according to Rodger Danner.

Granddaughter, Kim Danner had a picture of her grandmother, Anita "Zirpel" Danner, as a young girl. According to Kim her grandmother was on their farm playing around with her sister, who had taken the picture.

Kim said that if you look closely you would notice that Anita didn't have a shirt on, just a grass skirt. Kim had asked her grandmother about the picture, and her grandmother had gotten a little gleam in her eyes and proudly chuckled. Kim said that her grandmother, Anita had a free spirit, ahead of her time.

Robert L. Danner died on December 23, 2004 in Cottonwood, Shasta County, California at the age of 81 years old. Robert was cremated according to Rodger Danner.

Raymond Gideon Solomon Semmler & His Family*

Raymond Gideon Solomon Semmler, son of Solomon Semmler and Wilhemina Lagge, was born on February 1, 1920 in Douglas County, South Dakota. He was christened on February 4, 1920 in the Immanuel Lutheran Church, in Douglas County, South Dakota.

Raymond Semmler was recorded on the 1930 United States Census on April 2, 1930 by the Census Enumerator, Mrs. Ida Bertram living with his parents and family in Lincoln Township in Douglas County, South Dakota.[88] His father, Solomon was thirty-eight years old and a farmer and his birthplace was South Dakota.

His mother, Wilhelmina was thirty-six years old and her birthplace was Romania. There were eight children listed on the report: Solomon age 16 years old, Jonatha age 15 years old, Agatha age 12 years old, Raymond was listed as Gideon age 10 years old, Frieda age 9 years old, Benjamin age 6 years old, Gerhardt age 3 years old, and Rosa age 1 year old.

On April 26, 1940 on the 1940 United States Census, Raymond was still living in Lincoln Township in Douglas County, South Dakota with his parents and family according to the Census Enumerator, Lawrence Amend.[89]

His father, Solomon was working about 80 hours a week as grain farm operator while Raymond was doing family work on the farm for about 70 hours a week. Children listed on the report were Benjamin age 17 years old, Gerhardt 13 years old, Rosie 12 years old, Anita 10 years old, Roland 6 years old and Eldora 4 years old.

Violet Bernice Zirpel & Raymond Gideon S. Semmler Marriage & Family*

Violet Bernice Zirpel, daughter of Robert Hermann and Bertha Rosina Riecke Zirpel, married Raymond Gideon Solomon Semmler, son of Solomon Semmler and Wilhemina Lagge, on February 28, 1946 in Armour in Douglas County, South Dakota by Rev. M. F. Amelung, according to the South Dakota Marriage records.[90]

Raymond Gideon Solomon and Violet Bernice Semmler had six children: Barbara Ann, Solomon Gideon, Stanley Ray, Margaret Lou, Lawrence Lee, and Michael John Semmler.

Violet Bernice and Raymond Solomon Gideon Semmler Wedding Day [37]

Barbara Ann Semmler was born on November 7, 1948 in Parkston, Hutchinson County, South Dakota.

Solomon Gideon Semmler was born on April 3, 1950 in Douglas County, South Dakota and he was christened on April 30, 1950 in Douglas County, South Dakota.

Stanley Ray Semmler was born on May 24, 1952 in Douglas County, South Dakota and he was christened in Douglas County, South Dakota.

Margaret Lou Semmler was born on October 6, 1953 in Douglas County, South Dakota.

Lawrence Lee Semmler was born on February 22, 1955 in Douglas County, South Dakota and he was christened in Douglas County, South Dakota.

Michael John Semmler was born on February 28, 1957 in Douglas County, South Dakota and he was christened in Douglas County, South Dakota.

Raymond Semmler served in the U.S. Army during World War II as a Tec5 in the 2703 Engr. Lt. Equip. Company.

Violet Bernice & Raymond Gideon Solomon Semmler - The Later Years*

Raymond Gideon Solomon Semmler died on September 11, 1958 in Sioux Falls in Minnehaha County, South Dakota and his burial was in Parkston Cemetery, Parkston, Hutchinson County, South Dakota.

Violet Bernice Semmler died on March 17, 1989 in Stanley County, South Dakota and her burial was in the St. John' Lutheran Church Cemetery in Douglas County, South Dakota.

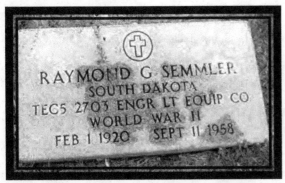

Raymond G. S. Semmler Grave located at the Parkston Cemetery, Parkston, South Dakota [38]

Barbara Ann Semmler & William Harry Schooler Marriage & Family*

Barbara Ann Semmler married William Harry Schooler on June 25, 1970 in Sioux Falls, Minnehaha County, South Dakota.

William Harry Schooler was born on May 1948 in Reliance, Lyman County, South Dakota and he died on November 30, 1977 in Collier County, Florida.

William Harry and Barbara Ann Schooler had two children: Gay Lynn, and Neida Marie Schooler.

Gay Lynn Schooler was born on January 23, 1972.

Neida Marie Schooler was born on August 1, 1974.

Gay Lynn Schooler & Martin Bernard Plamondon Marriage & Family*

Gay Lynn Schooler married Martin Bernard Plamondon on January 17, 1990 in Collier County, Florida.

Martin Bernard Plamondon was born on September 15, 1969.

Martin and Gay Lynn Plamondon had five children: Henrietta "Mavis", Harry B., Robert B., Renee, and Abby Plamondon.

Henrietta "Marvis" Plamondon was born on

March 9, 1993.

Harry B. Plamondon was born on September 22, 1994.

Robert B. Plamondon was born on November 4, 1997.

Renee Plamondon was born on September 9, 2002.

Abby Plamondon was born on December 6, 2004.

Neide Marie Schooler & Robert William Johnson Marriage & Family*

Neida Marie Schooler married Robert William Johnson on September 24, 2009.

Robert William and Neida Marie Johnson had two children: Dinah Marie and Nora G. Johnson.

Dinah Marie Johnson was born on February 26, 2006.

Nora G. Johnson was born on October 11, 2006.

Barbara Ann Schooler & John William King Marriage & Family*

Barbara Ann Schooler married John William King on July 7, 1978 in Collier County, Florida.

John William King was born on December 12, 1947 in Pennsylvania.

John William and Barbara Ann King had one child: John Thomas King. The marriage ended in divorce on July 18, 1978 in Naples, Florida.

John Thomas King was born on October 20, 1978.

Barbara Ann King & William Otto Unland Marriage *

Barbara Ann King married William Otto Unland on August 31, 2001 in, Naples, Collier County, Florida.

William Otto Unland was born on October 10, 1940 in Nashville, Davidson County, Tennessee.

Solomon Gideon Semmler & Cathryn Marie Haffner Marriage & Family*

Solomon Gideon Semmler married Cathryn

Marie Haffner, daughter of Edwin and Elizabeth Haffner on January 2, 1970 in Sioux Falls, Minnehaha County, South Dakota. The marriage ended in divorce on May 15, 1985.

Cathryn Marie Haffner was born on September 17, 1949 in Sioux Falls, Minnehaha County, South Dakota.

Solomon G. and Cathryn Marie Semmler had two children: Brandon Eugene and Amy Elizabeth Semmler.

Brandon Eugene Semmler was born on September 9, 1971 in San Diego, San Diego County, California and he was christened on December 5, 1971 in Sioux Falls, Minnehaha County, South Dakota.

Amy Elizabeth Semmler was born on September 2, 1975 in Sioux Falls, Minnehaha County, South Dakota and she was christened on October 12, 1975 in Sioux Falls, Minnehaha County, South Dakota.

Brandon Eugene Semmler & Paula Page Marriage & Family*

Brandon Eugene Semmler married Paula Page on November 5, 1994. Marriage ended in divorce.

Brandon Eugene and Paula Semmler had three children: Adam Leigh Page, Cameron Eugene, and Dilon Edward Semmler.

Adam Leigh Page was born on October 16, 1989. Adam is Brandon's step-son.

Cameron Eugene Semmler was born on April 5, 1995 in Sioux Falls, Minnehaha County, South Dakota and he was christened on July 23, 1995 in Hartford, Minnehaha County, South Dakota.

Dilon Edward Semmler was born on May 6, 1996 in Sioux Falls, Minnehaha County, South Dakota and he was christened in Sioux Falls, Minnehaha County, South Dakota.

Brandon Eugene Semmler's & Jodi Jeschke's Family*

Brandon Eugene Semmler and Jodi Jeschke had one child: Keaton Ryan Jeschke. They were never married.

Keaton Ryan Jeschke was born on January 3, 2006 in Sioux Falls, Minnehaha County, South Dakota .

He was christened on February 5, 2006 in Sioux Falls, Minnehaha County, South Dakota.

Brandon Eugene Semmler's & Kimberly Allington's Family*

Branon Eugene Semmler and Kimberly Allington had one child: Violet Rae Semmler. They were never married.

Violet Rae Semmler was born on August 14, 2008 in Sioux Falls, Minnehaha County, South Dakota.

She was christened on November 15, 2008 in Sioux Falls, Minnehaha County, South Dakota.

Amy Elizabeth Semmler & Jeffrey Phillip Bray Marriage & Family*

Amy Elizabeth Semmler married Jeffrey Phillip Bray, the son of Dennis Bray and Joyce Heaton on March 24, 2007 in Sioux Fall, Minnehaha County, South Dakota.

Jeffrey and Amy Bray had two children: Spencer Allen and Austin Jeffrey Bray.

Spencer Allen Bray was born on February 18, 2008 in Sioux Falls, Minnehaha County, South Dakota and he was christened on April 20, 2008 in Sioux Falls, Minnehaha County, South Dakota..

Austin Jeffrey Bray was born on May 13, 2009 in Sioux Falls, Minnehaha County, South Dakota and he was christened on July 19, 2009 in Brandon, Minnehaha County, South Dakota.

Solomon Gideon Semmler & Mary Jo Olson Marriage *

Solomon Gideon Semmler married Mary Jo Olson, the daughter of Oscar F. Olson and Phyllis H. Haugland, on July 17, 1990 in Sioux Falls, Minnehaha County, South Dakota.

Mary Jo Olsen was born on February 3, 1951 in Grand Rapids, Itasca County, Minnesota and she was christened in May 6, 1951 in Grand Rapids, Itasca County, Minnesota.

Stanley Ray Semmler & Barbara Jenkins Marriage & Family*

Stanley Ray Semmler married Barbara Jenkins on March 12, 1976 in Hawkinsville, Pulaski County, Georgia. The marriage ended in divorce in January of 2000.

Stanley Ray Semmler married Barbara Jenkins on March 12, 1976 in Hawkinsville, Pulaski County, Georgia. The marriage ended in divorce in January of 2000.

Barbara Jenkins was born on June 3, 1950.

Stanley Ray and Barbara Semmler had two children: Melissa Elizabeth and Megan Estelle Semmler.

Melissa Elizabeth Semmler was born on June 13, 1980 in Macon, Bibb County, Georgia and she was christened in Fort Pierre, Stanley County, South Dakota.

Megan Estelle Semmler was born on October 21, 1984 in Macon in Bibb County, Georgia and she was christened in the Hope Lutheran Church in Milledgeville in Baldwin County, Georgia.

Melissa Elizabeth Semmler & James Franklin Smallwood Marriage *

Melissa Elizabeth Semmler married James Franklin Smallwood on September 25, 2005. Their marriage ended in divorce.

Melissa Elizabeth Smallwood & Curtis Anthony Howard Marriage & Family*

Melissa Smallwood married Curtis Anthony Howard, son of Curt Howard and Becky Brown, on April 17, 2010 in Savannah, Chatham County, Georgia.

Curtis Anthony Howard was born in January 19, 1979.

Curtis and Melissa Howard had two children: Eli Kenneth and Ethan Ray Howard.

Eli Kenneth Howard and Ethan Ray Howard were born on February 18, 2011 and was christened on May 1, 2011 in the Lutheran Church of the Redeemer in Macon in Bibb County, Georgia.

Stanley Ray Semmler & Tammy Rae Ramsey Marriage & Family*

Stanley Ray Semmler married Tammy Rae Ramsey, daughter of Oliver Max Ramsey and Ida Mae Harper, on April 26, 2002 in Irwinton, Wilkinson County, Georgia.

Tammy Rae Ramsey was born on February

26, 1959 in Eatonton, Putnam County, Georgia and she was christened in November of 1969 in Putnam County, Georgia.

Stanley and Tammy had one child: Nicholas Stanton Semmler.

Nicolas Stanton Semmler was born on August 6, 1979 in Eatonton, Putnam County, Georgia and he was christened in May of 1988 in Eatonton, Putnam County, Georgia.

Frank William Schooler & His Family*

Frank William Schooler, the son of Kenneth L. and Ada M. Schooler, was born on February 13, 1940 in Reliance, Lyman County, South Dakota.

Frank was only 1 month old and was recorded on the 1940 United States Census in Bailey, Lyman County, South Dakota on April 2, 1940 by the Census Enumerator, Floyd Hollenback.[91]

His parents, Kenneth L. age 31 years old and Ada M. age 25 years old were at the home of Kenneth's parents, Will H. and Ann L. Schooler. Also recorded on the census report were two sisters: Viane age 5 years old and Agnar N. age 2 years old.

Margaret Lou Semmler & Frank William Schooler Marriage & Family*

Margaret Lou Semmler married Frank William Schooler on August 2, 1975 in Sioux Falls, Minnehaha County, South Dakota. The marriage ended in divorce in 1996.

Frank William and Margaret Lou Schooler had two children: Carmen Violet and Kenneth Lee Schooler.

Carmen Violet Schooler was born on November 2, 1977.

Kenneth Lee Schooler was born on July 22, 1979.

Frank Schooler died on January 26, 2008 and his burial was on February 2, 2008 in the Reliance Cemetery in Reliance, Lyman County, South Dakota.

Carmen Violet Schooler & Alan Charles Mavesen Marriage *

Carmen Violet Schooler married Alan

Charles Mavesen.

Alan Charles Mavesen was born on December 19, 1973 in Anoka, Anoka County, Minnesota.

Margaret Lou Schooler & Paul Fitt Marriage *

Margaret Lou Schooler married Paul Fitt on March 11, 1999. The marriage ended in divorce.

Margaret Lou Fitt & Larry Wendlandt Marriage *

Margaret Lou Fitt married Larry Wendlandt in August of 2008.

Margaret Lou Wendlandt, Kenneth Lee Schooler, Alan Charles Mavesen and Carmen Violet Mavesen. [39]

Lawrence Lee Semmler & Jonita Hubbard Marriage & Family*

Lawrence Semmler married Jolinta Hubbard on December 28, 1975.

Jolinta Hubbard was born on April 25, 1952.

Lawrence Lee and Jolinta Semmler had three children: Kristeen, Jacinta and Nickolas Semmler.

Kristeen Semmler was born on September 9, 1971.

Jacinta Semmler was born on February 12, 1973.

Nickolas Semmler was born on August 12, 1976.

Michael John Semmler & Karen J. Clark Marriage & Family*

Michael John Semmler married Karen J.

. Clark. The marriage ended in divorce.

Karen J. Clark was born on December 28, 1957.

Michael John and Karen J. Semmler had one child: Justine Semmler.

Justine Semmler was born on November 2, 1980.

Raymond Solomon Gideon and Violet Bernice Semmler's Children. Back row Stanley Ray Semmler, Michael John Semmler, and Lawrence Lee Semmler. Front row: Margaret Lou Semmler Fitt Wendlandt, and Barbara Semmler Unland in March 11, 1999. [40]

CHAPTER 5

Birth of John Gottlieb Zirpel*

John Gottlieb Zirpel, the second son of Johan and Augusta Zirpel, was born on March 20, 1888 in Douglas County, South Dakota.

He was christened on April 1, 1888 in the St. John's Lutheran Church, in Douglas County, South Dakota. His sponsors or God parents were Gottlieb Pietz, Daniel Rhode, Anna Titze and Katherina Baden.

John Gottlieb lived not quite a year, when he died on February 22, 1889, in Douglas County, South Dakota. His cause of death is unknown. His burial was on February 24, 1889 in the St. John's Lutheran Church Cemetery in Douglas County, South Dakota.

According to the Hillside Lutheran Cemetery Lutheran Records of the WPA Graves Registration Project in the early 1940s, John Gottlieb Zirpel's grave was recorded being located in Lot 43, Grave 5.

Birth of First Set of Twins: Bertha Auguste & Emma Katharina Zirpel*

The first set of twins, Bertha Auguste and Emma Katharina Zirpel, daughters of Johan and Augusta Zirpel, were born on January 17, 1890 in Douglas County, South Dakota.

They were christened on January 17, 1890 in the St. John's Lutheran Church in Douglas County, South Dakota. Their sponsors or God parents were Maria Rhode, Will Zirpel, Will Sperlich, and Katharina Baden.

Unfortunately, for both Bertha Auguste and Emma Katharina, they both died a day after their birth on January 18, 1890 in Douglas County, South Dakota. They were buried on January 20, 1890 in the St. John's Lutheran Church Cemetery in located in Douglas County, South Dakota.

According to the Hillside Lutheran Cemetery Lutheran Records of the WPA Graves Registration Project in the early 1940s, both Bertha Auguste and Emma Katherina Zirpel's grave was recorded being located in Lot 43, Grave 4 near their brother, John Gottlieb Zirpel.

John Gottlieb, the twins: Emma Katharina, and Bertha Auguste and Bertha Rosina Zirpel Headstones for their graves is located in the St. John's Lutheran Church Cemetery in Douglas County, South Dakota. [41]

Birth of Bertha Rosina Zirpel*

Bertha Rosina Zirpel, daughter of Johan and Augusta Zirpel, was born on February 10, 1891 in Douglas County, South Dakota.

She was christened March 15, 1891 in the St. John's Lutheran Church in Douglas County, South Dakota. Her sponsors or God parents were Gottlieb Pietz, Gottlieb Titze, and Maria Rhode.

Bertha Rosina lived a little over two years, when she died on April 16, 1893 in Douglas County, South Dakota. Her buried was in the St. John's Lutheran Church Cemetery in Douglas County, South Dakota.

Johan Zirpel Made Several Trips Back To Prussia To Visit His Sick Mother

Johan Zirpel made two trips back to the country where he was born to visit his mother, Johanna (Simonsek) Zirpel when she was sick.

His first return trip home to see his mother was approximately just two months prior to his marriage to Anna Augusta Sperlich in April of 1883.

No records for Johan Zirpel's trip from the United States to Schlesien have never been found.

According to a Hamburg Passenger List of 1850-1934 a copy of the ship manifest record was located for Johan Zirpel, who had left the Port of Hamburg on April 25, 1883 on the Steamboat,

"Westphalia" with a destination to arrive in the Port of New York in the United States.[92]

According to a translation of a copy of the ship manifest from German to English: the steam boat "Westphalia" had a Germany flag flying on it with Captain Ludwig in charge of the ship and owned by Hamburg-American Line, a joint stock company. The dimensions of the ship were 333.9 feet long and 40 feet wide. There were at least two levels on ship as Johan's accommodations were on the middle deck, which was steerage.

On the manifest, Johan Zirpel had originally left the residence of Kniegwitz, Schlesien in Germany and his age of twenty-five years old and his birth year of 1858 had been officially confirmed and he was register as a worker. Johan Zirpel was born in Steindorf, Kr Ohlau, Schlesien, Germany, it presumed that Kniegwitz must have been located near there.

Johan Zirpel made his second known trip in June of 1902 to visit his mother, Johanna Zirpel, who was sick again. With this information we know that Johanna Zirpel died after June of 1902 and we have found no records for her husband's death.

According to a copy of the ship passenger manifest for the "Graf Waldersee", it left the Port of Hamburg on June 13, 1902 and arrived in the Port of New York on June 26, 1902.[93] The manifest stated that Johan Zirpel was married, 44 years old and he had been certified as a citizen of the United States by a Clerk of Courts as a resident of Hillside. Johan was listed with the occupation of a farmer. His final destination was listed as Parkston, South Dakota. There were no record showing his actual accommodations on the ship, but it is presumed that he probably was in Third Class or Steerage.

The "Graf Waldersee" was owned by the Hamburg-American Line and one of four sister ships. The "Graf Waldersee" was named after General Alfred Graf von Waldersee, who had been born in Germany in 1832.[94] The dimensions of the ship were 586 feet long and 62 feet wide. It had accommodations for First Class, Second Class as well as Third Class or Steerage.

Johan Purchased More Land For A Second Home

Johan Zirpel purchased land from James Jobbins of Columbia County, Wisconsin on March 9, 1899 for $1,150 for Lot Three and Four and South-half of the North West quarter of Section Three located in "Lincoln" Township Ninety Nine North Range Sixty-two West of the 5th Principal Meridian and containing One hundred Sixty-One and Thirty Two One hundredth acres according to a government land survey.[95]

The deed was recorded by the Notary public, H. W. Johnson and witnessed by H. W. Johnson and W. K. Schalk according to a copy of the Deed Record located in Armour at the Douglas County Courthouse.

C. H. Brown, the Register of Deeds in Douglas County, South Dakota filed the Deed Record on March 9, 1899 at 5 PM, and recorded it in Book 12, page 235.[96]

Johan and August Zirpel continued living on their homestead property which located in Berlin or Washington Township in Douglas County, South Dakota as well as the Timber Culture property located in Lincoln Township to the west of the property Johan purchased from James Jobbins.

The Census Enumerator, Henry Ruff on June 21, 1900 recorded on the 1900 United States Census that Johan and Anna Augusta Zirpel were living on the property located in Berlin Township, Douglas County, South Dakota.[97] On the census report Johan owned his property, but there was a mortgage against it. It would be presumed that he borrow against that property in order to purchased the land from James Jobbins in Lincoln Township. There were seven children listed on the census report. They were Anna Emilie fifteen years old, Robert Herman thirteen years old, Emma Bertha seven years old, Wilhelm Otto four years old, Elisabeth Augusta three years old, Gottfried Johan three years old and Edward Richard Zirpel nine months old.

On April 26, 1910 on the 1910 United States Census was taken by the Census Enumerator, Walter L. Koehn, and Johan and Augusta Zirpel were still living on the homestead located in Berlin or Washington Township in Douglas County, South Dakota with six of their children still living with them: Emma Bertha seventeen years old, Wilhelm Otto fourteen years old, Gottfried John twelve years old, Elisabeth Augusta twelve years old, Edward Richard ten years old, and Bertha Rosina Zirpel five years old.[98]

Between 1900 and 1914, Johan actually began working for the second home in Lincoln

This Indenture, Made the 9th day of March in the year of our Lord One Thousand Eight Hundred and Ninety Nine, by and between James Jobbins single of the County of Columbia in the State of Wisconsin South Dakota, part of the first part, and Johann Zirpel of the County of Douglas in the State of South Dakota part of the second part; WITNESSETH, That the said part of the first part, for and in consideration of the sum of Eleven Hundred Fifty Dollars, to him in hand paid by the said part of the second part, the receipt whereof is hereby acknowledged, has Granted, Bargained, Sold and Conveyed, and by these presents do Grant, Bargain, Sell and Convey unto the said part of the second part, and to his heirs and assigns forever, all that certain piece or parcel of land situated in the County of Douglas, and State of South Dakota, described as follows, to-wit:

Lots Three (3) and Four (4) and South half of the North West quarter of Section Three (3) in Township Ninety Nine (99) north Range Sixty two (62) West of the 5th P.M. and containing one hundred Sixty one and thirty two one hundredths acres according to the Government survey thereof

[JJ 3-9-99 $1.50]

Together with all and singular the hereditaments and appurtenances thereunto belonging or in anywise appertaining.
TO HAVE AND TO HOLD The said premises, with the appurtenances, to the said part of the second part, his heirs and assigns forever, and the said James Jobbins for himself and his heirs, executors and administrators, do covenant and agree to and with the said part of the second part, his heirs and assigns, that he is well seized in fee of the land and premises aforesaid, and has good right and lawful authority to sell and convey the same in manner and form aforesaid, and that the same are free from all incumbrances whatsoever.

And further, that the said part of the first part, for himself and his heirs, and all and every other person lawfully claiming or to claim by, from or under him or them, shall and will from time to time, and at all times hereafter, make and execute, or cause and procure to be made and executed all such further deed or deeds whatsoever, for the further and more perfect assurance and confirmation of the said premises hereby granted, with the appurtenances, unto the said part of the second part, his heirs and assigns, as by him or them shall be required; and the above granted premises, in the quiet and peaceable possession of the said part of the second part, his heirs and assigns, against all persons lawfully claiming or to claim the same, or any part thereof, the said part of the first part, his heirs, executors and administrators, will warrant and forever defend.

IN WITNESS WHEREOF, the said party of the first part has hereunto set his hand and seal, the day and year first above written.

SIGNED AND DELIVERED IN PRESENCE OF

H. W. Johnson
W. H. Schalk

James Jobbins [SEAL.]
[SEAL.]
[SEAL.]
[SEAL.]

STATE OF SOUTH DAKOTA,
County of Douglas.
BE IT REMEMBERED, That on this 9th day of March, in the year One Thousand Eight Hundred and Ninety Nine before me H. W. Johnson a Notary Public within and for said County and State, personally appeared James Jobbins, single well known to me to be the person who is described in, and who executed the within and foregoing instrument, and severally duly acknowledged to me that he executed the same freely.
IN WITNESS WHEREOF, I have hereunto set my hand and official seal at said County, the day and year above written.

[seal]

H. W. Johnson
Notary Public.

Filed for record this 9th day of March A. D. 1899, at 5 o'clock P.M., recorded in Book 12, page 235.
By _____ Deputy. [seal] C. H. Brown Register of Deeds.

Deed Record between James Jobbins and Johan Zirpel on March 9, 1899. [42]

43

Chrisha Sandman 30	John Geidel Jr 320	John Geidel Jr. 160	Ernest Bialas 160	Fritz Wegehaupt 160	28	Christian Moege 240	Gottlieb Moege 320 27	Wilhelm Schnell 160	Gottlieb Wenzel 319	Robert A. Sawyer 320	25	Gottlieb Wenzel 320
Thedore Kursave 153		240 Gottlieb Gerlach	J G 30	Ernest Gerlach 160 29				Robert Reichert 160	26 Wilhelm Wenzel 240			
Daniel Tusman / Gott. Gerlach / Gustic Gerlach 70 31	Carl Olowskey 320	Ernest Gerlach 320 32	Ernest Hoffman 160 33		80 / 80	Herman Bialas	Johan Zirpel 160 34	Anna 20 Hemky / Karoline Storm 240	Sarah Dewey 160 / 35 C. Shultz 160	Robert A Sawyer 160 / W. Sperlich 160	School Land 36 640	
		Gustav Gerlach 320	Ernest Gerlach 160	Ernest Bertram 160								

On this recreation of the Plat Map in Berlin Township, Douglas County, South Dakota shows where the homestead property was located just north of the property in Lincoln Township. [43]

Gustav Gelach 160 6	Ernest Bertram 321	Ernest Bertram 160 4	Johan Zirpel 161	Johan Zirpel 321	Aug Luebke 240 3	Gott. Pietz 161	Wihelm Spelich 161 2	Joseph Smith 242	Joseph Mister.. 160 1
Aug. Mullers 425	Ernest Kumke 160 5 / Will Betram 160	E. B. Doolile 320				Ernest Hoff man160	Wm. Kahln 160	Ed Heidne 160	Joseph Horst man
G. H. Jameson 163 7	August Moith.. 160 / Eva Wenzel 160	Anna K. Streeter 160 8	Herman Sperlich / Ernest Kumke 9	Christian Moege 160 / Wilhelm Balzer160	Wilhelm Titze 160	Marie Liebschwager 160 10	Daniel Schunke 320 11	John G. Beiswanger 320 12	Conrad Munte.. 160
Michael Semml.. 150	Gottlieb 160 / Schultz 160	Ernest Bertram 160	Wilhelm Balzer 160		August Schuma.. 160	Aug Luebke 160 / Christ Reimp.. 160			Fred Unger 160

On this recreation of the Plat Map in Lincoln Township, Douglas County, South Dakota shows where the Timber Culture property was located just west of the property in Lincoln Township Where Johan and Anna Augusta would build their second home. [44]

Township. It is very possible the three sons that were living at home contributed to the building of the new home. It is also possible Robert Hermann helped with the building of the new home before and after his marriage.

According to Norbert Zirpel, a grandson of Johan Zirpel, his father, Gottfried Johann Zirpel helped with the installation and the hauling of the brick for house. Norbert said that all the brick were purchased in Sioux City, Iowa.

The cost of the bricks is unknown. In other places around the country in the 1900's bricks were sold for $20 per 1,000. but they would have been pretty expensive for the time period. Norbert said that all the bricks were transported from

Johann and Augusta Zirpel's 2nd home in Lincoln Township almost completed about 1900-1914. [45]

44

Johann and Augusta Zirpel's 2nd home completed with other buildings about 1914-1920. [46]

Sioux City, Iowa to Parkston, South Dakota by way of a train. After the bricks arrived in Parkston, Johan and the boys made a many trips as necessary to haul them by horse and buggy out to the farm.

Sometime between 1912-1914, the home was nearly completed. There was construction supplies sitting on the ground in front of the house in the picture. It was a very large and beautiful house for the time period, that may have cost between $1,800. to $2,000 or more to build.

According to a granddaughter to Johan and Augusta Zirpel, Mary Ellen (Zirpel) Mettenbrink there were 4-5 rooms on the first level and 3-4 rooms on the second level of the house. There was also a full walk in attic as well as cellar below the house. The walls were 12" thick. There were rocks in the walls of cellar which lets snakes come into the cellar according to Mary Ellen until her mother, Gertrude caulked the cracks to create a seal around the rocks. Mary Ellen said that they had a parlor instead of what we call a living room, pantry for the groceries and canned goods, and the rooms were very large.

Elmer Zirpel, another grandson to Johan and Augusta Zirpel, said that he put into the indoor bathroom when he had gotten older.

Johan Transfers Land To Sons, Robert & Gottfried Zirpel

On April 13, 1914, Johan and Augusta Zirpel transferred some property they owned in Lincoln Township to their oldest son, Robert Herman Zirpel for the amount of $1. The document was recorded by the Notary Public, James Steichen. It was recorded by the Register of Deeds, Chas M. Nowlaw on April 14, 1914 at 4 PM and recorded in Book 23, in Armour, Douglas County, South Dakota.

The property The South-Half of the South-West quarter (South Half of 8 West Quarter) of Section Three in Township Ninety-Nine North of Range Sixty-Two west of the 5th Principal Median containing 80 acres according the government land survey.

Robert Hermann Zirpel and his family lived on this property for several years. The Robert Zirpel family was recorded living in Lincoln Township in Douglas County, South Dakota on the 1940 United States Census. Sometime during the 1950's Robert Herman and Bertha Zirpel moved from the farm to Sioux Falls, South Dakota.

On January 7, 1920 according to the 1920 United States Census, Johan and Augusta Zirpel were living in Lincoln Township in Douglas County, South in their new home, by the report taken by the Census Enumerator, Mrs. Carl Bertram.[99] The report said that Johan owned his farm free of any mortgages in 1920. The children recorded on the report were Gottfried Johan twenty-two years old, Elisabeth Augusta Twenty-two years old, and Edward Richard Zirpel twenty years old.

Johan and Augusta continued to lived in their second home from 1912 or 1914 until 1926 when they sold the farm to their son, Gottfried Johan Zirpel for the amount of $5,000. A second generation of Zirpel ownership of this property.

45

Johan and Anna Augusta Zirpel Family about 1909-1912.
Back Row: Emma Bertha, Elisabeth Augusta, Anna Emilie, Gottfried Johann, Wilhelm Otto and
Robert Herman Zirpel. Front Row: Johan, Edward Richard and Anna Augusta Zirpel. [47]

WARRANTY DEED RECORD

Parklus Bros. Co., Printers and Binders, Sioux City, Iowa.

Know all Men by these Presents:
John Zirpel & Augusta Zirpel, his wife

grantor of Berlin Township, Douglas County, State of South Dakota for and in consideration

of Pay $___ no/100 ___ DOLLARS,
and other valuable consideration

GRANTS, CONVEYS AND WARRANTS TO
Robert Zirpel

grantee of Parkston, So. Dak. P. O., the following described real

estate in the County of DOUGLAS, in the State of South Dakota:

The South Half of the South West
quarter (S ½ of S W ¼) of Section Three (3) in Township Ninety Nine
(99) N. of Range Sixty Two (62) west of 5th P.M. containing 80 acres according to the Government survey thereof.

Dated this 13th day of April 1914.

John Zirpel
Augusta Zirpel

STATE OF SOUTH DAKOTA, Hutchinson COUNTY, ss.
On this 13th day of April in the year 1914, before me
a Notary Public
within and for said County and State, personally appeared John Zirpel &
Augusta Zirpel (his) wife

known to me to be the person who are described in and who executed the within and foregoing
instrument and acknowledged to me that they executed the same.

My Commission expires 19.
James Bleicher
Notary Public.

STATE OF SOUTH DAKOTA, COUNTY, ss.
On this day of in the year 19 , before me
, a Notary Public
within and for said County and State, personally appeared

known to me to be the person who described in and who executed the within and foregoing
instrument and acknowledged to me that he executed the same.

My Commission expires 19
Notary Public.

STATE OF SOUTH DAKOTA, COUNTY OF DOUGLAS, ss.
Filed for record this 14th day of April A. D. 1914, at 4 o'clock P. M., and recorded
in Book 23, Page 412
By
Chas H. Nowlan
Register of Deeds
Fees, $

Warranty Deed for property transferred to Robert Hermann Zirpel from his parents, Johan and Augusta Zirpel. [48]

46

The farm owned by Erwin and Olinda Zirpel between 1968 –1984 [49]

The deed was undersigned by the Notary Public, William H. Shaw on July 6, 1926 in Hutchinson County, South Dakota for Lots Three and Four and the South Half of the North West Quarter of Section Three in Township Ninety-Nine North of Range Sixty-Two West of the 5th Principal Meridian.[100] The document was also recorded by the Register of Deed, A Tecklenburg, at Armour in Douglas County, South Dakota on July 7, 1926 at 4:30 PM and recorded in Book 3C, on page 303.

Johan and Augusta Zirpel moved into Parkston in Hutchinson County, South Dakota to their third home, while Gottfried and Gertrude moved to the farm and raised their family. Gottfried and Gertrude Zirpel lived on the farm until about 1965-1968 at which time they moved into Parkston, South Dakota.

Erwin Karl and Olinda Leota Zirpel were joint tenants of the late Gottfried Johan Zirpel for the Northwest Quarter of Section Three in Township Ninety-Nine North of Range Sixty-two West of the 5th principal median; the North Half of the Southwest Quarter of Section Three in Township Ninety-nine north of Range Sixty-two of the 5th principal median; and the South Half of the Southeast Quarter of Section Four in Township Ninety-nine North of Range Sixty-two West of the 5th principal median for the amount of Thirty One Thousand dollars according to a copy of the Executor's Deed for Gottfried Johan Zirpel on January 18, 1978 by Norbert John Zirpel,

The Executor of the Last Will and Testament of Gottfried Johan Zirpel.[101] The document was witnessed by Henry Horstman Jr., Notary Public in Hutchinson County, South Dakota. June Altenburg, Register of Deeds, in Douglas County, South Dakota recorded the document for record on February 15, 1978 at 10 o'clock and 20 minutes AM and recorded in Book 45 of Deeds, on Page 396.

A third generation of Zirpel ownership of this property would occur.

In 1968, Erwin and Olinda Zirpel moved onto the farm. They purchased the farm, and raised their boys there. They lived on the farm until about 1984, when they moved into Parkston, South Dakota.

The house in 2002 was currently owned by Chad and Nikki Bialas. [50]

47

CHAPTER 6

Birth of
Emma Bertha Zirpel*

Emma Bertha Zirpel, the seventh child of Johan and Augusta Zirpel, was born on April 1, 1893 in Douglas County, South Dakota and she was christened on April 19, 1893 in the St. John's Lutheran Church in Douglas County, South Dakota.

Emma Bertha Zirpel appeared with her parents, Johan and Augusta on 1900 United States Census in Berlin Township, now known as Washington Township, Douglas County, South Dakota. Information was recorded on June 21, 1900 by Census Enumerator, Henry Ruff.[102]

Emma Bertha Zirpel was confirmed on March 24, 1907 in the Immanuel Lutheran Church in Douglas County, South Dakota.

On April 26, 1910, Emma Bertha Zirpel was recorded with her parents, Johan and Augusta Zirpel on the 1910 United States Census taken by the Census Enumerator, Walter L. Koehn were living on the homestead located in Berlin or Washington Township in Douglas County, South Dakota.[103]

George Peter Riecke
& His Family*

George Peter Riecke, son of Peter George Riecke and Anna Catherine Shottinger, was born on September 10, 1886 in Douglas County, South Dakota.

He was christened on January 12, 1912 in the Blooming Valley Lutheran Church, in Douglas County, South Dakota

George Peter Riecke was confirmed on 1903 in the St. John's Lutheran Church in Douglas County, South Dakota.

Emma Bertha Zirpel &
George Peter Riecke Marriage*

The marriage license for George Peter Riecke and Emma Bertha Zirpel was recorded by the Circuit Court, Clerk, T. J. Wohliord, of Douglas County, South Dakota on September 28, 1912.

Emma Bertha Zirpel, the daughter of Johan and Augusta Zirpel, married George Peter Riecke, the son of Peter George Riecke and Anna Catherine Shottinger, on October 6, 1912. Rev. B. Hemprel performed the ceremony in the Immanuel Lutheran Church in Douglas County, South Dakota.

George Peter and Emma Bertha Riecke had seven children: infant daughter, Sophie Alvina Elisabeth, Albert Wilhelm, Esther Frieda, Viola Elizabeth, Clara Elsie and George Gilbert Riecke.

George Peter and Emma Bertha Riecke
Wedding on October 6, 1912 [51]

Birth of Infant Riecke
Daughter*

On July 17, 1913, the first daughter of George Peter and Emma Bertha Riecke was born and died on July 17, 1913 as she was stillborn. The infant daughter was buried in Plot: Lot 13, grave 7 in the Blooming Valley Cemetery near Corsica in Douglas County, S. D. according to the Blooming Valley Cemetery records.

Headstone for George Peter and Emma Bertha Riecke's
stillborn infant in the Blooming Valley Cemetery
near Corsica in Douglas County, South Dakota. [52]

The Emma Bertha and George Peter Riecke Wedding taken at the Johan Zirpel farm. Sitting on the ground left to right: Martha Schrank holding baby, Clarence ?, Lottie Frahm. The other side on the ground: Martha Plamp, Annie Gerlach, Bertha Misterek, Annie Schrank, Ella Frahm, Edward Richard Zirpel. Sitting first row left to right: Carl Sperlich's son, Albert Storm, Grandma Rosina Sperlich, Martha Storm with Sophie sitting on her lap, Minnie Neugebauer, Wilhelm Otto Zirpel, Bertha Rosina Zirpel, Robert Hermann Zirpel, Bride: Emma Bertha Zirpel, Groom: George Peter Riecke, unknown, unknown, unknown, unknown. Second row: Rosina Frahm, Augusta Zirpel, Emelia Fitze, Emma Kreth, Mrs. (Gottlieb) Anna Titze, Marie Hoffman, Pauline Metzger, Mrs. (Carl) Augusta Sperlich, Mrs. (Wilhelm) Anna Titze, Louise Metgzer, Mrs. (Wilhelm) Augusta Sperlich, Mrs. Liebschwager, Mr. Liebschwager, unknown, unknown, unknown. Top row: Gottlieb Titze, Ernest Hoffman, Carl Sperlich, Wilhelm Titze, George Heidner, Johan Zirpel, Wilhelm Frahm, Herman Sperlich, Herman Metzger, Gustave Storm, Gottlieb Metzger, unknown, unknown, Wilhelm Sperlich, unknown, Carl Pietz, Gottfried John Zirpel and Gottlieb Pietz. [53]

Birth of Sophie Alvina Elisabeth Riecke*

Sophie Alvina Elisabeth, the second daughter of George Peter and Emma Bertha Riecke was born on May 13, 1914 in Hutchinson County, South Dakota and she was christened on June 14, 1914 at the St. John's Lutheran Church in Douglas County, South Dakota.

Sophie Alvina Elisabeth Riecke was confirmed on May 8, 1928 in the St. John's Lutheran Church in Douglas County, South Dakota.

Birth of Albert Wilhelm Riecke*

The first son of George Peter and Emma Bertha Riecke, Albert Wilhelm Riecke was born on February 14, 1916 in Parkston in Hutchinson County, South Dakota and he was christened on March 12, 1916 in the St. John's Lutheran Church in Douglas County, South Dakota.

Albert Riecke was confirmed in 1931 in the St. John's Lutheran Church in Douglas County, South Dakota.

Birth of Esther Frieda Riecke*

The third daughter of George Peter and Emma Bertha Riecke, Esther Frieda Riecke was born on July 27, 1918 in Davison County, South Dakota and she was christened on August 25, 1918 in the St. John's Lutheran Church in Douglas County, South Dakota.

A year and eleven months old, Esther Riecke died on June 16, 1920, forty days short of

Sophie Alvina Elisabeth, Esther Frieda
and Albert Wilhelm Riecke [54]

her 2nd birthday in Davison County, South Dakota. She was buried in the St. John's Lutheran Church Cemetery in Douglas County, South Dakota.

Headstone for Esther Frieda Riecke located in the St. John's Lutheran Church Cemetery in Douglas County, South Dakota. [55]

Birth of Viola
Alma Elizabeth Riecke*

Viola Alma Elizabeth Riecke, the fourth daughter of George Peter and Emma Bertha Riecke, was born on April 2, 1921 in Hillside in Douglas County, South Dakota and she was christened on May 15, 1921 in the St. John' Lutheran Church in Douglas County, South Dakota.

Viola Alma Elizabeth Riecke was confirmed in 1935 in the St. John's Lutheran Church in Douglas County, South Dakota.

Birth of
Clara Elsie Riecke*

Clara Elsie Riecke, the fifth daughter of George Peter and Emma Bertha Riecke, was born on October 8, 1923 in Davison County, South Dakota.

Clara Riecke was confirmed in 1937 in the St. John's Lutheran Church in Douglas County, South Dakota.

Birth of
George Gilbert Riecke*

The second son of George Peter and Emma Bertha Riecke, George Gilbert Riecke was born on February 10, 1928 in Corsica, Douglas County, South Dakota.

George Gilbert Riecke was confirmed on April 26, 1942 in the St. John's Lutheran Church in Douglas County, South Dakota.

Back row: Sophia Alvina Elisabeth, Emma Bertha, Albert Wilhelm, Front row: sitting George Peter holding Clara Elsie, standing Viola Alma Elizabeth Riecke.[56]

George Peter & Emma Bertha
Riecke - The Later Years*

George and Emma Riecke farmed in Hutchinson County, South Dakota for about three years. They had a farm in Baker Township for around 30 years.

George Peter Riecke and his wife, Emma Bertha appeared on the 1920 United States Census on March 2, 1920 according to the Census Enumerator, Floy Z. Bowers living in Baker

Township for around 30 years.

George Peter Riecke and his wife, Emma Bertha appeared on the 1920 United States Census on March 2, 1920 according to the Census Enumerator, Floy Z. Bowers living in Baker Township in Davison County, South Dakota.[104] There were three children recorded on the census record. Sophie Alvina Elisabeth was five years old. Albert Wilhelm was three years eleven months old. And Esther Frieda was six months old.

On April 2, 1930, the Census Enumerator, Francis Dohl, for the 1930 United States Census, recorded the George Riecke family still living in Baker Township in Davison County, South Dakota.[105] On this report George Peter and Emma Bertha Riecke had five children living with them. Sophie Alvina Elisabeth was fifteen years old. Albert Wilhelm was fourteen years old. Viola Alma Elizabeth was eight years old. Clara Elsie was six years old, and George Gilbert was two years and eleven months old.

The Riecke homestead near Armour, South Dakota. 57]

Gladys B. Moller, the Census Enumerator for the 1940 United States Census recorded George Peter family still living on their farm in Baker Township in Davison County, South Dakota.

George Peter was fifty-three years old and working as a farmer for about 40 hours a week on his farm. Emma Bertha was forty-seven years old. They had two children still living with them. Clara Elsie was sixteen years old and working as a housekeeper at home. George Gilbert was twelve years old.

George Peter and Emma Bertha Riecke [58]

George Peter Riecke died in the St. Benedict Hospital in Parkston in Hutchinson County, South Dakota on February 17, 1958.

His funeral service was held on Thursday, February 20, 1958 at the St. Paul Lutheran Church at 12:30 pm and also at the St. John's Lutheran Church at 2 pm with Rev. Haase officiating.

His burial was in the St. John's Lutheran Church Cemetery in Douglas County, South Dakota. The Pallbearer were Peter George Riecke, Ernest Gerlach, Walter Zirpel, Melvin Zirpel, Walter Gerlach and Donovan Anderson.

At the time of his death his was survived by his wife, Emma Bertha; two son: Albert Wilhelm of Mitchell, South Dakota and George Gilbert Jr. of Sioux Falls, South Dakota; three daughters: Mrs. Emil Semmler of Ethan, South Dakota; Mrs. Arnold Schuh of Mitchell, South Dakota; and Mrs. Kenneth Schrank of Corsica, South Dakota, as well as two brothers: William Riecke of Mount Vernon, South Dakota and August Riecke of Spencer, Iowa and one sister: Mrs. Robert Zirpel of Parkston, South Dakota and sixteen grandchildren.

Emma Bertha Riecke died at the home of her sister and husband, Mr. and Mrs. Oscar Gerlach in Parkston in Hutchinson County, South Dakota on May 25, 1962 at the age of 69 years old. The funeral services were held on Tuesday, May 29, 1962 at the St. Paul Lutheran Church and her burial was at the St. John's Lutheran Church Cemetery in Douglas County, South Dakota.

Emil Jacob Semmler
& His Family*

Emil Jacob Semmler was seventeen years old and recorded on the 1930 United States Census on April 22, 1930 by the Census Enumerator, Wm. Draayour living with his mother, Katherine and his step-father, John Hartmann in Valley Township in Douglas County, South Dakota.[106]

The record showed that Emil's mother, Katherine was born in Romania and she was about thirty-right years old. On the report was two sisters: Ottilia M. Semmler was sixteen years old and Esther E. Semmler was thirteen years old, as well as one brother: Christian M. Semmler was fifteen years old.

There were also four step-brothers and three step-sisters: Elmer Hartmann was eleven years old, Gideon D. Hartmann was ten years old, Olga L. Hartmann was nine years old, Viola K. Hartmann was eight years old, Helmet R. Hartmann was five years old, Arlene S. Hartmann was three years and six months old, and Leonard C. W. Hartmann was one year and eight months old.

The Marriage of
Sophie A. Elisabeth Riecke &
Emil Jacob Semmler*

Sophie Alvina Elisabeth Riecke, daughter of George Peter and Emma Bertha Riecke married Emil Jacob Semmler, son of Christian Semmler and Katherine Neu, on December 21, 1937 in Hillside in Douglas County, South Dakota. Rev. P. Teckenburg, a Lutheran minister performed the ceremony according to a copy of South Dakota Marriage Records.[107]

Emil Jacob and Sophie Alvina Elisabeth Semmler had no children.

On April 4, 1940, Emil and Sophie Semmler were recorded on the 1940 United States Census by the Census Enumerator, Henry Legtunberg living in Washington Township in Douglas County, South Dakota.[108] Emil was about twenty-seven years old and working about forty-eight hours as a farmer. Sophie was about twenty-five years old.

Emil and Sophie Semmler lived in Mitchell in Davison County, South Dakota approximately five years from 1953 until 1957.[109] At some point they moved to Ethan in Davison County, South Dakota remaining until their deaths. According to

Sophie Alvina Elisabeth Riecke & Emil Jacob Semmler
Wedding on December 21, 1937 [59]

the family Emil had been a Superintendent of the Sewer Department in Ethan or Mitchell South Dakota.

Emil Jacob Semmler died on July 17, 1983 in Ethan in Davison County, South Dakota and his burial was in the Sunset Memorial Park Cemetery in Mitchell in Davison County, South Dakota.

Sophie Alvina Elisabeth Semmler died December 1, 1996 in Ethan in Davison County, South Dakota.

Her funeral service was held at the New Home Lutheran Church on Thursday, December 5, 1996 at 2 pm in Mitchell, Davison County, South Dakota. Pastor Kathy Walz officiated.

Pallbearers were Bill Kretchmer, Garland Schrank, Dale Schmidt, Maylon Schuh, Bryan Schrank, and Gary Stadlman. The honorary pallbearers were Clifford Isaax, Kenneth Semmler, Chris Semmler and Wayne Tietz.

Her burial was in the Sunset Memorial Park Cemetery, in Mitchell in Davison County, South Dakota with her husband, Emil. Bittner Funeral Chapel handled the arrangements.

Erna Rosina Schuh
& Her Family*

Erna Rosina Schuh was fifteen years old

when she was recorded on the 1930 United States Census on April 2, 1930 by the Census Enumerator, P. E. Roheck living in Belmont Township in Douglas County, South Dakota with her mother, Mary R.[110] Mary R. was listed as forty-one years old.

There was no mention of her father on the report. On the report were three other children: Gideon E. was twelve years old, Arnold R. was eleven years old and Adeline was eight years old.

The Marriage of Albert Wilhelm Riecke & Erna Rosina Schuh*

Erna Rosina Schuh and Albert Wilhelm Riecke
Wedding on June 5, 1936. [60]

Albert Wilhelm Riecke, son of George Peter and Emma Bertha Riecke, married Erna Rosina Schuh, daughter of Leonhardt Bernard Schuh and Mary Regina Bietz, on June 5, 1936 in Hillside in Douglas County, South Dakota according to a copy of South Dakota Marriage records.[111]

Albert had received his father's consent on February 14, 1936 and Rev. P. Teckenburg performed the ceremony.

On April 23, 1940 according to the 1940 United States Census taken by the Census Enumerator, Anton F. Lingermann, Albert Wilhelm and Erna Rosina Riecke were living in Rome Township in Davison County, South Dakota.[112]

Albert was about twenty-four years old and

working about 72 hours a week farming. Erna was about twenty-five years old.

Erna Rosina and Albert Wilhelm Riecke [61]

Sophie Alvina Elizabeth Semmler and
Erna Rosina Riecke. [62]

Albert Wilhelm and Erna Rosina Riecke had no children. Albert and Erna lived in Mitchell in Davison County, South Dakota during their entire marriage.

Albert Wilhelm Riecke died on December 15, 1984 in Mitchell, Davison County, South Dakota and the location of his burial is unknown.

According to U.S. Public Records Index, Erna Rosina Riecke was still living in Mitchell, Davison County, South Dakota in 2001.[113]

The Marriage of Viola Alma Elizabeth Riecke & Arnold Reuben Schuh*

Viola Alma Elizabeth Riecke, daughter of George Peter and Emma Bertha Riecke, married Arnold Rueben Schuh, the son of Leonhardt Bernard Schuh and Mary Regina Bietz, on February 6, 1940 in O'Neil, in Holt County, Nebraska.

**Agatha Semmler, Gideon Schuh,
Viola Alma Elizabeth Riecke and Arnold Rueben Schuh
Wedding on February 6, 1940. [63]**

Arnold and Viola Schuh were recorded on the 1940 United States Census on April 12, 1940 by the Census Enumerator, John E. Sanger living at South Wisconsin Street in Mitchell, Davison County, South Dakota.[114] They living in the same house with Arnold's brother-in-law, Edwin Bietz and his wife, Laura D. was listed as twenty-one years old and working as a laborer in a local garage.

Arnold Rueben and Viola Alma Elizabeth Schuh had five children: Sheila Joan, Duane Arnold, Maylon Ray, Arlen Lee and Nola Mae Schuh.

Arnold and Viola lived in Scotland, South Dakota for sometime, while Arnold owned and operated a bar.

In 1950 they moved to Mitchell, South Dakota. Arnold drove a gas truck for Wudel Oil for two years and in 1952 he began painting with Fred Nagel.

Birth of
Sheila Joan Schuh*

Sheila Joan Schuh, daughter of Arnold Ruben and Viola Alma Elizabeth Schuh, was born on December 25, 1940 in Delmont, Douglas County, South Dakota and she was christened in the Immanuel Lutheran Church in Douglas County, South Dakota.

Birth of
Duane Arnold Schuh*

Duane Arnold Schuh, son of Arnold Ruben and Viola Alma Elizabeth Schuh, was born on January 29, 1947 in Delmont, Douglas County, South Dakota.

Birth of
Maylon Ray Schuh*

Maylon Lee Schuh, son of Arnold Ruben and Viola Alma Elizabeth Schuh, was born on January 8, 1949 in Scotland, Bon Homme County, South Dakota.

Birth of
Arlen Lee Schuh*

Arlen Lee Schuh, son of Arnold Ruben and Viola Alma Elizabeth Schuh, was born on April 7, 1952.

Birth of
Nola Mae Schuh*

Nola Mae, daughter of Arnold Ruben and Viola Alma Elizabeth Schuh, was born on May 11, 1954 in Mitchell, Davison County, South Dakota.

Arnold Rueben &
Viola Alma Elizabeth Schuh -
The Later Years*

In the later years of the 1950's he established Schuh Painting, and his sons, Duane and Arlen took over the business in 1972.

Viola Alma Elizabeth Schuh died on March 13, 1987 in Mitchell, Davison County, South Dakota.

Her funeral was held at Will Funeral Chapel on Tuesday, March 17, 1987 in Mitchell, South Dakota. Rev. Tim Stadem officiated.

Her burial was in the Graceland Cemetery in Mitchell, Davison County, South Dakota. The pallbearers were Larry Schrank, Delvon Schuh, Steve Schrank, Harlan Schuh, Garland Schrank

Arnold & Viola Schuh Family 1977 Back row: Duane Arnold, Nola Mae, and Sheila Joan Schuh.
Front row: Arlen Lee, Viola Alma Elizabeth, Arnold Rueben and Maylon Ray Schuh. [64]

Survivors included her husband, Arnold, five children: Gus & Sheila Wright of Detroit, Michigan; Duane Schuh, Arlen Schuh and Maylon Schuh, all of Mitchell, South Dakota. and Mrs. Nola Walinski of Appleton, Wisconsin; two sisters: Mrs. Clara Schrank of Mitchell, South Dakota and Mrs. Sophie Semmler of Ethan, South Dakota; thirteen grandchildren and two great-grand-children.

Arnold Rueben Schuh died at the age of 83 years old at this residence under hospice care in Mitchell, Davison County, South Dakota on Friday, April 26, 2002.

His funeral services were held at the First Lutheran Church in Mitchell, South Dakota.

His burial was next to his wife, Viola in the Graceland Memorial Cemetery in Mitchell, Davison County, South Dakota.

He was survived by his children: Duane Schuh and wife, Caroline of Rapid City; Maylon Schuh, and wife, Bonita of Mannheim, Germany; Arlen Schuh, and wife, Patricia of Mitchell, South Dakota; Nola Braiverman and husband, Marc of Appleton, Wisconsin; 13 grandchildren; 8 great-grandchildren; brothers: Gideon Schuh of Tripp, South Dakota; and Arthur Schuh and wife, Tillie of Delmont, South Dakota; and one sister: Erna Riecke of Parkston, South Dakota.

He was preceded in death by his wife, Viola

in 1987; a daughter, Sheila Wright in 2000; three brother; and two sisters.

Sheila Joan Schuh & Ronald Cripps Marriage & Family*

Sheila Joan Schuh, daughter of Arnold Ruben and Viola Alma Elizabeth Schuh, married Ronald Cripps on May 1, 1962. The marriage ended in divorce.

Ronald and Sheila Cripps had two children: Barbara and Kenneth Cripps.

Sheila Joan Cripps & William Wright Marriage *

Sheila Joan Cripps married William Wright.

Sheila Joan Wright died on October 6, 2000 at the Henry Ford Hospital in Wyandotte, Houghton County, Michigan.

The cause of her death was from Cholaugio Carcinoma. A carcinoma would have been a malignant tumor on an organ or a part the body and it may have spread to other parts of her body.

Her father, Arnold Schuh authorized the cremation of his daughter, Sheila and her ashes were buried in the Graceland Memorial Cemetery in Mitchell, Davison County, South Dakota.

Duane Arnold Schuh & Caroline Esther Zirpel Marriage & Family*

Duane Arnold Schuh, son of Arnold Ruben and Viola Alma Elizabeth Schuh, married Caroline Esther Zirpel, daughter of Waldemar Gotthelf Zirpel and Lillian Esther Moege, on May 1968 at the Zion Lutheran Church or the First Lutheran Church in Mitchell, Davison County, South Dakota. The marriage ended in divorce, then they remarried, they remarried again later.

Duane helped his parents to build the Schuh Painting & Papering contractor business which he later purchased.

Duane and Caroline moved to Rapid City, South Dakota sometime after 1970. Duane owned and operated his own painting business there. Duane has been awarded the "Craftsman Award" for his excellence in his field.

He later sold his business and worked at the Rapid City Regional Hospital. Caroline worked for the Black Hills Federal Credit Union in the Accounting Department.

Duane Arnold and Caroline Esther Schuh had two children: Paula Kay and Mark Duane Schuh.

Paula Kay Schuh was born on July 24, 1969 in Mitchell, Davison County, South Dakota.

Mark Duane Schuh was born on December 14, 1970 in Mitchell, Davison County, South Dakota.

Paula Kay Schuh & Jack Gray Marriage *

Paula Kay Schuh married Jack Gray, son of Charles and Edith Gray, on September 5, 1992. The marriage ended in divorce.

Paula Kay Gray & Tab D. Arthur Marriage & Family*

Paula Kay Gray married Tab D. Arthur, son of Eugene and Kaylynn Arthur, on September 6, 1996 in Gillette, Campbell County, Wyoming. Tab D. Arthur was born on October 18, 1959 in Wyoming.

Tab D. and Paula Kay Arthur had two children: Morgan and Lane James Arthur.

Morgan Arthur was born on April 29, 1997 in Gillette, Campbell County, Wyoming.

Lane James Arthur was born on March 19, 2000 in Gillette, Campbell County, Wyoming.

Josette Verzani & Mr. Wurdeman Marriage & Family*

Josette Verzani was born on August 5, 1970 in Norfolk County, Nebraska.

Josette Verzani married Mr. Wurdeman on a known date.

Mr. Wurdeman and Josette Wurdeman had two children: Ryan Edward and Candice Marie Wurdeman.

Ryan Edward Wurdeman was born on February 28, 1991.

Candice Marie Wurdeman was born May 24, 1993.

Candice has been attending Dakota Wesleyan College in Mitchell, South Dakota.

Mark Duane Schuh & Josette Wurdeman Marriage *

Mark Duane Schuh married Josette Wurdeman on July 10, 1999 in Rapid City, Pennington County, South Dakota.

Maylon Ray Schuh His Early Years*

Maylon Ray grew up in Mitchell, and at the age of 14 he quit high school to help with the family business "Schuh Painting and Papering Contractor". He enjoyed working with cars and took a night job as a "pump jockey" for his spending money with Eddie's Mobil. He spent many long hours working on cars, his own, for his friends and for customers.

March of 1966 Maylon enlisted in the South Dakota Army National Guard. He went to Fort Leonardwood, Missouri for his Basic Training and his Advanced Individual Training (AIT) was at Aberdeen Proving Grounds, Maryland. After he came back to South Dakota and continued to work for his parents.

Maylon Ray Schuh & Bonita Marie Young Marriage & Family*

Maylon Ray Schuh, son of Arnold Ruben and Viola Alma Elizabeth Schuh, married Bonita

Marie Young, daughter of Ralph John Young and Patricia Ann Chivington, on March 6, 1971 in the First Lutheran Church in Mitchell, Davison County, South Dakota.

Maylon and Bonita Schuh had five children: Aaron Ray, Schane Michael, Tanya Marie, Dawn Rene and Amanda Rose Schuh.

Aaron Ray Schuh was born on September 26, 1971.

Schane Michael Schuh was born on December 28, 1972.

Tanya Marie Schuh was born on February 14, 1974.

Dawn Rene Schuh was born on February 18, 1975 in the St. Joseph Hospital, Mitchell, Davison County, South Dakota.

Amanda Rose Schuh was born on July 23, 1976 in Sioux Falls, Minnehaha County, South Dakota.

Maylon Schuh Family Back Row: Aaron Ray, Schane Michael and Tanya Marie Schuh. Front Row: Maylon Ray, Bonita Marie, Amanda Rose and Dawn Rene Schuh [65]

Maylon Ray & Bonita Marie Schuh - The Later Years*

Maylon was brought on board as a full-time employee of the Combined Support Maintenance Shop #1 in Mitchell as a mechanic in December of 1971. He had started as the youngest, newest mechanic and worked his way "up the ladder" to the Shop Foreman. He was employed for 29 years, 9 months and took early retirement.

Maylon Schuh was a member of the 665th Maintenance Co for the South Dakota National Guard for nearly 43 years. He began as a Private First Class (PFC) and finished as a Warrant Officer 4 (CW 4). While he was in the military he

Maylon Ray Schuh, Warrant Officer 4 (CW 4) in the 665th Maintenance Co for the South Dakota Army National Guard. [66]

went back to school and obtained his GED, as well as earned several college credits towards a degree in Human Psychology.

Starting in 1976; and last 9 months, he was sent to thirteen different states doing airbrush murals on a semi trailer that had been transformed into CO_2 pellet rifle ranges and used as recruiting tools. Each state he included the seal, the bird, flower and some monument that was significant to that state. For South Dakota he painted Mount Rushmore and he did Stone Mountain for Georgia and so on. He was commissioned to all the murals, plaques and signs for the South Dakota National Guards Museum located in Pierre, South Dakota.

Following his early retirement as a mechanic, Maylon took the opportunity to serve in an active duty tour in Germany for 6 years, which actually turned into 7 years and 1 month!

Maylon Ray Schuh was awarded many medals during his military career. He received the Valley Forge Cross for Valor, the Soldier's Medal for Valor, both for his actions during the 1972 Rapid City Flood. He was awarded the Meritorious Service Medal for his 7 years of work in Europe for the National Guard Bureau. And when he retired January 8, 2009, he was awarded the Legion of Merit for his lifetime service to the military. Maylon was an expert shot, with a Chief's 50 Gold Medal to prove it. He also has a Silver Medal and a Bronze Medal. The most satisfying achievement was in 1984 when he was chosen as the South Dakota NCO of the Year and went on in 1985 to be chosen as the FORSCOM (Armed Forces Command) NCO of the Year, which is the highest as an enlisted person can go.

Maylon went on to train other soldiers in

South Dakota for the competition and in 1986 one of his students won the title and again in 1987 Bonita, his wife was chosen for the same honor. They were the only married couple that have ever won that title!

He has a love of classic cars, in particular "goats" GTOs. He has several of them that have been waiting for the retirement thing to happen so he has more time to restore them. They even had to build a "goat barn" to store them all in, each one has its own stall!

Since Maylon's retirement, his wife, Bonita and Maylon have been renovating their house by adding a new addition. They need more room to house all the antique furniture they purchased from Germany. They had 17 of the 21 rooms completed. Then they will paint the shop, and the cars, of course.

Bonita Marie and Maylon Ray Schuh [67]

Schane Michael Schuh & Paula R. Teeslink Marriage *

Schane Michael Schuh, son of Maylon Ray Schuh and Bonita Marie Young, married Paula R. Teeslink.

Paula was born in 1973.

Tanya Marie Schuh & Benjamin Lee Culver Marriage & Family*

Tanya Marie Schuh, daughter of Maylon Ray Schuh and Bonita Marie Young, married Benjamin Lee Culver.

Benjamin Lee and Tanya Marie Culver had three children: Cole Damon Schuh, Dominik Dean, Schuh and Korbin Jude Culver.

Cole Damon Schuh, son of Benjamin Lee and Tanya Marie Culver was born on December 16, 2002 in the Avera Queen of Peace Hospital in

Mitchell, Davison County, South Dakota.

Dominik Dean Schuh, son of Benjamin Lee and Tanya Marie Culver was born on January 30, 2003 in the Avera Queen of Peace Hospital in Mitchell, Davison County, South Dakota.

Korbin Jude Culver son of Benjamin Lee and Tanya Marie Culver was born on August 23, 2011 in the Avera Queen of Peace Hospital in Mitchell, Davison County, South Dakota.

Dawn Rene Schuh & Joshua Allen Pfiester Marriage & Family*

Dawn Rene Schuh, daughter of Maylon Ray Schuh and Bonita Marie Young, married Joshua Allen Pfiester on May 30, 2003. The marriage ended in divorce.

Joshua was born on August 28, 1975. Joshua and Dawn Pfiester had one child: Bonita Elizabeth Rose Pfiester.

Bonita Elizabeth Rose Pfiester was born on September 7, 2004 at the Avera Queen Peace Hospital in Mitchell, Davison County, South Dakota.

Dawn Rene Pfiester & Randy Botts Marriage *

Dawn Rene Pfiester married Randy Botts on June 1, 2009. Randy was born on September 8, 1964. The marriage ended in divorce in 2010.

Amanda Rose Schuh & Chester IV Farrell Marriage*

Amanda Rose Schuh, daughter of Maylon Ray Schuh and Bonita Marie Young, married Chester IV Farrell, son of Chester III Farrell and an unknown person, on September 14, 1995. Chester was born on March 18, 1971. The marriage ended in divorce in 1999.

Amanda Rose Ferrell & David Jacob Sheets II Marriage & Family*

David Jacob II and Jean Sheets had a child: Hannah Karon Sheets, before he had married Amanda Farrell.

Hannah Karon Sheets was born on November 8, 2002 in Rochester, Monroe County, New York.

Amanda Rose Farrell, married David Jacob

Sheets II, son of David and Vicki Sheets, on June 17, 2006 in Rochester, Monroe County, New York. David was born on March 15, 1971.

David Jacob II Sheets and Amanda Sheets had a child: David Jacob III Sheets.

David Jacob III Sheets was born on September 16, 2006 in Rochester, Monroe County, New York.

Amanda Rose, David Jacob III, Hannah Karon, And David Jacob Sheets II [68]

Arlen Lee Schuh & Patricia Joann Stahl Marriage & Family*

Patricia and Arlen Lee Schuh. [69]

Arlen Lee Schuh, son of Arnold Rueben and Viola Alma Elizabeth Schuh, married Patricia Joann Stahl on August 5, 1972 in the Zion Lutheran Church in Mitchell, Davison County, South Dakota. The marriage ended in divorce.

Patricia Joann Stahl was born on November 10, 1951.

Arlen Lee and Patricia Schuh had two children: Melissa Ann and Kristin Lea Schuh.

Melissa Ann was born on November 7, 1976.

Kristin Lea Schuh was born on July 20, 1980.

Melissa Ann Schuh & John Wayne Prunty Marriage & Family*

Melissa Ann Schuh married John Wayne Prunty. John was born in 1976.

John Wayne and Melissa Prunty had four children: Adelyn, William, Olivia and Ave Lynae Prunty.

Adelyn and William Prunty were born on August 25, 2005 in the Avera Queen of Peace Hospital in Mitchell, Davison County, South Dakota.

Olivia Prunty was born on August 11, 2007.

Ave Lynae Prunty was born on October 6, 2009.

Back row: John Wayne and Melissa Ann Prunty. Front row: William, Adelyn, Ava Lynae and Olivia Prunty. [70]

Nola Mae Schuh & Glenn Ray Walinski Marriage & Family*

Nola Mae Schuh, daughter of Arnold Rueben and Viola Alma Elizabeth Schuh, was born on May 12, 1953 in Mitchell, Davison County, South Dakota.

Nola Mae Schuh married Glenn Ray Walinski, son of George and Ginny Walinski, on May 11, 1974 in Mitchell, Davison County, South Dakota. The marriage ended in divorce.

Glenn Ray Walinski was born on September 1, 1952 in Wisconsin.

Glenn Ray and Nola Mae Walinski had two children: Ryan Glenn and Nikki. M. Walinski.

Ryan Glenn Walinski was born on May 20, 1978 in la Crosse, La Crosse County, Wisconsin.

Nikki M. Walinski was born on January 15, 1980.

Ryan Glenn, Nola Mae and Nikki M. Walinski. [71]

Ryan Glenn Walinski & Courtney Foster Marriage & Family*

Courtney Foster and Ryan Glenn Walinski Wedding day.[72]

Ryan Glenn Walinski married Courtney Foster, daughter of Stephen Foster and an unknown person, on October 9, 2004 in Denver, Denver County, Colorado.

Courtney Foster was born on Apr 12, 1983 in Centennial, Arapahoe County, Colorado.

Ryan Glenn and Courtney Walinski had two children: Jayla Mae and Callie Ann Walinski.

Jayla Mae Walinski was born on February 17, 2008.

Callie Ann Walinski was born on June 9, 2010.

Nicki M. Walinski & Greg Hauser Marriage *

Nikki M. Walinski married Greg Hauser on July 26, 2008.

Greg Hauser and Nikki M. Walinski Wedding Day [73]

Nola Mae Walinski & Marc Ross Braiverman Marriage *

Nola Mae Walinski married Marc Ross Braiverman on an unknown date. The marriage ended in divorce. Marc Ross Braiverman was born on March 22, 1952 in San Francisco, San Francisco County, California.

Nola Mae Braiverman & Douglas Wenzel Marriage*

Nola Mae Braiverman married Douglas Elliot Wenzel on August 30, 1988 in Appleton, Outagamie County, Wisconsin.

Douglas Elliot Wenzel was born on August 30, 1948.

Kenneth August Schrank & His Family*

Kenneth August Schrank, son of Charles Schrank and Emma M. Wicht[115], was born on May 30, 1921 in Douglas County, South Dakota.

Kenneth August Schrank was recorded on the 1930 United States Census at the age of eight years old living with his parents. The document was recorded by the Census Enumerator, Wm. Draayour on April 5, 1940 with the Schrank family living in Garfield Township in Douglas County, South Dakota.[116] The report said that Kenneth's father, Charley or Charles Schrank was

60

born in South Dakota and he worked as a farmer on his own farm and his was forty-three years old. Kenneth's mother, Emma M. Schrank was born in Nebraska and was thirty-eight years old.

Also list on that census report were five other children: Ella M. was twenty years old, Ralph D. was eighteen years old, Mabel L. was sixteen years old, Lloyd J. was ten years old and Helen I. was three years and eleven months old.

On April 24, 1940, the Census Enumerator, Henry Lightberg for the 1940 United States Census recorded Kenneth Schrank still living with his parents, Charles and Emma Schrank in Garfield Township, Douglas County, South Dakota.[117] Charles was listed as a farmer and his sons, Lloyd and Kenneth were working as farm laborer on the farm.

Daughters of Charles and Emma were also listed: one daughter, Helen worked as housekeeper; while the other daughter, Mabel was working as a waitress in a cafe.

Clara Elsie Riecke & Kenneth August Schrank Marriage & Family*

George Jones, Kenneth August Schrank, Clara Elsie Riecke, and Helen Jones on Wedding day. [74]

Clara Elsie Riecke, daughter of George Peter and Emma Bertha Riecke, married Kenneth A. Schrank, son of Charles Schrank and Emma M. Wicht, on December 20, 1941 in Hillside in Douglas County, South Dakota by Rev. P Tecklenburg, a Lutheran Minister according to a copy of a South Dakota Marriage record.[118]

Kenneth had gotten Charles Schrank, his father's consent on May 30, 1941, while Clara had gotten George Peter Riecke, her father's consent on October 8, 1941.

Kenneth August and Clara Elsie Schrank had ten children: Larry Dean, Harvey Lee, Janice Emma, Garland Kenneth, Barbara Lynn, Steven Charles, Julie Faye, Curtis Gene, Bryan Scott and Dawn Marie Schrank.

Kenneth Schrank Family. Back row: Clara Elsie and Kenneth August Schrank. Middle row: Larry Dean, Janice Emma, Barbara Lynn, and Garland Kenneth Schrank. Front row: Harvey Lee Schrank. [75]

Birth of Larry Dean Schrank*

Larry Dean Schrank, son of Kenneth August and Clara Elsie Schrank, was born on July 12, 1941 in Davison County, South Dakota.

Birth of Harvey Lee Schrank*

Harvey Lee Schrank, son of Kenneth August and Clara Elsie Schrank, was born on September 2, 1944.

Birth of Janice Emma Schrank*

Janice Emma Schrank, daughter of Kenneth August and Clara Elsie Schrank, was born on October 30, 1945.

Birth of Garland Kenneth Schrank*

Garland Kenneth Schrank, son of Kenneth August and Clara Elsie Schrank, was born on January 2, 1948 in Parkston in Hutchinson County, South Dakota.

Birth of
Barbara Lynn Schrank*

Barbara Lynn Schrank, daughter of Kenneth August and Clara Elsie Schrank, was born on July 7, 1949.

Birth of
Steven Charles Schrank*

Steven Charles Schrank, son of Kenneth August and Clara Elsie Schrank, was born on November 27, 1953 in the St. Benedict Hospital in Parkston in Hutchinson County, South Dakota.

Birth of
Julie Faye Schrank*

Julie Faye Schrank, daughter of Kenneth August and Clara Elsie Schrank, was born on April 9, 1957 in Parkston in Hutchinson County, South Dakota.

Birth of
Curtis Gene Schrank*

Curtis Gene Schrank, son of Kenneth August and Clara Elsie Schrank, was born on July 20, 1960 in Parkston in Hutchinson County, South Dakota.

Birth of
Bryan Scott Schrank*

Bryan Scott Schrank, son of Kenneth August and Clara Elsie Schrank, was born on November 6, 1961 in Parkston in Hutchinson County, South Dakota.

Birth of
Dawn Marie Schrank*

Dawn Marie Schrank, daughter of Kenneth August and Clara Elsie Schrank, was born on October 27, 1965 in Parkston in Hutchinson County, South Dakota.

Kenneth August & Clara Elsie Schrank - The Later Years*

Kenneth and Clara Schrank lived near Parkston, South Dakota for the early portion of their marriage as most of their children were born in Parkston. According to the U.S. City Directories Kenneth and Clara Schrank also lived at 32 Baker Corsica in Mitchell, South Dakota from 1950 through 1960.

Kenneth August Schrank died on January 17, 1983 in Mitchell in Davison County, South Dakota at the age of sixty-one years old.

His burial was in the Graceland Cemetery in Mitchell in Davison County, South Dakota.

Clara Elsie Schrank died on April 30, 1987 in Mitchell, Davison County, South Dakota.

Her burial was in Graceland Cemetery in Mitchell in Davison County, South Dakota next to her husband, Kenneth.

Larry Dean Schrank & Arlene Carol Herring Marriage & Family*

Larry Dean Schrank, son of Kenneth August and Clara Elsie Schrank, married Arlene Carol Herring, daughter of William Herring and Rachele Noldner, on March 15, 1969 in Mt. Vernon in Davison County, South Dakota.

Arlene Carol Herring was born on December 21, 1945 in the Methodist Hospital in Mitchell in Davison County, South Dakota.

Larry Dean and Arlene Carol Schrank had three children: Kristi K., Kevin K. and Darren Schrank.

Kristi K. Schrank was born on February 28, 1972 in the Methodist Hospital in Mitchell in Davison County, South Dakota.

Kevin K. Schrank was born on June 6, 1973 in the Methodist Hospital in Mitchell in Davison County, South Dakota.

Kylee Renee Schrank was born on February 3, 1997.

Darren Schrank was born on an unknown date.

Larry Dean Schrank died on March 3, 2001 in Trent in Moody County, South Dakota. It is not known where he is buried.

Kristi K. Schrank & John E. Harris Marriage*

Kristi K. Schrank married John E. Harris, son of unknown and Andrea Reynolds, on September 14, 1996 in Clear Lake in Deuel County, South Dakota. The marriage ended in divorce.

John E. Harris was born on November 20, 1973 in Hendricks, Lincoln County, Minnesota.

Kristi K. Harris & Todd J. Stark Marriage*

Kristi K. Harris married Todd J. Stark on April 17, 2005.

Todd J. Stark was born on December 3, 1974 in Watertown in Codington County, South Dakota.

Kevin K. Schrank & Jodi S. Bass Marriage & Family*

Kevin K. Schrank married Jodi L. Bass, daughter of Tom Bass and Carla Hill, on March 3, 1994 in Canton in Lincoln County, South Dakota.

Jodi L. Bass was born on January 12, 1974.

Kevin and Jodi Schrank had two children: Whitney Jo and Kylee Renee Schrank.

Whitney Jo Schrank was born on August 14, 1994 in Sioux Falls, Minnehaha County, South Dakota.

Kylee Renee Schrank was born on February 3, 1997.

Harvey Lee Schrank & Suzanne Mentele Marriage & Family*

Harvey Lee Schrank, son of Kenneth August and Clara Elsie Schrank, married Suzanne Mentele, on May 11, 1968.

Suzanne Mentele was on February 10, 1949.

Harvey Lee and Suzanna Schrank had three children: Lenny Lee, Michael Lee, and Randall Lee Schrank.

Lenny Lee Schrank was born on November 12, 1969.

Michael Lee Schrank was born on July 8, 1971.

Randall Lee Schrank was born on June 6, 1972.

Charles Joseph Mentele & His Family*

Charles Mentele's father, Robert Francis Mentele was born on December 17, 1898 in Epiphany in Minor County, South Dakota and he died on June 26, 1984 in Canova in Minor County, South Dakota.

Charles Mentele's mother, Ann Regina Lawrence was born in Eagle Butte in Dewey County, South Dakota and she died on October 19, 1986 in Canova in Miner County, South Dakota.

His parents, Robert Francis Mentele and Ann Regina Lawrence were married on April 28, 1941 by a Catholic Priest. Charles also had two brothers, James Francis and William Walter in his family.

Charles Joseph Mentele, son of Robert Francis Mentele and Ann Regina Lawrence, was born on May 19, 1946.

Janice Emma Schrank & Charles Joseph Mentele Marriage & Family*

Janice Emma Schrank, daughter of Kenneth August and Clara Elsie Schrank, married Charles Joseph Mentele, son of Robert Francis Mentele and Ann Regina Lawrence on July 15, 1967.

Charles and Janice Mentele had seven children: Tammara Sue, Donald John, Pamela Jean, Lynn Ann, Karen, Douglas Lee and John Paul Mentele.

Tammara Sue Mentele was born on December 8, 1968 in Mitchell, Davison County, S.D.

Donald John Mentele was born on January 10, 1970 in Mitchell, Davison County, South Dakota.

Pamela Jean Mentele was born on January 12, 1971.

Lynn Ann Mentele was born on November 6, 1972.

Karen Mentele was born on July 8, 1975.

Douglas Lee Mentele was born on June 13, 1981.

John Paul Mentele was born on September 15, 1984.

Janice Emma Mentele died on February 7, 2006 in Canova, Miner County, South Dakota.

Tammara Sue Mentele & Ray Ernest Reif Marriage & Family*

Tammara Sue Mentele married Ray Ernest Reif, son of Robert Reif and Darlene Bies, on June 20, 1992 in St. Mary's Church in Salem, McCook County, South Dakota.

Ray Ernest Reif was born on April 10, 1971 in Sioux Falls, Minnehaha County, South Dakota.

Ray and Tammara Reif had two children: Kristin Renee and Ryan John Reif.

Kristin Renee Reif was born on November

16, 1992 in Sioux Falls, Minnehaha County, South Dakota.

Ryan John Reif was born on July 25, 1996 in Sioux Falls, Minnehaha County, South Dakota.

Donald John Mentele & Karen Ann Glanzer Marriage & Family*

Donald John Mentele married Karen Ann Glanzer, daughter of David Glanzer and Ruth Ewert on April 8, 1989 in Emery, Hanson County, South Dakota.

Karen Ann Glanzer was born on July 10, 1970 in Mitchell, Davison County, South Dakota.

Donald and Karen Ann Mentele had three children: Kerry Ann, Derek John and Andrew David Mentele.

Kerry Ann Mentele was born on August 10, 1989 in Mitchell, Davison County, South Dakota.

Derek John Mentele was born on July 23, 1990 in Mitchell, Davison County, South Dakota.

Andrew David Mentele was born on April 8, 1993 in Mitchell, Davison County, South Dakota.

Kerry Ann Mentele & Joshua Lachnit Marriage & Family*

Kerry Ann Mentele married Joshua Lachnit.
Joshua and Kerry Ann Lachnit have one child: Kayden Lachnit.

Kayden Lachnit was born on September 11, 2009 in Mitchell, Davison County, South Dakota.

Pamela Jean Mentele & Ronald German Marriage & Family*

Pamela Jean Mentele married Ronald German.

Ronald and Pamela Jean German had two children: Emily and Shawna German.

Douglas Lee Mentele & Melissa Neugebauer Marriage*

Douglas Lee Mentele married Melissa Neugebauer on April 19, 2008 in the First United Methodist Church in Mitchell, Davison County, South Dakota.

Garland Kenneth Schrank & Jenelle Audrey Scott Marriage & Family*

Garland Kenneth Schrank, son of Kenneth August and Clara Elsie Schrank, married Jenelle Audrey Scott, daughter of Audrey Scott and Ovilla Madson, on April 30, 1967 in the Glenview Congregational Church.

Jenelle Audrey Scott was born on August 22, 1948 in the Methodist Hospital in Mitchell, Davison County, South Dakota.

Garland Kenneth and Jenelle Audrey Schrank had four children: Stacy Garnel, Wade Randall, Brandi Jo, and Ginger Leann Schrank.

Stacy Garnel Schrank was born on November 13, 1968 in Huron, Beadle County, South Dakota.

Wade Randall Schrank was born on October 4, 1969 in Huron, Beadle County, South Dakota.

Brandi Jo Schrank was born on July 8, 1978.

Ginger Leann Schrank was born on August 7, 1981 in Mitchell, Davison County, South Dakota.

Garland Kenneth Schrank Family. Back row: Jenelle Audrey and Garland Kenneth Schrank. Middle row: Brandi Jo and Wade Randall Schrank. Front row: Ginger Leann and Stacy Garnel Schrank [76]

Stacy Garnel Schrank & Melody Lynn Tunender Marriage & Family*

Stacy Garnel Schrank married Melody Lynn Tunender, daughter of Darrell Tunender and

Phyllis Branson, on May 31, 1991 in Emery, Hanson County, South Dakota.

Melody Lynn Tunender was born on June 18, 1969 in Sioux Falls, Minnehaha County, South Dakota.

Stacy Garnel and Melody Lynn Schrank had two children: Lauren Elizabeth and Patrick James Schrank.

Lauren Elizabeth Schrank was born on March 9, 1994 in Sioux Fall, Minnehaha County, South Dakota.

Patrick James Schrank was born on March 4, 1999.

Wade Randall Schrank & Sherry Lee Niles Marriage & Family*

Wade Randall Schrank married Sherry Lee Niles, daughter of Emil Don Niles and Shirley Mae Skjonsberg, on November 5, 1988 in Mitchell, Davison County, South Dakota.

Sherry Lee Niles was born on September 30, 1961 in Sisseton, Roberts County, South Dakota

Wade Randall and Sherry Lee Schrank had two children: Shelby Danielle and Zachary Wade Schrank.

Shelby Danielle Schrank was born about 1993.

No record of Zachary Wade Schrank's birth.

Wade Randall Schrank Family.
Back row: Wade Randall and Sherry Lee Schrank. Front row: Zachary Wade and Shelby Danielle Schrank. [77]

Brandi Jo Schrank & Jesse J. Uithoven Marriage*

Brandi Jo Schrank married Jesse J. Uithoven on June 7, 1997 in the First United Church in Mitchell, Davison County, South Dakota.

Ginger Leann Schrank Marriage & Family*

Ginger Leann Schrank is married to an unknown man. They have a daughter. Dates and locations unknown.

Barbara Lynn Schrank & Wayne Raymond Tietz Marriage & Family*

Barbara Lynn Schrank, daughter of Kenneth August and Clara Elsie Schrank, married Wayne Raymond Tietz, son of Laurence Tietz and Ann Schillinger, on February 5, 1972.

Wayne Raymond Tietz was born on April 5, 1945.

Wayne Raymond and Barbara Lynn Tietz had one son: Matthew Tietz.

Matthew Tietz was born on January 23, 1987 in Sioux Falls, Minnehaha County, South Dakota.

Barbara Lynn Tietz died in 1995.

Steven Charles Schrank & Norma Jean Van Noort Marriage & Family*

Norma Jean Van Noort was born on May 10, 1954 in the Methodist Hospital in Mitchell, Davison County, South Dakota.

Steven Schrank married Norma Noorst on May 9, 1975 at the St. Paul Cathedral Church in Stickney, Aurora County, South Dakota.

Julie Faye Schrank & Richard Clair Gustad Marriage & Family*

Julie Faye Schrank married Richard Clair Gustad on March 20, 1981 in Platte, Charles Mix County, South Dakota.

Richard Clair Gustad was born on February 6, 1944 in Brule County, South Dakota.

Richard Clair and Julie Faye Gustad had three children: Tawnya Marie, Christopher John, and Richard Clair Gustad Jr.

Richard Clair Gustad Jr. was born on September 4, 1970 in Platte, Charles Mix County, South Dakota.

Tawnya Marie was born on February 16, 1977.

Christopher John Gustad was born on September 11, 1981 in Mitchell, Davison County, South Dakota.

Richard Gustad Family. Back row: Richard Clair and Julie Faye Gustad. Front row: Christopher John, Tawnya Marie and Richard Clair Jr. Gustad. [78]

Richard Clair Gustad Jr. Marriage & Family*

Richard Clair Gustad Jr. was born on September 4, 1970 in Platte, Charles Mix County, South Dakota.

Richard Clair Gustad Jr. married an unknown person on September 5, 1999 in Platte, Charles Mix County, South Dakota.

Richard Clair Gustad and his wife had two children: Gavin Richard and Clayton Allen Gustad.

Gavin Richard Gustad was born on June 28, 2004.

Clayton Allen Gustad was born on March 11, 2007.

Bryan Scott Schrank & Sherri Schoon Marriage & Family*

Bryan Scott Schrank married Sherri Schoon on September 21, 1991 in the Zion Lutheran Church in Mitchell, Davison County, South Dakota.

Sherri Schoon was born on March 10, 1969 in Sioux Falls, Minnehaha County, South Dakota.

Bryan Scott and Sherri Schrank have one daughter: Joslyn Clara Schrank.

Joslyn Clara Schrank was born on June 26,

2001 in Sioux Falls, Minnehaha County, South Dakota.

Dawn Marie Schrank & Jae Miller Marriage & Family*

Dawn Marie Schrank married Jae Miller on December 1, 1984.

Jae Miller was born on June 19, 1964.

Jae and Dawn Marie Miller had two children: Larissa Marie and Kayle Dawn Miller.

Larissa Marie Miller was born on June 7, 1985 in Mitchell, Davison County, South Dakota.

Kayle Dawn Miller was born on June 23, 1986 in Mitchell, Davison County, South Dakota.

Larissa Marie Miller & John Bain Marriage & Family*

Larissa Marie Miller married John Bain on August 1, 2009 in Aberdeen, Brown County, South Dakota.

John and Larissa Marie Bain had one child: Mia Christine Bain.

Kayle Dawn Miller & Mr. Heidzig Marriage & Family*

Kayle Dawn Miller married Mr. Heidzig.

Mr. Heidzig and Kayle Dawn Heidzig had one daughter: Jazmyne Marie Heidzig.

Bernice Vreugedenhil & Her Family*

Bernice Vreugdenhil, daughter of Teunis and Johanna Vreugdenhil was born on September 5, 1926 in Aurora Center in Aurora County, South Dakota.

Bernice Vreugdenhil was recorded living with her parents, Teunis and Johanna Vreugdenhil of the 1930 United States Census by the Census Enumerator, Nicholas Paelstra on April 14, 1930.[119]

On this report, the family was living in Joubert in Douglas County, South Dakota. Her father, Teunis was recorded with his birthplace in Netherlands while her mother, Johanna was recorded with her birthplace in South Dakota.

Also on the report was a brother, Edwin who was 8 months old as well as Bernice 2 years and 6 months old.

On April 4, 1940 the Teunis Vreugdenhil family was recorded living in Truro in Aurora County, South Dakota on the 1940 United States Census by the Census Enumerator, Arie Nydam.[120]

The family had lived in the same place since 1935. Teunis was thirty-eight years old while his wife, Johanna was thirty-nine years old. Bernice was thirteen years old and she had completed the 7th grade in school. Also recorded on the report was Edwin ten years old and Eunice seven years old.

George Gilbert Riecke & Bernice Vreugedenhil Marriage & Family*

George Gilbert Riecke and Bernice Vreugdenhil Wedding on December 14, 1944.[79]

George Gilbert Riecke, son of George Peter and Emma Bertha Riecke married Bernice "Bonnie" Vreugdenhil, daughter of Teunis and Johanna Vreugdenhil on December 14, 1944 in the St. John's Lutheran Church in Douglas County, South Dakota by Rev. P. Tecklenburg. George had received his parents content to marry Bernice on February 10, 1944 according a copy of a South Dakota Marriage Record.[121]

According to Lois Bialas they were married at the Redeemer Lutheran Church in Armour, Douglas County, South Dakota.

George Gilbert and Bernice Riecke had five children: Gloria Kaye, Mavis Jean, Doreen Faye, Georgia Sue and Brenda Lynn Riecke.

Birth of Gloria Kaye Riecke*

Gloria Kaye Riecke, daughter of George Gilbert and Bernice Riecke, was born July 22, 1945 in Aurora County, South Dakota.

Birth of Mavis Jean Riecke*

Mavis Jean Riecke, daughter of George Gilbert and Bernice Riecke, was born on June 13, 1947 in Stickney, Aurora County, South Dakota.

Birth of Doreen Faye Riecke*

Doreen Faye Riecke, daughter of George Gilbert and Bernice Riecke, was born on June 21, 1953.

Birth of Georgia Sue Riecke*

George Sue Riecke, daughter of George Gilbert and Bernice Riecke, was born on February 11, 1955.

Birth of Brenda Lynn Riecke*

Brenda Lynn Riecke, daughter of George Gilbert and Bernice Riecke, was born on April 27, 1964.

George Gilbert & Bernice Riecke - The Later Years*

George Gilbert and Bernice Riecke lived on a farm until 1952, after which they moved into Mitchell in Davison County, South Dakota. According to the U.S. City Directories, 1821-1989, George and Bernice Riecke lived at 601 E. Hanson in Mitchell, Davison County, South Dakota in 1953. George worked at the Anderson Packing Company until 1955.

Between 1958 and 1959, according to the U. S. City Directories, 1821-1989, George and Bernice lived at 530 S. Marion in Sioux Falls, Minnehaha County, South Dakota. George also worked at Greenlee Packing Company in Sioux

Falls and he owned the Riecke's Bait Shop.

In 1973, he moved to Rapid City, where George was employed at Black Hills Packing Company until retiring in 1989.

They moved to Colton, South Dakota in 1992.

Bernice Riecke died on September 22, 1996 in Rapid City, Pennington County, South Dakota. Have no records of where she is buried.

George moved to Paige, Nebraska in 1996, then later he moved to Verdigre, Nebraska around 2002.

George was a member of the Wayne Township Fire Department for sixteen years, the Crooks Gun Club and he enjoyed fishing, hunting, playing cards and taking his family on yearly vacations.

In 2006, George moved to Sioux Falls, where he was a resident at the Southridge Healthcare Center until his death on Friday, February 19, 2010.

George Gilbert Riecke [80]

The funeral services for George Gilbert Riecke were held on Wednesday, February 24, 2010 at the St. John's Lutheran Church in Douglas County. His burial was in the St. John's Lutheran Cemetery.

He was survived by five daughter: Gloria Schmidt and husband, Dale of Sioux Falls, South Dakota; Mavis Kiggins and husband, Ronald of Harrisburg, South Dakota; Doreen Thoelke of Rapid City, South Dakota; Georgian Honstein and fiancé, Bernie Carr of Torrington, Wyoming; Brenda Brown and husband, Kent of Rapid City, South Dakota; thirteen grandchildren, seventeen great-grandchildren, and one sister-in-law, Erna Riecke of Mitchell, South Dakota

He was preceded in death by his wife, Bernice, one brother, Albert Riecke, and four sisters:

Sophie Semmler, Viola Schuh, Clara Schrank and Esther Riecke; two grandchildren, one great-grandchild and a special friend, Fern Boelter.

George Gilbert Riecke Family, Back Row: George Gilbert Riecke, Gloria Faye Schmidt. Middle row: Mavis Jean Kiggins, Doreen Faye Thoeke. Font row: Georgia Sue Honstein, Bernice Riecke, and Brenda Lynn Brown[81]

Gloria Kaye Riecke & Dale L. Schmidt Marriage & Family*

Gloria Kaye Riecke, daughter of George Gilbert and Bernice Riecke, married Dale L. Schmidt, son of Fred Schmidt and Winnie Davis, on June 24, 1967 in Sioux Falls, Minnehaha County, South Dakota.

Dale L. Schmidt was born on January 28, 1942 in Brookings County, South Dakota.

Dale L. and Gloria Kaye Schmidt had three children: Laurie, Natalie and Amanda Schmidt.

Laurie Schmidt was born on April 5, 1973 in Sioux Falls, Minnehaha County, South Dakota.

Natalie Schmidt was born on January 26, 1975 in Sioux Falls, Minnehaha County, South Dakota.

Amanda Schmidt was born on May 31, 1979 in Sioux Falls, Minnehaha County, South Dakota. According to Bonnie Schuh, Amanda grew up in Sioux Falls, South Dakota. In 1997 they moved to Missoula, Montana, where she attended the University of Montana. Amanda still resides in Missoula, Montana.

Amanda Schmidt's best family memory was the memories they created with their annual family camping trips to the Black Hills, fishing on Center Lake, and midnight something were the best parts of every trip. Amanda and one of her sisters have made a pack to continue bringing their families to the Black Hills.

Natalie Schmidt & Erik Kafka
Marriage & Family*

Natalie Schmidt married Erik Kafka on June 23, 2007 in Izaac Walton League in Sioux Falls, Minnehaha County, South Dakota.

Erik Kafka was born on July 21, 1980 in Sioux Falls, Minnehaha County, South Dakota.

Erik and Natalie Kafka have one daughter: Branawen Schmidt Kafka.

Branawen Schmidt Kafka was born on May 31, 2000 in Sioux Falls, Minnehaha County, South Dakota.

Mavis Jean Riecke & Ronald J. Kiggins
Marriage & Family*

Mavis Jean Riecke, daughter of George Gilbert and Bernice Riecke, married Ronald J. Kiggins, son of Walter L. Kiggins and Fern L. Heasley, on October 4, 1941 in Sioux Falls, Minnehaha County, South Dakota.

Ronald J. Kiggins was born on October 4, 1941 in Sioux Falls, Minnehaha County, South Dakota.

Ronald J. and Mavis Jean Kiggins had five children: Rhonda Jean, Ronald John, Walter Allen, Michael Ray and Jeanette Lillian Kiggins.

There is no record date or location of the birth for Rhonda Jean Kiggins.

There is no record date or location of the birth for Ronald John Kiggins.

Walter Allen Kiggins was born on January 20, 1970 in Sioux Falls, Minnehaha county, South Dakota.

Michael Ray Kiggins was born on July 4, 1972 in Sioux Falls, Minnehaha County, South Dakota.

Jeanette Lillian Kiggins was born on July 4, 1972 in Sioux Falls, Minnehaha County, South Dakota.

Ronald John Kiggins
Marriage & Family*

Ronald John Kiggins is married. They have two children: Morgan and Tamara Kiggins.

There is no record date or location of the birth for Morgan and Tamara Kiggins.

Walter Allen Kiggins
Marriage & Family*

Walter Allen Kiggins is married. They have two children: Brian Campbell and Autumn Kiggins.

Brian Campbell Kiggins was born on November 23, 1991.

There is no record date or location of the birth for Autumn Kiggins.

Michael Ray Kiggins
Marriage & Family*

Michael Ray Kiggins is married. They have three children: Julie, Jeremiah and Austin Kiggins.

Julie Kiggins was born on January 18, 1994.

There is no record date or location of the birth for Jeremiah and Austin Kiggins.

Doreen Faye Riecke & Van William Thoelke
Marriage & Family*

Doreen Faye Riecke, daughter of George Gilbert and Bernice Riecke, married Van William Thoelke.

Van William Thoelke was born on May 27, 1954.

Van William and Doreen Faye Thoelke have one daughter: Christina Jean Thoelke.

Christina Jean Thoelke was born on August 2, 1977 in Rapid City, Pennington County, South Dakota.

Christina Jean Thoelke
Marriage & Family*

Christina Jean Thoelke is married. They have two children: Hannah Mae Thoelke and Trace Victor Smolik.

There is no record date or location of the birth for Hannah Mae Thoelke and Trace Victor Smolik.

Georgia Sue Riecke & Dave Honstein
Marriage & Family*

Georgia Sue Riecke, daughter of George Gilbert and Bernice Riecke, married Dave Honstein on September 21, 1975. The marriage ended in divorce.

Dave and Georgia Sue Honstein had three children: Lisa Marie Honstein, Kimberly Sue Honstein, and Cory Lee Honstein.

There is no record date or location of the

birth for Lisa Marie Honstein.

There is no record date or location of the birth for Kimberly Sue Honstein.

Cory Lee Honstein was born on December 12, 1986.

Kimberly Sue Honstein & Brent Huseman

Marriage & Family*

Kimberly Sue Honstein married Brent Huseman. They had one daughter: Aubrey Amelia Huseman.

There is no record date or location of the birth for Aubrey Amelia Huseman.

Cory Lee Honstein & Shauna Marriage & Family*

Cory Lee Honstein married Shauna in June of 2008. They have one son: Gunther Honstein.

There is no record date or location of the birth for Gunther Honstein.

Brenda Lynn Riecke & Kent Eldon Brown Marriage & Family*

Brenda Lynn Riecke, daughter of George Gilbert and Bernice Riecke, married Kent Eldon Brown on June 2, 1984.

Kent Eldon Brown was born on August 10, 1962,

Kent Eldon and Brenda Lynn Brown have tow children: Ashley Nicole and Kayla Marie Brown.

Ashley Nicole Brown was born on April 27, 1990.

Kayla Marie Brown was born on June 4, 1993 and she died on November 27, 1993.

CHAPTER 7

Birth of
Wilhelm Otto Zirpel*

Wilhelm or "William" Otto Zirpel, son of Johan and Anna Augusta Zirpel, was born on September 4, 1895 in Douglas County, South Dakota.

He was christened on September 14, 1895 in the St. John Lutheran Church in Douglas County, South Dakota. His sponsors or God parents were Gohf Lebeiswager, Johanna Bialas, Gohf Pietz, Maria Jatrielei.

Wilhelm Otto appeared with his parents, Johan and Anna Augusta Zirpel on the 1900 United States Census report living in Berlin Township, now known as Washington Township in Douglas County, South Dakota according to the Census Enumerator, Henry Ruff.[121]

The brother and sisters listed on the same report were Anna Emilie fifteen years old, a set of twins: Gottfried Johan and Elisabeth three years old, and Edward Richard 9 months old.

Their father, Johan was listed as a general farmer and his own his property.

He was confirmed on March 20, 1910 at the Immanuel Lutheran Church in Douglas County, South Dakota according the St. Lutheran Church records. His parents, Johan and Anna Augusta Zirpel as well as his brothers and sisters were present during the confirmation.

On April 26, 1910, Wilhelm Otto Zirpel appeared on the 1910 United States Census still living with his parents, Johan and Anna Augusta Zirpel in Berlin Township, now called the Washington Township in Douglas County, South Dakota according to the records of the Census Enumerator, Walter L. Koehn.[122]

Wilhelm at the age of fourteen was working as a farm laborer on his father's farm.

There were five children listed on the census report. They were Emma Bertha, Gottfried Johan, Elisabeth, Edward Richard, and Bertha Rosina Zirpel.

Wilhelm Otto Zirpel registered himself on the World War I Draft Registration according to S. H. Hildeward recording the information in Hutchinson County, South Dakota on June 8-9, 1917.[123] Wilhelm was single as well as a farmer. He was described as being of medium in height

Wilhelm Otto Zirpel the year is unknown [82]

with a slender built. He also had gray colored eyes with dark hair according to the document.

A year later on June 24, 1918, Wilhelm Otto enlisted into the United States Army during World War I and he was released on May 12, 1919 as a Private.[124]

Emma Martha Marie Reichert & Her Family*

Emma Martha Marie Reichert, the daughter of Robert P. Reichert and Emma Wegehaupt, was born on September 15, 1902 in Douglas County, South Dakota.

She was christened on April 30, 1922 in the Immanuel Lutheran Church located in Douglas County, South Dakota.

On April 15, 1910, the Census Enumerator, Walter L. Koehn reported that Emma Martha Maria was living with her parents, Robert P. and Emma Reichert in Berlin Township in Douglas County, South Dakota.[125]

On the report, Robert P. Reichert was born in Germany and he worked as a farmer. It also said that Emma Reichert was also born in Germany. There were four children list on the report. They were Emma Martha Maria seven years old, Johanna six years old, Hulda three years old, and Arnold eight months old. Also registered was a Carl W. Riechert seventy-five years old.

Emma Martha Maria Reichert was confirmed on April 16, 1916 at the Immanuel Lutheran Church in Douglas County, South Dakota.

Emma Martha Maria Reichert was still living with her parents, Robert P. and Emma in the Washington Township in Douglas County, South Dakota according the 1920 United States Census on January 17, 1920 by the Census Enumerator, Mrs. Carl Bertram.[126]

The report stated that Robert P. was forty-six years old and his wife, Emma was thirty-eight years old.

The following children on the register were Emma Martha Maria seventeen years old, Johanna fifteen years old, Arnold ten years old, and Hattie four years old.

The report said that Robert P. had immigrated to the United States in the year of 1883.

On the 1930 United States Census according the Census Enumerator, Mrs. Ida Bertram on April 16, 1930 the Robert P. and Emma Reichert family was still living in the Washington Township in Douglas County, South Dakota.[127]

On the report the children that were still living a home were Johanna twenty-six years old, Hulda twenty-three years old, Arnold twenty years old and "Bertha" or Hattie fourteen years old.

According to the Friedhof Cemetery records on Find a grave, Robert P. Reichert died in 1956 and his wife, Emma died in 1958. The records said that both, Robert P. and Emma Reichert were buried in the Friedhof Cemetery, Douglas County, South Dakota.

Wilhelm Otto Zirpel & Emma Martha Maria Reichert Marriage & Family*

Wilhelm Otto Zirpel, son of Johan and Anna Augusta Zirpel, married Emma Martha Maria Reichert, daughter of Robert P. Reichert and Emma Wegehaupt, on April 20, 1922 in the Immanuel Lutheran Church located in Douglas County, South Dakota.

Wilhelm Otto Zirpel & Emma Martha Maria Reichert Wedding.
The three men in back row: Robert P. Reichert, Johan Zirpel and George Peter Riecke Sr. New row: Arnold Reichert, Hulda Reichert, Emma Reichert, Anna Augusta Zirpel, Emma Riecke, Gottfried Zirpel, Gertrude Zirpel, Oscar Gerlach, and Elisabeth Gerlach. Next row: Elizabeth Wegehaupt, Johanna Reichert, Edward Zirpel, Emma Martha Maria Zirpel, Wilhelm Otto Zirpel, unknown lady friend of bride, Otto Sperlich, Fritz Wegehaupt, Two flower girls: Sophie Alvina Elizabeth Riecke and Hertha Reichert. [83]

Wilhelm Otto and Emma Martha Maria Zirpel had seven children: Waldemar Gotthelf, Wilma Norma, John Robert, Martin Wilhelm, Malvin Otto, Margaret Maria and Edna Emma Zirpel.

Birth of
Waldemar Gotthelf Zirpel*

Waldemar Gotthelf Zirpel, son of Wilhelm Otto and Emma Martha Maria Zirpel, was born on May 13, 1924 in Hutchinson County, South Dakota.

He was christened on June 8, 1924 in the Immanuel Lutheran Church in Douglas County, South Dakota.

Birth of
Wilma Norma Zirpel*

Wilma Norma Zirpel, daughter of Wilhelm Otto and Emma Martha Maria Zirpel, was born on October 22, 1925 in Hutchinson County, South Dakota.

She was christened on November 15, 1925 in the Immanuel Lutheran Church in Douglas County, South Dakota.

Wilma Norma Zirpel was confirmed on June 4, 1930 by Rev. Paul Hempel at the Immanuel Lutheran Church in Douglas County, South Dakota.

Birth of
John Robert Zirpel*

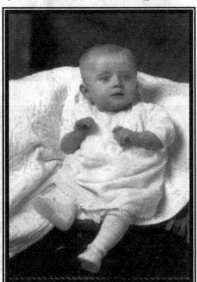

John Robert Zirpel 9 months old, son of Wilhelm Otto and Emma Martha Maria Zirpel 1930 [84]

John Robert Zirpel, son of Wilhelm Otto and Emma Martha Maria Zirpel, was born on January 20, 1929 in Hutchinson County, South Dakota.

He was christened on February 29, 1929 in the Immanuel Lutheran Church in Douglas County, South Dakota.

John Robert Zirpel only lived for thirteen years, as he died on December 13, 1942 in Hutchinson County, South Dakota.

He was buried in the Friedhof Cemetery also known as the Immanuel Lutheran Cemetery on December 13, 1942.

Gravestone for John Robert Zirpel located in the Immanuel Lutheran Cemetery in Douglas County, South Dakota. [85]

Wilhelm Otto and Emma Martha Maria Zirpel were recorded on the 1930 United States Census on April 16, 1930 by the Census Enumerator, Franklin Jssenhusth living in the Susquehanna Township in Hutchinson County, South Dakota.[128] Wilhelm Zirpel was listed as a farmer on the report. The children listed on the report were Waldmar Gotthelf five years old, Wilma Norma four years and five months old, and John Robert Zirpel one year and 2 months old.

Birth of Twins - Malvin Otto & Martin Wilhelm Zirpel*

Martin Wilhelm and Malvin Otto Zirpel, twin sons, of Wilhelm Otto and Emma Martha Maria Zirpel, were born on November 6, 1932 in Parkston, Hutchinson County, South Dakota.

They were christened on December 4, 1932 in the Immanuel Lutheran Church in Douglas County, South Dakota.

Martin Wilhelm and Malvin Otto Zirpel were confirmed in 1947 in the Immanuel Lutheran Church in Douglas County, South Dakota.

**Johan Zirpel holding his twin grandsons,
Left Malvin Otto and right Martin Wilhelm [86]**

Malvin Otto &
Martin Wilhelm Zirpel -
Their Early Years *

Martin Wilhelm and Malvin Otto Zirpel both attended grade school as well as high school in Parkston, Hutchinson County, South Dakota. They graduated in 1951 from the Parkston High School in Parkston, Hutchinson County, South Dakota.

While attending high school Martin Wilhelm had been a candidate for king in the homecoming festivities, and he also had been elected for go to the Boys State.

Birth of
Margaret Maria Zirpel*

Margaret Maria Zirpel, daughter of Wilhelm Otto and Emma Martha Maria Zirpel, was born on June 1, 1937 in Hutchinson County, South Dakota.

She was christened on June 27, 1937 in the Immanuel Lutheran Church in Douglas County, South Dakota.

Margaret Maria Zirpel was confirmed in 1951 at the Immanuel Lutheran Church in Douglas County, South Dakota.

On April 19, 1940, the Census Enumerator, Aaron S. Mellueger recorded Wilhelm Otto and Emma Martha Maria Zirpel on the 1940 United States Census still living in Susquehanna Town-ship in Hutchinson County, South Dakota.[129]

Wilhelm Zirpel was recorded working an average of 70 hours a week. They owned their home and it was valued at $700. Also Wilhelm had only completed the 7th grade in school. On the report, their son, Waldemar Gotthelf was fifteen years old and he worked as a farm laborer on his father's farm.

There were five other children listed on the report. They were Wilma Norma fourteen years old, John Robert ten years old, Malvin Otto and his twin brother, Martin Wilhelm seven years old, and Margaret Maria three years old.

Birth of
Edna Emma Zirpel*

Edna Emma Zirpel, daughter of Wilhelm Otto and Emma Martha Maria Zirpel, was born on May 2, 1944 in South Dakota.

She was christened on May 24, 1944 in the Immanuel Lutheran Church in Douglas County, South Dakota.

Wilhelm Otto & Emma Martha
Maria Zirpel - The Later Years*

**Wilhelm Otto and Emma Martha Maria Zirpel
40th Wedding Anniversary in 1972 [87]**

**Wilhelm Otto and Emma Martha Maria Zirpel
50th Wedding Anniversary in 1982 [88]**

The Reichert farm in 1931 south of Flensburg. Back row left to right in a zig-zag pattern: Helen Reichert, Wilhelm Otto Zirpel, Arnold Reichert, Emma Martha Maria Zirpel holding her son, John Robert Zirpel, Fritz Wegehaupt and his wife, Otille Wegehaupt, Hulda Reichert, Lizzie Wegehaupt Laufer, Edward Richard Zirpel holding Walter Robert Zirpel his adopted son, Johanna Reichert, Mathilda L. Zirpel, and Bill Reichert in hat and overalls. Next row left to right: Waldemar Gotthelf Zirpel, Johan Zirpel, Robert P. Reichert, Wilma Norma Zirpel, Emma Reichert, Helen Wegehaupt (you can only see her hair), the 3 boys in wagon: Carlie Laufer, Arthur Wegehaupt and Bob Wegehaupt. Front row left to row: Paul Laufer, Alfrieda Laufer, Hertha Reichert, Esther Laufer, Melvin Wegehaupt, Adeline Wegehaupt, George Wegehaupt.
Oscar Laufer took the picture. [89]

Wilhelm Otto Zirpel died on May 9, 1978 in Parkston, Hutchinson County, South Dakota at the age of 82 years old.

He was buried in the Immanuel Lutheran Cemetery in Douglas County, South Dakota.

Emma Martha Maria Zirpel died on December 6, 1996 in Parkston, Hutchinson County, South Dakota.

She was buried by her husband, Wilhelm in the Immanuel Lutheran Cemetery in Douglas County, South Dakota.

Lillian Esther Moege & Her Family*

Carl R. and Clara Moege were recorded on the 1930 United States Census living in the Washington Township in Douglas County, South Dakota according to the Census Enumerator, Mrs. Ida Bertram.[130] On the report both Carl and Clara were born in Germany.

Lillian Esther Moege, daughter of Carl R. and Clara Moege, was born on August 25, 1930. She was christened on September 21, 1930 in the Immanuel Lutheran Church in Douglas County, South Dakota.

Lillian Esther Moege was confirmed on June 20, 1943 in the Immanuel Lutheran Church in Douglas County, South Dakota.

Emma Martha Maria Zirpel on her 94th Birthday 1996. Back row standing: Margaret Maria Bertram, and Edna Emma Stoebner. Front row seated: Wilma Norma Reimnitz, Emma Martha Maria Zirpel and Martin Wilhelm Zirpel. [90]

Waldemar Gotthelf Zirpel & Lillian Esther Moege Marriage & Family*

Lillian received her father's consent on August 25, 1947 according to a copy of a South Dakota Marriage Record and she married Waldemar Gotthelf Zirpel.[131] The marriage ceremony was held on June 6, 1948 in the Immanuel Lutheran Church in Douglas County, South Dakota by Rev. John DeWald, a Lutheran Pastor.

Waldemar Gotthelf and Lillian Esther Zirpel had five children: Caroline Esther, William Roger, James Waldemar, Rita Kay and Robert John Zirpel.

Birth of Caroline Esther Zirpel*

Caroline Esther Zirpel, daughter of Waldemar Gotthelf and Lillian Esther Zirpel, was born on August 1, 1949 in Parkston, Hutchinson County, South Dakota.

She was christened in 1949 in the Immanuel Lutheran Church in Douglas County, South Dakota.

Birth of William Roger Zirpel*

William Roger Zirpel, son of Waldemar Gotthelf and Lillian Esther Zirpel, was born on December 5, 1950.

He was christened in 1950 in the Immanuel Lutheran Church in Douglas County, South Dakota.

Birth of James Waldemar Zirpel*

James Waldemar Zirpel, son of Waldemar Gotthelf and Lillian Esther Zirpel, was born on November 22, 1957 in South Dakota.

Birth of Rita Kay Zirpel*

Rita Kay Zirpel, daughter of Waldemar Gotthelf and Lillian Esther Zirpel was born on September 26, 1959 in South Dakota.

Birth of Robert John Zirpel*

Robert John Zirpel, son of Waldemar Gott-

helf and Lillian Esther Zirpel, was born on July 27, 1967 in South Dakota.

Waldemar Gotthelf Zirpel Family. Back row: William Roger Zirpel, James Waldemar Zirpel, and Robert John Zirpel. Front row: Rita Kay Pope, Lillian Esther Zirpel and Caroline Esther Schuh. [91]

Caroline Esther Zirpel & Duane Arnold Schuh Marriage & Family*

Duane Arnold Schuh, son of Arnold Ruben and Viola Alma Elizabeth Schuh, married Caroline Esther Zirpel, daughter of Waldemar Gotthelf Zirpel and Lillian Esther Moege, on May 1968 at the Zion Lutheran Church or the First Lutheran Church in Mitchell, Davison County, South Dakota. The marriage ended in divorce, then, they remarried again later.

Duane helped his parents to build the Schuh Painting & Papering contractor business which he later purchased.

Duane and Caroline moved to Rapid City, South Dakota sometime after 1970. Duane owned and operated his own painting business there. Duane has been awarded the "Craftsman Award" for his excellence in his field.

He later sold his business and worked at the Rapid City Regional Hospital. Caroline worked for the Black Hills Federal Credit Union in the Accounting Department.

Duane Arnold and Caroline Esther Schuh had two children: Paula Kay and Mark Duane Schuh.

Paula Kay Schuh was born on July 24, 1969 in Mitchell, Davison County, South Dakota.

Mark Duane Schuh was born on December 14, 1970 in Mitchell, Davison County, South Dakota.

Paula Kay Schuh & Jack Gray Marriage *

Paula Kay Schuh married Jack Gray, son of Charles and Edith Gray, on September 5, 1992. The marriage ended in divorce.

Paula Kay Gray & Tab D. Arthur Marriage & Family*

Paula Kay Gray married Tab D. Arthur, son of Eugene and Kaylynn Arthur, on September 6, 1996 in Gillette, Campbell County, Wyoming.

Tab D. Arthur was born on October 18, 1959 in Wyoming.

Tab D. and Paula Kay Arthur had two children: Morgan and Lane James Arthur.

Morgan Arthur was born on April 29, 1997 in Gillette, Campbell County, Wyoming.

Lane James Arthur was born on March 19, 2000 in Gillette, Campbell County, Wyoming.

Duane Arnold Schuh Family. Back row: Paula Kay Arthur, Mark Duane Schuh, and Josette Schuh. Front row: Morgan Arthur, Duane Arnold Schuh, Caroline Esther Schuh and Lane James Arthur. [92]

Josette Verzani & Mr. Wurdeman Marriage & Family*

Josette Verzani was born on August 5, 1970 in Norfolk County, Nebraska.

Josette Verzani married Mr. Wurdeman on a known date.

Mr. Wurdeman and Josette Wurdeman had two children: Ryan Edward and Candice Marie Wurdeman.

Ryan Edward Wurdeman was born on February 28, 1991.

Candice Marie Wurdeman was born May 24, 1993.

Candice has been attending Dakota Wesleyan College in Mitchell, South Dakota.

Mark Duane Schuh & Josette Wurdeman Marriage *

Mark Duane Schuh married Josette Wurdeman on July 10, 1999 in Rapid City, Pennington County, South Dakota.

James Waldemar Zirpel & Becky Peterson Marriage*

James Waldemar Zirpel, son of Waldemar Gotthelf and Lillian Esther Zirpel, married Becky Peterson on March 4, 1978 in the United Methodist Church in Viborg, Turner County, South Dakota.

Becky Peterson was born on December 11, 1955.

James Waldemar and Becky Zirpel [93]

William Roger Zirpel & Kathy Erickson Marriage*

Kathy and William Roger Zirpel [94]

William Roger Zirpel, son of Waldemar Gotthelf and Lillian Esther Zirpel, married Kathy Erickson on August 25, 1972 in the Zion Lutheran Church in Mitchell, Davison County, South Dakota.

Kathy Erickson was born on December 25, 1950.

Rita Kay Zirpel & Jimmie Pope II Marriage & Family*

Rita Kay Zirpel, daughter of Waldemar Gotthelf and Lillian Esther Zirpel, married Jimmie Pope II on April 20, 1985.

Jimmie Pope II was born on September 19, 1957.

Jimmie II and Rita Kay Pope had two children: Makaela Kay and Jimmie Pope III.

Makaela Kay was born April 27, 1991.

Jimmie Pope III was born on November 13, 1994.

Jimmie Pope III, Rita Kay Pope and Makaela Kay Pope. [95]

Robert John Zirpel & Carolyn Luken Marriage & Family*

Robert John Zirpel, son of Waldemar Gotthelf and Lillian Esther Zirpel, married Carolyn Luken on March 24, 1990.

Carolyn Luken was born on May 14, 1967 in Omaha, Douglas County, Nebraska.

Robert John and Carolyn Zirpel had two children: Hannah Leann and Justin Robert Zirpel.

Hannah Leann Zirpel was born on May 18, 2000.

Justin Robert Zirpel was born on June 3, 2004.

Back row: Robert John Zirpel.
Front row: Justin Robert Zirpel, Carolyn Zirpel and Hannah Leann Zirpel. [96]

Back row: Kathy Zirpel, William Roger Zirpel, James Waldemar Zirpel, Becky Zirpel, Duane Arnold Schuh, and Robert John Zirpel. Front row: Rita Kay Pope, Lillian Esther Zirpel, Caroline Esther Schuh and Carolyn Zirpel. [97]

Fourth row: Dennis Allen Stoebner holding granddaughter, Samantha Gannon, Martin Wilhelm Zirpel, Mildred Zirpel, Larry Leonard Reimnitz, David Lee Renshaw, Leo (Jerry) Jerome Leonard party hidden. Third row: Ernest William Bertram, Edna Emma Stoebner, James Waldemar Zirpel, Wilma Norma Reimnitz, Judy Renshaw, and Jay Alan Van Den Hock. Second row: Margaret Maria Bertram, Marlys Moege, Lillian Esther Zirpel, Mira Susanna Leonard holding son, Jamie Jerome Leonard, Michelle Bertram, Marcia Leann Van Den Hoek, and Thomas William Zirpel. First row: Dennis Malvin Zirpel, Leanne Lyn Zirpel, Lynn Gannon holding Hannon Gannon, Alexas Noel Gannon, Gerald Moege, Donald Lee Zirpel, Anne Moege, and Maynard Moege. The two people behind Donald Lee Zirpel and Ann Moege are Ryan William Bertram and Bonita Lou Zirpel. [98]

Waldemar Gotthelf & Lillian Esther Zirpel - The Later Years*

According to the United States Directories, from 1891-1989, Waldemar Gotthelf and Lillian Esther Zirpel were living in Mitchell, Davison County, South Dakota.

In 1984, Waldemar Gotthelf and Lillian Esther Zirpel were living in a Rural Route address closed to Mitchell, South Dakota according to the United States Public Records Index, Volume 1.

At the age of sixty-eight years old, Waldemar Gotthelf Zirpel died on February 3, 1993 in Alexandria, Hanson County, South Dakota.

He was buried in the Immanuel Lutheran Church Cemetery in Douglas County, South Dakota.

Lillian Esther Zirpel & Leonard Robert Zirpel

Marriage*

Lillian Esther Zirpel married Leonard Robert Zirpel, son of Gottfried Johan and Gertrude Anna Zirpel, on February 26, 1994 in Parkston, Hutchinson County, South Dakota.

The United States Public Records Index, said that Leonard Robert & Lillian Esther Zirpel lived within Mitchell in Davison County, South Dakota between 1994 throughout 1998.

Leonard Robert Zirpel died on October 20, 198 in Sioux Falls, Minnehaha County, South Dakota.

He was buried in the Protestant Cemetery located in Parkston, Hutchinson County, South Dakota.

Leonard Gottlieb Adolf Reimnitz & His Family*

According to records that Darlene Horst had, Paul Robert Reimnitz was born on July 23, 1890 and he died on November 15, 1967. His wife, Lena Louise Blume was born on June 21, 1890 and she died on September 15, 1968. Darlene said that the couple were married on March

18, 1919.

Leonard Gottlieb Adolf Reimnitz, son of Paul Robert Reimnitz and Lena Louise Blume, was born on October 9, 1922 in Mount Vernon, Davison County, South Dakota.

He was christened on October 29, 1922 in the Immanuel Lutheran Church in Douglas County, South Dakota.

On April 5, 1930, Leonard Gottlieb Adolf Reimnitz was living with his parents, Paul Robert and Lena Louise Reimnitz in Tobin Township in Davison County, South Dakota according to the 1930 United States Census taken by the Census Enumerator, Mrs. Lena S. Van Metze.[132] The census report said that Paul Robert was a farmer. Also on this report was a total of six children. They were Louis E. ten years old, Dorothy M. nine years old, Leonard G. seven years old, George R. six years old, Lydia E. three years old, and Lena L. one year old.

Leonard Gottlieb Adolf Reimnitz was confirmed on July 5, 1936 by the Rev. Paul Hempel at the Immanuel Lutheran Church in Douglas County, South Dakota.

On the 1940 United States Census Leonard's family was still living in Tobin Township in Davison County, South Dakota on April 30, 1940 according to the Census Enumerator, Frank L. Patterson.[133]

The report said that Leonard had only completed the eighth grade and he was a unpaid worker on the farm with his father. There were seven children listed on the report. They were Louis E. twenty years old, Leonard G. seventeen years old, George A. sixteen years old, Lydia E. thirteen years old, Lena L. eleven years old, Robert L. nine years old and Paul D. seven years old.

Wilma Norma Zirpel & Leonard Gottlieb Adolf Reimnitz Marriage & Family*

Wilma Norma Zirpel, daughter of Waldemar Gotthelf and Lillian Esther Zirpel, married Leonard Gottlieb Adolf Reimnitz, the son of Paul Robert Reimnitz and Lena Louise Blume, on June 14, 1944 in the Immanuel Lutheran Church in Douglas County, South Dakota by Rev. John DeWald according to a copy of a South Dakota Marriage Record.[134] Also the marriage document said that Leonard Reimnitz received his father's consent on October 9, 1943, while Wilma Zirpel received her father's consent later

on October 22, 1943.[135]

Leonard Gottlieb Adolf and Wilma Norma Reimnitz had six children: Darlene Marie, Larry Leonard July Ellen, Sallie Rose, Samuel Paul and John William Reimnitz.

Birth of Darlene Marie Reimnitz*

Darlene Marie Reimnitz, daughter of Leonard Gottlieb Adolf and Wilma Norma Reimnitz, was born at the home of Wilhelm Otto and Emma Martha Maria Zirpel in Parkston, Hutchinson County, South Dakota on May 12, 1945.

She was christened by Rev. John DeWald in the Immanuel Lutheran Church in Douglas County, South Dakota. Her sponsors or God parents were Waldemar Gotthelf Zirpel, Lena Bialas, and Dorothy Stahl.

Darlene Marie Reimnitz was confirmed on March 22, 1959 by Rev. Leonard A. Eberhard at the Immanuel Lutheran Church in Douglas County, South Dakota.

Birth of Larry Leonard Reimnitz*

Larry Leonard Reimnitz, son of Leonard Gottlieb Adolf and Wilma Norma Reimnitz, was born on June 21, 1947 in the Parkston Hospital in Parkston, Hutchinson County, South Dakota.

He was christened by Rev. John DeWald on July 13, 1947 in the Immanuel Lutheran Church in Douglas County, South Dakota.

Larry Leonard Reimnitz was confirmed by Rev. Leonard A. Eberhard on March 26, 1961 at the Immanuel Lutheran Church in Douglas County, South Dakota.

Birth of Judy Ellen Reimnitz*

Judy Ellen Reimnitz, daughter of Leonard Gottlieb Adolf and Wilma Norma Reimnitz, was born in the Parkston Hospital in Parkston, Hutchinson County, South Dakota.

She was christened by Rev. Wild of Delmont, on July 9, 1950 in the Immanuel Lutheran Church in Douglas County, South Dakota.

Judy Ellen Reimnitz was confirmed in 1964 in the Immanuel Lutheran Church in Douglas County, South Dakota.

Back row: Judy Ellen Renshaw, John William Reimnitz, Larry Leonard Reimnitz, and Sallie Rose Brink. Font row: Samuel Paul Reimnitz, Wilma Norma Reimnitz, Leonard Gottlieb Adolf Reimnitz, and Darlene Marie Horst. [99]

Birth of
Sallie Rose Reimnitz*

Sallie Rose Reimnitz, daughter of Leonard Gottlieb Adolf and Wilma Norma Reimnitz, was born on September 9, 1952 at the Armour Hospital in Armour, Douglas County, South Dakota.

She was christened by Rev. John DeWald on January 1, 1953 at the Immanuel Lutheran Church in Douglas County, South Dakota. Her sponsors or God parents were Margaret Bertram, Lydia Sigmund, and Louis Reimnitz.

Sallie Rose Reimnitz was confirmed in March of 1967 by Rev. Leonard A. Eberhard at the Immanuel Lutheran Church in Douglas County, South Dakota.

Birth of
Samuel Paul Reimnitz*

Samuel Paul Reimnitz, son of Leonard Gottlieb Adolf and Wilma Norma Reimnitz, was born on September 18, 1956 at the Armour Hospital in Armour, Douglas County, South Dakota.

He was christened on October 7, 1956 in the Immanuel Lutheran Church by Rev. Leonard A. Eberhard. His sponsors or God parents were Erna Eberhard, George Reimnitz, and Paul Reimnitz.

Samuel Paul Reimnitz was confirmed on May 10, 1970 by Rev. Leonard A. Eberhard at the Immanuel Lutheran Church in Douglas County, South Dakota.

Birth of
John William Reimnitz*

John William Reimnitz, son of Leonard Gottlieb Adolf and Wilma Norma Reimnitz, was born at the Parkston Hospital in Parkston, Hutchinson County, South Dakota on December 17, 1963.

He was christened on January 5, 1964 in the Immanuel Lutheran Church in Douglas County, South Dakota by Rev. Leonard A. Eberhard.

John William Reimnitz was confirmed in 1978 at the Immanuel Lutheran Church in Douglas County, South Dakota.

Leonard Gottlieb Adolf &
Wilma Norma Reimnitz -
The Later Years*

Leonard Gottlieb Adolf Reimnitz died on January 20, 2003 in the Queen of Peace Hospital in Mitchell, Davison County, South Dakota from cancer.

Rev. Anthony Steinronn officiated at the

funeral which was held on June 22, 2003 in the Immanuel Lutheran Church Cemetery in Douglas County, South Dakota.

Wilma Norma Reimnitz 80th Birthday 2005 Back row: Darlene Marie Horst, Ronald William Horst, Sallie Rose Brink, Leon Arnold Brink, and Nancy Jean Renshaw. Front row: Stephanie Anne Reimnitz, John William Reimnitz, Wilma Norma Reimnitz, Larry Leonard Reimnitz, and Lynn Dianne Reimnitz. [100]

Ronald William Horst & His Family*

Ronald William Horst was born on May 6, 1942 in Valentine, Cherry County, Nebraska.

He was christened on May 31, 1942 in Mission, Todd County, Nebraska by Rev. Richard Stiemke at the Zion Lutheran Church, Wis. Synod. His sponsors or God parents were Jack Horst, Lodema and Irene Hideman.

Ronald William Horst was confirmed on June 9, 1957 in Chamberlain, Brule County, South Dakota by Rev. Walter Klipp at the Zion Lutheran Church, Mo. Synod.

Darlene Marie Reimnitz & Ronald William Horst Marriage & Family*

Darlene Marie Reimnitz, daughter of Leonard Gottlieb Adolf and Wilma Norma Reimnitz, married Ronald William Horst, son of Richard William Horst and Violet Ann Hideman on November 23, 1961 in the Immanuel Lutheran Church in Douglas County, South Dakota by Rev. Leonard A. Eberhard.

Ronald William and Darlene Marie Horst had three children: Robin Lee, Tracy Sue and Tanya Lee Horst.

Birth of Donald Joseph Minsky*

Donald Joseph Minsky was born on September 12, 1956 in Berlin, Green Lake County, Wisconsin.

Ronald William and Darlene Marie Horst were also foster parents to Donald Joseph Minsky from November 15, 1971 until September 12, 1974.

Birth of Robin Lee Ann Horst*

Robin Lee Ann Horst, daughter of Ronald William and Darlene Marie Horst, was born at the Platte Memorial Hospital in Platte, Charles Mix County, South Dakota on June 20, 1962.

Robin Lee Ann Horst was christened on June 22, 1962 by the Rev. George W. Mock, as a member of the Emma Lutheran Church of Tripp, South Dakota, at the Platte Memorial Hospital in Platte, Charles Mix County, South Dakota. Her sponsors or God parents were Roger Horst, Steven Horst and Larry Leonard Reimnitz.

Back Row: Ronald William and Darlene Marie Horst. Front row: Robin Lee Ann Horst [101]

Robin Lee Ann Horst died on April 7, 1969 at the age of six years old in South Dakota.

She was buried in the Immanuel Lutheran Church Cemetery in Douglas County, South Dakota.

The cause of her death was contributed to by Downs Syndrome, Pneumonia complicated with heart failure.

Robin is remember by her family as the "Heaven's Very Special Child".

Birth of
Tracy Sue Horst*

Tracy Sue Horst, daughter of Ronald William and Darlene Marie Horst, was born on November 19, 1976 in Friendship, Adams County, Wisconsin.

She was christened by Rev. Paul F. Dawson from Plymouth, Wisconsin, on August 19, 1979 at the Taycheedah Chapel, Taycheedah, Fond du Lac County, Wisconsin. Her sponsors or God parents were Ronald William and Darlene Marie Horst.

Tracy Sue Horst was confirmed by Rev. Robert Eckelamn of the Peace Lutheran Church at Great Falls, Cascade County, Montana on May 5, 1991.

Birth of
Tanya Lee Horst*

Tanya Lee Horst, daughter of Ronald William and Darlene Marie Horst, was born on January 6, 1978 in Waco, McLennan County, Texas.

She was christened by Rev. Paul F. Dawson from Plymouth, Wisconsin on August 19, 1979 at the Taycheedah Chapel, Taycheedah, Fond du Lac County, Wisconsin. Her sponsors or God parents were Ronald William and Darlene Marie Horst.

Back row: Darlene Marie and Ronald William Horst. Front row: Tracy Sue and Tanya Lee Horst [102]

Tracy Sue & Tanya Lee Horst
Formal Adoption*

Tracy Sue and Tanya Lee Horst were foster children on January 16, 1979 for Ronald William and Darlene Marie Horst. They are full sisters.

Tracy Sue and Tanya Lee were formally adopted on November 10, 1981 by Ronald William and Darlene Marie Horst.

Tracy Sue Horst &
Kenneth H. C.
Mowrey Houston Family*

Tracy Sue Horst and Kenneth H. C. Mowrey had one child: Codi Horst. Tracy and Kenneth were never married.

Codi Horst was born on November 27, 1995 in Salem, Caldwell County, Missouri.

She was christened by Rev. David Kettner on December 31, 1995 at the Salem Lutheran Church in Salem, Caldwell County, Missouri. His sponsors or God parents were Shannon Renshaw and Tanya Lee Horst.

Codi Horst was confirmed by Rev. Al Althoff on August 30, 2009 at the St. John Lutheran Church in Gregory, Gregory County, South Dakota.

Tracy Sue Horst &
Jade Richard Siewert
Marriage & Family*

Back row: Tracy Sue Siewert. Front row: Codi Horst, Emil Siewert Jade's grandfather, Jayden Thomas Siewert, and Jade Richard Siewert. [103]

Tracy Sue Horst married Jade Richard Siewert on February 26, 2001 in Burke, Gregory County, South Dakota. Deborah Serr performed the ceremony the Gregory County Courthouse in

Gregory, Gregory County, South Dakota.

Jade Richard Siewert was born on September 1, 1970.

Jade Richard and Tracy Sue Siewert have one child: Jayden Thane Siewert.

Birth of
Jayden Thane Siewert*

Jayden Thane Siewert was born on May 21, 2002 in Gregory, Gregory County, South Dakota.

He was christened by Rev. Wade Harr on August 4, 2002 at the St. John Lutheran Church in Gregory, Gregory County, South Dakota. His sponsors or God parents were Tanya Cerney and Jessica Shaffer.

Scott Wade Cerney &
Chrissy Kahler
Marriage & Family*

Scott Wade Cerney was born on January 21, 1971.

Scott Wade Cerney married Chrissy Kahler on September 18, 1993. The marriage ended in divorce.

Scott Wade and Chrissy Cerney had two children" Caleb Wade and Calla Ann Cerney.

Caleb Wade Cerney was born on January 6, 1994.

Calla Ann Cerney was born on September 11, 1995.

Tanya Lee Horst &
Scott Wade Cerney Marriage*

Back row: Tanya Lee Horst or Cerney, and Caleb Wade Cerney. Front row: Calla Ann Cerney, and Scott Wade Cerney. [104]

Tanya Lee married Scott Wade Cerney on October 9, 1999. They were divorced on 2010, and Tanya changed her name back to Horst, but she still used Cerney, since they have gotten back together, but they are not remarried.

Darlene Marie and Ronald William Horst [105]

Larry Leonard Reimnitz &
Unknown Person & Family*

Larry Leonard Reimnitz and a unknown person had one child: Ann Marie Reimnitz.

Ann Marie Reimnitz was born on August 24, 1967.

Ann Marie Reimnitz &
Mr. Nelson
Marriage & Family*

Back row: Brittney Ann Nelson. Middle row: Ann Marie Nelson and Cassidy Quinn Nelson. Front row: Austin Blake Nelson[106]

Ann Marie Reimnitz married Mr. Nelson

Ann Marie and Mr. Nelson had three children: Brittney Ann, Austin Blake, and Cassidy Quinn Nelson.

Brittney Ann Nelson was born on March 27, 1990.

Austin Blake was born on August 23, 1993.

Cassidy Quinn was born on June 2, 1997.

Larry Leonard Reimnitz & Lynn Dianne Baker Marriage & Family*

Larry Leonard Reimnitz, son of Leonard Gottlieb Adolf and Wilma Norma Reimnitz, married Lynn Dianne Baker on December 16, 1972 in the Mt. Calvary Lutheran Church in Huron, Beadle County, South Dakota.

Lynn Dianne Baker was born on March 6, 1941.

Larry Leonard and Lynn Dianne Reimnitz have four children: Wendy Wolf, Kelly Wolf, Liz Smith and Blaine Smith.

Wendy Wolf was born on June 18, 1957.

Kelly Wolf was born on September 3, 1958.

Blaine Smith was born on June 30, 1961.

Back row: Larry Leonard Reimnitz and Kelly wolf. Middle row: Liz Smith Blaine Smith and Wendy Wolf. Front row: Lynn Dianne Reimnitz.[107]

Judy Ellen Reimnitz & David Lee Renshaw Marriage & Family*

Judy Ellen Reimnitz, daughter of Leonard Gottlieb Adolf and Wilma Norma Reimnitz, married David Lee Renshaw on August 30, 1968 in the Immanuel Lutheran Church in Douglas County, South Dakota. The marriage ended in divorce on September 25, 2003.

David Lee and Judy Ellen Renshaw had four children: Shannon Lee, Travis Howard, Melinda Sue and Teresa Marie Renshaw.

Birth of Shannon Lee Renshaw*

Shannon Lee Renshaw was born on May 19, 1969 in Parkston, Hutchinson County, South Dakota.

She was christened in 1969 in the Immanuel Lutheran Church in Douglas County, South Dakota.

Shannon Lee Renshaw & Troy Michael Schrempp Marriage & Family*

Back row: Shannon Lee Schrempp and Troy Michael Schrempp. Front row: Regan David Schrempp, Elvis the dog, and Aspen Amelia Schrempp.[108]

Shannon Lee Renshaw married Troy Michael Schrempp on August 2, 1996.

Troy Michael Schrempp was born on August 23, 1969 in Yankton, Yankton County, South Dakota.

Troy Michael and Shannon Lee Schrempp had two children: Aspen Amelia and Regan David Schrempp.

Aspen Amelia Schrempp was born on November 16, 1997 in Minneapolis, Hennepin County, Minnesota.

Regan David Schrempp was born on April 12, 2001 in Brainerd, Crow Wing County, Minnesota.

Birth of Travis Howard Renshaw*

Travis Howard Renshaw was born on August 17, 1970 in Armour, Douglas County, South Dakota.

He was christened in 1970 in the Immanuel Lutheran Church in Douglas County, South Dakota.

Travis Howard died on October 1, 1970 a result of SIDS or Sudden Infant Death Syndrome in Armour, Douglas County, South Dakota.

He was buried in the Immanuel Lutheran Church Cemetery in Douglas County, South Dakota.

Birth of
Melinda Sue Renshaw*

Melinda Sue Renshaw was born on May 22, 1971 in Armour, Douglas County, South Dakota.

Unfortunately, she died on May 22, 1971 from premature birth problems.

Melinda Sue Renshaw was buried in the Immanuel Lutheran Church Cemetery in Douglas County, South Dakota.

Birth of
Teresa Marie Renshaw*

Teresa Marie Renshaw was born on May 19, 1974 in Yankton, Yankton County, South Dakota.

She died on May 24, 1974 as a result of premature birth problems.

Teresa Marie Renshaw was buried in the Immanuel Lutheran Church Cemetery in Douglas County, South Dakota.

Ronald Edward Vanderheiden & unknown Person & Family*

Ronald Edward Vanderheiden was born on March 7, 1950 in Platte, Charles Mix County, South Dakota.

Ronald Edward Vanderheiden and a unknown person had a child: Lyndsey Vanderheiden.

Lyndsey Vanderheiden was born on January 1, 1984.

Lyndsey Vanderheiden & Unknown Person & Family*

Lyndsey Vanderheiden and a unknown person had a child: Berkley Addison Vanderheiden.

Berkley Addison Vanderheiden was born on October 11, 2008 in Sioux Falls, Minnehaha

County, South Dakota.

Ronald Edward Vanderheiden, Lyndsey Vanderheiden holding Berkley Addison Vanderheiden, and Judy Ellen Vanderheiden [108]

Judy Ellen Renshaw &
Ronald Edward Vanderheiden
Marriage*

Judy Ellen Renshaw married Ronald Edward Vanderheiden on February 20, 2006 in the First Reformed Lutheran Church in Platte, Charles Mix County, South Dakota. The marriage ended in divorce on May 31, 2012. Judy took back Renshaw for her last name.

Sallie Rose Reimnitz &
Leon Arnold Brink
Marriage & Family*

Back row: Stephanie Lynn Brink holding Madison Rose Brink, Adam Leon Brink, Leon Arnold Brink, and Sallie Rose Brink. Front row: Helena Brink holding Logan Alexander Brink [109]

Sallie Rose Reimnitz married Leon Arnold Brink on April 7, 1973 in the Immanuel Lutheran Church in Douglas County, South Dakota.

Leon Arnold Brink was born on July 12, 1949.

Leon Arnold and Sallie Rose Brink had two children: Adam Leon and Stephanie Lynn Brink.

Adam Leon Brink was born on June 30, 1976 in Sioux Falls, Minnehaha County, South Dakota.

Stephanie Lynn was born on July 12, 1979 in Sioux Falls, Minnehaha County, South Dakota.

Adam Leon Brink & Nicole Herring Marriage *

Adam Leon Brink married Nicole Herring on December 4, 1999. The marriage end in divorce in April of 2002.

Adam Leon Brink & Helena Johnson Marriage & Family*

Adam Leon Brink married Helena Johnson on June 18, 2004.

Helena Johnson was born on June 5, 1979.

Adam Leon and Helena Brink have one child: Logan Alexander Brink.

Logan Alexander Brink was born on June 3, 2003 in Huntsville, Madison County, Alabama.

Logan Alexander Brink, Adam Leon Brink and Helena Brink. [110]

Stephanie Lynn Brink & Craig Nelson Family*

Stephanie Lynn Brink and Madison Rose Brink. [111]

Stephanie Lynn Brink and Craig Nelson had one child: Madison Rose Brink. They are not married.

Madison Rose Brink was born on November 1, 2001 in Sioux Falls, Minnehaha County, South Dakota.

Samuel Paul Reimnitz & Nancy Jean Scholten Marriage & Family*

Samuel Paul Reimnitz, son of Leonard Gottlieb Adolf and Wilma Norma Reimnitz, married Nancy Jean Scholten on October 17, 1975 in the Immanuel Lutheran Church in Douglas County, South Dakota.

Nancy Jean Scholten was born on September 6, 1956.

Samuel Paul and Nancy Jean Reimnitz had four children: Jordon Samuel, Lindsey Marie, Seth Cameron, and Lacy Jean Reimnitz.

Jordon Samuel Reimnitz was born on May 3, 1983 in Mitchell, Davison County, South Dakota.

Lindsey Marie Reimnitz was born on July 31, 1984 in Mitchell, Davison County, South Dakota.

Seth Cameron Reimnitz was born on July 16, 1989 in Mitchell, Davison County, South Dakota.

Lacey Jean Reimnitz was born on June 18, 1992 in Mitchell, Davison County, South Dakota.

Back row: Seth Cameron Reimnitz, Lindsey Marie Reimnitz, and Samuel Paul Reimnitz. Front row: Jordon Samuel Reimnitz, Sarah Danielle Reimnitz holding Lauryn Marie Reimnitz, Lacey Jean Reimnitz, and Nancy Jean Reimnitz. [112]

Jordon Samuel Reimnitz & Sarah Danielle Kennedy Marriage & Family*

Jordon Samuel Reimnitz married Sarah Danielle Kennedy on July 30, 2005.

Sarah Danielle Kennedy was born on February 20, 1985.

Jordon Samuel and Sarah Danielle Reimnitz had two children: Lauryn Marie and Ethan Samuel Reimnitz.

Lauryn Marie Reimnitz was born on December 20, 2005 in Armour, Douglas County, South Dakota.

Ethan Samuel Reimnitz was born on July 13, 2009 at the Douglas County Hospital in Armour, Douglas County, South Dakota.

Jordon Samuel Reimnitz holding Ethan Samuel Reimnitz, and Sarah Danielle Reimnitz holding Lauryn Marie Reimnitz. [113]

John William Reimnitz & Stephanie Anne Olsen Marriage & Family*

John William Reimnitz, son of Leonard Gottlieb Adolf and Wilma Norma Reimnitz, married Stephanie Anne Olsen on July 16, 1988 in the Immanuel Lutheran Church in Bertrand, Phelps County, Nebraska.

Stephanie Anne Olsen was born on August 29, 1966.

John William and Stephanie Anne Reimnitz had three children: Kaitlin Anne, Kevin John, and Trevor Allen Reimnitz.

Kaitlin Anne Reimnitz was born on March 4, 1991.

Kevin John Reimnitz was born on November 11, 1992.

Trevor Allen was born on November 7, 1994.

Back row: Ronald William Horst, Darlene Marie Horst, David Lee Renshaw, Judy Ellen Renshaw, Samuel Paul Reimnitz, Nancy Jean Reimnitz, John William Reimnitz, Stephanie Anne Reimnitz, Larry Leonard Reimnitz, and Lynn Dianne Reimnitz. Front row: Sallie Rose Brink, Leonard Gottlieb Adolf Reimnitz, Wilma Norma Reimnitz, and Leon Arnold Brink. [114]

Back row: Stephanie Anne Reimnitz, John William Reimnitz, and Kevin John Reimnitz, Front row: Kaitlin Ann Reimnitz, and Trevor Allen Reimnitz.[115]

Marlys Martha & Mildred Mae Leischner Twins & Their Family*

Edward Emanuel Leischner, son of Gustaf M. and Lydia Leischner, was born on October 19, 1900 in Parkston, Hutchinson County, South Dakota.

Martha Louise Tiede, daughter of David and Dorothea Tiede, was born on June 9, 1908 in Parkston, Hutchinson County, South Dakota.

Edward Emanuel Leischner married Martha Louise Tiede on April 24, 1932 in Hutchinson County, South Dakota according to South Dakota Marriages, 1905-1949.[136]

Edward Emanuel and Martha Louise Leischner were recorded on the 1940 United States Census were living in Kulm Township, Hutchinson County, South Dakota on April 10, 1940 according to the Census Enumerator, Alvin A. Delperdeng.[137] Edward Emanuel was thirty-nine years old and his wife Martha Louise was thirty-one years old on the report. On this same report was twin sisters: Marlys Martha and Mildred Mae five years old and Calvin E. nine months old.

Mildred and her sister, Marlys attended grade school at the Welcome School, in District 317.

Edward Emanuel Leischner died on August 12, 1966 in Parkston, Hutchinson County, South Dakota and he was buried in the Parkston Protestant Cemetery in Parkston, Hutchinson County, South Dakota.

Martha Louise Leischner died on November 7, 1999 in Parkston, Hutchinson County, South Dakota and she was buried in the Parkston Protestant Cemetery in Parkston, Hutchinson County, South Dakota.

Double Wedding Twin Zirpel Brothers Marry Twin Leischner Sisters*

Back row: Norbert John Zirpel, Martin Wilhelm Zirpel, Mildred Mae Leischner, Marlys Martha Leischner, and Malvin Otto Zirpel, and Calvin Leischner. Bridesmaids: Dorothy Tiede and Margaret Zirpel. Front row: Garry Freier, Judy Reimnitz, Caroline Zirpel and Kenneth Leischner.[116]

There was a double wedding ceremony held on November 15, 1953 in the Congregational Church in Parkston, Hutchinson County, South Dakota, when twin Zirpel brothers, Martin and Malvin married twin Leischner sisters, Mildred and Marlys.

Martin Wilhelm, son of Wilhelm Otto and Emma Martha Maria Zirpel, married Mildred Mae Leischner, daughter of Ed Emanuel and Martha Louise Leischner, while Malvin Otto Zirpel, son of Wilhelm Otto and Emma Martha Maria Zirpel, married Marlys Martha Leischner, daughter of Ed Emanuel and Martha Louise Leischner, together on November 15, 1953.

Martin Wilhelm Zirpel & Mildred Mae Leischner Marriage & Family*

Mildred Mae Zirpel is a member of the Faith Lutheran church of which she is a Chartered Member. She is also a member of the Lutheran Women's Missionary League and the Lutheran Laymen's League. Mildred has also served as a Den Mother for the Cub Scouts. Mildred enjoys such hobbies like embroidering, crocheting, and also traveling.

Martin Wilhelm and Mildred Mae Zirpel had six children: Daniel Martin, Geraldine Mae, Karen Ann, Donald Lee, Brian Scott, and Thomas William Zirpel.

Birth of Daniel Martin Zirpel*

Daniel Martin Zirpel, son of Martin Wilhelm and Mildred Mae Zirpel was born on February 3, 1956.

He was christened in 1956 in the Immanuel Lutheran Church in Douglas County, South Dakota.

Birth of Geraldine Mae Zirpel*

Geraldine Mae Zirpel, daughter of Martin Wilhelm and Mildred Mae Zirpel, was born on August 11, 1957.

Birth of Karen Ann Zirpel*

Karen Ann Zirpel, daughter of Martin Wilhelm and Mildred Mae Zirpel, was born on September 15, 1961.

Birth of Donald Lee Zirpel*

Donald Lee Zirpel, son of Martin Wilhelm and Mildred Mae Zirpel, was born on January 10, 1965.

Birth of Brian Scott Zirpel*

Brian Scott Zirpel, son of Martin Wilhelm and Mildred Mae Zirpel, was born on April 3, 1969.

Birth of Thomas William Zirpel*

Thomas William Zirpel, son of Martin Wilhelm and Mildred Mae Zirpel, was born on November 7, 1977.

Daniel Martin Zirpel & Lynn Boddicker Marriage & Family*

Daniel Martin Zirpel married Lynn Boddicker on June 12, 1976 in the Sacred Heart Catholic Church in Parkston, Hutchinson County, South Dakota. The marriage ended in divorce in May of 1983.

Lynn Boddicker was born on November 10, 1956.

Daniel Martin and Lynn Zirpel had a child: Brooke Lynn Zirpel.

Brooke Lynn Zirpel was born on March 15, 1983.

Brooke Lynn Zirpel was a 2000 graduate of the Parkston High School in Parkston, South Dakota. She also graduated in 2005 from SDSU in Brooking, South Dakota, where she earned a Bachelor's Degree in Nursing. She was employed with the Medical Center of Aurora, Colorado, as well as working as a surgical nurse in the operating room.

Brooke Lynn Zirpel & Gregory Alan Morehouse Marriage & Family*

Brooke Lynn Zirpel married Gregory Alan Morehouse, son of Mark and Deb Morehouse, on December 3, 2005 in the Faith Lutheran Church in Parkston, Hutchinson County, South Dakota.

Gregory Alan Morehouse was born on November 11, 1981. Gregory was also a 2000 graduate of the Parkston High School in Parkston, South Dakota. He later graduated from SDSM & T in Rapid City, South Dakota, where he earned a Bachelor's Degree in Industrial Engineering. He has worked for Lockhead Martin as a mechanical designer in the Atlas Program in Littleton, Colorado.

Gregory Alan and Brooke Lynn Morehouse had two children: Kennedy Lynn and Emersyn Debra Morehouse.

Kennedy Lynn Morehouse was born on May 13, 1007.

Emersyn Debra Morehouse was born on May 13, 2010.

Gregory Alan Morehouse, Brooke Lynn Morehouse holding Emersyn Lynn Morehouse, Natalie Ann Zirpel, Dustin Daniel Zirpel, Deborah Zirpel and Daniel Martin Zirpel[117]

Daniel Martin Zirpel & Deborah Kaufman Marriage *

Daniel Martin Zirpel married Deborah Kaufman on May 28, 1983.

Deborah Kaufman was born on June 21, 1950.

Daniel Martin and Deborah Zirpel had one child: Dustin Daniel Zirpel.

Dustin Daniel Zirpel was born on September 17, 1984.

Dustin Daniel Zirpel & Natalie Ann Weber Marriage *

Dustin Daniel Zirpel married Natalie Ann Weber on January 7, 2012 in the Sacred Heart Catholic Church in Parkston, Hutchinson County, South Dakota.

Natalie Ann Weber was born on September 23, 1988 in Parkston, Hutchinson County, South Dakota.

Geraldine Mae Zirpel & William Sudbeck Marriage & Family*

Geraldine Mae Zirpel married William Sudbeck on October 14, 1978 in the Faith Lutheran Church in Parkston, Hutchinson County, South Dakota.

William Sudbeck was born on August 27, 1957.

William and Geraldine Mae Sudbeck had three children: Sara Maria, Adam William, and Jeremy James Sudbeck.

Sara Maria Sudbeck was born on October 5, 1981.

Adam William Sudbeck was born on August 2, 1984.

Jeremy James Sudbeck was born on September 15, 1989.

Sara Maria Sudbeck & Toby Privett Marriage & Family*

Back row: Toby Privett holding Addilynn Marie Privett, and Jeremy James Sudbeck. Middle row: Sara Marie Sudbeck, Megan Marie Sudbeck, Adam William Sudbeck, Geraldine Mae Sudbeck and William Sudbeck. Front row: Tayge James Privett. [118]

Sara Maria Sudbeck married Toby Privett on June 17, 2006 in the Faith Lutheran Church in Parkston, Hutchinson County, South Dakota.

Back row: Brian Scott Zirpel, Daniel Martin Zirpel, Donald Lee Zirpel, and Geraldine Mae Sudbeck. Front row: Karen Ann Farris, Mildred Mae Zirpel, Thomas William Zirpel and Martin Wilhelm Zirpel. [119]

Toby Privett was born on May 11, 1981.

Sara has been employed by the Sioux Valley Hospital in Sioux Falls, South Dakota, while Toby has been employed at the First Premier Bankcard in Sioux Falls, South Dakota.

Toby and Sara Maria Privett have two children: Tayge James and Addilynn Marie Privett.

Tayge James Privett was born on August 5, 2007.

Addilynn Marie Privett was born on January 22, 2010.

Karen Ann Zirpel & Rick Farris Marriage & Family*

Karen Ann Zirpel married Rick Farris on October 2, 1982 in the Faith Lutheran Church in Parkston, Hutchinson County, South Dakota.

Rick Farris was born on June 11, 1958.

Rick and Karen Ann Farris had two children: Eric Jon and Lauren Marie Farris.

Eric Jon Farris was born on December 30, 1990.

Lauren Marie Farris was born on March 7, 1995.

Donald Lee Zirpel & Bonita Lou Fergen Marriage*

Back row: Karen Ann and Rick Farris.
Front row: Lauren Marie Farris, Koda the dog, and Eric Jon Farris. [120]

Donald Lee and Bonita Lou Zirpel [121]

92

Back row: Rick Farris, Karen Ann Farris, Deborah Zirpel, Daniel Martin Zirpel, Brian Scott Zirpel, Bonita Lou Zirpel, and Donald Lee Zirpel . Middle row: William Sudbeck, Geraldine Mae Sudbeck, Martin Wilhelm Zirpel, Mildred Mae Zirpel, Thomas William Zirpel, Kristi Kay Zirpel, Shelba Petrik holding son, Bently Petrik and David Petrik. Front row: Alyssa Marie Zirpel, Zachary Zirpel and Caleton Shedeed. [122]

Donald Lee Zirpel married Bonita Lou Fergen on June 20, 1987 in the Sacred Heart Catholic Church in Parkston, Hutchinson County, South Dakota.

Bonita Lou Fergen was born on March 16, 1965.

Brian Scott Zirpel & Angie Kruger Marriage & Family*

Brian Scott Zirpel, Alyssa Marie Zirpel, Angie Zirpel and Zachary Zirpel. [123]

Brian Scott Zirpel married Angie Kruger on August 15, 1992.

Angie Kruger was born on August 1, 1969.

Brian Scott and Angie Zirpel have two children: Alyssa Marie and Zachary Zirpel.

Alyssa Marie Zirpel was born on May 4, 1999.

Zachary Zirpel was born on April 30, 2002.

Thomas William Zirpel & Holly Steiner Marriage*

Thomas William Zirpel married Holly Steiner on August 30, 2003 in the Faith Lutheran Church in Parkston, Hutchinson County, South Dakota. The marriage ended in divorce in July of 2009.

Thomas William Zirpel & Kristi Kay Irwin Marriage *

Thomas William and Kristi Kay Zirpel [124]

Thomas William Zirpel married Kristi Kay Irwin on July 4, 2012 at the Chapel in the Hill at

Rapid City, Pennington County, South Dakota.

Kristi Kay Irwin was born on October 23, 1969 in Wager, Charles Mix County, South Dakota.

Malvin Otto Zirpel & Marlys Martha Leischner Marriage & Family*

Malvin Otto and Marlys Martha Zirpel had two children: Dennis Malvin and Carol Marlys Zirpel.

Birth of Dennis Malvin Zirpel*

Dennis Malvin Zirpel, son of Malvin Otto and Marlys Martha Zirpel, was born on December 1, 1955.

He was christened in 1955 in the Immanuel Lutheran Church in Douglas County, South Dakota.

Dennis Malvin Zirpel was confirmed in 1970 at the Immanuel Lutheran Church in Douglas County, South Dakota.

Birth of Carol Marlys Zirpel*

Carol Marlys Zirpel, daughter of Malvin Otto and Marlys Martha Zirpel, was born on January 27, 1958 in Parkston, Hutchinson County, South Dakota.

She was christened in the Faith Lutheran Church in Parkston, Hutchinson County, South Dakota.

Carol Marlys Zirpel was confirmed in 1972 at the Immanuel Lutheran Church in Douglas County, South Dakota.

Dennis Malvin Zirpel & Leanne Lyn Reichert Marriage & Family*

Leanne Lyn Reichert was born on October 5, 1957.

Leanne Lyn Reichert was confirmed in 1971 at the Immanuel Lutheran Church in Douglas County, South Dakota.

Dennis Malvin Zirpel married Leanne Lyn Reichert on December 19, 1975 in the Immanuel Lutheran Church in Douglas County, South Da-

kota.

Dennis Malvin and Leanne Lyn Zirpel have two children: Christopher Dennis and Joshua Lee Zirpel.

Christopher Dennis Zirpel was born on June 22, 1976 and he was christened in 1976 in the Immanuel Lutheran Church in Douglas County, South Dakota.

Joshua Lee Zirpel was born on January 29, 1983.

Christopher Dennis Zirpel & Katie Lawrence Marriage & Family*

Christopher Dennis Zirpel married Katie Lawrence on April 27, 2002 in the St. John Lutheran Church in Yankton, Yankton County, South Dakota.

Katie Lawrence was born on March 9, 1979.

Christopher Dennis and Katie Zirpel had one child: Jordon Jean Zirpel.

Jordon Jean Zirpel was born on May 28, 2003.

Back row: Christopher Dennis Zirpel, Katie Zirpel, Joshua Lee Zirpel, and Melissa Zirpel. Front row: Jordon Jean Zirpel, Dennis Malvin Zirpel holding Justice Laurel Zirpel, Marlys Martha Moege, Leanne Lyn Zirpel holding Jonas Harold Zirpel. [125]

Joshua Lee Zirpel & Melissa Nickerson Marriage & Family*

Joshua Lee Zirpel married Melissa Nickerson on May 10, 2008.

Melissa Nickerson was born on January 29, 1983.

Joshua Lee and Melissa Zirpel have two children: Jonas Harold and Justic Laurel Zirpel.

Twins: Jonas Harold and Justic Laurel Zirpel were born on March 24, 2007.

Carol Marlys Zirpel & Michael Lawrence Bialas
Marriage & Family*

Michael Lawrence was born on July 10, 1955 in Parkston, Hutchinson County, South Dakota.

He was christened in 1955 in the Immanuel Lutheran Church in Douglas County, South Dakota.

Michael Lawrence Bialas was confirmed in 1970 at the Immanuel Lutheran Church in Douglas County, South Dakota.

Carol Marlys Zirpel attended school in Parkston and later country school near Dimock, South Dakota. She graduated college in Sioux Falls, South Dakota with a Degree as a Medical Assistant.

Carol Marlys Zirpel married Michael Lawrence Bialas, son of Lawrence Harold Bialas and Bernice Elizabeth Gerlach, on October 21, 1977 in the Immanuel Lutheran Church in Douglas County, South Dakota. The marriage ended in divorce on October 5, 1994.

Michael Lawrence and Carol Marlys Bialas had four children: Christen Carol, Matthew Michael, Emily Elizabeth and Mandy Marie Bialas.

Birth of Christen Carol Bialas*

Christen Carol Bialas was born on November 26, 1980 in Sioux Falls, Minnehaha County, South Dakota.

She was christened in 1980 in the Immanuel Lutheran Church in Douglas County, South Dakota.

Birth of Matthew Michael Bialas*

Matthew Michael Bialas was born on January 5, 1983 in Sioux Falls, Minnehaha County, South Dakota.

Birth of Emily Elizabeth Bialas*

Emily Elizabeth Bialas was born on July 10, 1987 in Sioux Falls, Minnehaha County, South Dakota.

Birth of Mandy Marie Bialas*

Mandy Marie Bialas was born on July 10, 1988 in Mitchell, Davison County, South Dakota.

Christen Carol Bialas & Tim James Wermers Jr.
Marriage & Family*

Christen Carol Bialas married Tim James Wermers Jr. on September 22, 2001 in the Faith Lutheran Church in Parkston, Hutchinson County, South Dakota.

Tim James Jr. and Christen Carol Wermers have one child: Sophie Carol Wermers.

Sophie Carol Wermers was born on September 13, 2011.

Matthew Lawrence Bialas & Danielle Wonch - Girl Friend*

In 2013, Matthew Michael Bialas had a special girl friend, Danielle Wonch.

Danielle Wonch was born on October 24, 1980.

Back row: Tim James Wermers Jr. holding his daughter, Sophie Carol Wermers, Matthew Michael Bialas, and Keith Goehring.
Front row: Christen Carol Wermers, Marlys Martha Moege, and Emily Elizabeth Bialas. [126]

Carol Marlys Bialas & Keith Allen Goehring Marriage*

On March 16, 2002, Carol Marlys Bialas married Keith A Goehring, son of Marvin and Shirley Goehring in the Faith Lutheran Church in Parkston, Hutchinson County, South Dakota. The ceremony was performed by Rev. Carl Rockrohr.

Parents of the couple were Marlys Moege of

Carol Marlys Bialas and Keith Allen Goehring. [127]

Dimock, South Dakota and Marvin and Shirley Goehring of Parkston, South Dakota.

The attendants for the couple were Christen Carol and Tim James Wermers. Carol, the bride was escorted down the aisle by her son, Matthew Michael Bialas. The Candle lighters were Emily Elizabeth Bialas and Mandy Marie Bialas.

Carol Marlys & Keith Allen Goehring - The Later Years*

Carol Marlys Goehring had worked as a secretary for Lloyd Mahan, Toshiba and County Fair Mitchell, as well as Parkston Food Center in Parkston, South Dakota.

Keith Allen Goehring was an attorney in Parkston, South Dakota.

Carol Marlys Goehring died from cancer on October 31, 2007 at the Avera McKennan Hospital in Sioux Falls, Minnehaha County, South Dakota.

Her funeral services were held on November 2, 2007 at the Faith Lutheran Church in Parkston, Hutchinson County, South Dakota.

Her burial was in the Parkston Protestant Cemetery in Parkston, Hutchinson County, South Dakota.

Carol Marlys Goehring had been a member of the Faith Lutheran Church, and she had been active as the Church Organist, Sunday School Teacher, and a member of the LWML. She enjoyed gardening, cooking or baking, as well as bowling, her greatest pleasure was spending time with her family.

Malvin Otto Zirpel - His Later Years*

Malvin Otto Zirpel died in South Dakota on January 20, 1964 and he was buried in the Parkston Protestant Cemetery in Parkston, Hutchinson County, South Dakota.

Herbert Gottlieb Moege & His Family*

Herbert Gottlieb Moege, son of Ernest and Serena Moege, was born on February 6, 1922 in his parent's home in Dimock, Hutchinson County, South Dakota.

Herbert Gottlieb Moege was recorded living in Washington Township, Douglas County, South Dakota with his parents, Ernest and Serena Moege on the 1930 United States Census taken by the Census Enumerator, Mrs. Ida Bertram on April 15, 1930.[138] Herbert Gottlieb was eight years old. His father, Ernest was forty years old while he mother, Serena was thirty-three years old.

Marlys Martha Zirpel & Herbert Gottlieb Moege Marriage & Family*

Marlys Martha Zirpel & Herbert Gottlieb Moege. [128]

Marlys Martha Zirpel married Herbert Gottlieb Moege on August 19, 1966 in South Dakota

Herbert Gottlieb and Marlys Martha Moege had four addition children: Gerald Herbert, Maynard Edward, Cheryl Ann and Lynette Edna Moege.

Birth of
Gerald Herbert Moege*

Gerald Herbert Moege was born on June 22, 1967 in the Parkston Hospital in Parkston, Hutchinson County, South Dakota.

Birth of
Maynard Edward Moege*

Maynard Edward Moege was born on August 1, 1968 in the Parkston Hospital in Parkston, Hutchinson County, South Dakota.

Birth of
Cheryl Ann Moege*

Cheryl Ann Moege was born on July 16, 1970 in the Parkston Hospital in Parkston, Hutchinson County, South Dakota.

Birth of
Lynette Edna Moege*

Lynette Edna Moege was born on November 1, 1971 in the Parkston Hospital in Parkston, Hutchinson County, South Dakota.

Gerald Herbert Moege &
Suzanne Ceclia Lampe -
Girl Friend*

In 2013, Gerald Herbert Moege's girl friend was Suzanne Ceclia Lampe.

Suzanna Ceclia Lampe was born on December 2, 1964.

Suzanne Ceclia Lampe, Marlys Martha Moege, and Gerald Herbert Moege. [129]

Maynard Edward Moege &
Anna Marie Reiman
Marriage*

Maynard Edward Moege married Anne Marie Reiman on November 27, 1992.

Anna Marie Reiman was born on July 16, 1968.

Anne Marie Moege, Marlys Martha Moege and Maynard Edward Moege. [130]

Cheryl Ann Moege &
Kelly Joseph Mogck
Marriage & Family*

Cheryl Ann Moege married Kelly Joseph Mogck in 1990.

Kelly Joseph Mogck was born on September 2, 1964.

Kelly and Cheryl Mogck had two children: Samantha Ann and Mariah Jo Mogck.

Samantha Ann Mogck was born on May 25, 1992.

Mariah Jo Mogck was born on January 20, 1994.

Back row: Cheryl Ann Mogck and Kelly Joseph Mogck. Front row: Samantha Ann Mogck, Marlys Martha Moege, and Mariah Jo Mogck. [131]

Lynette Edna Moege &
Lance John Konrad
Marriage & Family*

Lynette Edna Moege married Lance John Konrad on April 5, 1991.

Lance John and Lynette Konrad had two children: Jamie Lyn and Lane John Konrad.

Jamie Lyn was born on August 26, 1993.

Lane John Konrad was born on January 25, 1996.

Back row: Lane John Konrad and Jamie Lyn Konrad. Front row: Lynette Edna Konrad, Marlys Martha Moege, and Lance John Konrad. [132]

Herbert Gottlieb Moege - The Later Years*

Herbert Gottlieb Moege died on June 4, 1997 in Parkston, Hutchinson County, South Dakota. His burial was in the Immanuel Lutheran Church Cemetery in Douglas County, South Dakota.

Margaret Maria Zirpel & William John Bertram

Marriage & Family*

William John Bertram, son of Ernest William and Viola Bertram was born on October 26, 1935.

Margaret Maria Zirpel, daughter of Wilhelm Otto and Emma Martha Maria Zirpel, married William John Bertram, son of Ernest William and Viola Bertram on October 28, 1956 in Emmaus Lutheran Church in Tripp, Hutchinson County, South Dakota.

William John and Margaret Maria Bertram had five children: Marcia Leann, Maria Diann, Ernest William, Mira Susann, and Erin Lee Bertram.

Birth of Marcia Leann Bertram*

Marcia Leann Bertram was born on September 1957 in South Dakota.

Birth of Maria Diann Bertram*

Marcia Diann Bertram was born on August 2, 1960 in South Dakota.

Birth of Ernest William Bertram*

Ernest William Bertram was born on July 8, 1964 in South Dakota.

Birth of Mira Susann Bertram*

Mira Susann Bertram was born on February 19, 1969 in South Dakota.

Birth of Erin Lee Bertram*

Erin Lee Bertram was born on November 23, 1975 in South Dakota.

Marcia Leann Bertram & Jay Alan Van Den Hoek Marriage *

Marcia Leann Bertram married Jay Alan Van Den Hoek on December 12, 1987 in the Redeemer Lutheran Church in Armour, Douglas County, South Dakota.

Jay Alan Van Den Hoek was born on June 20, 1975.

Maria Diann Bertram & John Edward Meyer Marriage & Family*

Maria Diann Bertram married John Edward Meyer on May 9, 1981.

John Edward Meyer was born on November 20, 1957.

John Edward and Maria Diann Meyer had three children: Stacy Sue, Nathaniel John and Ashley Diann Meyer.

Stacy Sue Meyer was born on February 28, 1985.

Stacy Sue Meyer married Joshua Daniel Clay Billard on August 6, 2005.

Joshua Daniel Clay Billard was born on March 5, 1984.

Nathaniel John Meyer was born on March 10, 1988.

Ashley Diann Meyer was born on April 7, 1999.

Ernest William Bertram & Michelle Thompson Marriage & Family*

Ernest William Bertram married Michelle Thompson on November 9, 1991.

Michelle Thompson was born on April 25, 1972.

Ernest William and Michelle Bertram had two children: Ryan William and Ethan Lee Bertram.

Ryan William Bertram was born on June 17, 1997.

Ethan Lee Bertram was born on September 26, 2005.

Mira Susann Bertram & Leo Jerome Leonard Marriage & Family*

Mira Susann Bertram married Leo Jerome Leonard on June 1, 1991 in the Redeemer Lutheran Church in Armour, Douglas County, South Dakota.

Leo Jerome Leonard was born on July 29, 1968.

Leo Jerome and Mira Susann Leonard had three children: Jamie Jerome, Micah William, and Marissa Susan Leonard.

Jamie Jerome Leonard was born on September 6, 1998 in the Queen of Peace Hospital, Mitchell, Davison County, South Dakota.

Micah William Leonard was born on May 4, 2004 in the Queen of Peace Hospital, Mitchell, Davison County, South Dakota.

Marissa Susan Leonard was born on July 28, 2008 in the Queen of Peace Hospital, Mitchell, Davison County, South Dakota.

Erin Lee Bertram & Kari Van Der Werff Marriage & Family*

Erin Lee Bertram married Kari Van Der Werff on June 20, 1998.

Kari Van Der Werff was born on December 24, 1977.

Erin Lee and Kari Bertram had three

children: Emma Nicole, Alley May and Sara Kate Bertram.

Emma Nicole Bertram was born on October 21, 2001.

Ally May Bertram was born on August 31, 2003.

Sara Kate Bertram was born on November 26, 2008.

Margaret Maria and William John Bertram
50th Wedding Anniversary in 2006. [133]

Dennis Allen Stoebner & His Family*

Ruben Emil Stoebner married Edna Semmler on September 16, 1941 in Hutchinson County, South Dakota, according to South Dakota Marriages, 1905-1949.[139]

Dennis Allen Stoebner, son of Ruben Emil Stoebner and Edna Semmler, was born on November 17, 1943 in Parkston, Hutchinson County, South Dakota.

Dennis Allen Stoebner's parents, Ruben and Edna farmed west of Tripp, Hutchinson County, South Dakota for nearly 45 years before they moved into Tripp, South Dakota.

According to cemetery records, Ruben Emil Stoebner was born on January 6, 1914 and he died on November 27, 2001. Ruben's wife, Edna was born on May 19, 1921 and she died on May 6, 2008.

Edna Emma Zirpel & Dennis Allen Stoebner Marriage & Family*

99

Back row : Marcia Leann Van Den Hoek, Jay Alan Van Den Hoek, Nathaniel John Meyer, Maria Diann Meyer, John Edward Meyer, Joshua Daniel Clay Billard and Stacy Sue Billard. Middle row : Leo Jerome Leonard, Micah William Leonard, William John Bertram, Ashley Diann Meyer, Margaret Maria Bertram, and Ernest William Bertram. Front row : Jamin Jerome Leonard, Mira Susann Leonard, Ally May Bertram, Kari Bertram, Emma Nicole Bertram, Ryan William Bertram, Michelle Bertram, and Ethan Lee Bertram. [134]

Edna Emma Zirpel, daughter of Wilhelm Otto and Emma Martha Maria Zirpel, married Dennis Allen Stoebner, son of Ruben Edwin and Edna Stoebner, on May 24, 1964 on May 24, 1964 in the Faith Lutheran Church in Parkston, Hutchinson County, South Dakota.

Dennis Allen and Edna Emma Stoebner. [135]

Dennis Allen and Edna Emma Stoebner had two children: Lynn Marie and David Allen Stoebner.

Lynn Marie Stoebner was born on September 19, 1968 in Wagner, Charles Mix County, South Dakota.

David Allen Stoebner was born on March 21, 1972 in Wagner, Charles Mix County, South Dakota.

Dennis Allen and Edna Emma Stoebner were living in Aberdeen, South Dakota in 2012.

Lynn Marie Stoebner & Leo Gannon Marriage & Family*

Lynn Marie Stoebner married Leo Gannon on October 22, 1994.

Leo Gannon was born on March 12, 1966.

Leo and Lynn Marie Gannon had six children: Alexas Noel, Hanna Marie, Samantha, Rachel, Sarah, and Elizabeth Gannon.

Alexas Gannon was born on December 28, 1995 in Mitchell, Davison County, South Dakota.

Hanna Marie Gannon was born on March 10, 1998 in Mitchell, Davison County, South Dakota.

Back row: Alex Noel Gannon, Hannah Marie Gannon, Samantha Gannon, Leo Gannon, Lynn Marie Gannon, Elizabeth Gannon, Edna Emma Stoebner, Dennis Allen Stoebner, Heidee Stoebner, and David Allen Stoebner, Front row: Sarah Gannon, Rachel Gannon, Katelin Stoebner and Dillon Stoebner. [136]

Samantha Gannon was born on October 7, 1999 in Mitchell, Davison County, South Dakota.

Rachel Gannon was born on January 14, 2004 in Sioux Falls, Minnehaha County, South Dakota.

Sarah Gannon was born on August 17, 2005 in Sioux Falls, Minnehaha County, South Dakota.

Elizabeth Gannon was born on January 3, 2008 in Sioux Falls, Minnehaha County, South Dakota.

Leo and Lynn Marie Gannon lived in Aberdeen, South Dakota in 2009.

David Allen Stoebner & Heidee Osborn
Marriage & Family*

David Allen Stoebner married Heidee Osborn on August 2, 1997.

Heidee Osborn was born on August 1, 1969.

David Allen and Heidee Stoebner had three children: Collin David, Dillion and Katelin Stoebner.

Collin David Stoebner was born in Aberdeen, Brown County, South Dakota.

Dillon Stoebner was born on May 13, 2001 in Aberdeen, Brown County, South Dakota.

Katelin Stoebner was born on March 3, 2004 in Aberdeen, Brown County, South Dakota.

Edna Emma and Dennis Allen Stoebner. [137]

CHAPTER 8

Birth of Gottfried John Zirpel - A Twin*

Gottfried John Zirpel was a twin, son of Johan and Augusta Zirpel was born on April 25, 1897 in Douglas County, South Dakota. His twin sister was Elisabeth Augusta Zirpel. According to his the birth certificate document filed on June 13, 1942, his birth place was Parkston-P.O. in Douglas County, South Dakota. The evidence of his birth was taken from a Baptismal Certificate Record, issued by Rev. Ernest Bruegel, Pastor of the Evangelical Lutheran Church at Hillside, South Dakota before the Notary Public, M. C. Sullivan.

He was christened on May 23, 1897 in the Immanuel Lutheran Church in Douglas County, South Dakota.

Gottfried John Zirpel was three years old when he appeared with his parents, Johan and Anna Augusta Zirpel on the 1900 United States Census located in Berlin Township, now known as Washington Township, Douglas County, South Dakota according to the census report taken on June 21, 1900, by the Census Enumerator, Henry Ruff.[140]

His brothers and sisters listed on the census report: Anna Emilie was fifteen years old, Robert Hermann was thirteen years old, Emma Bertha was seven years old, Wilhelm Otto was four years old, Elisabeth Augusta was three years old, and Edward Richard was nine months old. His father, Johan was listed as general farmer and owning his farm.

On April 26, 1910, Gottfried John Zirpel appeared on the 1910 United State Census living with his parents, Johan and Anna Augusta in Berlin Township, now called Washington Township at the age of twelve years according to the Census Enumerator, Walter L. Koehn.[141] The other siblings listed on the census report were Emma Bertha, Wilhelm Otto, Elisabeth Augusta, Edward Richard and Bertha Rosina.

Gottfried John Zirpel was confirmed on March 31, 1912 in the Immanuel Lutheran Church in Douglas County, South Dakota.

According to the World War I draft card registration card for Gottfried John Zirpel by W. M. Scholes in Douglas County, South Dakota on June 5, 1918, Gottfried was twenty-one years

old, single, and he was still living with his parents.[142] He was described as having brown hair and brown eyes according to the document.

Gottfried John Zirpel and Elisabeth Augusta Zirpel Confirmation on March 31, 1912. [138]

On the 1920 United States Census on January 7, 1920 recorded by the Census Enumerator, Mrs. Carl Bertram, Gottfried John was living in Lincoln Township, Douglas County, South Dakota with his parents, Johan and Anna Augusta Zirpel, his twin sister, Elisabeth Augusta Zirpel and a brother, Edward Richard Zirpel.[143] On this report, Gottfried John was working as a farm laborer on his father's farm.

Gertrude Anna Gerlach & Her Family*

Gertrude Anna Gerlach's grandparents were Johann Gottlieb Moke and Ann Susanna Misch.

Johann Gottlieb Moke, son of Paul Karl Moke and Rosina Hoffman, was born on March 12, 1853 in Ottag, Ohlau, Schlesien, Germany. He died on January 9, 1908 in Douglas County, South Dakota and he was buried in the St. John's Lutheran Church Cemetery in Douglas County, South Dakota.

Johann Gottlieb Moke married Ann Susanna Misch on January 1, 1876 in Stad Free Church, Ohlau, Silesia, Germany.

STATE OF SOUTH DAKOTA.

County of __Douglas__ }ss.

I, __Janet R. Morris__ , Clerk of Courts and local registrar of vital statistics and keeper of the files and records of births and deaths within and for said county and state, do hereby certify that the said records show the following facts regarding the birth of __3 Gottfried John Zirpel__ :

Full name at birth __Gottfried John Zirpel__ ; sex __male__ ; date of birth __April 25th. 1897 __19; birthplace __Parkston-P.O.__

City or Town
__Douglas__ County, South Dakota; color __white__ ;

father's full name __John Zirpel__ ; father's age __38__ ;

father's birthplace __Germany__ ;

State or Country

mother's maiden name __Augusta Sperlich__ ; mother's age __28__ ;

mother's birthplace __Germany__ ; by whom the birth was

State or Country

reported __Christiane Moege__ ; address __Parkston, S.D.__ ;

was abstract of supporting evidence filed? __Yes. Evidence taken from a Baptismal Certificate record,issued by Rev Ernest Bruegel,pastor of the Evangelical Lutheran church at Hillside, S.D. shows date of birth as April 25th. 1897 before M.C. Sullivan as Notary Public.__ I further certify that the report of said birth was filed in my office on the __13th.__ day of __June__ , 19 __42__, and that it was recorded in Record of Births No. __THREE__

Established

and entered as number __3244-E__ , on page __10__ .

IN TESTIMONY WHEREOF I have hereunto set my hand and affixed the seal of the Circuit Court in my office in the city of __Armour__ in said county and state this __13th.__ day of __June__ 19__42__

Janet R. Morris

By _____ Clerk of Courts.
Deputy.

Gottfried John Zirpel's Birth Certificate. [139]

STATE OF SOUTH DAKOTA.

County of __Douglas__ }ss.

I, __Janet R. Morris__ , Clerk of the Circuit Court within and for said County and State, and keeper of the files and records of births and deaths within and for said County, do hereby certify that the said records show the following facts regarding the birth of __Gertrude Gerlach__

Name __Gertrude Gerlach__

Sex __female__ ; Date of birth __February 19th__ A. D. 19__1903__ ; Place of birth __Hillside Berlin Twp.Douglas__ County, South Dakota; Father's name __Carl Gerlach__

Age __33__ ; Father's color __white__ ; Father's birthplace __Germany__

Father's occupation __-__ ; Father's residence __Hillside, S.D.__

Mother's maiden name __Anna Moke__ ; Age __26__ ; Mother's birthplace __Germany__ ; Mother's residence __Hillside, S.D.__

Number of children previously born to her __--__ By whom the birth was reported

(father) __Carl Gerlach__

I FURTHER CERTIFY, that the report of said birth was filed in my office on the __13th.__ day of

Established

__June__ , A. D. 19__42__, and that it was recorded in Record of Births No. __THREE__

and entered as number __3245-E__ , on page __11__ .

IN TESTIMONY WHEREOF I have hereunto set my hand and affixed the seal of the Circuit Court in my office in the City of __Armour__ and said County and State, this __13th.__ day of __June__ A. D. 19__42__.

Janet R. Morris

Clerk of the Circuit Court.

By _____ Deputy Clerk.

Gertrude Anna Gerlach's Birth Certificate. [140]

Ann Susanna (Misch) Moke was born on September 3, 1858 in Ottag, Kreis Ohau, Silesia, Germany and she died on June 1, 1936 in Douglas County, South Dakota.

Ann Susanna Moke was buried in St. John's Lutheran Cemetery in Douglas County, South Dakota.

Johann Gottlieb and Ann Susanna Moke had ten children: Annie Rosina, Emma Dorothea, Bertha, Gottfried Karl, Dorothy Martha (Dorothea), Selma Clara, Frederick Wilhelm, Gottlieb Johann, Karl Otto and Gertrude Louise.

The family of Johann Gottlieb and Ann Susanna Moke was recorded on the 1900 United States Census taken on June 18, 1900 by the Census Enumerator, Henry Ruff, living in Valley Township, Douglas County, South Dakota.[144]

On the report, Johann Gottlieb and Ann Susanna Moke had twelve children with only ten living. The children listed on the report were Bertha was seven years old, Gottfried Karl was fourteen years old, Dorothea Martha was eleven years old, Selma Clara was nine years old, Frederick Wilhelm was seven years old, Gottlieb Johann was five years old, Karl Otto was two years old, and Gertrude Louise was one year old.

On April 20, 1910 according the Census Enumerator, Walter L. Koehn, Ann Susanna Moke was listed as a widow on the 1910 United States Census.[145] Only three children was listed on the report, Gottlieb, Otto and Gertrude.

Ann Susanna Moke was recorded on the 1920 United States Census on January 14, 1920 by the Census Enumerator, Mrs. Carl Bertram living in Washington Township, Douglas County, South Dakota with three of her children: Gottlieb, Otto, and Gertrude.[146]

Anna Rosina Moke was confirmed in 1882 at the St. Lutheran Church in Douglas County, South Dakota.

On the 1930 United States Census, Ann Susanna Moke was living in Washington Township, Douglas County, South Dakota with her son, Gottlieb and his wife, Hattie on April 18 or 19, 1930 according to the Census Enumerator, Mrs. Ida Bertram.[147]

Carl John Gerlach was born on September 20, 1870 in Gruentanne, Schlesien, Germany.

In 1883 he came to the United States with his father, who had located near Hillside.

In 1885, Carl joined the St. John Lutheran Church in that community.

Anna Rosina Moke, daughter of Johann Gottlieb Moke and Ann Susanna Misch, married Carl John Gerlach on March 3, 1897 at the St. John Lutheran Church in Douglas County, South Dakota.

Carl John Gerlach and Anna Rosina Moke on Wedding Day March 3, 1897 [141]

Carl John and Anna Rosina Gerlach had ten children: Bertha, Karl Bernhard, Erich Frederick, Gertrude Anna, Laura D., Fredrick G., Leonard Gilbert, Gerda Agnes, Verna Selma, and Eldor Gottlieb Gerlach.

Carl John and Anna Rosina Gerlach were living in Lincoln Township, Douglas County, South Dakota with two of their children, Bertha and Karl Bernhard on June 4, 1900 according to The Census Enumerator, William Pfiefer on the 1900 United States Census.[148]

The children listed on this report were Bertha and Karl Bernhard Gerlach. The report said Anna Rosina had immigrated in 1881 with her family.

Gertrude Anna Gerlach, daughter of Carl John Gerlach and Annie Rosina Moke was born on February 19, 1903 at Hillside in Berlin Township, Douglas County, South Dakota according to the Certificate of Birth filed by the Clerk of the Circuit Court, Janet R. Morris, on June 13, 1942 in the city of Armour, Douglas County, South Dakota. She was christened on March 15, 1903 in the St. Lutheran Church in Douglas County, South Dakota.

Carl John and Anna Rosina (Moke) Gerlach [142]

On May 7, 1910 on the 1910 United States Census, the Census Enumerator, Bert E. Fenenga, reported the family of Carl Gerlach living in Valley Township, Douglas County, South Dakota. [149]

The children listed on this report were Bertha was twelve years old, Karl Bernhard was ten years, Gertrude Anna was seven years old, Laura D. was four years old, Fredrick G. was three years and Leonard Gilbert was two months old.

Gertrude Anna Gerlach Confirmation 1917 [143]

Gertrude Anna Gerlach was confirmed on March 18, 1917 at the Immanuel Lutheran Church in Douglas County, South Dakota.

On the 1920 United States Census recorded by the Census Enumerator, Tony Tinkelenberg

on April 23rd and 24th, 1920 reported that the Carl Gerlach family had moved from Valley Township in Douglas County to Garfield Township in Douglas County, South Dakota. [150]

There were nine children listed on the report: Karl Bernhard twenty years old, Erich Freidrich eighteen years old, Gertrude Anna seventeen years old, Laura D. fifteen years old, Leonard Gilbert seven years old, Verna Selma five years old, and Eldor Gottlieb two years old.

Annie Rosina Gerlach died on October 8, 1927 in Douglas County, South Dakota and she was buried in the St. John Lutheran Cemetery.

Hedwig Naether was born on December 25, 1880, in Grobosterhausen, near Eisleben, Germany.

On January 12, 1901 she had been united in marriage to her first husband, Reinhold Otto in the city of Boderslaben near Querfurt. The Rev. Reinhold performed this ceremony.

Reinhold and Hedwig Otto had three children were born to this union and one son, Reinhold died when he was only 6 days old.

In 1912, the Otto family came to the United States and settled in Gates Center, Kansas, where they remained for a few years and later moved to Robert, Idaho, where they took up a homestead. The extreme drought conditions induced them to moved to South Dakota in 1924 and they settled in the Wittenberg community in South Dakota.

On August 26, 1926, Hedwig's first husband, Reinhold Otto died. Hedwig and her daughter moved to Parkston on February 4, 1927.

Carl John and Hedwig (Otto) Gerlach [144]

After Annie Rosina's death, Carl John Gerlach married Hedwig Otto on December 6, 1928 in Parkston, Hutchinson County, South Dakota. They were married by Rev. John Lambertus.

Carl John Gerlach farmed until 1929 after which he moved into Parkston in Hutchinson County, South Dakota.

Carl John and Hedwig Gerlach were living in Parkston in Hutchinson County, South Dakota on April 14, 1930 according to the 1930 United States Census recorded by the Census Enumerator, Mueller.[151]

The report said that Hedwig's birthplace had been Germany. There were only two children recorded still living at home. They were Verna Selma sixteen years old and Eldora Gottlieb twelve years old.

Carl John and Hedwig were still living in Parkston, Hutchinson County, South Dakota on April 5, 1940 according to the 1940 United States Census recorded by the Census Enumerator, R. Adeline Friedrich.[152]

On this report Carl Gerlach had completed the 8th grade on school, he owned his home and the home was valued at $1,500. Carl was recorded at the age of sixty-nine years old and Hedwig was fifty-nine years old.

Hedwig Gerlach, the second wife of Carl John Gerlach died on September 15, 1949 in Hutchison County, South Dakota and she was buried in the Wittenberg Cemetery in Hutchinson County, South Dakota.

According to a copy of Mrs. Carl Gerlach's obituary the funeral was held on Sunday afternoon at the Salem Lutheran Church with Dr. M. F. Amelung officiating. The burial was in the Wittenberg Cemetery. The Thompson funeral home had been charge of the funeral arrangements.

Hedwig Gerlach had been member of the Lutheran church and during the last twenty-two years of her life a member of the Salem Lutheran Congregation.

Hedwig Gerlach was mourned by her husband, Carl John and 12 children: Mrs. Christ Baumiller, Parkston, South Dakota; Karl Bernard Gerlach of Mitchell, South Dakota; Erich Friedrich Gerlach of West Bend, Wisconsin; Gertrude Anna (Gerlach) Zirpel of Parkston, South Dakota; Mrs. Edwin Bietz of Mitchell, South Dakota; Fredrick G. Gerlach of Mitchell, South Dakota; Leonard Gilbert Gerlach of Mount Vernon, South Dakota; Mrs. Reinhold Baumiller of Wittenberg Township, Hutchinson County, South Dakota; Verna Selma (Gerlach) Cross of Barton, Wisconsin; and Eldora Gottlieb Gerlach of Mitchell, South Dakota.

Hedwig was also survived by a sister back in Germany, 52 grandchildren and 16 great-grandchildren.

Carl John Gerlach lived in his home in Parkston until a short time before his death. After that time his life was spent between the Carl Dorzak home in West Bend, Wisconsin and the home of Edwin Bietz in Mitchell, South Dakota.

Carl John Gerlach died on Thursday, January 4, 1951, that evening while in the Mitchell Hospital in Mitchell, Davison County, South Dakota. The Rev. M. F. Amelung officiated at the services and the burial which was held in the Hillside Cemetery in Douglas County, South Dakota under the direction of the Thompson Funeral Home.

Survivors were Mrs. Dorzak and Erich Freidrich Gerlach, West Bend, Wisconsin; Bernard Gerlach, Mrs. Edwin Bietz, Fredrick G. Gerlach and Eldor Gottlieb Gerlach, Mitchell, South Dakota; Mrs. Gottfried Zirpel, Mrs. Reinhold Baumiller and Mrs. Christ Baumiller, Parkston, South Dakota; Leonard Gilbert Gerlach, Mount Vernon, South Dakota; Mrs. Melvin Cross, Barton, Wisconsin; Mrs. Arthur Newell, Eagle, Indiana; 43 grandchildren; 23 great-grandchildren; and a sister, Mrs. Christina Moege, Mitchell, South Dakota.

Gottfried Johan Zirpel & Gertrude Anna Gerlach
Marriage & Family*

Gottfried John Zirpel and Gertrude Anna Gerlach [145]

After Gertrude Anna Gerlach received her father's consent on February 19, 1921.[153] Gertrude Anna Gerlach, daughter of Carl John Gerlach and Anna Rosina Moke, married Gottfried Johan Zirpel, son of Johan and Anna Augusta

106

Gottfried John Zirpel and Gertrude Anna Gerlach Wedding . Back row: Edward Richard Zirpel, Mathilda L. Zirpel, Wilhelm Otto Zirpel, Emma Martha Maria Zirpel, Oscar Carl Gerlach, Elisabeth Augusta Gerlach Front row left to right: Gottfried John Zirpel and Gertrude Anna Zirpel. Flowers girls: Verna Selma Gerlach and Evelyn Stahl. [146]

Zirpel, on a snow-covered day, February 2, 1922 in the St. John Lutheran Church in Douglas County, South Dakota. Rev. P. Tecklenburg, Lutheran Minister performed the ceremony.

According to various family members the previous day snow had fell and there was around three feet of snow on the ground, and many thought that the wedding would surely be postponed. With all the amount of snow everyone was afraid it would make it impossible for the guests to arrive safely.

Their wedding reception was held in the home of Carl John and Anna Rosina Gerlach home, the bride's parents.

Gottfried John was fairly certain that there would be no wedding, because of all the snow. However, the best man, Wilhelm Otto Zirpel was the one to start shoveling the snow and the wedding was not cancelled.

The cooks arrived around 12 noon and eagerly began preparing the meal with hopes that all the guests would be able to get there.

Gottfried John and Gertrude Anna Zirpel settled on the Johan Zirpel farm, two miles north and eight one-half miles west of Parkston, South Dakota.

Together, they became members of the Immanuel Lutheran Church in Douglas County, South Dakota.

In 1926, they purchased the farm from Johan Zirpel and continued to live there until 1965.

Gottfried John and Gertrude Anna Zirpel had eight children: Leonardt Robert, Wilbert Erich, Erwin Karl, Elmer Gottfried, Norbert John, Harold Arnold, Rosalene Gertrude, and Mary Ellen Ruth Zirpel.

On the 1930 United States Census on April 10th-11th, 1930, the family of Gottfried Johan Zirpel was living in Lincoln Township, Douglas County, South Dakota according to the Census Enumerator, Mrs. Ida Bertram.[154]

Gottfried John Zirpel was as farmer who owned his home. The report also noted that Gottfried John was not veteran of the U.S. Military. There were five children listed on the census report. They were Leonardt Robert six years old,

Wilbert Erich five years old, Erwin Karl three years old, Elmer Gottfried two years old, and Norbert John five months old.

Gottfried John and Gertrude Anna Zirpel and their children were still living in Lincoln Township, Douglas County, South Dakota on April 26, 1940, on the 1940 United States Census according to the Census Enumerator, Lawrence N. Amend.[155]

According to the report, Gottfried John was a grain farmer, he owned his home, it was valued at $1,000 and he had only completed the 3rd grade in school. There were seven children listed on the report living with their parents. They were Leonardt Robert sixteen years old, Wilbert Erich fifteen years old, Erwin Karl thirteen years old, Elmer Gottfried twelve years old, Norbert John ten years old, and, Rosalene Gertrude one year old.

When they retired in November of 1965, Gottfried John and Gertrude Anna Zirpel moved from the farm into Parkston, Hutchinson County, South Dakota.

At that time they joined the Faith Lutheran Church in Parkston, South Dakota.

Birth of
Leonardt Robert Zirpel*

Leonardt Robert Zirpel, son of Gottfried John Zirpel and Gertrude Anna Gerlach was born on May 14, 1923 in Douglas County, South Dakota and her was christened in 1923 in the Immanuel Lutheran Church in Douglas County, South Dakota.

Leonard Robert Zirpel Confirmation 1937. [147]

Leonard Robert Zirpel was confirmed on July 4, 1937 at the Immanuel Lutheran Church in Douglas County, South Dakota.

Birth of
Wilbert Erich Zirpel*

Wilbert Erich Zirpel Confirmation 1939. [148]

Wilbert Erich Zirpel, son of Gottfried John Zirpel and Gertrude Anna Gerlach, was born on November 24, 1924 in Parkston, Hutchinson County, South Dakota and he was christened on December 14, 1924 in the Immanuel Lutheran Church in Douglas County, South Dakota

Wilbert Erich Zirpel was confirmed on June 4, 1939 at the Immanuel Lutheran Church in Douglas County, South Dakota.

Birth of
Erwin Karl Zirpel*

Erwin Karl Zirpel Confirmation 1941. [149]

Erwin Karl Zirpel, son of Gottfried John Zirpel and Gertrude Anna Gerlach, was born on July 29, 1926 in Douglas County, South Dakota and he was christened on August 22, 1926 in the Immanuel Lutheran Church in Douglas County, South Dakota.

Erwin Karl Zirpel was confirmed on June 15, 1941 at the Immanuel Lutheran Church in Douglas County, South Dakota.

Birth of
Elmer Gottfried Zirpel*

Elmer Gottfried Zirpel, son of Gottfried John Zirpel and Gertrude Anna Gerlach, was born on November 25, 1927 in Douglas County, South Dakota and he was christened on January 6, 1938 in the Immanuel Lutheran Church in Douglas County, South Dakota.

Elmer Gottfried Zirpel was confirmed on June 28, 1942 at the Immanuel Lutheran Church in Douglas County, South Dakota.

Birth of
Norbert John Zirpel*

Norbert John Zirpel, son of Gottfried John Zirpel and Gertrude Anna Gerlach, was born on November 13, 1929 in Douglas County, South Dakota and he was christened on December 8, 1929 in the Immanuel Lutheran Church in Douglas County, South Dakota.

Norbert John Zirpel was confirmed on March 31, 1943 at the Immanuel Lutheran Church in Douglas County, South Dakota.

Birth of
Harold Arnold Zirpel*

Harold Arnold Zirpel Confirmation 1951. [150]

Harold Arnold Zirpel, son of Gottfried John Zirpel and Gertrude Anna Gerlach, was born on March 10, 1936 in Mitchell, Davison County, South Dakota and he was christened on April 5, 1936 in the Immanuel Lutheran Church in Douglas County, South Dakota.

Harold Arnold Zirpel was confirmed in 1951 in the Immanuel Lutheran Church in Douglas County, South Dakota.

Wilbert Erich Zirpel took the picture. Elmer Gottfried Zirpel, Harold Arnold Zirpel sitting on bike, Leonard Robert Zirpel, Walter Robert Zirpel, Erwin Karl Zirpel and Norbert John Zirpel in front house on the farm about 1940. [151]

Birth of
Rosalene Gertrude Zirpel*

Rosalene Gertrude Zirpel, daughter of Gottfried John Zirpel and Gertrude Anna Gerlach, was born on February 11, 1939 and she was christened on March 5, 1939 in the Immanuel Lutheran in Douglas County, South Dakota.

Rosalene Gertrude Zirpel was confirmed in 1953 at the Immanuel Lutheran Church in Douglas County, South Dakota.

Rosalene Gertrude Zirpel Confirmation 1953. [152]

Birth of
Mary Ellen Ruth Zirpel*

Mary Ellen Ruth Zirpel Confirmation 1958. [153]

Mary Elizabeth Poe
& Her Family*

Francis Marion Poe, son of Marion Cortez Poe and Iva Lenore Blackburn, was born on Au-

Francis Marion Poe, son of Marion Cortez Poe and Iva Lenore Blackburn, was born on August 21, 1906 in Fairplay, Jefferson County, Ohio, he died January 29, 1970 in Hopedale, Harrison County, Ohio and was buried in the Bloomingdale Cemetery in Bloomingdale, Jefferson County, Ohio at the age of 63, according to Ohio cemetery records.[156]

Eunice Emma Gault, daughter of William W. Gault and Dora Ferguson, was born on April 29, 1906 in Reed Mill, Jefferson County, Ohio, she died on February 16, 1990 in Steubenville, Jefferson County, Ohio and was buried in the Bloomingdale Cemetery in Bloomingdale, Jefferson County, Ohio at the age of 83, according to Ohio Cemetery records.[157]

Mary Elizabeth Poe, daughter of Francis M. Poe and Eunice E. Gault was born May 26, 1928 in Broadacre, Jefferson County, Ohio.

On the 1930 United States Census recorded by the Census Enumerator, Frank A. Boyd in April of 1930, Mary Elizabeth Poe living in Bloomfield, Jefferson County, Ohio with her parents, Francis M. and Eunice E. Poe.[158]

Francis Poe was recorded working as State Board driver. Francis was twenty or twenty-three years old and he was born in Ohio. Eunice Poe was twenty-four years old and also born in Ohio. Mary Elizabeth Poe was two years on the census report.

Mary Elizabeth Poe at the age of eleven years old was recorded on the 1940 United States Census on April 2, 1940 by the Census Enumerator, Ivan H. Wallan, living on Main Street Route U. S. 22 in Bloomfield, Jefferson County, Ohio.[159]

Mary Elizabeth Poe had completed the 5th grade in elementary school. Francis Poe was working as grader operator for the County Highway Department.

Leonard Robert Zirpel &
Mary Elizabeth Poe
Marriage & Family*

Mary Elizabeth Poe, daughter of Francis M. Poe and Eunice E. Gault, married Leonard Robert Zirpel, son of Gottfried John Zirpel and Gertrude Anna Gerlach, on January 27, 1946 in Jefferson County, Ohio.

According to Ohio cemetery records Leonard Robert Zirpel and Mary Elizabeth Poe were married in Canton, Stark County, Ohio.[160]

Leonard Robert Zirpel [154]

Unknown person, Leonard Robert Zirpel,
Mary Elizabeth Poe and unknown person on
January 27, 1946 in Jefferson County, Ohio [155]

Leonard Robert and Mary Elizabeth Zirpel
had two children: one daughter, Susanna Jo Zirpel
and one son, Garnet Lee Zirpel. Their marriage
ended in divorce.

Birth of
Susanna Jo Zirpel*

Susanna Jo Zirpel [156]

Susanna Jo Zirpel, daughter of Leonard Robert and Mary Elizabeth Zirpel was born on January 6, 1948 in Steubenville, Jefferson County,
Ohio.

Birth of
Garnet Lee Zirpel*

Garnet Lee Zirpel, son of Leonard Robert
and Mary Elizabeth Zirpel was born in 1952 and
he died in 1952. Garnet Lee was buried in the
Bloomingdale Cemetery in Bloomingdale, Jefferson County, Ohio according to the Ohio cemetery records.

Garnet Lee Zirpel Gravestone in the Bloomingdale
Cemetery in Jefferson County, Ohio [156]

Mary Elizabeth Zirpel died on February 17,
1956 in Steubenville, Jefferson County, Ohio and
she was buried in the Bloomingdale Cemetery in
Bloomingdale, Jefferson County, Ohio.

Mary Elizabeth (Poe) Zirpel Gravestone in the
Bloomingdale Cemetery, Jefferson County, Ohio [157]

Susanna Jo Zirpel &
Charles Edward Pratt
Marriage & Family*

Susanna Jo Zirpel [158]

Charles Edward Pratt, son of Robert Charles Pratt and Lucille Louise Cline, was born on November 7, 1943 in West Virginia.[161]

Charles Edward Pratt, son of Robert Charles Pratt and Lucille Cline, married Susanna Jo Zirpel, daughter of Leonard Robert Zirpel and Mary Elizabeth Poe. Their marriage is believed to have happen in before November of 1965 in Jefferson County, Ohio.

Charles Edward and Susanna Jo Pratt had three children: Rebecca L., Brian C., and Phillip E. Pratt. Their marriage ended in divorce on May 7, 1970 in Jefferson County, Ohio.[162] The grounds for the divorce was gross neglect and extreme cruelty according to the Ohio Divorce Index.

Birth of
Rebecca L. Pratt*

Rebecca L. Pratt was born on November 6, 1965. It is believed she was born in Jefferson County, Ohio, but no official records have found.

Birth of
Brian C. Pratt*

Brian C. Pratt Cresap was born on December 9, 1967. It is believed he was born in Jefferson County, Ohio, but no official records have found.

Birth of
Phillip E. Pratt*

Philip E. Cresap was born on May 5, 1969. It is believed he was born in Jefferson County, Ohio, but no official records have found.

Charles Edward Pratt died on April 5, 1997 in Tuscarawas County, Ohio in a long term care facility according the Ohio Deaths.[163] That same report stated that Charles Edward Pratt had been mining machine operator in the coal mining. There is no record of where he might be buried.

Susanna Jo Pratt &
David J. Cresap
Marriage *

David J. Cresap was born around 1947.

Susanna Jo Pratt, daughter of Leonard Robert and Mary Elizabeth Zirpel, married David Cresap in Jefferson County, Ohio in 1977.[164]

Both Susanna Jo and David J. Cresap had been living in Steubenville, Jefferson County, Ohio when their marriage ended in divorce on May 19, 1977 according to the Ohio Divorce Index.[165]

Apparently, Suzanna Jo Cresap remarried David J. Cresap on November 23, 1977 in Jefferson County, Ohio according to marriage records located.[166]

Susanna Jo Cresap died on April 14, 1984 after a lengthy illness in the Ohio Valley Medical Center located in Wheeling, Ohio County, West Virginia according to an obituary found in the *"Steubenville Herald Star"* on April 15, 1984.[167] There had been an autopsy done for certification purposed.

The obituary from the *"Steubenville Herald Star"* on April 15, 1984 said that Susanna had lived in Amsterdam, Auglaize County, Ohio with her husband, David J. Cresap.

Susanna Jo Cresap had been member of the Bloomingdale United Presbyterian Church.

She was survived by her husband, David J. Cresap, two sons: Brian C. and Phillip E. Pratt, both at home; a daughter: Mrs. Jack (Rebecca L.) Milligan of Germany; her maternal grandmother, Eunice Emma Poe of Steubenville, Ohio; and a grandson.

The funeral had been under the direction of Dunlope-Williams Funeral Home.

Susanna Jo Cresap's body laid in state on Wednesday at the Bloomingdale United Presbyterian Church in Bloomingdale, Jefferson County, Ohio.

Rev. Arthur C. Tennies officiated with the service at the Bloomingdale Cemetery, in Jefferson County, Ohio.

Rebecca L. Pratt & Jack L. Milligan Marriage & Family*

Jack L. Milligan was born on November 2, 1962 in Steubenville, Jefferson County, Ohio, according to the Ohio Birth Index.[168]

Rebecca L. Pratt, daughter of Charles Edward and Susanna Jo Pratt, married Jack L. Milligan on November 17, 1988 in Jefferson County, Ohio according to Ohio Marriage Index.[169]

It is believed that Jack L. and Rebecca L. Milligan had two children: Jack and Julie Milligan as there were two minor children list on the divorce records.

On May 22, 1990 Jack L. Milligan lived in Harrison County, Ohio while Rebecca L. Milligan lived in Steubenville, Jefferson County, Ohio when their marriage was dissolved according to Ohio Divorce Index.[170]

Rebecca L. Milligan & Robert J. Kirk Marriage *

Robert J. Kirk was born on December 24, 1963 in Steubenville, Jefferson County, Ohio according to Ohio Birth Index.[171]

There was a record of a marriage between Rebecca L. Milligan and Robert J. Kirk on February 6, 1991 in Jefferson County, Ohio.[172]

Unfortunately the marriage ended in divorce on April 22, 1992 according to the Ohio Divorce Index.[173]

Rebecca L. Kirk & David M. Lamb Marriage *

David M. Lamb was born about 1967.

There was a record of a marriage between Rebecca L. Kirk and David M. Lamb on May 12, 1992 in Jefferson County, Ohio according to the Ohio Marriage Index.[174] On the record, Rebecca L. Kirk had been married 3 times.

There was no record of a divorce was ever located.

Rebecca L. Lamb & Todd A. Rupert Marriage & Family *

Todd A. Rupert was born on June 14, 1970.

There was a record of a marriage between Rebecca L. Lamb and Todd A. Rupert on February 24, 1999, in Jefferson County, Ohio according the Ohio Marriage Index.[175]

Todd A. Rupert died on October 8, 2006 at the Weirton Medical Center after a lengthy illness.

Todd A. Rupert was survived by his mother; his wife, Rebecca of Mingo Junction, Ohio; a son, Erick Rupert; a daughter, Tabatha Rupert; a stepson, Jack Milligan; a step-daughter, Julie Milligan of Mingo Junction, Ohio; a brother, James H. Rupert and his wife, Karen and a sister, Kelly Williams, and a nephew, Dominic Williams, all of Mingo Junction, Ohio.

Phillip E. Pratt & Lynda S. Stoddard Marriage *

Phillip E. Pratt, son Charles Edward and Susanna Jo Pratt, married Lynda S. Stoddard on January 22, 1993 in Mahoning County, Ohio.[176]

Leonard Robert Zirpel & Carol Marriage *

Leonard Robert Zirpel married Carol in April of 1954 in Springfield, Illinois according to the family.

According to the U.S. City Directories, 1821-1989, Leonard Zirpel was living at 715 S. 7th in Springfield, Sangamon County, Illinois in 1953. On this report, Leonard was working as mechanic.

Leonard Robert and Carol Zirpel were living at 41 W. Edward in Springfield, Sangamon County, Illinois according to U.S. City Directories 1821-1989. Carol Zirpel was working as typist.

In 1956, Leonard Robert Zirpel and his wife Carol were living in Springfield, Sangamon County, Illinois according to the U.S. City Directories, 1821-1989. On this report, Leonard was working as a Assistant Service Manager.

Their marriage ended in divorce in 1959.

Shortly after this divorce Leonard Zirpel moved to White Lake, Aurora County, South Dakota where he work as a mechanic with brother, Wilbert Erich Zirpel.

Leonard Robert Zirpel & Maud "Johnny" Hawbaker Marriage *

Maud B. "Johnny" Hawbaker was born on December 27, 1903.

Leonard Robert Zirpel married Maud B. Hawbaker on April 11, 1968 in Springfield, Sangamon County, Illinois.

Maud B. "Johnny" Zirpel died on December 1, 1992.

Leonard Robert Zirpel & Lillian Esther "Moege" Zirpel Marriage *

Leonard Robert Zirpel married Lillian Esther (Moege) Zirpel on February 26, 1994 in Parkston, Hutchinson County, South Dakota.

Between 1994 and 1998, Leonard Robert and Lillian Esther Zirpel lived at 1401 S. Main Street #42 in Mitchell, Davison County, South Dakota according to U.S. Public Records Index.

Leonard Robert Zirpel died on October 20, 1998 in Sioux Falls, Minnehaha County, South Dakota from a heart attack and he was buried in the Parkston Protestant Cemetery located in Parkston, Hutchinson County, South Dakota.

Rev. Jerome Troester officiated over the funeral which was held in Faith Lutheran Church in Parkston, Hutchinson County, South Dakota. The music was provide by the Faith Lutheran Adult Choir with accompanist, Lynette Konrad and the organist, Carol Esther Bialas.

Pall bearers were John Frederick Zirpel, Randolph Scott Zirpel, Mark Anthony Zirpel, Bryan Allen Zirpel, Gaylen Clifford Roth and Allen Richard Mehlhaff.

Wilbert Erich Zirpel - His Early Years *

Wilbert Erich Zirpel [159]

Wilbert Erich Zirpel were among eleven men from Douglas County who entered were inducted into the Armed Forces on Friday, May 11, 1945 according to "*The Chronicle*," in Armour, Douglas County, South Dakota.

All the members left Armour on the noon train and travel to Sioux City, Iowa which includ-

ed Arthur Pekoske from Armour; Harold F. Noteboom, Donald W. Borman, and Walter F. Schrank Jr. from Corsica; Arnold G. Goldammer of Dimock; Wilbert E. Zirpel and Norbert P. Neugebauer from Parkston; Orville P. Olsen, Ruben Liebert, and Norman P. Serr from Delmont; John E. Hasseler Jr. from Harrison.

Wilbert Erich Zirpel was installed into the Army of the United States, on May 25, 1945 when he entered the service at Ft. Snelling, Minnesota.

Wilbert E. Zirpel was in Separation Center Ft. Lewis, Wisconsin, when he was honorable discharge as Technician Fourth Grade Co. A. 714st Sig BV BN by J. Willard Wager, Lieutenant Colonel AGD on December 10, 1946. The reason for the separation was the Convenience of the Government RR Demobilization AR 615 365 December 15, 1944.

Wilbert's Military Occupation Specialty was Auto Mech 014 and his Military Qualification was MM M 1 Rifle 1 Cl G LMG.

Wilbert spent one year, nine days serving in a foreign country, while only serving six months and twenty days in the United States.

Wilbert spent part of his service time on the General John Pope while in Japan. He received the Asiatic Pacific Service Medal, Victory Medal and Army of Occupation Medal (Japan).

Wilbert E. Zirpel served on the General John Pope During World War II [160]

Audrey May Beutner & Her Family*

Audrey May Beutner, daughter of Gustave George and Viola Iva Minor, was born on November 9, 1925 in Crow Lake, Jerauld County, South Dakota.

On the 1930 United States Census taken on April 30, 1930 by Census Enumerator, R. E. Brown, Audrey May Beutner was living with her parents, Gustave George and Viola Iva in White Lake, Aurora County, South Dakota.[177] Also list on this report was True Gustave was six years old, Audrey May was four years old and four months old, Eugene Wayne was two years and seven months old, and Ruth Minnie was one year and three months old. It said that Gustave George was born in South Dakota while his wife, Viola Iva was born in Iowa.

The Gustave Beutner family was recorded still living in White Lake, Aurora County, South Dakota on the 1940 United States Census on April 2-3, 1940 by the Census Enumerator, Ann E. Mahoney.[178]

The family's address was DC Gillis Co., I Add. in White Lake on the report. The parents listed were Gustave George age thirty-nine years old, Viola Iva was thirty-four years old. The children listed on the census report were True Gustave fifteen years old, Audrey May fourteen years old, Eugene Wayne twelve years old and Ruth Minnie ten years old.

Audrey was confirmed by Rev. Tobias Buehner at St. Martin Lutheran Church in 1941.

Wilbert Erich Zirpel & Audrey May Beutner Marriage & Family*

Gottfried John Zirpel, Gertrude Ann Zirpel, Viola Iva Beutner and Gustave George Beutner. Parents of Wilbert Erich Zirpel & Audrey May Beutner [161]

Wilbert Erich Zirpel, son of Gottfried John and Gertrude Anna Zirpel, married Audrey May Beutner, daughter of Gustave George Beutner and Viola Iva Minor, on December 19, 1948 by Rev. Steve Persa the St. Martin Lutheran Church in White Lake, Aurora County, South Dakota.[179]

Wilbert Erich and Audrey May Zirpel had

seven children: Ruby Audrey, Ruth Dianne, Wilbert Lee, Wayne Erich, Clyde Dwane, Mary Ann, and Bryan Allen.

Wilbert ran a repair shop in White Lake, South Dakota before the family moved to Woonsocket, Sanborn County, South Dakota. His brother, Leonard Zirpel work in the garage with him in White Lake as well as in Woonsocket.

Birth of Twins - Ruby Audrey & Ruth Dianne Zirpel*

Ruby Audrey and Ruth Dianne Zirpel, daughters of Wilbert Erich and Audrey May Zirpel, were born on September 29, 1949 in Parkston, Hutchinson County, South Dakota. They were christened on October 19, 1949 in the Immanuel Lutheran Church in Douglas County, South Dakota.

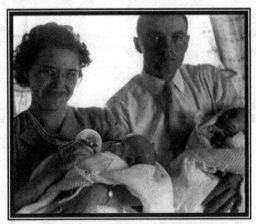

Audrey May and Wilbert Erich Zirpel holding Ruth Diane and Ruby Audrey 1949 [162]

Birth of Wilbert Lee Zirpel*

Wilbert Lee Zirpel, son of Wilbert Erich and Audrey May Zirpel, was born on December 24, 1950 in Parkston, Hutchinson County, South Dakota.

Birth of Wayne Erich Zirpel*

Wayne Erich Zirpel, son of Wilbert Erich and Audrey May Zirpel, was born on April 28, 1952 in Mitchell, Davison County, South Dakota.

Birth of Clyde Dwane Zirpel*

Clyde Dwane, Zirpel, son of Wilbert Erich

Right to Left: Olinda Zirpel, Ruth Minnie (Beutner) Lutz, Audrey May Zirpel, Wilbert Erich Zirpel, Norbert John Zirpel and Erwin Karl Zirpel December 19, 1948. [163]

Wilbert Lee Jr., Ruth Diane, Ruby Audrey and Clyde Dwane Zirpel in the jumper 1956 [164]

and Audrey May Zirpel, was born on February 28, 1956 in Mitchell, Davison County, South Dakota. His actual birthdate was February 29, 1956, but official records go with the 28th. He was christened on March 18, 1956 in the Trinity Lutheran Church in White Lake, Aurora County, South Dakota.

Clyde Dwane Zirpel was confirmed by Pastor, Richard O. Meyer at the Mt. Olive Lutheran

Church in Woonsocket, Sanborn County, South Dakota.

Birth of
Mary Ann Zirpel*

Mary Ann Zirpel, daughter of Wilbert Erich and Audrey May Zirpel, was born on March 29, 1961 in Mitchell, Davison County, South Dakota. She was christened in White Lake, Aurora County, South Dakota.

Birth of
Bryan Allen Zirpel*

Bryan Allen Zirpel, son of Wilbert Erich and Audrey May Zirpel, was born on August 5, 1964 in Mitchell, Davison County, South Dakota and he was christened on August 1964 in the Trinity Lutheran Church, White Lake, Aurora County, South Dakota.

Wilbert Erich & Audrey May
Zirpel - The Later Years*

Wilbert Erich and Audrey May Zirpel lived

From about 1965 until 1968, this building was used by The Zirpel Bros. Garage in Woonsocket, S. D. [165]

in White Lake, where Wilbert done some farming, prior to moving to Woonsocket in 1965.

Wilbert operated the Zirpel and Sons Garage. He was member of the American Legion and Veterans of Foreign Wars and the Woonsocket Fire Department.

Wilbert and Audrey Zirpel were both members of the Mt. Olive Lutheran Church in Woonsocket, Sanborn County, South Dakota.

Audrey enjoyed gardening, baking, dancing, playing cards and taking care of her family.

Wilbert Erich Zirpel died on Sunday, August 18, 1974 in the St. Mary's Hospital in Rochester, Olmstead County, Minnesota after a accident. The funeral service was held at the Mt. Calvary Lutheran Church in Huron, Beadle County, South Dakota, with the Rev. Richard O. Meyer of the Mt. Olive Lutheran Church of Woonsocket officiating. His burial was in the Eventide Cemetery, Woonsocket, Sanborn County, South Dakota with military rites by the Woonsocket American Legion.

The pallbearers were Leonard Robert Zirpel, Erwin Karl Zirpel, Elmer Gottfried Zirpel, Norbert John Zirpel, Harold Arnold Zirpel and Eugene Wayne Beutner.

Survivors included his widow, Audrey Zirpel, Woonsocket, South Dakota; four sons: Wilbert Lee Zirpel Jr., of McGuire AFB, New Jersey; Wayne Erich Zirpel, of Los Alamos, New Mexico; Clyde Dwane and Bryan Allen Zirpel, of Woonsocket, South Dakota; three daughters: Mrs. Ronald (Ruth) Nelson, of Huron, South Dakota; Mrs. Darrel (Ruby) Hoxsie, and Mary Ann Zirpel, of Woonsocket, South Dakota; four grandchildren; his parents: Mr. and Mrs. Gottfried John

Erwin Karl Zirpel and Norbert John Zirpel, of Parkston, South Dakota; Elmer Gottfried Zirpel, of Beloit, Wisconsin; Harold Arnold Zirpel, of San Jose, California; two sisters: Mrs. Clifford (Rosalene) Roth, of Huron, South Dakota; and Mrs. Richard (Mary Ellen) Mehlhaff, of Sioux City, Iowa.

Audrey May Zirpel died on Sunday, March 13, 2011, at the Violet Tschetter Memorial Home in Huron, Beadle County, South Dakota.

Service was held on March 16, 2011 at the Mt. Calvary Lutheran Church with Rev. Daniel Domke and Rev. Kelly Smith officiating in Huron, South Dakota. Her burial was in the Eventide Cemetery in Woonsocket, Sanborn County, South Dakota.

Casket bearers were Daniel Marotteck, Jarrod Lee Nuss, Daniel Harding Hoxsie, Doyle Erich Hoxsie, Michael Duane Zirpel, Jeffrey Paul Hagman and Erich Leroy Dammann.

Those grateful for having shared in her life were four sons: Wilbert Lee Zirpel Jr. of Buffalo, Wyoming; Wayne Erich and Laurie Zirpel, of Rio Rancho, New Mexico; Clyde Dwane and Mona Zirpel, of Lane, South Dakota: two daughters: Ruth & Ronald Nelson, of Huron, South Dakota; and Mary Ann and Steve Dammann, of Woonsocket, South Dakota; son-in-law, Darrell Hoxsie of Sioux City, Iowa; nineteen grandchildren; forty-four great-grandchildren; brother: Eugene Wayne Beutner, of Hot Springs, South Dakota; sister: Ruth and Tom Lutz, of Bassett, Nebraska; and many nieces and nephews.

Audrey was preceded in death by her parents: Gustave George and Viola Iva Beutner, her husband: Wilbert Erich Zirpel Sr.; daughter: Ruby Audrey Hoxsie; great-granddaughter: Haley Marie Weideman; brother: True Gustave Beutner; and step-father: Paul Hoes.

Ruby Audrey Zirpel 1968 [166]

Wilbert Erich Sr. and Audrey May Zirpel Family in 1989.
Back row: Mary Ann (Zirpel) Dammann and Bryan Allen Zirpel. Front row: Wilbert Lee Zirpel Jr., Ruby Audrey (Zirpel) Hoxsie, Audrey May Zirpel, Ruth Diane (Zirpel) Nelson and Clyde Dwane Zirpel [167]

Ruby Audrey Zirpel &
Darrell Harding Hoxsie
Marriage & Family*

Darrell H. Hoxsie and Ruby A. Hoxsie 1968 [168]

Darrel Harding Hoxsie, son of Delbert Harding Hoxsie and Lilly Mae Gumb, was born on April 4, 1949, in O'Neil, Holt County, Nebraska.

Sometime after 1935, his family loved to Woonsocket, Sanborn County, South Dakota.

Ruby Audrey Zirpel, daughter of Wilbert

Erich and Audrey May Zirpel, married Darrell Harding Hoxsie, son Delbert Harding Hoxsie and Lilly Mae Gumb, on August 15, 1968 in Woonsocket, Sanborn County, South Dakota.

Darrel Harding and Ruby Audrey Hoxsie had four children: Rochelle Audrey, Daniel Harding, Renae Jean, and Doyle Erich Hoxsie.

Birth of
Rochelle Audrey Hoxie*

Rochelle Audrey Hoxie, daughter of Darrell Harding and Ruby Audrey, was born on January 9, 1972 in Albuquerque, Bernalillo County, New Mexico and she was christened in January of 1972 in Albuquerque, Bernalillo County, New Mexico.

Birth of
Daniel Harding Hoxsie*

Daniel Harding Hoxsie, son of Darrell Harding and Ruby Audrey, was born on September 1, 1973 in Albuquerque, Bernalillo County, New Mexico and he was christened in September of 1973 in Albuquerque, Bernalillo County, New Mexico.

118

Birth of
Renae Jean Hoxsie*

Renae Jean Hoxsie, daughter of Darrell Harding and Ruby Audrey, was born on February 9, 1978 in Wessington Springs, Jerauld County, South Dakota and she was christened in April of 1978 in Woonsocket, Sanborn County, South Dakota.

Birth of
Doyle Erich Hoxsie*

Doyle Erich Hoxsie, son of Darrell Harding and Ruby Audrey, was born on October 13, 1979 in Wessington Springs, Jerauld County, South Dakota and he was christened in October of 1979 in Woonsocket, Sanborn County, South Dakota.

Back row left to right: Ruby Audrey holding Doyle Erich, and Darrel Harding holding Renae Jean Hoxsie. Front row left to right: Daniel Harding and Rochelle Audrey Hoxie November of 1980 [169]

Rochelle Audrey Hoxsie &
James Joseph Weideman
Marriage & Family*

Rochelle Audrey Hoxsie married James Joseph Weideman, son of Thomas Weideman (Step-father) and Mary Ellen Bennett, on July 17, 1999 in the Lathem Memorial Park, Sioux City, Woodbury County, Iowa.

James Joseph Weideman was born on May 10, 1964 in Sioux City, Woodbury County, Iowa and he was christened in Sioux City, Woodbury County, Iowa.

James Joseph and Rochelle Audrey Weideman had one child: Haley Marie Weideman.

Haley Marie Weideman was born on January 8, 2001 in Sioux City, Woodbury County, Iowa. Unfortunately, she died on January 8, 2001 in Sioux City, Woodbury County, Iowa and she is buried in Sioux City, Woodbury County, Iowa.

Daniel Harding Hoxsie &
Angela Marie Ryan
Marriage & Family*

Daniel Harding Hoxsie married Angela Marie Ryan on May 21, 2005 in the Redeemer Lutheran Church in Sioux City, Woodbury County, Iowa.

Daniel Harding and Angela Marie Hoxsie have five children: Blake Harding, Jacob Daniel, Zane, Shayla Daniela, and Ann Hoxsie.

Blake Harding Hoxsie was born on April 7, 1996 in Sioux City, Woodbury County, Iowa.

Jacob Daniel Hoxsie was born on August 18, 2000 in Sioux City, Woodbury County, Iowa.

Zane Hoxsie was born on June 8, 2003.

Shayla Daniela Hoxsie was born on July 8, 2007.

Ann Hoxsie was born on May 21, 2005.

Daniel Harding Hoxsie work as sheet metal worker at the Interstate Mechanical in Sioux City, Woodbury County, Iowa.

Angela Marie Hoxsie works at the Whispering Creek Active Retirement Center in Sioux City, Woodbury County, Iowa.

Renae Jean Hoxsie &
Stas Anthony Szczepanik
Marriage & Family*

Renae Jean Hoxsie married Stas Anthony Szczepanik, son of Stanley Anthony Szczepanik Sr. and Ann Marie Hampton, on August 5, 200 in the St. Peter's Church in Jefferson, Union County, South Dakota. The marriage ended in divorce January of 2011.

Stas Anthony Szczepanik was born on May 24, 1968 in Alton, Madison County, Illinois.

Stas Anthony and Renae Jean Szczepanik had one child: Anthony Vincent Szczepanik.

Anthony Vincent Szczepanik was born on May 8, 2001 in Sioux City, Woodbury County, Iowa.

Doyle Erich Hoxsie & Melinda Jordon Family*

Doyle Erich Hoxsie and Melinda lived together but they are engaged not married.

Melinda Jordon was born on August 26, 1975 in Pender, Thurston County, Nebraska.

The family lives in Dakota City, Dakota County, Nebraska and there are three children in the household: Taylor, Trenton and Kourtney.

Taylor Jordon was born on February 13, 1993 in Pender, Thurston County, Nebraska.

Trenton Jordon was born on June 13, 1994 in Pender, Thurston County, Nebraska.

Kourtney Bowman was born on August 15, 1996 in Pender, Thurston County, Nebraska.

Ruby Audrey & Darrel Harding Hoxsie - The Later Years*

The Darrell Hoxsie family moved from Woonsocket, South Dakota to Sioux City in Woodbury County, Iowa in 1981. There they made their home.

Ruby Audrey Hoxsie died on July 29, 2010 in Sioux City, Woodbury County, Iowa. Her funeral was on August 2, 2010 at the Redeemer Lutheran Church in Sioux City, Woodbury County, Iowa with Rev. David Zirpel, officiating. She was buried in the Memorial Park Cemetery in Sioux City, Woodbury, Iowa.

Pall bearers were Jim Weideman, Rick Allison, Charles Hoxsie, Stas Szczepanik, Steve Dammann, and Richard Mees.

Ruby worked for more than 29 years as a restorative care aide at Indian Hills Care Center, now known as Touchstone Living Center, where she enjoyed her work helping the residents of the facility.

Ruby also enjoying raising her own family and seeing them grow as individuals. Ruby enjoyed her hobbies of crocheting, reading and she was a huge fan of Elvis.

She was survived by her husband: Darrell Hoxsie of Sioux City, Iowa; her four children: Daniel Harding and Angela Hoxsie of Sioux City, Iowa; Doyle Erich and his special friend, Melinda Jordon of Dakota City, Nebraska; Rochelle and Jim Weideman, and Renae Jean and Stas Szczepanik of Sioux City, Iowa.

Ruby was also survived by her eleven grandchildren; her mother: Audrey May Zirpel; her four

brothers: Wilbert Lee Zirpel Jr., Wayne Erich and Laurie Zirpel, Clyde Dwane and Mona Zirpel, Bryan Zirpel and special friend, Lisa Wolf, and two sisters: Ruth Dianne and Ronald Nelson, and Mary Ann and Steve Dammann.

Ruby was preceded in death by her father, Wilbert Erich Zirpel Sr., and one granddaughter, Haley Marie Weideman.

Darrel Harding Hoxsie, of Sioux City, Iowa passed away at his residence on Thursday, March 6, 2014.

The funeral services were held on Tuesday, March 11, 2014 at the Rustin Avenue United Methodist Church in Sioux City, Iowa with Rev. David N. Zirpel officiating.

Interment with Military Honors was in the Memorial Park Cemetery in Sioux City, Iowa.

Darrel served his country as a member of the United States Air-Force from 1969-1973. Following his discharge he returned to Woonsocket, South Dakota where he working in the lumber business.

The family moved to Sioux City, Iowa in 1981, and Darrel continued his work in the lumber industry at the Jordan Millwork and Wallensky Lumber Company. He had retired only two weeks before his death.

Darrell enjoyed woodworking, tinkering, and attending tractor pulls. He was a loving father who cherished the time he could spend with his grandchildren.

His life was loving remembered by his family which included his sons: Daniel and his wife, Angela of Sioux City, Iowa, and Doyle and his Fiancée, Melinda Jordon, Dakota City, Nebraska; his daughters: Rochelle Weideman and her husband, James of Sioux City, Iowa and Renae Sczepanik of Sioux City, Iowa; and his eleven grandchildren.

He is also survived by two sisters: Linda Mees and her husband, Richard of Alpena, South Dakota, and Sheryl Smith and her husband, Don of Woonsocket, South Dakota.

Darrel was preceded in death by his parents, his wife, Ruby, a granddaughter, Haley Weideman and brother, Charles.

Ruth Dianne Zirpel & Ronald Eugene Nelson Marriage & Family*

Ruth Dianne Zirpel, daughter of Wilbert Erich and Audrey May Zirpel, married Ronald

Ruth Diane Zirpel [170]

Eugene Nelson, son of Palmer and Lucy Nelson, on February 26, 1971.

Ronald Eugene Nelson was born on September 19, 1948 in Roberts Road on the bridge, Roberts County, South Dakota.

Ronald Eugene and Ruth Dianne had three children: Ronette Jean, Ronda Gene, and Roni Ann Nelson.

Birth of
Ronette Jean Nelson*

Ronette Jean Nelson, daughter of Ronald Eugene and Ruth Dianne Nelson, was born on July 28, 1971 in Huron, Beadle County, South Dakota.

Birth of
Rhonda Gene Nelson*

Rhonda Gene Nelson, daughter of Ronald Eugene and Ruth Dianne Nelson, was born on September 14, 1974 in Huron, Beadle County, South Dakota and she was christened on June 30, 1991 in the Mt. Calvary Lutheran Church in Huron, Beadle County, South Dakota.

Birth of
Roni Ann Nelson*

Roni Ann Nelson, daughter of Ronald Eugene and Ruth Dianne Nelson, was born on August 15, 1979 in Huron, Beadle County, South Dakota and she was christened on June 30, 1991 in the Mt. Calvary Lutheran Church in Huron, Beadle County, South Dakota.

Ronette Jean Nelson &
Daniel Marotteck
Marriage & Family*

Daniel and Ronette Jean Marotteck[171]

Ronette Jean, daughter of Ronald Eugene and Ruth Dianne Nelson, married Daniel Marotteck, on June 5, 1993 in Huron, Beadle County, South Dakota.

Daniel Marotteck was born on December 22, 1963 in Bethesda, Montgomery County, Maryland and he was christened on December of 1963 in Bethesda, Montgomery County, Maryland.

Daniel and Ronette Jean Marotteck had one child: Christine Shantel Marotteck.

Christine Shantell Marotteck 2012 [172]

Christine Shantel Marotteck was born on November 9, 1993 in Huron, Beadle County, South Dakota and she was christened on December 5, 1993 in the Mt. Calvary Lutheran Church in Huron, Beadle County, South Dakota.

Ronda Gene Nelson & Jarrod Lee Nuss Marriage & Family*

Back row left to right: holding on to parents are Jeana Lynn and Tanner Lee Nuss. Front row left to right: Ronda Gene, Jackie Gene and Jarrod Lee Nuss. [173]

Ronda Gene Nelson, daughter of Ronald Eugene and Ruth Dianne Nelson, married Jarrod Lee Nuss, son of Martin Richard Nuss and Karen Joan Zeeb, on December 16, 1995 in the Friedens Reform Church in Tripp, Hutchinson County, South Dakota.

Jarrod Lee Nuss was born on March 11, 1969 in Armour, Douglas County, south Dakota and he was christened on April 27, 1969 in Friedens Reform Church, Tripp, Hutchinson County, South Dakota.

Jarrod Lee and Ronda Gene Nuss have three children: Tanner Lee, Jeana Lynn and Jackie Gene Nuss.

Tanner Lee Nuss was born on January 12, 1996 in Mitchell, Davison County, South Dakota and he was christened on March 2, 1997 in the Friedens Reform Church in Tripp, Hutchinson County, South Dakota. In 2003, Tanner liked to play T-ball during the summer.

Jeana Lynn Nuss was born on March 5, 1998 in Mitchell, Davison County, South Dakota and she was christened in the Friedens Reform Church in Tripp, Hutchinson County, South Dakota.

In 2003, Jeana traveled to Minnesota with Ronda's older sister, Ronette Marotteck and she spent two weeks with them during the summer.

Jackie Gene was born on June 9, 2000 in Mitchell, Hutchinson County, South Dakota and she was christened on September 3, 2000 in the Friedens Reform Church in Tripp, Hutchinson County, South Dakota.

Roni Ann Nelson & Shae Poage Marriage & Family*

Roni Ann, daughter of Ronald Eugene and Ruth Dianne Nelson, had a common law marriage to Shae Poage in Enid, Garfield County, Oklahoma. The marriage ended in divorce on November 9, 2001.

Shae and Roni Ann Poage had one child: Hannah Marie Poage.

Hannah Marie Poage was born on August 16, 1997 in Enid, Garfield County, Oklahoma and she was christened on September 13, 1997 in the St. Paul Lutheran Church in Enid, Garfield County, Oklahoma.

Roni Ann Poage & Justin Bundy Marriage & Family*

Roni Ann Poage married Justin Bundy on April 2, 2004 in Enid, Garfield County, Oklahoma. The marriage ended in divorce.

Justin Bundy was born on December 30, 1973.

Justin and Roni Ann Bundy had one child: Adrienne Ty Bundy.

Adrienne Ty Bundy was born on June 8, 2000 in St. Mary's Hospital in Enid, Garfield County, Oklahoma.

Roni Ann Bundy & Mr. Bueno & Family*

Mickayla Ann Bueno, Hannah Marie Poege, and Adrienne Ty Bundy [174]

Back row left to right: Jarrod Lee Nuss, Ronda Gene Nuss holding Jackie Gene Nuss, Roni Ann Poage holding Hannah Marie Poage, unknown, Ronette Jean Marotteck and Daniel Marotteck. Front row left to right: Ronald Eugene Nelson holding Adrienne Ty Bundy and Jeana Lynn Nuss, Christine Shantel Marotteck and Ruth Dianne Nelson holding Tanner Lee Nuss. Ronald and Ruth Nelson 30th Wedding Anniversary. [175]

Roni Ann Nelson and Mr. Bueno had one children: Mickayla Ann, but they were never married.

Mickayla Ann Bueno was born on February 28, 2007 in the Huron Medical Center in Huron, Beadle County, South Dakota.

Wilbert Lee Zirpel Jr.*

Wilbert Lee Zirpel Jr. 1969 [176]

Wilbert Lee Zirpel went to Dakota State University in Madison, Lake County, South Dakota from August of 1969 until May of 1973.

Wilbert served in the United States Air Force from January 1974 until 1978. Two years of his military service was spent in Germany and the remaining two years were spent at the Air Force Base, Fort Dix, Burlington County, New Jersey. After getting out of the service Wilbert lived with his mother, Audrey May Zirpel in Woonsocket, Sanborn County, South Dakota for awhile.

Wilbert Lee Zirpel Jr. in the U. S. Air Force [177]

Between 1994 and 1995, Wilbert lived and work at North of Buffalo in Buffalo, Wyoming.

Between 1996 and 2002, Wilbert lived and work in as electric Technician on Autos 118-1/2 S. Gillette Avenue in Gillette, Campbell County, Wyoming.

Wilbert also spent two years taking Paralegal Schooling in Colorado.

Wilbert moved to 601 E. Parmelee St., Lot 7 in Buffalo, Johnson County, Wyoming.

In 2013, he moved back to South Dakota where Wilbert lived in a apartment closed to his sister, Ruth Dianne Nelson lived in Huron, Beadle County, South Dakota.

Wayne Erich Zirpel & Laurie Rose Roberts
Marriage & Family *

Wayne Erich Zirpel 1970 [178]

Wayne Erich Zirpel in the U. S. Army [179]

Wayne Erich Zirpel served in the United State Army around 1970 until 1972.

Wayne Erich Zirpel, son of Wilbert Erich and Audrey May Zirpel, married Laurie Rose Roberts, daughter of Merle and Doris Roberts on April 7, 1973 in New Mexico.

Laurie Rose Roberts was born on August 9, 1953.

Wayne Erich and Laurie Rose Zirpel had five children: Virginia Rae, Michael Wayne, Jamie Suzanne, Samantha Rose and Joshua Merle Zirpel.

Birth of
Virginia Rae Zirpel*

Virginia Rae Zirpel, daughter of Wayne Erich and Laurie Rose Zirpel, was born on Feb 1, 1973 in Rio Rancho, Sandoval County, New Mexico.

Birth of
Michael Wayne Zirpel*

Michael Wayne Zirpel, son of Wayne Erich and Laurie Rose Zirpel, was born on January 13, 1975 in Rio Rancho, Sandoval County, New Mexico.

Birth of
Jamie Suzanne Zirpel*

Jamie Suzanna Zirpel, daughter of Wayne Erich and Laurie Rose Zirpel, was born on January 29, 1980 in Rio Rancho, Sandoval County, New Mexico.

Birth of
Samantha Rose Zirpel*

Samantha Rose Zirpel, daughter of Wayne Erich and Laurie Rose Zirpel, was born on July 29, 1985 in Rio Rancho, Sandoval County, New Mexico.

Birth of
Joshua Merle Zirpel*

Joshua Merle Zirpel, son of Wayne Erich and Laurie Rose Zirpel, was born on November 23, 1989 in Rio Rancho, Sandoval County, New Mexico.

Virginia Rae Zirpel & Steven Robert Allen Marriage & Family*

Stephanie Jeanette Allen [180]

Back row left to right: Michael Wayne Zirpel, Linda Diane Zirpel, Jamie Suzanne Zirpel, Steven Robert Allen, Virginia Rae Allen holding Katelyn Rose Allen. Middle row left to right: Laurie Rose Zirpel holding Christopher Andrew Zirpel, Wayne Erich Zirpel holding Stephanie Jeanette Allen, Front row left to right: sitting Bryan James Zirpel, Kevin Michael Zirpel, Joshua Merle Zirpel and Samantha Rose Zirpel [181]

Virginia Rae Zirpel married Steven Robert Allen on March 1, 1995 in Bernalillo County, New Mexico. Their marriage ended in divorce.

Steve Robert Allen was born on October 10, 1968 in Franklin County, New Mexico.

Steve Robert and Virginia Rae Allen have four children: Stephanie Jeanette, Katelyn Rose, Jacob, and Megan Allen.

Stephanie Jeanette Allen was born on April 17, 1996 in Rio Rancho, Sandoval County, New Mexico.

Katelyn Rose Allen was born on August 1, 1998 in Rio Rancho, Sandoval County New Mexico.

Jacob Allen was born on February 11, 2003.

Megan Allen was born on November 25, 2006.

Virginia Rae Allen & Mike Kimura Marriage *

Virginia Rae Allen married Mike Kimura on May 28, 2012 in New Mexico.

Mike and Virginia Rae Kimura [182]

Michael Wayne Zirpel & Linda Diane Garcia

Marriage & Family*

Michael Wayne Zirpel married Linda Diane Garcia on July 7, 1994 in Bernalillo County, New Mexico. Their marriage ended in divorce

125

Linda Diane Garcia was born on March 4, 1973 in Albuquerque County, New Mexico. Michael Wayne and Linda Diane Zirpel had three children: Brian James, Kevin Michael and Christopher Andrew Zirpel.

Brian James Zirpel was born on November 17, 1992 in Rio Rancho, Sandoval County, New Mexico.

Brian James Zirpel was working as an Electronics Engineer Test Specialist at Target in New Mexico.

Kevin Michael Zirpel was born on December 21, 1994 in Rio Rancho, Sandoval County, New Mexico.

Kevin Michael Zirpel worked at Algodones Volunteer Fire Department in Bernalillo County, New Mexico.

Christopher Andrew Zirpel was born on October 18, 1995 in Rio Rancho, Sandoval County, New Mexico.

Christopher Andrew Zirpel works with all kinds of landscaping.

Michael Wayne and Brian James Zirpel [183]

Brian James, Kevin Michael and
Christopher Andrew Zirpel [184]

Michael Wayne Zirpel &
Shannon Marriage & Family*

Michael Wayne Zirpel married Shannon sometime after 1995.

Shannon Zirpel had two son: Nicholas and Elijah.

Michael Wayne Zirpel worked at the Swift Transportation Company in New Mexico.

Jamie Suzanne Zirpel &
Michael E. Verretta

Marriage & Family*

Mike E. and Jamie Suzanna Verretta [185]

Jamie Suzanne Zirpel married Mike E. Verretta on June 17, 2000 in Rio Rancho, Sandoval County, New Mexico.

Mike E. Verretta was born on September of 1980.

Mike E. and Janie Suzanne Verretta had two children: Samantha and Britney Rae Verretta.

Samantha Verretta was born in August of 1996.

Britney Rae Verretta was born on September 10, 2007.

Samantha Rose Zirpel &
John Andy Estes
Marriage & Family*

Samantha Rose Zirpel married John Andy Estes in May of 2005.

John Andy and Samantha Rose Estes have one child: Scotty Estes.

Scotty Estes was born on August 11, 2006.

Samantha Rose and John Andy Estes [186]

Laurie Rose Zirpel and Samantha Rose Estes [187]

Joshua Merle Zirpel & Cheyenne Shakira Catalina Newkowski Marriage *

Joshua Merle Zirpel married Cheyenne Shakira Catalina Newkowski on June 22, 2013 in the First Baptist Church in Rio Rancho, Sandoval County, New Mexico.

Joshua Merle and Cheyenne Shakira
Catalina Zirpel Wedding 2013 [188]

Wayne Erich Zirpel and Bryan Allen Zirpel 2013. [189]

Mona Clydene Spear & Family *

Clyde Edward Spear, son of Willie Edward Spear and Mary Ruth Henderson was born on May 4, 1921 in Hall County, Georgia.

Ramona Eileen Stebbins, daughter of Edwin Layton Sereno Stebbins and Leah Lolita Peterson, was born on July 15, 1929, in Miller, Hand County, South Dakota.

Clyde Edward Spear and Ramona Eileen Stebbins were married on August 21, 1947 in Rapid City, Pennington County, South Dakota. Ramona Eileen Spear filed for divorce in Milledgeville, Georgia, according to Probate Court Records, Milledgeville, Baldwin County at a divorce in 1953. Their divorce was finalized on July 13, 1953.

Clyde Edward Spear died on May 3, 1978 in Augusta, Richmond County, Georgia and he was buried in Sparta, Hancock County, Georgia.

Freeman Edward Clark was born on October 6, 1913 in Jerauld County, South Dakota.

Ramona Eileen Spear married Freeman Edward Clark on September 7, 1963 in Mitchell, Davison County, South Dakota.

Freeman Edward Clark died on March 12, 1985 in Wessington Springs, Jerauld County, South Dakota and he was buried in Beadle County, South Dakota.

Mona Clydene Spear, daughter of Clyde Edward Spear and Ramona Eileen Stebbins, was born on September 25, 1956 in the North Shore Hospital, Miami, Dade County, Florida with the assistance of Helen C. Dayton M.D. She was christened on June 22, 1975 in the Mt. Olive Lutheran Church in Woonsocket, South Dakota.

Ramona Eileen Clark died on April 29, 1998 in Lane, Jerauld County, South Dakota. She was cremated.

Mona C. Spear & Lawrence A. Land Marriage & Family*

Mona Clydene Spear married Lawrence Allen Land on June 21, 1973 in Chambers County, Texas. The marriage ended in divorce in March of 1975.

Lawrence Allen and Mona Clydene Land had one child: John Henry Land.

John Henry Land was born on April 19, 1974 and he died on September 7, 1974. He was buried in plot 5, Lot E, Grave 43 in Graceland Cemetery in Mitchell, Davison County South Dakota.

Clyde Dwane Zirpel & Mona Clydene Spear Marriage & Family*

Clyde Dwane Zirpel and Mona Clydene Spear
1973 High School Prom [190]

Mona Clydene and Clyde Dwane Zirpel
June 28, 1975 [200]

Mona Clydene Zirpel was baptized and confirmed as an adult, at the Mt. Olive Lutheran Church in Woonsocket, Sanborn County, South Dakota by Pastor Richard O. Meyer.

Clyde Dwane Zirpel, son of Wilbert Erich and Audrey May Zirpel, married daughter of Clyde Edward Spear and Ramona Eileen Stebbins on June 28, 1975 in the Mt. Olive Lutheran Church with Pastor Richard O. Meyer officiating in Woonsocket, Sanborn County, South Dakota. Wilbert Lee Zirpel Jr. and Mary Ann Zirpel were the witnesses.

Clyde Dwane Zirpel in SD National Guards [201]

Clyde Dwane and Mona Clydene Zirpel had two children: Michael Duane and Rebecca Jean Zirpel.

Clyde Dwane joined the South Dakota National Guards on July 23, 1975, he served as Sgt. for a period of 20 years, 10 months and 31 days in the Detachment 1, Company C 153D Engineers Battalion (C) (Mech). Sgt. Clyde Dwane Zirpel received a Honorable Discharge on October 31, 1995.

Mona Clydene holding Rebecca Jean, and
Clyde Dwane and Michael Duane Zirpel [202]

Birth of
Michael Duane Zirpel*

Michael Duane Zirpel was born on February 11, 1978 in St. John's Regional Medical Center in Huron, Beadle County, South Dakota. He was christened on March 26, 1978 in the Mt. Olive Lutheran Church in Woonsocket, Sanborn County, South Dakota by Pastor John D. Sanstrom. His God parents were Richard Clark and Ruby Audrey Hoxsie.

Michael Duane Zirpel was confirmed in the Mt Olive Lutheran Church in Woonsocket, Sanborn County, South Dakota on June 7, 1992 by Pastor August C. Roesler and witnessed by John E. White and Clyde Dwane Zirpel.

Birth of
Rebecca Jean Zirpel*

Rebecca Jean Zirpel was born on September 20, 1981 in the Weskota Memorial Medical Center in Wessington Springs, Jerauld County, South Dakota. She was christened on November 8, 1981 in the Mt. Olive Lutheran Church in Woonsocket, Sanborn County, South Dakota. Her God parents were Steve Dammann and Connie Stebbins.

Rebecca was confirmed on May 5, 1996 in the Zion Lutheran Church in Wessington Springs, Jerauld County, South Dakota by Pastor August C. Roessler, and witnessed by Elmer Kludt and Ray Ohhegge.

Michael Duane Zirpel &
Victoria Lynn Miller
Marriage & Family*

Michael Duane Zirpel in US Marine Corp. [203]

Michael Duane graduated from the Wessington Springs High School in Wessington Springs, South Dakota in May of 1996. He missed his graduation ceremony as he was in United States Marine Corp Basic Training.

Michael Duane Zirpel served in the United States Marine Corp for 4 years. He signed up in March of 1996 and He received his discharge in 2000 or 2001 as a Corporeal. After his basic training and school, Michael spent 1 year in Okinawa, Japan and he returned to the United States to Camp Lejeune, North Carolina.

Victoria Lynn and Michael Duane Zirpel [204]

Michael Duane Zirpel, son of Clyde Dwane and Mona Clydene Zirpel, married Victoria Lynn Miller, daughter of Homer Dewy Miller III and Debra Jane Kimmons, on June 23, 2001 in the First Baptist Church in North Spartanburg, Spartanburg County, South Carolina.

Victoria Lynn Miller was born on January 6, 1979 on Spartanburg, Spartanburg County, South Carolina.

Bailey Jane, Colin Michael, and
Mikayla Lynn Zirpel [205]

Michael Duane and Victoria Lynn Zirpel had three children: Mikayla Lynn, Bailey Jane, and Colin Michael Zirpel.

Mikayla Lynn Zirpel was born on June 3, 2004 in Spartanburg, Spartanburg County, South Carolina.

Bailey Jane Zirpel was born on May 10, 2007 in Spartanburg, Spartanburg County, South Carolina.

Colin Michael was born on March 28, 2011 in Spartanburg, Spartanburg County, South Carolina.

Rebecca Jean Zirpel & Travis Joe Stunes Marriage & Family*

Travis Joe Stunes and Rebecca Jean Zirpel engagement [206]

Rebecca Jean Zirpel, daughter of Clyde Dwane and Mona Clydene Zirpel, married Travis Joe Stunes, son of Roger Edward Stunes and Leana Alta Shonley, on August 20, 2005 in Mitchell, Davison County, South Dakota.

Travis Joe Stunes was born on August 26, 1978 in Mitchell, Davison County, South Dakota.

Travis Joe and Rebecca Jean Stunes had four children: Tegan Elizabeth, Ashleigh Katherine, Jaeda Lyn and Jacey Leigha Stunes. Travis adopted Tegan Elizabeth and Ashleigh Katherine.

Tegan Elizabeth Stunes was born on September 17, 1999 in Mitchell, Davison County, South Dakota and she was christened on November 14, 1999 in the Zion Lutheran Church, Wessington Springs, Jerauld County, South Dakota.

Ashleigh Katherine Stunes was born on September 9, 2001 in the Avera Queen of Peace Hospital in Mitchell, Davison County, South Dakota and she was christened on September 13, 2001 in

the Zion Lutheran Church in Wessington Springs, Jerauld County, South Dakota.

Jaeda Lyn Stunes was born on October 24, 2006 in the Avera Queen of Peace Hospital in Mitchell, Davison County, South Dakota and she was christened on December 17, 2006 in the Zion Lutheran Church in Wessington Springs, Jerauld County, South Dakota.

Jacey Leigha Stunes was born on February 24, 2010 in the Avera Queen of Peace Hospital in Mitchell, Davison County, South Dakota and she was christened in the Zion Lutheran Church in Wessington Springs, Jerauld County, South Dakota.

Back row: Rebecca Jean holding Jacey Leigha, Ashleigh Katherine, Tegan Elizabeth and Travis Joe Stunes. Front row: Jaeda Lynn Stunes [207]

Mary Ann Zirpel & Steven Linn Dammann Marriage & Family*

Mary Ann Zirpel [208]

Mary Ann Zirpel, daughter of Wilbert Erich and Audrey May Zirpel, married Steven Linn

Dammann, son of LeNor Dammann and Arlene Einck, March 29, 1980 in Wessington Springs, Jerauld County, South Dakota.

Steven Linn Dammann was born on November 21, 1956 in Wessington Springs, Jerauld County, South Dakota and he was christened in Jerauld County, South Dakota.

Steven Linn and Mary Ann Dammann had two children: Tasha Deann and Erich Leroy Dammann.

Tasha Deann Dammann was born on August 18, 1980 in Mitchell, Davison County, South Dakota and she was christened in September of 1980 in Wessington Springs, Jerauld County, South Dakota.

Back row: Steven Linn and Mary Ann Dammann
Front row: Tasha Deann Dammann
and Erich Leroy Dammann [209]

Erich Leroy Dammann was born on March 26, 1983 in Wessington Springs, and he was christened in April of 1983 in Wessington Springs, Jerauld County, South Dakota.

In December of 2000, Mary Ann Dammann said that when she was younger, she enjoyed getting together at Christmas time with all the relatives on her father' side of the family to see everyone, it was fun. Then at Easter they would go to Grandma's place (Viola's home in White Lake) and be with all the relatives on her mother's aide of family.

Tasha Deann Dammann & Jeffrey Paul Hagman Marriage & Family*

Tasha Deann Dammann, daughter of Steven

Tasha Deann Dammann, daughter of Steven Linn and Mary Ann Dammann married Jeffrey Paul Hagman, son of Fred Hagman and Kathy Huis, on April 27, 2002 in the St. Winfred's Catholic Church in Woonsocket, Sanborn County, South Dakota.

Jeffrey Paul Hagman was born on December 13, 1978.

Tasha Deann and Jeffrey Paul Hagman [210]

Whitney Ann, Waverly Lynn and
Westin Jeffrey Hagman [211]

Jeffrey Paul and Tasha Deann Hagman had three Children: Westin Jeffrey, Whitney Ann and Waverly Lynn Hagman.

Westin Jeffrey Hagman was born on October 15, 2004 in the Avera Queen Of Peace Hospital in Mitchell, Davison County, South Dakota and he was christened in April of 2005 in Woonsocket, Sanborn County, South Dakota.

Whitney Ann Hagman was born on March 9, 2006 in the Avera Queen of Peace Hospital in Mitchell, Davison County, South Dakota and she was christened in August of 2006 in Woonsocket, Sanborn County, South Dakota.

Waverly Lynn Hagman was on August 6,

2009 in the Avera Queen of Peace Hospital in Mitchell, Davison County, South Dakota.

Bryan Allen Zirpel *

Bryan Allen Zirpel, S.D. National Guards [212]

Bryan Allen Zirpel joined the South Dakota National Guards in Woonsocket, Sanborn County, South Dakota in 1982. He continued to served in the 153 Engineer BN until 1995. In 1996 until 2006 Bryan served in 665 Maintenance Co. He also had some training in Germany while in the South Dakota National Guards.

Bryan Allen Zirpel & Darla Mae Parisien Marriage & Family*

Bryan Allen Zirpel and Bryton Erich Neil Zirpel [213]

Bryan Allen Zirpel, son of Wilbert Erich and Audrey May Zirpel, Darla Mae Parisien on June 24, 1989 in the First United Methodist Church in Huron, Beadle County, South Dakota. The marriage ended in divorce.

Bryan Allen and Darla Mae Zirpel had one child: Bryton Erich Neil Zirpel.

Bryton Erich Neil Zirpel was born on July 2, 1990 in Huron, Beadle County, South Dakota and he was christened in the First Methodist Church in Huron, Beadle County, South Dakota.

Bryton Erich Neil Zirpel and Stephanie Nemec [214]

Bryton Zirpel works as am Assistant Buyer for SCS Direct, a distribution Company for Amazon.com and he resided in Stratford, Connecticut.

Stephanie Nemec, daughter of John and Theresa Fawver, was born on December 1, 1982 in Bridgeport, Fairfield County, Connecticut. She was raised in Stratford, Fairfield County, Connecticut.

Stephanie Nemec works as an Office Manager for Victoria Souza Photography and she resides in Stratford, Connecticut.

Bryan Allen Zirpel & Teresa Marie Williams Marriage & Family*

Bryan Allen Zirpel, son of Wilbert Erich and Audrey May Zirpel, married Teresa Marie Williams, daughter of James and Mary Williams, on December 29, 1995 in the Holy Family Catholic Church in Mitchell, Davison County, South Dakota. Their marriage ended in divorce.

Bryan Allen and Teresa Marie Zirpel had two children: Kendra and Nathaniel Lee Zirpel.

Kendra Zirpel [215]

Kendra Zirpel was born on May 22, 1997 in Mitchell, Davison County, South Dakota and she was christened in the Holy Family Catholic Church in Mitchell, Davison County, South Dakota.

Nathaniel Lee Zirpel [216]

Nathaniel Lee Zirpel was born on January 18, 1999 in Mitchell, Davison County, South Dakota and he is christened in the Holy Family Catholic Church in Mitchell, Davison County, South Dakota.

Bryan Allen Zirpel & Lisa Jean Wolf Marriage *

Bryan Allen and Lisa Jean Zirpel [217]

Wallace E. Podhradsky was born on August 3, 1930 in South Dakota and he died in June 14, 2002 in Mitchell, Davison County, South Dakota.

Sharon Alice Mathis was born on September 16, 1938 in Aurora County, South Dakota and she died on November 12, 2013 in Mitchell, Davison County, South Dakota.

Wallace E. Podhradsky married Sharon Alice (Mathis) Morgan on August 13, 1965 in Woonsocket, Sanborn County, South Dakota.

Wallace E. and Sharon Alice Podhradsky had two children: Craig and Lisa Jean Podhradsky.

Lisa Jean Podhradsky was born on August 3, 1966 in Mitchell, Davison County, South Dakota.

Bryan Allen Zirpel, son of Wilbert Erich and Audrey May Zirpel, married Lisa Jean Wolf, daughter of Wallace Podhradsky and Sharon Alice Mathis, on August 4, 2012 in Hitchcock Park in Mitchell, Davison County, South Dakota by Rev. Mindy Ehrke and their best man was Doug Dewward and the maid of honor was Joan McCord.

Olinda Leota Laib & Her Family*

Conrad Heinrich Laib Jr., son of Conrad Heinrich Sr. and Katherina Meerroth was born on August 14, 1858 in Fredensthal, Bessarabia, Russia, according to the Bessarabia Village Records, 185x.

Sophia Marz was born on October 28, 1861 in Fredensthal, Bessarabia, Russia.

Conrad Heinrich Laib Jr., son of Conrad Heinrich Sr. and Katherina Meerroth, married Sophia Marz on October 30, 1880 in a unknown location in Russia.

Conrad Heinrich Laib Jr. and Sophia (Marz) Laib [218]

Conrad Heinrich Jr. and Sophia Laib had seven of their nine children in Fredensthal, Bessarabia, Russia. The children born in Russia were Katherine, John, Maria, Conrad, Frederick, Michael and Andrew Laib.

According to New York, Passenger Lists, 1820-1957, Konrad Laib and his family left the port of Bremen and they arrived on April 21,

1898 in the Port of New York, New York on the ship named Trave.[180]

The family left New York and settled in Tripp in Hutchinson County, South Dakota for a few years until they located land in which to build their home. They had two children in South Dakota: Theresa and Emma Laib.

The family moved to Lincoln Township in Douglas County, South Dakota sometime before June 9, 1900, when the family was recorded on the 1900 United States Census by the Census Enu-merator, William Pfeifer.[181] There were eight children listed on this report. They were Katherine age 18 years old, John 16 years old, Maria 14 years old, Conrad 11 years old, Frederick 8 years old, Michael 5 years old, Andrew 3 years old and The-resa months old.

Then the family moved north of Delmont in Belmont Township, Douglas County, South Dakota.

On the 1910 United States Census recorded on April 15-16, 1910 by the Census Enumerator, D. E. Whittenmore, Conrad and Sophia Laib were living in Belmont Township, Douglas County, South Dakota.[182]

Conrad Heinrich Jr. and Sophia Laib were recorded on the 1920 and 1930 United States Census still living in Belmont Township in Douglas County, South Dakota.

Sometime after 1930 the family moved to Delmont in Belmont Township, Douglas County, South Dakota according to the 1940 United States Census report taken by the Census Enumerator, Math J. Loss on April 6, 1940.[183]

Conrad Heinrich Laib Jr. died on February 22, 1944 and his wife, Sophia Laib died on March 4, 1948.

Emma Johanna and Frederick Laib [219]

Frederick Laib, son of Conrad Heinrich Jr. and Sophia Laib married Emma Johanna Schulz, daughter of Gottlieb Schulz and Wilhelmina Ratke on April 1, 1917 in Parkston Salem Lutheran Church in Parkston, Hutchinson County, South Dakota.

Emma Johanna Schulz was born on December 8, 1887 in Hutchinson County, South Dakota.

Frederick and Emma Johanna Laib had five children: Arnold, Leona, Olinda, Roland and Delores Laib.

On the 1920 United States Census the Fred Laib family was living in Independence Township in Douglas County, South Dakota on January 3rd, 4th, and 5th, 1920 according to the Census Enumerator, Francis P. Gallagher.[184] On this report, Fred Laib was born about 1892 in Russia along with his parents, while Emma J., his wife was born in South Dakota and she was 22 years old. Also recorded on this report was one son, Arnold W. 4 months old.

Olinda Leota Laib, daughter of Frederick Laib and Emma Johanna Schulz was February 8, 1927 in Douglas County, South Dakota.

Olinda Leota Laib [220]

On April 3, 1930 on the 1930 United States Census, the Census Enumerator, Gerrit F. Drasselburys recorded the Frederick Laib family still living in Independence Township in Douglas County, South Dakota.[185] On this report Frederick was 37 years old and his wife, Emma Johanna was 32 years old. The children listed on the report were Arnold 10 years old, Leona 8 years old and Olinda 3 years and 11 months old.

The Frederick Laib family was listed on the 1940 United States Census living in Independence

Township, Douglas County, South Dakota with five children listed on the report.[186] The children were Arnold 20 years old, Leona 18 years old, Olinda 13 years old, Roland 9 years old and Delores 6 years old. On this report Olinda Laib had completed the 8th grade in elementary school.

Emma Johanna Laib died at the St. Benedict Hospital in Parkston, Hutchinson County, South Dakota on July 9, 1976. She was buried in the Parkston Protestant Cemetery in Parkston, Hutchinson County, South Dakota.

Frederick Laib died on November 12, 1981 while in the Parkston Hospital in Parkston, Hutchinson County, South Dakota. He was buried in the Parkston Protestant Cemetery November 15, 1981 by his wife, in Parkston, Hutchinson County, South Dakota.

He was survived by two sons: Arnold and Roland Laib, Delmont, South Dakota; three daughters: Mrs. Erwin (Leona) Goehring, Sioux Falls, South Dakota; Mrs. Erwin (Olinda) Zirpel, Parkston, South Dakota; and Mrs. Arnold (Delores) Kirchhevel, Armour, South Dakota; a brother, Andrew Laib, Mobridge, South Dakota; a sister, Emma Fink Drefs, Delmont, South Dakota; 18 grandchildren; and seven great grandchildren.

He was preceded in death by his parents, his wife, Emma Johanna, three sisters and three brothers.

Olinda Leota Laib attended and graduated from Amour High School in Armour in Douglas County, South Dakota.

Southern State Teachers College where Olinda Laib received a degree in Education. It was a one-year course for elementary teachers. She received her certificate on June 15, 1945 and it was signed by Superintendent of Public Schools, J. F. Hines.

Olinda taught in a school in Douglas County, South Dakota between 1945 until 1946 according to the County Superintendent, Albert Vander Twin.

Then Olinda taught intermediate grades in a school in Alpena, Jerauld County, South Dakota between 1946 until 1947 according to the County Superintendent, Earl C. Gregory.

Olinda transferred back to Douglas County, South Dakota and taught in a school between 1947 until 1949 according to County Superintendent, Albert Vander Twin.

Olinda taught in the St. John's School in Hutchinson County, South Dakota between 1952 until 1953 according to the Superintendent of Public Instruction, Harold S. Freeman after she had married Erwin Zirpel.

Edwin Karl Zirpel & Olinda Leota Laib Marriage & Family*

Roland Laib, Norbert John Zirpel, Elmer Gottfried Zirpel, Erwin Karl Zirpel, Olinda Leota Laib, Deloris Laib, Inez Baumiller, and Betty Bietz. Flowers girls are Mary Ellen Ruth Zirpel and Betty Jean Goehring [221]

135

Erwin Karl Zirpel left the farm in Douglas County, South Dakota October of 1946 and he traveled to West Bend, in Washington County, Wisconsin where he joined International Union, United Automobile Workers of America according to L. D. Melius, Finance Secretary. He continue until September 16, 1947, when he withdrew from the International Union according to President of the Union, Ben Heiting, and Financial Secretary of the Union, Floyd Melius.

It is presumed that Erwin return to South Dakota after this.

Erwin Karl and Olinda Leota Zirpel 1949 [222]

Erwin Karl Zirpel, son of Gottfried John Zirpel and Gertrude Anna Gerlach married Olinda Leota Laib, daughter of Frederick Laib and Johanna Schultz on April 8, 1949 in the St. Peter's Lutheran Church by Armour in Douglas County South Dakota. The Rev. J. Haber performed the double ring ceremony.

The maid of honor was, Delores Laib, sister of the bride. The bridesmaids, cousins of the groom were Inez Baumiller and Betty Bietz. The best man was Elmer Gottfried Zirpel, brother of the groom. The other attendants of the groom were Norbert John Zirpel, brother of the groom and Roland Laib, brother of the bride. The flower girls were Betty Jean Goehring, a niece of the bride, and Mary Ellen Ruth Zirpel, a sister of the groom.

Following the ceremony, a wedding dinner was served at the church parlors by the Ladies Aid of the Church with about 140 guests. The reception was held at the home of the grooms.

During the evening, Rev. J. DeWald gave a very appropriate talk, after which two hymns were sung by Mrs. Arnold Laib, Gertrude and Lorentina Semmler.

The young couple lived on a farm a mile west of Armour, in Douglas County, South Dakota and Erwin was engaged in farming.

Erwin Karl and Olinda Leota Zirpel had two children that they adopted: John Frederick and Darwin James Zirpel.

Birth of
John Frederick Zirpel*

John Frederick Zirpel was born on May 31, 1961 and he was adopted on June 23, 1961.

John Frederick Zirpel was confirmed in 1975 at the Immanuel Lutheran Church in Douglas County, South Dakota.

John Frederick Zirpel [223]

Birth of
Darwin James Zirpel*

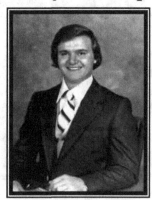

Darwin James Zirpel [224]

136

Darwin James Zirpel was born on September 20, 1963 and he was adopted on January 30, 1964.

Darwin James Zirpel was confirmed in 1977 at the Immanuel Lutheran Church in Douglas County, South Dakota.

John Frederick Zirpel & Laurie Dawn Pries Marriage & Family*

Darwin James Zirpel, Laurie Dawn Zirpel, John Frederick Zirpel, Olinda Leota Zirpel and Erwin Karl Zirpel [225]

John Frederick Zirpel married Laurie Dawn Pries, daughter of Gerald E. and Delores C. Pries on July 30, 1983 at the Faith Lutheran Church in Parkston, Hutchinson County, South Dakota, Rev. August C. Roessler performed the ceremony. Attending the couple were: maid of honor, Kim Bernhard, Vermillion, South Dakota; bridesmaids were Shelley Muntefering, Tripp, South Dakota, and Tina Bartels, Hawarden, Iowa; best man, Darwin James Zirpel, Parkston, South Dakota; and groomsmen were James Slack and Rich Gaffin, both of Harrisburg, South Dakota. Stephanie Pries, Troy, Michigan served as flower girl and Kara Pries, El Paso, Texas was ring bearer. Ushers were Dan Nelson, Minneapolis, Minnesota and Clark Huffman, Harrisburg, South Dakota. The bride's personal attendants were Kellee Haub, Sioux Falls, South Dakota and Cathy Weber, Dimock, South Dakota. Pinning flowers was Annette Staz, Omaha, Nebraska.

A reception was held at the Holiday Inn, Mitchell, South Dakota with Mr. and Mrs. Donald Herrick, Mitchell, South Dakota, aunt and uncle of the bride; and Mr. and Mrs. Clifford Roth, Huron, Huron, South Dakota, aunt and uncle of the

groom, serving as hosts. Jeanette Neugebauer, Yankton, South Dakota registered the guests and Marjo Zirpel and Lisa Melhaff, cousins of the groom, had charge of the gift table. Dianne Pries, el Paso, Texas and Renee Pries, Troy, Michigan, were in charge of the punch table. Cake servers were Mrs. Fred Gerlach, Mitchell, South Dakota, god-mother of the groom and Mrs. Gene Kammerer, Groton, South Dakota, god-mother of bride.

The bride and groom were graduates of the Parkston High School in Parkston, Hutchinson County, South Dakota and both had been attending the University of South Dakota in Vermillion, South Dakota.

Laurie Dawn Pries was born on February 6, 1962.

Michael John, Laurie Dawn, Taryn Leigh, and John Frederick Zirpel [226]

Michael John, Laurie Dawn, Taryn Leigh, and John Frederick Zirpel [227]

John Frederick and Laurie Dawn Zirpel had two children: Michael John and Taryn Leigh Zirpel. Their marriage ended in divorce on August 14, 2009.

Michael John Zirpel was born on October 4, 1988. In 2003, Michael was confirmed in May and also graduated the 8th grade as Salutatorian. Michael started Keller High School that same year and he enjoyed playing school basketball and tried out for soccer that next spring.

Taryn Leigh Zirpel was born on November 18, 1991. In 2003, Taryn started her confirmation studies. She enjoyed school at Crown of Life, She played the flute in the band.

Darwin James Zirpel & Renae Ann Kleinschimdt
Marriage *

Darwin James Zirpel in SD Army National Guards [228]

Darwin James Zirpel enter the Army National Guard of South Dakota on October 3, 1983, in Co C (-) 153rd Engr. Bn. (C) (A) in Parkston, Hutchinson County, South Dakota. Darwin was a PFC E3 and his primary AFSC was 12B10 combat Engineer with his secondary AFSC 51R10electrician. He was honorably discharged on October 3, 1986. He received a ASR for Marksman Badge M-16 rifle.

Renae Ann and Darwin James Zirpel [229]

Darwin James Zirpel married Renae Ann Kleinschmit, daughter of Ronald Kleinschmit and the late Phyllis (Eckmann) Kleinschmit on July 1, 1995 in the Faith Lutheran Church in Parkston, Hutchinson County, South Dakota. Rev. Jerome Troester performed the ceremony.

The maid of honor was Lisa Kleinschmit, sister of bride; the bridesmaid was Julie Loecker; and the flower girl was Taryn Leigh Zirpel, niece of the groom. The best man was John Frederick Zirpel, brother of groom; the groomsmen was Jeff Pekas; and the ring bearer was Michael John Zirpel, nephew of the groom. Their marriage ended in divorce.

Erwin Karl & Olinda Leota Zirpel - The Later Years*

Back row: Erwin Karl, John Frederick, and Darwin James Zirpel.
Front row: Olinda Leota Zirpel [230]

Erwin Karl Zirpel's Farm between 1966-1982 [231]

Erwin Karl and Olinda Leota Zirpel lived on a farm a mile west of Armour, in Douglas County, South Dakota for a few years.

Erwin Karl and Olinda Leota Zirpel also farmed in Aurora, Davison, and Hutchinson Counties in South Dakota for nearly thirty four years.

When Gottfried John Zirpel and his wife, Gertrude Anna retired from the farm, they moved in Parkston, South Dakota.

Erwin had been raised on his grandfather, Johan Zirpel's homestead as he sold it to Gottfried John Zirpel and then Gottfried sold it to Erwin Karl Zirpel between 1966-1968.

Erwin Karl Zirpel had a good humor and he loved animals August of 1978 [232]

The family lived and farmed on the homestead property.

For nearly thirty–six years of Erwin's life he worked as a Pioneer Seed Salesman within the surrounding counties where they lived as well as farmed on his land. He had received various awards while selling seeds for Pioneer.

In June of 1982, Erwin decided to retire from farming and the family left the farm and moved into a house that Olinda's parents, Fred and Emma J. Laib had owned in Parkston, Hutchinson County, South Dakota. There new home was across the street from his parents, Gottfried John and Gertrude Anna Zirpel. When they moved into town, Erwin sold the farm.

Erwin Karl and Olinda Leota had been member of the Immanuel Lutheran located in Douglas County, South Dakota.

Both Karl and Olinda Leota Zirpel join the Faith Lutheran Church in Parkston, South Dakota and were active members of the Faith Lutheran Church after moving to Parkston. Erwin throughout the years served in various positions which included the Lutheran Laymen League chairman, AAL/Thrivent Chairman, Sunday School Teacher, Dartball Chairman, and the Church Council President-chairman. Olinda was a member of LWML in the Faith Lutheran Church. Erwin was also active with the Parkston Historical Society, and many other clubs and organizations.

In 1998, Erwin Karl and Olinda Leota had their Fifth Wedding Anniversary. After which Erwin, Olinda, their son, John Frederick and his family, Laurie, Michael and Taryn Zirpel went to Europe on a trip. They spent a special time together touring eight different countries: London; England; Paris, France; Germany; Hungry; Italy; Switzerland; Austria; and Brussels.

Over 5,000 cups and 400 Calendar photos in his garage behind the house 1999 [233]

During the years Erwin worked as a Pioneer Seed salesman he was also collect coffee cups or mugs. Every trip that he had been taken to see relatives or friends the collection really began to grow.

According to Scott E. Ehler, of the Parkston Advance Newspaper in Parkston, South Dakota in 1999 Erwin say that he had over 5,000 mugs, 400 calendar photos that he had framed the wooden strips as well as beer and soda cans, and other memorabilia over the past 51 years.[187] After Erwin's retirement from selling Pioneer seed, he began building display cases and rows of hooks in the ceiling of the large metal building behind his house, where had kept bags of Pioneer seed. His display were limited to walls and ceiling, so that he could still park a vehicle in the building. Erwin really loved collecting things from the past.

Over 6,000 coffee mugs mounted in his garage, walls and ceiling in Erwin Zirpel's collection in 2001 [234]

Erwin Karl Zirpel's 75th Birthday [235]

Erwin had told Mary Gales Askren, a reporter for The Daily Republic Newspaper of Mitchell, South Dakota in 2001 that he was a collector by nature and had an estimated 6,000 coffee mugs mounted in his garage: on the walls, on the ceiling and in display cases he had built.[188] After he had stopped farming and selling Pioneer-brand seeds in the late 1980's, collecting coffee mugs with advertisements on them was something to do.

Some of coffee cups came from friends and family members, rummage sales, thrift stores, flea markets, Salvation Army stores, gathered them on the many vacations and trips when visiting their children in Texas. It was not unusual for him to bring home a suitcase full of coffee mugs when visiting other relatives around the country.

While Erwin was still in the seed business, he began displaying the mugs around the outside walls of the barn he used to store the seed and he continued to display them in his garage as well.

Erwin Karl Zirpel died on Friday, November 21, 2003 while in the Heart Hospital in Sioux Falls, Minnehaha County, South Dakota at the age of 77 years. His funeral service was held on November 25, 2003 at the Faith Lutheran Church in Parkston, South Dakota and the Rev. Vic Dorn officiated. The music was furnished by the Faith Lutheran choir and Bev Scheets, the organist.

Erwin Karl Zirpel was buried in the Parkston Protestant Cemetery in Hutchinson County, South Dakota. The casket bearers were Kevin Branick, Myles Konopasek, Gary Wenzel, Todd Fruedenthal, Tim Tiede, and Daniel Zirpel.

He was survived by his wife, Olinda Leota; two sons: John Frederick Zirpel, and wife Laurie, Keller, Texas; and Darwin James Zirpel, Yankton, South Dakota; two grandchildren: Michael John and Taryn Leigh Zirpel, both of Keller, Texas; two sisters: Rosalene Roth and husband, Clifford, Huron, South Dakota and Mary Ellen Mettenbrink and husband, Harold, Sioux City, Iowa; three brothers, Elmer Gottfried Zirpel and wife, Luella, Appleton, Wisconsin; Norbert John Zirpel and wife, Elaine, Parkston, South Dakota; and Harold Arnold Zirpel and wife, Virginia, San Jose, California; four sister-in-laws: Audrey May Zirpel, Woonsocket, South Dakota; Lillian Esther Zirpel, Mitchell, South Dakota; Delores Kirchhevel, Parkston, South Dakota; and Rosemary Laib, Armour, South Dakota, and numerous nieces and nephews.

He had been preceded in death by both of his parents, his mother-in-law and father-in law, Frederick and Emma Johanna Laib; two brothers,

Leonard Robert Zirpel and Wilbert Erich Zirpel; various in-laws: Arnold Kirchhevel, Roland Laib, Erwin and Leona Goehring, Arnold and Magdalena Laib and Richard Mehlhaff.

Olinda Leota Zirpel died on Monday, April 3, 2006, at her home in Parkston, Hutchinson County, South Dakota.

Her funeral services were held at the Faith Lutheran Church in Parkston, South Dakota. She was buried in the Parkston Protestant Cemetery in Hutchinson County, South Dakota.

She was survived by her two sons: John Frederick Zirpel and wife, Laurie, Keller, Texas and Darwin James Zirpel, Yankton, South Dakota; two grandchildren; and one sister, Delores Kirchhevel, Parkston, South Dakota.

She was preceded in death by her husband, Erwin Karl Zirpel, her parents, two brothers: Roland and Arnold Laib; one sister, Leona Goehring.

Luella M. Frey & Her Family*

Luella Mae Frey's grandparents were Fred and Katie Frey. Both of her grandparents were born in South Dakota.

On the 1900 United States Census Fred and Katie lived in Township 96 in Bon Homme County, South Dakota according to the census report taken by the Census Enumerator, Julius O. Smith on June 1-2, 1900.[189] On this report was a son Reinhold Christian Frey only three months old.

Reinhold Christian Frey, son of Fred and Katie Frey was born on February 17, 1900 in Bon Homme County, South Dakota.

Ida Stoebner, daughter of Andrew Stoebner and Magdalena Pietz, was born on July 14, 1900 in Tripp, Hutchinson County, South Dakota.

According to the South Dakota Marriages, 1905-1949, Reinhold Christian Frey married Ida Stoebner on February 27, 1927. The couple was married by Rev. W. J. Krieger in the Reformed Church in Tripp, Hutchinson County, South Dakota.[190]

The Census Enumerator, B. A. Neidermult recorded Reinhold Christian Frey and his wife, Ida on April 15, 1930 living in German, Hutchinson County, South Dakota on the 1930 United States Census.[191] On child was listed on the report as Velda R. Frey 2 years and 6 months old.

Luella Mae Frey, daughter of Reinhold Christian Frey and Ida Stoebner was born on May 23, 1932 in German Township, Hutchinson County, South Dakota. She was christened on July 6, 1932 in the Bethel Reformed Church.

The Reinhold Frey family was found on the 1940 United States Census living in German Township, Hutchinson County, South Dakota according to the report taken on April 22, 1940 by the Census Enumerator, Alvin A. Delperdang.[192] Reinhold Christian Frey was listed as a farmer owning his home that was valued at $600. There were three children listed on this report. They were Velda R. 12 years old, Luella M. 7 years old, and Marvin M. 4 years old. Also list on the report was Fred Frey 64 years old.

Elmer Gottfried Zirpel & Luella Mae Frey Marriage & Family*

Elmer Gottfried Zirpel [236]

Elmer Gottfried Zirpel [237]

Elmer Gottfried Zirpel, son of Gottfried John Zirpel and Gertrude Anna Gerlach, married

Elmer Gottfried and Luella Mae Zirpel [238]

Luella Mae Frey, daughter of Reinhold Christian Frey and Ida Stoebner, were married on June 5, 1955 in the Friedens Reformed Church in Tripp, Hutchinson County, South Dakota.

The maid of honor was Rosalene Gertrude Zirpel, sister of groom and the bridesmaids were Noreen Bertram, friend of the groom and Sylvia Anderson, 2nd cousin of the groom. The best man was Marvin Frey, brother of bride and the groomsmen were Harold Arnold Zirpel, brother of the groom and Reno Stoebner, 2nd cousin of

the bride. The ring bearer was Harlan Gjorass and the flower girls were Ruth Diane and Ruby Audrey Zirpel.

Elmer Gottfried and Luella Mae Zirpel had five children: Kathleen Kay, Richard Lee, Karen Ann, Ronald Allen, and Randolph Scott Zirpel.

Birth of
Kathleen Kay Zirpel*

Kathleen Kay Zirpel [239]

Kathleen Kay Zirpel was born June 25, 1956 in Huron, Beadle County, South Dakota and she Christened on July 15, 1956 in the Mt. Calvary Lutheran Church in Huron, Beadle County, South Dakota.

Reno Stoebner, Harold Arnold Zirpel, Marvin Frey, Elmer Gottfried Zirpel, Luella Mae Zirpel,
Rosalene Gertrude Roth, Noreen Bertram, Sylvia Martha Anderson.
Ring bearer: Harlan Gjorass and flower girls: Ruth Dianne and Ruby Audrey Zirpel [240]

Kathleen Kay Zirpel Gravesite in the Parkston Protestant Cemetery in Parkston, South Dakota [241]

Unfortunately, Kathleen Kay Zirpel died suddenly on June 14, 1970 while she was in the Fairmont Hospital in Fairmont, Martin County, Minnesota.

The funeral for Kathleen Kay Zirpel was held on Wednesday, June 16, 1970 at the St. Paul's Lutheran Church in Fairmont, Minnesota. There were also services held later that day at the Faith Lutheran Church in Parkston, South Dakota. Her burial was at the Parkston Protestant Cemetery in Parkston, South Dakota.

Birth of
Richard Lee Zirpel*

Richard Lee Zirpel was born on November 3. 1957 in Huron, Beadle County, South Dakota and he was christened on November 10, 1957 in Mt. Calvary Lutheran Church, in Huron, Beadle County, South Dakota.

Richard Lee Zirpel [242]

Birth of
Karen Ann Zirpel*

Karen Ann Zirpel was born on October 31, 1960 in Huron, Beadle County, South Dakota and he was christened on November 13, 1960 in Mt. Calvary Lutheran Church, in Huron, Beadle County, South Dakota.

Karen Ann Zirpel [243]

Birth of
Ronald Allen Zirpel*

Ronald Allen Zirpel was May 14, 1962 in St. John's Hospital, in Huron, Beadle County, South Dakota and he was christened on November 10, 1957 in Mt. Calvary Lutheran Church, in Huron, Beadle County, South Dakota.

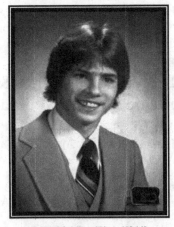

Ronald Allen Zirpel[244]

Birth of
Randolph Scott Zirpel*

Randolph Scott Zirpel was born August 18, 1965 in Aberdeen, Brown County, South Dakota and he was christened in September of 1965 in the St. Paul Lutheran, Aberdeen, Brown County, South Dakota.

143

Randolph Scott Zirpel [245]

Richard Lee Zirpel & Barbara Jean Blank Marriage & Family*

Richard Lee Zirpel married Barbara Jean Blank on June 3, 1984 in Neenah, Winnebago County, Wisconsin. The marriage ended in divorce on July 14, 1985 in Oshkosh, Winnebago County, Wisconsin.

Barbara Jean Blank was born on July 29, 1962 in Neenah, Winnebago County, Wisconsin.

Richard Lee and Barbara Jean Zirpel had one child: Anthony Richard Zirpel.

Anthony Richard Zirpel was born on April 27, 1984 in Neenah, Winnebago, Wisconsin and he was christened on June 24, 1984 in Neenah, Winnebago County, Wisconsin.

Richard Lee Zirpel & Amiee Sue Eggert Marriage *

Richard Lee Zirpel married Amiee Sue Eggert on June 17, 1989 in Appleton, Outagamie County, Wisconsin.

Amiee Sue Eggert was born on May 17, 1958 in Appleton, Outagamie County, Wisconsin and she was christened in May 1958 in Appleton, Outagamie County, Wisconsin.

Richard worked in a Post office in 2003, and Amiee worked as a Nurse that same year.

Karen Ann Zirpel & Peter Johan Bekx Marriage & Family*

Karen Ann Zirpel married Peter Johan Bekx on July 29, 1989 in Appleton, Outagamie County, Wisconsin.

Peter Johan Bekx was born on April 21, 1961 in Appleton, Outagamie County, Wisconsin and he was christened on May 2 1961 in the St. Paul Lutheran Church.

Peter Johan and Karen Ann Bekx had three children: Jordan Johan, Amanda Nicole and Parker Logan Bekx.

Jordon Johan Bekx was born on June 13, 1991 in Appleton, Outagamie County, Wisconsin and he christened on August 4, 1991 in Appleton, Outagamie County, Wisconsin.

Bekx family November 2012.
Back row standing: Parker Logan and Jordon Johan Bekx. Middle row: Amanda Nicole and Karen Ann Bekx. Front row: Peter Johan Bekx. [246]

Amanda Nicole Bekx was born on January 4, 1995 in Appleton, Outagamie County, Wisconsin and she was christened on June 4, 1995 in Kaukauna, Outagamie County, Wisconsin.

Parker Logan Bekx was born on May 2, 1997 in Appleton, Outagamie County, Wisconsin and he was christened on June 8, 1997 in Kaukauna, Outagamie County, Wisconsin.

In 1998, Karen had gotten a new job in August and worked for U.S. Oil Company and also she worked as a part-time Human Resource Manager.

In 1998, Peter work for Wisconsin Tissue. In 2003 Peter was working in finance at a converting Company.

Ronald Allen Zirpel & Ann Marie Vetter Marriage *

Ronald Allen Zirpel married Ann Marie Vetter on June 6, 1987 in the Peace Lutheran Church in Neenah, Winnebago County, Wisconsin. The marriage ended in divorce on October 9, 1989 in Appleton, Outagamie County, Wisconsin.

Ann Marie Vetter was born on September 12, 1966 in Nebraska.

Ronald Allen Zirpel & Melissa Lynn Schreiber
Marriage & Family*

Ronald Allen Zirpel married Melissa Lynn Schreiber on November 1, 1997 in the Bethany Lutheran Church in Kaukauna, Outagamie County, Wisconsin.

Melissa Lynn Schreiber was born on April 10, 1969 in Saint Elizabeth Hospital, Appleton, Outagamie County, Wisconsin and she was christened on April 27, 1969 in the Holy Angles Catholic Parish, Appleton, Outagamie County, Wisconsin.

Ronald Allen and Melissa Lynn Zirpel had two children: Connor Alan and Preston Clay Zirpel.

Conner Alan Zirpel was born on December 18, 1998 in the Appleton Medical Center in Appleton, Outagamie County, Wisconsin and he was christened on March 14, 1999 in the Bethany Lutheran church, Kaukauna, Outagamie County, Wisconsin.

Preston Clay Zirpel was born on January 3, 2002 in the Appleton Medical Center in Appleton, Outagamie County, Wisconsin and he was christened on March 10, 2002 in the Bethany Lutheran Church in Kaukauna, Outagamie County, Wisconsin.

In 1998, Ronald had changed employer's in November, and he started at U.S. Oil Company. In 1998, Melissa worked in payroll for Valmet.

Randolph Scott Zirpel & Lori Volkman Marriage*

Randolph Scott Zirpel married Lori Volkman on August 1, 1987. The marriage ended in divorce.

Lori Volkman was born on March 4, 1967.

Randolph Scott Zirpel & Renee Lee Marcks
Marriage & Family*

Randolph Scott Zirpel married Renee Lee Marcks on November 1, 1997.

Renee Lee Marcks was born on August 23, 1971 in Appleton, Outagamie County, Wisconsin and she was christened in Shiocton, Outagamie County, Wisconsin.

Randolph Scott and Renee Lee Zirpel had one child: Riley Owen Zirpel.

Riley Owen Zirpel was born on September 5, 2000 in Neenah, Winnebago County, Wisconsin and he was christened on October 7, 2000 in Neenah, Winnebago County, Wisconsin.

In 2003, Randolph managed his own company, Fox Valley Asphalt.

In 2003, Renee worked as a payroll manager at Metso.

Back row: Renee Lee Zirpel, and Randolph Scott Zirpel. Front row: Riley Owen Zirpel [247]

Elmer Gottfried & Luella Mae Zirpel - The Later Years*

The family of Elmer Gottfried Zirpel lived in Huron, Beadle County, South Dakota from 1956 until around 1964.

According to the U.S. Public Records, 1821-1989, Elmer was working as a clerk in Huron, South Dakota and he changed jobs in 1960, when he began working as a salesman.

The Elmer Zirpel family must have moved to Aberdeen in Brown County, South Dakota before Randolph Scott Zirpel was born in August of 1965.

Sometime in 1993, Elmer Gottfried and

Luella Mae Zirpel moved in Yankton, Yankton County, South Dakota. According to the U.S. Public Records Index, Volume 1, they lived in Yankton until 2002.

Luella Mae and Elmer Gottfried Zirpel 1973 [248]

Richard Lee Zirpel, Karen Ann Bekx,
Luella Mae Zirpel, Elmer Gottfried Zirpel,
Ronald Allen Zirpel, and Randolph Scott Zirpel [249]

Luella Mae, Olinda Leota, Erwin Karl,
and Elmer Gottfried Zirpel [250]

Elmer Gottfried Zirpel [251]

In 1998, Elmer drove the school bus and he also had the opportunity that summer to drive bus for some of the prisoners in Yankton prison.

In 2003, Elmer Zirpel was driving for the handicap, taking them to work and home again. He also joined a golf league with the guys from work and he went to the golf course at least once a week.

According to the U.S. Public Records Index, Volume 1, Elmer and Luella Zirpel moved from Yankton, South Dakota to Appleton in Outagamie County, Wisconsin where they would be closer to their children who lived around the area.

Elmer Gottfried Zirpel, 86, passed away on Monday, January 6, 2014 in Appleton, Outagamie County, Wisconsin from brain cancer.

A funeral service was held at the Trinity Lutheran Church, Menasha, Wisconsin on Friday, January 10, 2014 and Rev. Steven S. Billings officiated.

A Memorial service was held at the Faith Lutheran Church in Parkston, Hutchinson County, South Dakota and Rev. David Zirpel officiated.

The burial was held at the Parkston Protestant Cemetery in Parkston, Hutchinson County, South Dakota. Pallbearers were Jordan Bekx, Amanda Bekx, Parker Bekx, Conner Zirpel, Riley Zirpel, and Preston Zirpel.

Elmer Zirpel served in the United States Army during the Korean War. He worked for the Gambles Department Store for 25 years and drove school bus for 30 years before he retired.

Elmer was survived by his wife, Luella Mae Zirpel and four children: Richard Lee Zirpel and wife, Amiee; Karen Ann Bekx and husband, Peter; Ronald Allen Zirpel and wife, Melissa; and Randolph Scott Zirpel and wife, Renee; and six children: Jordan Johan Bekx, Amanda Nicole Bekx, Parker Logan Bekx, Conner Allen Zirpel, Preston Clay Zirpel, and Riley Owen Zirpel; one brother, Norbert John Zirpel, Parkston, South Dakota; two sisters: Rosalene Roth, Huron, South Dakota and Mary Ellen Mettenbrink, Sioux City, Iowa.

He was preceded in by his daughter, Kathleen Kay Zirpel and his parents: Gottfried John and Gertrude Anna Zirpel, and four brothers: Leonard Robert Zirpel, Wilbert Erich Zirpel, Erwin Karl Zirpel and Harold Arnold Zirpel.

Elaine Evangeline Frey & Her Family*

Hulda Weisser, daughter of Gottlieb and Rosie Weisser, was born on February 12, 1907 in South Dakota.

Hulda Weisser was recorded on the 1910 United States Census by the Census Enumerator on April 30, 1910 living with her parents, Gottlieb and Rosie Weisser in Avon, Emanuel Precinct in Bon Homme County, South Dakota.[193] On this report Gottlieb was twenty-nine years old and his wife, Rosie was twenty-six years old. There were one year old and Paul two months old. Also listed on this report were the grandparents, Fred Weisser sixty-eight years old and his wife, Margelina sixty-eight years old.

On the 1920 United States Census according to the Census Enumerator, Fred C. Platter, on January 12, 1920, the Gottlieb Weisser family was still living in the Emanuel Township in Bon Homme County, South Dakota.[194] There were nine children listed on the census report: Hulda 13 years old, Alfred 11 years old, Paul nine years old, Ruben 8 years old, Rebecca 8 years old, Alma 5 years old, Ernest 3 years old, Albert 1 year old and Laintina 2 months old.

April 19, 1930, the Census Enumerator, Ruth F. Bangert, recorded the Gottlieb Weisser family on the 1930 United States Census living in Emanuel Township in Bon Homme County, South Dakota.[195] Gottlieb and Rosie Weisser had twelve children and eleven of them were listed on the census report. They were Alfred 21 years old, Paul 20 years old, Rebecca 18 years old, Ruben 18 years old, Alma 15 years old, Ernest 14 years old, Albert 12 years old, Laintina 10 years old, Arthur 9 years old, Leo 7 years old and Otto 5 years old.

On the 1940 United States Census recorded

Otto Frey Family. Back row: Ernest Frey, Violet Frey, and Elmer Frey
Front row: Darlene Frey, Otto Frey, Hulda Frey and Elaine Frey. [252]

147

on April 30 and May 1, 1940 by the Census Enumerator, William G. Kucera the Gottlieb Weisser family was still living in Emanuel Township in Bon Homme County, South Dakota.[196] Gottlieb was 59 years old and his wife Rosie was 57 years old. There were six children living with their parents. They were Alma 25 years old, Albert 22 years old, Laintina 20 years old, Arthur 19 years old, Leo 17 years old, and Otto 15 years old. The report said that Gottlieb owned his home and it was valued at $2,500.

Otto Frey, son of Phillip Frey and Katharina Mock, was born on February 3, 1909 in South Dakota.

There is a record of Phillip and Katharina Frey on the 1910 United States Census on April 25, 1910 according to the Census Enumerator, J. M. G. Gross, living in Stickel Township, McPherson County, South Dakota with five children.[197] The report stated that Phillip had immigrated in 1889 to the United States from his birthplace of Russia. On the report Katharina was also born in Russia. The five children were Phillip 9 years old, Albert 7 years old, Emma 5 years old, Pauline 3 years old and Ida 1 month old.

According to South Dakota Marriages, 1905-1949, Otto Frey married Hulda Weisser on April 13, 1930 in Bon Homme County, South Dakota.

Otto and Hulda Frey were recorded on the 1930 United States Census at the home of Otto's parents, Phillip and Katharina Frey in Oak Hollow Township, Hutchinson County, South Dakota in April of 1930 by the Census Enumerator, Peter J. Hofer.[198] On this report Otto was working as a farm laborer. The report said that Phillip Frey was born in Russia while his wife, Katherina was born in South Dakota. Phillip Frey was listed as farmer. There were three other children listed on the report: Gotthelf was thirty-three years old, Emil was thirty years old, and Emma was twenty-six years old.

Elaine Evangeline Frey, the daughter of Otto and Hulda Frey was born on February 25, 1939 in the Shaw Hospital in Tripp, Hutchinson County, South Dakota. She was christened in the Frieden's United Church of Christ in Tripp, Hutchinson County, South Dakota.

On the 1940 United States Census, the Census Enumerator, Edwin H. Pope found Otto and Hulda Frey living in Oak Hollow Township in Hutchinson County, South Dakota with four chil-

dren, Otto's mother, Katherina and Otto's brother, Gotthelf.[199] The children listed on the report were Violet nine years old, Ernest six years old, Elmer two years old, and Elaine one year old. The grandmother Katharina Frey were also listed on the report. Katharina was 63 years old. A brother, Gotthelf 43 years old was also listed in the report.

Elaine Evangeline Frey grew up west of Tripp on Highway 18 and she was confirmed into the Lutheran faith at the Immanuel Lutheran Church in Douglas County, South Dakota under the direction of Rev. Leonard Eberhardt.

She attended elementary school at Prairie Mound Country School and later graduated from the Tripp High School in 1957.

Norbert John Zirpel & Elaine Evangeline Frey

Marriage & Family*

Norbert John Zirpel [253]

Between 1943 until 1951 Norbert John Zirpel worked as a farmer for Waldemar Zirpel of Parkston, in Hutchinson County, South Dakota.

Norbert John Zirpel, U. S. Air Force [254]

Back row: Ray DeWald, Ivan Baumiller, Elmer Zirpel, and Ernest Frey.
Middle row: Carol Erck, Marlene Albrecht, Norbert Zirpel, Elaine Zirpel, Darlene Frey and Rosalene Zirpel.
Ring bearer: Wayne Zirpel. Flower girl: Sandra Thum.[255]

On July 10, 1951, Norbert John Zirpel left Parkston, Douglas County, South Dakota and went to Sioux Fall, South Dakota to enter into active service in the U.S. Air Force. Norbert received training in A & E Mech. and B-29 Special Course at the Air Force Base in Sheppard, Texas. He also trained at Chanute Air Force Base in Elect, General as well as Navigation, Inc. in F-86D, Elect. He was a SSgt (T) in the Air Force before he was discharged.

Norbert John Zirpel, AF 17334573 was honorably discharged from the U.S. Air Force on July 9, 1955, according to 1st LT USAF, Lavon J. Bender. He was released from active duty at the Sioux City Air Base, Sioux City, Iowa after serving four years. Norbert received the National Defense Service Medal and the Good Conduct Medal.

Norbert John Zirpel, son of Gottfried Johan Zirpel and Gertrude Anna Gerlach, married Elaine Evangeline Frey, daughter of Otto Frey and Hulda Weisser, on June 30, 1957 at the Friedens Reformed Church in Tripp, Hutchinson County, South Dakota. The Rev. Blaufuss officiated.

The maid of honor was Darlene Frey and

Norbert John & Elaine Evangeline Zirpel[256]

149

the bridesmaid were Rosalene Zirpel, Marlene Albrecht, and Carol Erck.

The best man was Elmer Zirpel and his attendants were Ernest Frey, Ivan Baumiller, and Ray DeWald.

The ushers were Rau Thum and Wilbert Zirpel. The flower girl was Sandra Thum while Wayne Zirpel was the ring bearer.

There was a reception with about 420 guests held in the Legion Hall. Erwin Zirpel was the toastmaster during the program. Others who assisted were Mrs. Marvin Haase, Lucille Herr, Martin Zirpel, Stuart Oberg, Mrs. Clarence Haase, Alice Reiner, Mrs. Leo Weisser, Mrs. Ray Thum, Luella Zirpel, Olinda Zirpel, Marlene Haase.

After a short wedding trip, Norbert and Elaine made their first home south and southwest of Parkston, and in 1964, they moved to their new home and farm, 2 miles west and 2 1/2 miles south of the Parkston Airport.

Norbert John and Elaine Evangeline Zirpel had seven children: Charlotte Ann, David Norbert, Mark Anthony, Marjo Marie, Bruce Allen, Troy Lynn, and Kayla Rae Zirpel.

Birth of
Charlotte Ann Zirpel*

Charlotte Ann Zirpel, daughter of Norbert and Elaine Zirpel, was born on August 12, 1959 in Parkston, Hutchinson County, South Dakota.

Charlotte Ann Zirpel [257]

Birth of
David Norbert Zirpel*

David Norbert Zirpel, son of Norbert and Elaine Zirpel, was born on November 6, 1960 in Parkston, Hutchinson County, South Dakota.

David Norbert Zirpel [258]

Birth of
Mark Anthony Zirpel*

Mark Anthony Zirpel, son of Norbert and Elaine Zirpel, was born on March 27, 1962 in Parkston, Hutchinson County, South Dakota.

Mark Anthony Zirpel [259]

Birth of
Marjo Marie Zirpel*

Marjo Marie Zirpel [260]

150

Marjo Marie, daughter of Norbert and Elaine Zirpel, was born on May 4, 1967 in Parkston, Hutchinson County, South Dakota.

Birth of
Bruce Allen Zirpel*

Bruce Allen Zirpel [261]

Bruce Allen Zirpel, son of Norbert and Elaine Zirpel, was born on July 27, 1968 in Parkston, Hutchinson County, South Dakota.

Birth of
Troy Lynn Zirpel*

Troy Lynn Zirpel, son of Norbert and Elaine Zirpel, was born on July 2, 1973 in Parkston, Hutchinson County, South Dakota.

Troy Lynn Zirpel [262]

Birth of
Kayla Rae Zirpel*

Kayla Rae Zirpel, daughter of Norbert and Elaine Zirpel, was born on February 7, 1982 in Parkston, Hutchinson County, South Dakota.

Kayla Rae Zirpel [263]

Charlotte Ann Zirpel &
Gary James Adamson
Marriage & Family*

Charlotte Ann and Gary James Adamson [264]

Charlotte Ann Zirpel married Gary James Adamson on August 13, 1983 in the Faith Lutheran Church in Parkston, Hutchinson County, South Dakota.

Gary James Adamson was born on June 9, 1952.

Gary James Adamson had a daughter with a unknown person: Nicole Adamson.

Nicole Adamson was born on March 7, 1972.

Nicole Adamson married Mr. Reece.

Mr. Reece and Nicole Reece had two children: Jessica Marie and Dillion James Reece. The marriage ended in divorce.

Jessica Marie Reece was born on January 9, 1992.

Dillion James Reece was born on August 27, 1993.

Nicole Reece married Matthew Metcalf on June 26, 1999,

Matthew Metcalf was born on June 17, 1968.

Matthew and Nicole Metcalf had three children: Krisha, Carrie and Savanah Metcalf.

Krisha Metcalf was born on July 6, 1989.

Carrie Metcalf was born on July 9, 1992.

Savanah Metcalf was November 17, 1996.

In 1998, Nicole and her children moved to Texas, where she was going to school.

Gary James and Charlotte Ann Adamson had another child: Tara Leigh Adamson.

Tara Leigh Adamson was born on October 31, 1985.

In 1998, Tara worked hard at her basketball, the swim team, and confirmation. In 2003, Tara was selected to go to All State where she was also named the player of the year on the volleyball team. She also went to State for Declam and won.

Charlotte Adamson worked as a teacher in 1998, and also worked at her brother-in-laws steak house on weekends.

Gary Adamson worked as an electrician in 1998. He also enjoys hunting and fishing.

Pamela Suzan Fenske & Family*

Eugene Ernest Fenske, the son of Ernest Fenske and Christina Jerke, was born on July 10, 1933 in Beadle County, South Dakota.

Eugene Ernest Fenske married Virginia "Gin" Walz on May 20, 1953 in Pipestone, Pipestone County, Minnesota.

Eugene served in the U.S. Air Force.

Eugene Ernest and Virginia Fenske had two children: Gregory and Pamela Suzan Fenske.

Pamela Suzan Fenske was born on December 26, 1954.

Gregory Fenske was born in a unknown year and his death was in 1989.

Eugene Ernest Fenske died on Friday, March 7, 2014 at the SunQuest Healthcare Center in Huron, Beadle County, South Dakota. He was buried in Riverside Cemetery, in Huron, Beadle County, South Dakota with Military honors.

David Norbert Zirpel & Pamela Suzan Fenske Marriage & Family*

Pamela Suzan and David Norbert Zirpel [265]

David Norbert Zirpel married Pamela Suzan Fenske, daughter of Eugene and Virginia Fenske on August 10, 1985 in the Faith Lutheran Church in Parkston, Hutchinson County, South Dakota.

David Norbert and Pamela Suzan Zirpel have three children: Christina Ann, Caleb David and Zac Zirpel.

Christina Ann Zirpel was born on January 16, 1990.

In 1998, Christina Zirpel was busy with piano, violin, dance, Church and Sunday School choir.

In 2002, Christina Zirpel was busy with confirmation, violin as well as other school and church activities.

In 2003, Christina Zirpel was in confirmation, volleyball, basketball, gymnastics as well as playing the violin.

Caleb David Zirpel was born on June 9, 1995.

In 2003, Caleb Zirpel enjoyed swimming. Zac Zirpel was born on September 25, 1997.

In 1998, Pamela Zirpel was teaching and working on her Masters Degree. In 2003, Pamela was working as a substitute teacher.

Christina Ann, David Norbert, Pamela Suzan and Caleb David Zirpel [266]

In May of 2002, David Norbert Zirpel took a call to Sioux City. It was a large change from a small church to a large one, as well as moving from a small town into a large city. David bought their first home.

David Norbert Zirpel, formerly of Parkston, South Dakota was installed as an Associate Pastor at the Redeemer Lutheran Church in Sioux City, Iowa at 3 pm on Sunday June 2, 2002, at the church.

David Norbert Zirpel was a 1991 graduate of the Concordia Seminary in St. Louis, Missouri and he was ordained into the office of Holy Ministry.

David Norbert Zirpel was a pastor for the eight years at the Concordia Lutheran Church in Bourbon, Missouri.

Before entering the seminary, David had been a high school English Teacher in Phillip, South Dakota.

Mark Anthony Zirpel & Lori Ann Thuringer Marriage & Family*

Mark Anthony Zirpel married Lori Ann Thuringer on August 18, 1984 in the Faith Lutheran Church in Parkston, Hutchinson County, South Dakota.

Lori Ann Thuringer was born on August 8, 1965.

Mark Anthony and Lori Ann Zirpel have four children: Ryan Mark, Tyler Jerome, Myles Wendlin and Callie Christine Zirpel.

Ryan Mark Zirpel was born on May 21, 1986. In 2003, Ryan enjoyed football, wresting and basketball.

Tyler Jerome Zirpel was born on May 27, 1988. In 2003, Tyler also enjoyed football, wresting, and basketball.

Lori Ann and Mark Anthony Zirpel [267]

Back row: Lori Ann and Mark Anthony Zirpel. Front row: Tyler Jerome, Ryan Mark and Myles Wendlin Zirpel [268]

Myles Wendlin Zirpel was born on November 15, 1989. Myles enjoyed football, wresting and basketball as his brothers.

Callie Christine Zirpel was born on August 5, 1993. In 2003, Callie enjoyed basketball, piano and church choir.

Mark keeps himself busy running the farm. The kids even had a few sheep.

In 1998, Lori started a new job as a wicker saleswoman. In 2002, Lori started working at the new Grain Elevator in Parkston. In 2002, Lori was the Youth Director at Faith Lutheran Church.

Ryan Mark Zirpel [269]

Tyler Jerome Zirpel & Mallory Marie Muntefering Marriage *

Mallory Marie and Tyler Jerome Zirpel [270]

Mallory Marie Muntefering, daughter of Mike Muntefering and Denice Freier, was born on January 1, 1989.

Mallory is a 2007 graduate of Parkston High School in Parkston, South Dakota. Mallory also a 2011 graduate of South Dakota State University with a bachelor's degree in pharmaceutical science and she received her doctor of Pharmacy in 2013. She works as a Pharmacist at the Avera St. Benedict Hospital in Parkston, South Dakota and Lewis Drug in Mitchell, South Dakota.

Tyler Jerome Zirpel is a graduate of Parkston High School in Parkston, South Dakota. Tyler is

also a graduate of South Dakota State University with a bachelor's degree in general agriculture. Tyler works as a Syngenta seed advisor in Parkston, South Dakota.

Tyler Jerome Zirpel, son of Mark Anthony and Lori Ann Zirpel, married Mallory Marie Muntefering, daughter of Mike Muntefering and Denice Freier on June 29, 2013 in the Salem United Church of Christ in Parkston, Hutchinson County, South Dakota.

Marjo Marie Zirpel & Roger Lawrence Soukup Marriage & Family*

Marjo Marie and Roger Lawrence Soukup [271]

Marjo Marie Zirpel married Roger Lawrence Soukup, son of Lawrence David Soukup and Shirley Cihak, on January 3, 1992.

Roger Lawrence Soukup was born on February 16, 1960.

Roger Lawrence and Marjo Marie Soukup have five children: Tyrel Lawrence, Austin Lee, Gina Jo, Kristan Kay, and Lance Joseph Soukup.

Tyrel Lawrence Soukup was born on February 2, 1984.

Austin Lee Soukup was born on April 16, 1994.

Gina Jo Soukup was on January 31, 1996.

Kristan Kay Soukup was born on April 30, 1998.

Lance Joseph Soukup was born on February 16, 2001.

In 1998, Marjo Soukup worked a Representative of AAL. In 2003, Marjo still worked with AAL Insurance and also at the hospital as a nurse.

Roger Soukup kept himself busy with cattle and farming.

Bruce Allen Zirpel & Kara Lynn Larson Marriage & Family*

Back row: Bruce Allen and Kara Lynn Zirpel
Front row: Brenna Kathryn and Brock Allen Zirpel [273]

Kara Lynn and Bruce Allen Zirpel [272]

Bruce Allen Zirpel married Kara Lynn Larson on August 7, 1992.

Kara Lynn Larson was born on December 14, 1968.

Bruce Allen and Kara Lynn Zirpel have three children: Ashley, Brenna Kathryn and Brock Allen Zirpel.

Ashley (Hicks) Zirpel was born in March of 1991.

Brenna Kathryn Zirpel was born on January 4, 1998.

Brock Allen Zirpel was born on June 5, 2001.

Bruce Zirpel worked with AAL Insurance in 2003.

In 1998, Kara helped Bruce with office work.

Troy Lynn Zirpel & Heather Dawn Van Leuven Marriage & Family*

Troy Lynn and Heather Dawn Zirpel [274]

Heather Dawn Van Leuven had two children: Jordan Clark and Kylee Hope Van Leuven.

Jordon Clark Van Leuven was born on June 26, 1991.

Kylee Hope Van Leuven was born on July 16, 1993.

Troy Lynn Zirpel married Heather Van Leuven on June 16, 2007.

Troy Lynn and Heather Dawn Zirpel have one additional child: Brody James Zirpel.

Brody James Zirpel was born on September 4, 2008.

In 1998, Troy Zirpel was working with Pri-America Financial Services in Mesa, Arizona. In 2003, Troy was living in Arizona and working with Investments.

Norbert John Zirpel's family in 2000. Back row: Tara Leigh Adamson, Lori Ann Zirpel, Mark Anthony Zirpel, Charlotte Ann Adamson, Gary James Adamson, Troy Lynn Zirpel, Pamela Suzan Zirpel, David Norbert Zirpel, and Kayla Rae Zirpel. Middle Row: Roger Lawrence Soukup holding Kristina Kay Soukup, Marjo Marie Soukup, Callie Christine Zirpel, Elaine Evangeline Zirpel, Norbert John Zirpel, Kara Lynn Zirpel holding Brenna Kathryn Zirpel, Bruce Allen Zirpel. Front row: Gina Jo Soukup, Christina Ann Zirpel, Tyler Jerome Zirpel, Austin Lee Soukup, Ryan Mark Zirpel, Myles Wendlin Zirpel, and Caleb David Zirpel. [275]

Norbert John Zirpel's family in 2007.
4th row: David Norbert Zirpel, Roger Lawrence Soukup, Myles Wendlin Zirpel, Mark Anthony Zirpel, Tyler Jerome Zirpel, and Gary James Adamson. 3rd row: Jordan Clark Van Leuven, Troy Lynn Zirpel, Christina Ann Zirpel, Norbert John Zirpel, Elaine Evangeline Zirpel, Ryan Mark Zirpel, Reece Proctor, Tara Leigh Adamson, and Bruce Allen Zirpel. 2nd row: Kylee Van Leuven, Heather Dawn Zirpel, Pamela Suzan Zirpel, Marjo Marie Soukup, Lori Ann Zirpel, Kayla Rae Zirpel-Proctor, Charlotte Ann Adamson, and Kara Lynn Zirpel. 1st row: Caleb David Zirpel, Austin Lee Soukup, Lance Joseph Soukup, Callie Christine Zirpel, Brock Allen Zirpel and Brenna Kathryn Zirpel. [276]

Kayla Rae Zirpel & Mark Proctor Marriage & Family*

In 1998, Kayla Rae Zirpel was excited when she was chosen as first chair Flute in the All-State Orchestra. She had auditions against forty other flutists. She also tubed down the Niobrara River as well as attended the National Youth Gathering in Atlanta, Georgia.

In 2003, Kayla was a junior at Brooking, South Dakota, she worked at Perkins and cleaned homes. Kayla also went to California with the State Marching Band in the New Year's Parade as they were the fifth entry.

In 2003, Kayla graduated from college in May, she planned on attending chiropractic school that next fall.

Kayla Rae Zirpel married Mark Proctor on June 19, 2004 in the Pierre State Capital Rotunda, Pierre, Hughes County, South Dakota.

Kayla Rae and Mark Proctor [277]

Reece, Mark and Kayla Rae Proctor [278]

Mark Proctor was born on June 19, 1969.

Mark and Kayla Proctor have one son: Reece Proctor.

Reece Proctor was born on July 1, 1992.

Norbert John & Elaine Evangeline Zirpel - The Later Years*

Norbert John and Elaine Evangeline Zirpel
50th Wedding Anniversary [279]

In 1998, Norbert sold seed and oil. He was the Church Secretary for one year.

In 2002 and 2003 Norbert kept busy reading and studying the markets as well as working seed and oil orders and also helping Mark with the farm.

Elaine planted large gardens, raised chickens, ducks, and geese. She canned (pickles were her specialty), and baked bread as well as kuchen.

Elaine also taught Sunday School and VBS and participated in the LWML and Valentine Luncheon projects at Faith Lutheran Church. In the community Elaine volunteered in the Farmer's Union and Thrivent (AAL) projects for 30 years. She enjoyed visiting with people and she always made time for her children and grandchildren by cooking for them, playing cards, and Arizona aggravations, and attending their activities.

Elaine Zirpel received an award from Bonnie Geyer, South Dakota Farmer Union, for 30 years of service. The award was presented at the annual Farmers Union Educational Honors Luncheon

157

which was held during the 95th annual South Dakota Farmers Union convention.

Bonnie Geyer and Elaine Evangeline Zirpel [280]

German Kuchen by Elaine Zirpel

1/4 cup of granulated sugar
1 cup Milk, scalded
1 tsp. salt
1/4 cup salad oil
3 1/4 cups of flour
cinnamon
1 large beaten egg
1 pkg. dry yeast
Any kind of fruit or
Cottage cheese or
Poppy seed

Pour the warm milk over the sugar and yeast; let set for about 5-10 minutes. Add salt, egg, oil, and flour. Mix until soft, might be a little sticky. Let rise until double. Roll out like pie crust 1/4 inch thick. Fit into greased pie tins. You can use a little more flour if needed to roll out. Add any kind of fruit you want. Put custard on top. Sprinkle with cinnamon. Let rise; bake at 350 degrees for about 20 minutes. Top and bottom should be golden brown.

CUSTARD FILLING:

1 cup cream or half and half
1/2 cup sugar
1 tsp. Vanilla
1 egg beaten
1 Tsp. Flour (1 1/2 Tsp. if half and half used)

Mix first 4 ingredients together. Cook this in the microwave until think, stir about every 5 minutes. Add the vanilla. VARIATIONS: Take some of filling and add cottage cheese, as much as you like. Or add poppy seed that has been soaking in milk to part of the filling.

STREUSEL TOPPING:

3/4 cup sugar   3/4 cup flour
1/4 cup oleo or margarine

Mix until crumbly, Put on top of fruit and filling; sprinkle with cinnamon. Or you can just spread the dough with butter and put the streusel on top. You can spread the dough with butter and sprinkle with graduated sugar and cinnamon to top.

FOR CINNAMON BREAD:

Take some sweet dough as for kuchen and roll out. Spread oleo or butter; sprinkle lots of cinnamon on top. Roll up and put into a greased bread pan and let rise; bake at 350 degrees for about 20-30 minutes.

FOR TEA BUNS:

Roll the kuchen dough into small balls in your hand and pinch the ends. Put in greased bread pan; let rise and bake at 350 degrees for 20 minutes.

FOR CARMEL ROLLS:

Roll the kuchen dough and spread with oleo or butter and sugar; sprinkle cinnamon. Put about 1/4 cup brown sugar on the bottom of a 9 x 13 pan. Pour 3/4 cup of warm water around the rolls that have been cut 1/4 inch thick and placed into pan. Bake at 350 degrees for about 20 minutes. Tip upside down on cookie sheet and leave 5 minutes so caramel can drip off.

Elaine Evangeline Zirpel died on January 8, 2013 while in the Avera McKennan Hospital in Sioux Falls, Minnehaha County, South Dakota. Her funeral was held at the Faith Lutheran Church in Parkston, South Dakota with Rev. Kenneth Soyk officiating. She was buried in the Parkston Protestant Cemetery, Parkston, South Dakota.

Survivors included her husband, Norbert John Zirpel; 7 children: Charlotte Ann (Gary James) Adamson of Centerville, South Dakota; David Norbert (Pamela Suzan) Zirpel of Sioux City, Iowa; Mark Anthony (Lori Ann) Zirpel of Parkston, South Dakota; Marjo Marie (Roger Lawrence) Soukup of Lake Andes, South Dakota; Bruce Allen (Kara Lynn) Zirpel of Omaha, Nebraska; Troy Lynn (Heather Dawn) Zirpel of Maricopa, Arizona; and Kayla Rae (Mark) Proctor of St. Paul, Minnesota. 21 grandchildren, 8 great-grandchildren and 1 great-great grandchild; 1 sister, Darlene (Marvin) Holce of Tabor, South Dakota and 1 brother, Elmer (Marlene) Frey of West

Bend, Wisconsin; in-laws: Lillian Esther Zirpel of Mitchel, South Dakota, Elmer Gottfried and Luella Mae Zirpel of Appleton, Wisconsin, Clifford E. (Rosalene Gertrude) Roth of Huron, South Dakota, Harold Walter (Mary Ellen Ruth) Mettenbrink of Sioux City, Iowa; 2 aunts: Mrs. Otto (Lorraine) Weisser and Mrs. Albert (Esther) Weisser, and 36 nieces and nephews.

Preceding her in death were her parents: Otto and Hulda Frey; brother: Ernest Frey; sister: Violet Thum; in-laws: Ray Thum, Marlene Frey, William Wenzel, Leonard and Johnny (Maud B.) Zirpel, Wilbert Erich and Audrey May Zirpel, Erwin Karl and Olinda Leota Zirpel, Harold Arnold and Virginia Margaret Zirpel, and Richard Edwin Mehlhaff, and 7 nieces and nephews.

Virginia Margaret Weber & Her Family*

William Adam Weber, son of John G. and Mary E. Weber was born on November 4, 1900 in Hutchinson County, South Dakota. William was also Virginia Weber's father.

William Adam Weber was recorded on the 1920 United States Census living with his parents, John G. and Mary E. Weber, in Cross Plains Township, Hutchinson County, South Dakota on January 21, 1920 by the Census Enumerator, Roscoe Daniels.[200] On this report John G. Weber was 48 years old and he was born in Wisconsin. Also on this report Mary E. Weber was 45 years old and she was born in Iowa. There were eight children listed on the report. They were Charles H. 20 years old, William A. 19 years old, Anna M. 17 years old, Joseph A. 15 years old, George A. 13 years old, Elizabeth S. 12 years old, Francis K. 10 years old and Eleanor E. 8 years old.

Elizabeth Mary Weber, daughter of Henry and Margaret Weber, was born on August 21, 1900 in South Dakota. Elizabeth was also Virginia Weber's mother.

Elizabeth Mary Weber was recorded on the 1920 United States Census living with her parents, Henry and Margaret Weber on January 30, 1920 in Rome Township, Hutchinson County, South Dakota by the Census Enumerator, Michael J. Loyne.[201] Both Henry and Margaret Weber were born in Wisconsin. Henry was listed as 46 years old while Margaret was 41 years old. There were seven children on the report. They were Elizabeth M. nineteen years old, Frank N. seventeen years

old, Rosa K. fifteen years old, Michael H. thirteen years old, Martha M. ten years old, Arthur F. seven years old and Katherine M. three years old.

William Adam Weber, son of John G. and Mary E. Weber married Elizabeth Mary Weber, daughter of Henry and Margaret Weber on on January 22, 1924 in Dimock, Hutchinson County, South Dakota according to the South Dakota Marriage Index.[202]

William Adam and Elizabeth Mary Weber were recorded on the 1930 United States Census on April 25, 1930 living in Cross Plains Township, Hutchinson County, South according to the Census Enumerator, J. B. Mueller.[203] William and Elizabeth were twenty-nine years old. There were three children listed on the report. They were Delbert five years old, Alfred three years and five months old, and Velora M. nine months old.

Virginia Margaret Weber, daughter of William Adam and Elizabeth Mary Weber was born on November 21, 1937 in Parkston, Hutchinson County, South Dakota.

On April 13, 1940, the Census Enumerator, Otto M. Lundy, recorded Virginia Margaret living with her parents, William Adam and Elizabeth Mary Weber in Cross Plains Township, Hutchinson County, South Dakota.[204] There were six children listed on the report. They were Delbert fifteen years old, Alfred thirteen years old, Velora Mae ten years old, Jeanette four years old and Virginia two years old.

Harold Arnold Zirpel & Virginia Margaret Weber Marriage & Family*

Harold Arnold and Virginia Margaret Zirpel 1957 [281]

Harold Arnold Zirpel served in the U.S. Navy for four years, between 1954 and 1958.

Harold Arnold Zirpel, son of Gottfried John Zirpel and Gertrude Anna Gerlach, married Virginia Margaret Weber, daughter of William Adam and Elizabeth Mary Weber, on July 13, 1957 in San Jose, San Diego County, California.

Harold Arnold and Virginia Margaret Zirpel had one child: Douglas William Zirpel.

Birth of
Douglas William Zirpel*

Douglas William Zirpel was born on June 23, 1958 in San Diego, San Diego County, California. He was christened in September of 1958 at the home of Gottfried John and Gertrude Anna Zirpel's home in Lincoln Township, Douglas County, South Dakota according to his Aunt Mary Ellen Mettenbrink.

Douglas William Zirpel confirmation. [282]

Douglas William Zirpel [283]

Kevin Eugene Fazendin &
Georgia Carol Mayer
Marriage & Family*

Georgia Carol Mayer was born on September 14, 1952 in Townsend, Broadwater County, Montana and she was christened on October 13, 1952 in Helena, Lewis and Clark County, Montana.

Kevin Eugene Fazendin was born on May 28, 1950.

There is a record of Kevin Eugene Fazendin serving in the Military between April 30, 1969 until January 31, 1973, according to the U.S. Department of Veterans Affair BIRDS Death File, 1850-2010.

Kevin Eugene Fazendin married Georgia Carol Mayer on July 31, 1971 in San Joaquin County, California according to California Marriage Index, 1960-1985. No record of a divorce was located.

Kevin Eugene and Georgia Carol Fazendin had one child: Tonya Rochelle Fazendin.

Tonya Rochelle Fazendin was born on January 21, 1974 in Sonora, Tuolumne County, California. She was christened on July 9, 1981 in Manteca, San Joaquin County, California.

Kevin Eugene Fazendin died on February 13, 1978 according to the California Death Index, 1940-1997.

He was buried in Greenlawn Memorial Park in Bakersfield, Kern County, California according to the California, Find a Grave Index, 1775-2012.

Georgia Carol Fazendin either took her maiden back after a divorce from Kevin or after his death, no record of change found.

Douglas William Zirpel &
Georgia Carol Mayer
Marriage & Family*

Georgia Carol (Mayor) Zirpel [284]

Douglas William Zirpel married Georgia Carol Mayer on May 17, 1980 in San Jose, San Diego County, California. The marriage ended in divorce 1995.

Douglas William and Georgia Carol Zirpel had two children: Eryn Elizabeth and Karl Douglas Zirpel.

Eryn Elizabeth Zirpel was born on May 26, 1981 in Manteca, San Joaquin County, California and she was christened on July 19, 1981 in Manteca, San Joaquin County, California.

Douglas William Zirpel holding Eryn Elizabeth Zirpel, Tonya Rochelle Fazendin standing in front of Georgia Carol Zirpel, Virginia Margaret Zirpel and Harold Arnold Zirpel 1982. [285]

Karl Douglas Zirpel, Tonya Rochelle Fazendin and Eryn Elizabeth Zirpel 1991 [286]

Karl Douglas Zirpel was born on November 3, 1983 in Stockton, San Diego County, California and he was christened on January 19, 1984 in Manteca, San Joaquin County, California.

In 1998, Eryn was the Homecoming Queen in October of that year. Eryn also received some awards for her volleyball.

In 2002, Eryn Elizabeth Zirpel had completed her second year of college and graduated with her Associate Arts Degree that May. She also coached the High School Volleyball and worked at a local market.

In 2003, Eryn Elizabeth Zirpel was a junior at Stanislaus State College and she had been working on her business major.

In 1998, Karl Douglas Zirpel received award for his soccer.

In 2002, Karl graduated High School that May and in the fall enrolled as a freshman at Cal State College in Long Beach, California. He was an active member of the SAE Fraternity.

In December 2003, Karl Zirpel started a new job as host at a local restaurant.

In March of 2011, according Douglas Zirpel, his father, Karl Douglas Zirpel had taken a new position and he lived closer to the Kodak Theater and he was only four blocks away fro the Academy Awards.

In 2002 and 2003, Douglas William Zirpel was working at Dun & Bradstreet. He had been with the company for over 20 years.

Douglas William Zirpel enjoyed riding his Harley in his spare time.

Harold Zirpel Family 2003.
Back row standing:
Karl Douglas Zirpel, Tonya Rochelle Fazendin, Eryn Elizabeth Zirpel and Douglas William Zirpel.
Front row sitting: Harold Arnold and Virginia Margaret Zirpel. [287]

Eryn Elizabeth Zirpel & Aaron Michael Bowers Marriage & Family*

Eryn Elizabeth Zirpel married Aaron Michael Bowers on July 5, 2005 in Oakdale, Stanislaus County, California.

Aaron Michael Bowers was born on July 31, 1981 in San Jose, San Diego County, California.

Aaron Michael Bowers is a purchasing agent for Florsheim Homes in Stockton, California.

In 2006, Eryn Elizabeth and Aaron Michael Bowers were living in Modesto, California. Eryn had been working as a High School Teacher at East Union High School in Manteca, California.

In March of 2011, according to Douglas William Zirpel, his son-in-law, Aaron Michael Bowers was in Construction Management for the Stockton Unified School District.

In March of 2011, according to Douglas William Zirpel, his daughter, Eryn Elizabeth Bowers was a High School Business Teacher.

Aaron Michael and Eryn Elizabeth Bowers have one child: Payton Aryn Bowers.

Aaron Michael, Payton Aryn and
Eryn Elizabeth Bowers [288]

Birth of
Payton Aryn Bowers*

Payton Aryn Bowers [289]

Payton Aryn Bowers was born on September 18, 2011 in Fort Pierre, Stanley County, South Dakota.

Harold Arnold &
Virginia Margaret Zirpel -
The Later Years*

Harold Arnold and Virginia Margaret Zirpel
25th Wedding Anniversary 1982 [290]

Harold Arnold and Virginia Margaret Zirpel moved to the San Jose, California area in 1959 and they continued living there until 2004 when they moved to Manteca, California.

Harold Arnold Zirpel retired from the Pacific Gas and Electric Company in San Jose, California after 25 years of service.

Harold Arnold Zirpel 2001 [291]

Harold Arnold Zirpel like to create stuff with coins and wooden. He created a picture with coins for a friend who had been having a 50th Wedding Anniversary.

Harold Arnold Zirpel with his bird house Mailbox [292]

Harold also loved to work with wood, and he made a bird house mailbox and also a box for playing Bingo.

Harold Arnold Zirpel with his box for playing Bingo [293]

Virginia Margaret Zirpel died on September 25, 2006 in Manteca, San Joaquin County, California after thirteen and 1/2 years and 67 chemotherapy treatments for ovarian cancer.

Her funeral service was held on September 27, 2006 at the Parkview Cemetery on the French Cap Road and Funeral Home in Stockton, San Diego County, California. It is assumed that Virginia was buried in the Parkview Cemetery, but no records are found.

Virginia Margaret Zirpel was survived by her husband, Harold Arnold Zirpel of Manteca, California; a son, Douglas William Zirpel of Manteca, California; three grandchildren: Tonya Rochelle Fazendin, Eryn Elizabeth Bowers, and Karl Douglas Zirpel; a brother, Alfred Weber, of Whittier, California; a sister, Jeanette Weiss, of Mitchell, South Dakota.

She was preceded in death by her parents, William Adam and Elizabeth Mary Weber; a brother, Delbert Weber; and a sister, Velora Bocker.

Harold Arnold Zirpel died on April 1, 2007 while in the Memorial Medical Center in Modesto, Stanislaus County, California. His funeral services were held at the Parkview Funeral Home in Manteca, California on April 5, 2007. His Burial was in the Parkview Cemetery on the French Cap Road in Manteca, San Joaquin County, California.

He was a member of the United Lutheran church in Manteca, California.

Harold was survived by his son, Douglas William Zirpel of Manteca, California; two brothers: Norbert John Zirpel, of Parkston, South Dakota; and Elmer Gottfried Zirpel, of Appleton, Wisconsin; two sisters: Rosalene Gertrude Roth, of Huron, South Dakota; and Mary Ellen Ruth Mettenbrink, of Sioux City, Iowa; three grandchildren: Eryn Elizabeth Bowers and Tonya Rochelle Fazendin, of Manteca, California; and Karl Douglas Zirpel, of Pasadena, California; sister-in-laws: Jeanette Weiss, of Mitchell, South Dakota; and Doris Weber, of Whitehouse, Texas; brother-in-law: Alfred Weber, of Whittier, California; and numerous nieces and nephews.

He was preceded in by his wife, and his parents, and brothers: Wilbert Erich Zirpel, Leonard Robert Zirpel, and Erwin Karl Zirpel.

Clifford Edwin Roth & His Family*

Lehart G. Roth, son of George Roth and Elizabeth Sayler was born on November 6, 1904 in Hutchinson County, South Dakota.

William Sedlezky, Elsie Sedlezky's father [294]

163

William Sedlezky was born on January 1, 1877 in a unknown location.

Amalia Ibis was born on September 29, 1873in a unknown location.

William Sedlezky married Amalia Ibis on October 27, 1912 in a unknown location.

Elsie Sedlesky, daughter of William Sedlezky and Amalia Ibis was born on April 25, 1912 in South Dakota.

Amalia (Ibis) Sedlezky, Elsie Sedlezky's mother [295]

Lehart G. Roth, son of George Roth and Elizabeth Sayler married Elsie Sedlezky, daughter of William Sedlezky and Amalia Ibis on June 28, 1931 in Freeman, Hutchinson County, South Dakota.

Lehart and Elsie Sedlezky [313]

Clifford Edwin Roth, son of Lehart G. Roth and Elsie Sedlezky, was born on November 28, 1937 in South Dakota.

Clifford Edwin Roth Confirmation 1953 [297]

Clifford Edwin Roth 1956 [298]

William Sedlezky died on August 6, 1949 and Amalia Sedlezky died on July 20, 1972.

Clifford Edwin Roth was recorded on April 18, 1940 by the Census Enumerator, Paul P. Kleinsasser, living with his parents, Lehart G. and Elsie Roth in Wolf Creek Township, Hutchinson County, South Dakota.[205] Lehart was listed as 35 years old and a wage or salary worker in Government work. Elsie was listed as 27 years old. There were four children reported on the census.

There were Violet seven years old, Lillian six years old, Arnold four years old and Clifford two years old.

Lehart G. Roth died in January of 1977 in Edinburg, Hidalgo County, Texas. He was buried in the Freeman Unity Lutheran Cemetery in Freeman, Hutchinson County, South Dakota.

Elsie Roth died on March 6, 2006 and she was buried in the Freeman Unity Lutheran Cemetery in Freeman, Hutchinson County, South Dakota.

Rosalene Gertrude Zirpel & Clifford Edwin Roth Marriage & Family*

Rosalene Gertrude and Clifford Edwin Roth [299

Rosalene Gertrude Zirpel, daughter of Gottfried John Zirpel and Gertrude Anna Gerlach, married Clifford Edwin Roth, son of Lehart G. Roth and Elsie Sedlezky, on November 24, 1957 in the Immanuel Lutheran Church in Douglas County, South Dakota.

Clifford Edwin and Rosalene Gertrude Roth had six children: Cynthia Rose, Gaylen Clifford, Carla Jean, Carol Ann, Darin Lee and Stacy Rae Roth.

Birth of Cynthia Rose Roth*

Cynthia Rose Roth was born on October 24, 1958 in Parkston, Hutchinson County, South Dakota.

Cynthia Rose Roth [300]

Birth of Gaylen Clifford Roth*

Gaylen Clifford Roth was born on April 13, 1960 in Huron, Beadle County, South Dakota.

Gaylen Clifford Roth [301]

Birth of Carla Jean Roth*

Carla Jean Roth was born on September 1961 in Huron, Beadle County, South Dakota.

Unfortunately, Carla Jean Roth who had been in the third grade at the Wilson School died on January 20, 1970 in Huron, Beadle County, South Dakota.

Carol Baumiller, Jerry Roth, Mary Ellen Ruth Zirpel, Arnold Roth, Rosalene Gertrude Roth, Clifford Erwin Roth, Elaine Evangeline Zirpel, Norbert John Zirpel, Lillian Roth and Harley Thomas.
Flower Girl: Trudy Roth. Ring Bearer: Wilbert Lee Zirpel. [302]

Carla Jean Roth about 1964 [303]

kota; four grandparents: Lehart G. and Elsie Roth and Gottfried Johan and Gertrude Anna Zirpel, all of Parkston, South Dakota; and one great-grandparent, Mrs. William Sedlesky, of Freeman, South Dakota.

Funeral service were held on January 23, 1970 at the American Lutheran Church in Huron, South Dakota. The Rev. Erling Erickson officiated.

Survivors were her parents, Clifford Edwin and Rosalene Gertrude Roth; two brothers: Gaylen Clifford Roth and Darin Lee Roth, of Huron, South Dakota; two sisters: Cynthia Rose Roth and Carol Ann Roth, of Huron, South Da-

Carla Jean Roth [304]

166

Birth of
Carol Ann Roth*

Carol Ann Roth was born on December 21, 1963 in Huron, Beadle County, South Dakota.

Carol Ann Roth [305]

Birth of
Darin Lee Roth *

Darin Lee Roth was born on January 28, 1967 in Huron, Beadle County, South Dakota.

Darin Lee Roth [306]

Birth of
Stacy Rae Roth*

Stacy Rae Roth was born on August 26, 1976 in Huron, Beadle County, South Dakota.

Stacy Rae Roth [307]

Cynthia Rose Roth &
John Brinks Marriage *

Cynthia Rose Roth married John Brinks on May 1, 1982. The marriage ended in divorce. John Brinks was born September 13, 1956.

Cynthia Rose Brinks &
Brent Bernell York
Marriage & Family*

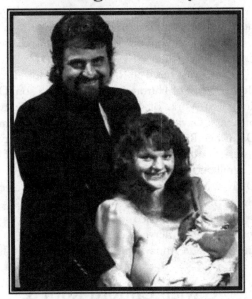

Brent Bernell, Cynthia Rose and
Dakota Red York [308]

Cynthia Rose (Roth) Brinks married Brent Bernell York on December 18, 1991 in Terre Haute, Vigo County, Indiana.

167

Brent Bernell York was born on July 21, 1953.

Brent Bernell and Cynthia Rose York had one child: Dakota Red York.

Dakota Red York was born on December 8, 1991 in Indiana.

Dakota Red York [309]

Cynthia Rose York died at her home on December 17, 2011 in Huron, Beadle County, South Dakota.

There was a memorial service at the Welter Funeral Home with cremains burial in the Riverside Cemetery on December 21, 2011.

Cynthia Rose York loved to paint and spent time with her family.

She was survived by her husband, Brent Bernell York of Huron, South Dakota; a son, Dakota Red York, of Huron, South Dakota; two brothers: Gaylen Clifford and Rebecca Roth, and Darin Lee Roth, all of Huron, South Dakota; two sisters: Carol Ann and Wayne Lester Thedorff of Vermillion, South Dakota and Stacy Bertera of Detroit, Michigan; and many aunts, uncles, nieces and nephews.

She was preceded in death by a sister, Carla Jean Roth and her grandparents: Gottfried John and Gertrude Anna Zirpel; and Lehart and Elsie Roth.

Gaylen Clifford Roth & Rebecca Marie Kuehl Marriage & Family*

Rebecca Marie Kuehl, daughter of Marcus J. and Anita Kuehl was born on December 21, 1962

in Yale, Beadle County, South Dakota.

Gaylen Clifford Roth, son of Clifford Edwin and Rosalene Gertrude Roth, of Huron, married Rebecca Marie Kuehl, daughter of Marcus J. and Anita Kuehl, of Yale, South Dakota, on January 16, 1982 by the Rev. James Hahn at the Trinity Lutheran Church in Yale, South Dakota.

Attendants included Dawn Boetel, maid of honor; Russell Mager, best man; Victoria Squire and Jennifer Kuehl, bridesmaids; Leo Pollock and Sherman Roth, groomsmen.

Usher were Mark Kuehl and John Frederick Zirpel.

Laurie Bich was the personal attendant.

The bride was a 1981 graduate of Iroquois High School and employed by Country Kitchen.

The groom was a 1978 Huron High School graduate and was employed at Roth Plumbing and Heating.

Gaylen Clifford and Rebecca Marie Roth had two children: Ryan Gaylen and Patrick Clifford Roth.

Gaylen Clifford and Rebecca Marie Roth [310]

Ryan Gaylen Roth, Patrick Clifford Roth and Clifford Edwin Roth [311]

168

Ryan Gaylen Roth was born on July 15, 1984 in Casper, Natrona County, Wyoming.

Patrick Clifford Roth was born on April 25, 1988 in Casper, Natrona County, Wyoming.

Ryan Gaylen Roth & Kadie Jo Floberg Marriage & Family*

Kadie Jo and Ryan Gaylen Roth [312]

Ryan Gaylen Roth married Kadie Jo Floberg, daughter of Leonard and Nancy Floberg on June 30, 2006 in Detroit Lake, Becker County, Minnesota.

Kadie Jo Floberg was born on November 1, 1983.

Ryan Gaylen and Kadie Jo Roth have two children: Kayleigh and Rylen James Roth.

Kayleigh Jo Roth was born on October 18, 2007 in Fargo, Cass County, North Dakota.

Rylen James Roth was born on November 3, 2010 in Fargo, Cass County, North Dakota.

Rylen James and Kayleigh Jo Roth [313]

Kadie Jo, Rylen James, Ryan Gaylen and Kayleigh Jo Roth [314]

Carol Ann Roth & Russell Mager Marriage & Family*

Carol Ann Roth married Russell Mager on July 3, 1981. The marriage ended in divorce.

Russell and Carol Ann Mager had one child: Jared Wayne Mager.

Jared Wayne Mager was born on November 25, 1981.

Carol Ann Mager & Wayne Lester Thedorff Marriage & Family*

Carol Ann, Wayne L., and Jared Wayne Thedoroff [315]

Carol Ann Mager married Wayne Lester Thedorff on October 4, 1986 in Vermillion, Clay County, South Dakota.

Wayne Lester Thedorff adopted Jared Wayne Mager.

Wayne Lester Thedorff was born on October 4, 1986 in South Dakota.

Wayne Lester and Carol Ann Thedorff had one child: Tyler Clair Thedorff.

Tyler Clair Thedorff was born on March 26, 1989 in Yankton, Yankton County, South Dakota.

Tyler Clair Thedorff [316]

Jared Wayne Thedorff & Andrea Rae Blaha Marriage & Family*

Andrea Rae, Owen Charles, and Jared Wayne Thedoroff [317]

Jared Wayne Thedorff married Andrea Rae Blaha on August 12, 2006 in Vermillion, Clay County, South Dakota.

Andrea Rae Blaha was born on August 5, 1981 in South Dakota.

Jared Wayne and Andrea Rae Thedorff had two children: Owen Charles and Cole Lincoln Thedorff.

Owen Charles Thedorff was born on June 3, 2010 in Rapid City, Pennington County, South Dakota.

Cole Lincoln Thedorff was born on may 3, 2012 in Rapid City, Pennington County, South Dakota.

Cole Lincoln Thedoroff [318]

Stacy Rae Roth & William Anthony Bertera III Marriage & Family*

Back row: Amanda Rose. Middle row: William Anthony III, and Samantha Rae. Front row: Stacy Rae Bertera. [319]

Stacy Rae Roth married William Anthony Bertera III on March 8, 1997 in Livonia, Wayne County, Michigan.

William Anthony Bertera III was born on July 25, 1970 in Wayne County, Michigan.

William Anthony III and Stacy Rae Bertera had two children: Amanda Rose and Samantha Rae Bertera.

Amanda Rose Bertera was born on June 1, 1992 in Huron, Beadle County, South Dakota.

Samantha Rae Bertera was born on August 6, 1998 in Michigan.

Amanda Rose Bertera [320]

Back row: Gaylen Clifford, Darin Lee, and
Clifford Edwin Roth. Middle row: Cynthia Rose,
Carol Ann and Rosalene Gertrude Roth.
Front row: Stacy Rae Roth. [323]

Samantha Rae Bertera [321]

Rosalene Gertrude & Clifford Edwin Roth - The Later Years*

Rosalene Gertrude and Clifford Edwin Roth 2008 [324]

Richard Edwin Mehlhaff & His Family*

Clifford Edwin and Rosalene Gertrude Roth
25th Wedding Anniversary [322]

Fred D. and Amelia (Koth) Mehlhaff,
Richard Edwin Mehlhaff's grandparents [325]

Freidrich D. Mehlhaff was born on April 19, 1882 in South Dakota.

Amelia Koth was born about 1890 in South Dakota.

Freidrich D. Mehlhaff married Amelia Koth, the daughter of Daniel Koth and Regina Baldzer in South Dakota on an unknown date.

Herbert Mehlhaff, son of Freidrich D. and Amelia Mehlhaff, was born on April 7, 1909 in Tripp, Hutchinson County, South Dakota.

Freidrich D. and Amelia Mehlhaff with their children were recorded on the 1930 United States Census living in Sharon Township, Hutchinson County, South Dakota by the Census Enumerator, Wm. R. D. Rehemamm on April 7, 1930.[206] On the report Freidrich D. was 46 years old and his wife, Amelia was 40 years old.

There were six children listed on the report. They were Herbert 20 years old, Arlene 17 years old, Nettie 11 years old, Walter 8 years old, Albert 4 years and 8 months old and Norman 2 years and 4 months old.

Anna Engel was born on April 27, 1909 in Bismarck, Burleigh County, North Dakota.

According to South Dakota Marriages, 1905-1949, Herbert Mehlhaff married Anna Engel on March 6, 1932 in Tripp, Hutchinson County, South Dakota.[207]

The family of Herbert and Anna Mehlhaff was recorded on April 13, 1940 by the Census Enumerator, Leo Vanormy, living in Wittenberg Township, Hutchinson County, South Dakota.[208] Herbert was a farmer and he rented their home.

Five of Richard Edwin's older siblings were listed on the census report. They were Howard B. 7 years old, LaVelle V. 5 years old, Elvira A. 4 years old, Bertha M. 2 years old and Numia 1 month old.

Richard Edwin, son of Herbert and Anna Mehlhaff was born on December 6, 1943 in Kaylor Township, Hutchinson County, South Dakota.

Herbert Mehlhaff died on January 6, 1960 in Parkston, Hutchinson County, South Dakota and he was buried in the Parkston Protestant Cemetery in Parkston, Hutchinson County, South Dakota.

Anna Mehlhaff died on June 7, 1976 in Parkston, Hutchinson County, South Dakota and she was buried in the Parkston Protestant Cemetery in Parkston, Hutchinson County, South Dakota.

Gravestone for Herbert and Anna Mehlhaff located in the Parkston Protestant Cemetery in Parkston, Hutchinson County, South Dakota. [326]

Mary Ellen Ruth Zirpel & Richard Edwin Mehlhaff Marriage & Family*

Mary Ellen Ruth Zirpel [327]

Mary Ellen Ruth and Richard Edwin Mehlhaff [328]

Back row: Bertha Preheim, Rosalene Gertrude Roth, Mary Ellen Ruth Zirpel, Richard Edwin Mehlhaff, Alvin Mehlhaff, and Elmer Gottfried Zirpel. Front row: John Frederick Zirpel, Flower girls, Mary Ann Zirpel and (Carla Jean Roth not in the picture) and ring bearer, Scott Preheim. [329]

Mary Ellen Ruth Zirpel, daughter of Gottfried John and Gertrude Anna Zirpel married Richard Edwin Mehlhaff, son of Anna Mehlhaff and the late Herbert Mehlhaff on May 17, 1964 in the Immanuel Lutheran Church in Douglas County, South Dakota. The Rev. Leonard Eberhardt officiated at the wedding.

Mary Lou Schnell, soloist, and Norma Geidel, organist, provided the nuptial music.

Rosalene Gertrude Roth was matron of honor with Bertha Preheim and Carla Jean Roth, as bridesmaids. Alvin Mehlhaff was best man with Elmer Gottfried Zirpel and John Frederick Zirpel as attendants. Leonard Robert Zirpel and Howard B. Mehlhaff were ushers. Mary Ann Zirpel was the flower girl and Scott Preheim was the ring bearer.

The Ladies Aid served at the reception assisted by Elaine Evangeline Zirpel, Mrs. Ray Fredrick, Olinda Leota Zirpel, Mrs. Menno Kaufman, LaVelle Mehlhaff, Betty Young, Norma Gerlach, Bob Sinkbeil, Gloria Dorzak, Edna Zirpel, Geraldine Geidel, Janet Lippert, Dennis Stoebner, Dewayne Bialas, Richard Tiede, Ronnie Young, Marlys Gerlach, Ruth Diane Zirpel, Jeanette Bialas, Brenda Gerlach, Wilbert Lee Zirpel Jr., Doyle Bertram, Douglas Luebke, Ruby Audrey Zirpel, Yvonne Gerlach, Phyllis Bertram and Dale Gerlach.

Mary Ellen Ruth Mehlhaff was a 1962 graduate of Parkston High School in Parkston, Hutchinson County, South Dakota.

Richard Edwin and Mary Ellen Ruth made their home on Presho, in Lyman County, South Dakota. Mary Ellen worked at the Frontier Drive-In Cafe while Richard worked at Anderson Gas and Appliances.

Richard Edwin and Mary Ellen Ruth Mehlhaff had two children: Allen Richard and Lisa Rose Mehlhaff.

Birth of Allen Richard Mehlhaff*

Allen Richard Mehlhaff was born on March 11, 1967 in the Lutheran Hospital in Sioux City, Woodbury County, Iowa and he was christened in the Redeemer Lutheran Church in Sioux City, Woodbury County, Iowa.

Birth of Lisa Rose Mehlhaff*

Lisa Rose Mehlhaff was born on November 7, 1969 in Sioux City, Woodbury County, Iowa.

Lisa Rose, Mary Ellen Ruth, Richard Edwin and
Allen Richard Mehlhaff 1971. [330]

Allen Richard Mehlhaff &
Heather Sue Hasenkamp
Marriage & Family*

Allen Richard Mehlhaff [331]

In 1998, Allen worked for DHL and he attended a computer school in Omaha, Nebraska.

Allen Richard Mehlhaff married Heather Sue Hasenkamp on October 10, 1998 in the Christ Lutheran Church in Lincoln, Lancaster County, Nebraska.

Heather Sue Hasenkamp was born on April 29, 1970.

In 1998, Heather worked as a Physical Therapist in Lincoln, Nebraska.

Allen Richard and Heather Sue Mehlhaff had three children: Lucy Violet, Ivy Kate and Maggy Faith Mehlhaff.

Lucy Violet Mehlhaff was born on September 16, 2003 in Lincoln, Lancaster County, Ne-

Back row: Allen Richard Mehlhaff. Front row:
Lucy Violet, Maggy Faith, Heather Sue
and Ivy Kate Mehlhaff [332]

braska.

Ivy Kate Mehlhaff was born on September 23, 2005 in Lincoln, Lancaster County, Nebraska.

Maggy Faith Mehlhaff was born on July 13, 2007 in Lincoln, Lancaster County, Nebraska.

In 2003, Allen Richard was working for a computer company while Heather Sue went back to work part-time.

Lisa Rose Mettenbrink &
John Lee Haver
Marriage & Family*

Lisa Rose Mehlhaff [333]

Lisa Rose Mehlhaff married John Lee Haver on November 8, 1997 in the Church of Masters in Omaha, Douglas County, Nebraska.

John Lee Haver was born on December 9, 1968.

John Lee and Lisa Rose Haver had two children: Delaney Rose and Carly Lee Haver.

Delaney Rose Haver was born on May 25, 2000.

Carly Lee Haver was born on March 26, 2003.

In 1998, Lisa worked with Exectrain a computer firm.

In 1998, John was working as a attorney for Mutual of Omaha. In 2003, John had gotten promotion with Mutual of Omaha.

Back row: John Lee and Delaney Rose Haver.
Front row: Carly Lee, Bently, Lisa Rose Haver. [334]

Richard Edwin Mehlhaff - The Later Years*

Richard Edwin Mehlhaff died as result of a heart attack on June 7, 1980 in Sioux City, Woodbury County, Iowa. He was buried in the Memorial Park Cemetery in Sioux City, Woodbury County, Iowa.

Harold Walter Mettenbrink & His Family*

Rudolph F. Mettenbrink was born on December 16, 1905 in Nebraska.

Dorothea Catherine Pauly, daughter of Henry Pauly and Caroline Lena Kraft, was born on August 7, 1907 in Nebraska.

Harold Walter Mettenbrink was born on August 5, 1933 in a house in Grand Island, Hall County, Nebraska and he was christened in the Trinity Lutheran Church in Grand Island, Hall County, Nebraska.

On the 1940 United States Census on April 26, 1940 Rudolph F. and his wife, Dorothea and children were recorded living on West 4th Street in Hall, in Hastings Township, in Adams County, Nebraska by the Census Enumerator, E. J. Bassett.[209] Rudolph F. was 34 years old and a manager of a Milling Company. His wife, Dorothea was 31 years old. There were two children listed on the report. They were Harold Walter 6 years old and James 1 year old.

Rudolph F. Mettenbrink died in March of 1968 in Arcadia, Valley County, Nebraska.

Dorothea Catherine Mettenbrink died in November of 1982 in Arcadia, Valley County, Nebraska.

Harold Walter Mettenbrink married Arieta Fern Greenland.

Areita Fern Greenland was born on August 24, 1938.

Harold Walter and Arieta Fern Mettenbrink had two children: Michael James and Ellen Lynn Mettenbrink.

Birth of Michael James Mettenbrink*

Michael James Mettenbrink was born on January 20, 1965 in the Bishop Bergon Hospital in Omaha, Douglas County, Nebraska and he was christened in the St. Marks Church in Omaha, Douglas County, Nebraska.

Birth of Ellen Lynn Mettenbrink*

Ellen Lynn Mettenbrink was born on April 3, 1968 in the Lutheran Hospital, Sioux City, Woodbury County, Iowa and she was christened in the Redeemer Lutheran Church in Sioux City, Woodbury County, Iowa.

Michael James Mettenbrink & Laurie Jo Kerkeide Marriage & Family*

Laurie Jo and Michael James Mettenbrink [335]

175

Michael James Mettenbrink married Laurie Jo Kerkeide on April 20, 1996 in Marshall, Lyon County, Minnesota.

Laurie Jo Kerkeide was born on May 24, 1969.

Michael James and Laurie Jo Mettenbrink had three children: Collin Michael, Evan Matthew and Gilliam Arieta.

Collin Michael Mettenbrink was born on April 4, 1997.

Evan Matthew Mettenbrink was born on December 29, 1998.

Gilliam Arieta Mettenbrink was born on February 13, 2002.

Mary Ellen Ruth Mehlhaff & Harold Walter Mettenbrink Marriage *

Mary Ellen Ruth and Harold Walter Mettenbrink [336]

Areita Fern Mettenbrink died July 23, 1983 from Cancer and she was buried in Grand Island, Hall County, Nebraska.

Mary Ellen Ruth Mehlhaff, daughter of Gottfried John Zirpel and Gertrude Anna Gerlach married Harold Walter Mettenbrink, son of Rudolph F. Mettenbrink and Dorothea Catherine Pauly on July 6, 1985 in the Redeemer Lutheran Church in Sioux City, Woodbury County, Iowa.

In 1998, Harold was the Treasurer for the Kiwanis and the AAL Branch, as well as working at a fund raising for the Boy Scouts.

In 2002, Harold worked at a funeral home when needed. Harold was still a member of the

Kiwanis, the new Leadership Council at the church and the choir.

In 1998, Mary Ellen was working with LORI and the Altar Guild.

In 2002, Mary Ellen was still involved with LORI, the Altar Guild and the choir.

Mary Ellen Ruth & Harold Walter Mettenbrink 2002 [337]

Gottfried John & Gertrude Anna Zirpel- The Later Years*

Gertrude Anna and Gottfried John Zirpel 1972 [338]

Gottfried John Zirpel farmed on his father's farm until 1965 when he retired. Gottfried John and Gertrude Anna Zirpel moved into Parkston in Hutchinson County, South Dakota.

Gottfried John Zirpel died unexpectedly at his home in Parkston on November 12, 1975. He

Back row: Elmer Gottfried, Leonard Robert, Norbert John, Wilbert Erich and Erwin Karl Zirpel.
Front row: Rosalene Gertrude, Gertrude Anna, Mary Ellen Ruth, Gottfried John and Harold Arnold Zirpel. [339]

Gertrude Anna and Gottfried John Zirpel 50th Wedding Anniversary. Back row: Elmer Gottfried, Norbert John, Harold Arnold, Wilbert Erich, and Leonard Robert Zirpel. Next row: Mary Ellen Ruth Mehlhaff, Gertrude Anna, Gottfried John, Rosalene Gertrude Roth, and Erwin Karl Zirpel.[340]

was buried in the Parkston Protestant Cemetery in Parkston, South Dakota.

He was survived by his wife, Gertrude; five sons: Leonard Robert of Springfield, Illinois; Erwin Karl and Norbert John of Parkston, South Dakota; Elmer Gottfried of Beloit, Wisconsin, Harold Arnold of San Jose, California; two daughters: Rosalene Roth of Huron, South Dakota and Mary Ellen Mehlhaff of Sioux City, Iowa.

Gertrude Anna Zirpel died on December 21, 1986 in Parkston, Hutchinson County, South Dakota and she was buried next to her husband.

CHAPTER 9
Birth of Elisabeth Augusta Zirpel - A Twin*

Elisabeth Augusta & Gottfried John Zirpel [341]

Elisabeth Augusta Zirpel was a twin, daughter of Johan and Augusta Zirpel was born on April 25, 1897 in Douglas County, South Dakota. His twin brother was Gottfried John Zirpel. She was christened on May 23, 1897 in the St. John Lutheran Church in Douglas County, South Dakota.

Elisabeth Augusta Zirpel was confirmed on March 12, 1912 at the Immanuel Lutheran Church in Douglas County, South Dakota.

Elisabeth Augusta and Gottfried John Zirpel
Confirmation 1912. [342]

According to the 1900 United States Census report taken on June 21, 1900, by the Census Enumerator, Henry Ruff, Elisabeth Augusta Zirpel was 3 years old when she appeared with her parents, Johan and Augusta Zirpel in Berlin Township, now known as Washington Township, Douglas County, South Dakota.[210] Her brothers and sisters listed on the census report. Anna Emilie was fifteen years old. Robert Hermann was thirteen years old. Emma Bertha was seven years old. Wilhelm Otto was four years old. Gottfried John was three years old. Edward Richard was nine months old. His father, Johan was listed as general farmer and owning his farm.

On April 26, 1910, Elisabeth August Zirpel appeared on the 1910 United States Census living with her parents, Johan and Augusta in Berlin Township, now called Washington Township at the age of 12 years according to the Census Enu-merator, Walter L. Koehn.[211] The other siblings listed on the census report were Emma Bertha, Wilhelm Otto, Gottfried John, Edward Richard and Bertha Rosina.

Oscar Karl Gerlach & His Family*

Oscar Karl Gerlach's grandfather, Christian Gerlach was born in Germany on August 10, 1823. No records found for his parents.

Christian Gerlach married Christiane on August 5, 1855 in Ehningen, Ehningen, Württemberg, Germany. No records found for Christiane's last name, or the date of her birth and death.

Oscar Karl Gerlach's father, Ernest Gerlach Sr., son of Christian and Christiane Gerlach was born on July 31, 1858 in Silesia, Germany.

It is presumed that Christian Gerlach's family came to America in 1883 according to four different United States Census records for Oscar Karl Gerlach.

According to the 1900 United States Census Dorothea Kuinke was born in August of 1838 in Germany and her husband, Gottlier Kuinke was born in July of 1829 in Germany taken by the Census Enumerator, Alvin Mahan on June 6, 1900 in Starr Township, in Hutchinson County, South Dakota.[212] The report said that their parents were born in Germany also. They had been married over 40 years. Gottlier was seventy years old and Dorothea was sixty-one years old. They had one child living out of three children born.

Tombstone for Christian Gerlach located
in the Immanuel Lutheran Church Cemetery in
Douglas County, South Dakota. [343]

Gottlier Kuinke died sometime between 1900 and 1910, as Dorothea Kuinke was listed as a widow, on the 1910 United States Census taken on April 22, 1910 by the Census Enumerator, Charles H. Reuland, in Starr Township in Hutchinson County, South Dakota.[213] Dorothea was also listed as a grandmother living with Ernest and Hedwig Baumgart.

Augusta Dorothea Kuinke, daughter of Gottlier and Dorothea Kuinke was born on September 27, 1875 in Peisterwitz, Germany.

Christian Gerlach died on January 10, 1896 and he was buried in the Immanuel Lutheran Church Cemetery in Douglas County, South Dakota.

Augusta Dorothea Kuinke, daughter of Gottlier and Dorothea Kuinke, married Ernest Gerlach Sr., son of Christian and Christiane Gerlach, on December 1, 1896 in Douglas County, South Dakota.

Ernest Sr. and Augusta Dorothea Gerlach had at least twelve children: William, Oscar Karl, John Ernest, Alvin, Alma, Hilda, Reinhold, Herbert, Albert, Bertha, Eitel, Martin Walter Gerlach.

Oscar Karl Gerlach was born on December 4, 1899 in Douglas County, South Dakota and he was Christened on January 7, 1900 in the St. John Lutheran Church in Douglas County, South Dakota.

On June 21, 1900, the Census Enumerator, Henry Ruff recorded Ernest and Augusta Gerlach living in Valley Township, Douglas County, South Dakota on the 1900 United States Census.[214] Two sons were listed on the report. William was two years old and Oscar Karl was one year old.

The Ernest Gerlach Sr. family moved to Washington Township in Douglas County, South Dakota sometime after the 1900 United States Census was taken.

Walter L. Koehn, the Census Enumerator, for the 1910 United States Census recorded the Ernest Sr. Gerlach family on April 25 & 26, 1910 living in Berlin Township of Douglas County, South Dakota.[215] On this report Ernest owned his farm. Ernest and Augusta Dorothea Gerlach had eight children living with them. William was eleven years old, Oscar Karl was nine years old, John Ernest Jr. was eight years old, Alvin was seven years old, Emil was four years old, Alma was five years old, Hilda was three years old, and Reinhold was 1 year and two months old.

Oscar Karl Gerlach registered himself on the World War I Draft Registration according to O. W. Laufer recording the information in Hutchinson County, South Dakota on September 12, 1918.[216] Oscar Karl was single as well as a farmer with his father, Ernest Gerlach. He was described as being medium in height and built. He had blue eyes and brown hair according to the document.

Ernest and Augusta Dorothea Gerlach along with their thirteen children were recorded living in Washington Township in Douglas County, South Dakota on the 1920 United States Census according to the Census Enumerator, Mrs. Carl Bertram on June 23, 1920.[217] The children on the report were William, Oscar Karl, John Ernest, Alvin, Alma, Hilda, Emil, Reinhold, Herbert, Albert, Bertha, Eitel, and Martin Walter Gerlach.

The Ernest Sr. Gerlach family was recorded on the 1930 United States Census by the Census Enumerator, Mrs. Ida Bertram still living in Washington Township, Douglas County, South Dakota on April 18 & 19, 1930.[218] There were seven children still living with them.

On the 1940 United States Census Ernest & Augusta Dorothea Gerlach were still living in Washington Township, Douglas County, South Dakota on April 4, 1940 with their son, Martin Walter according to the Census Enumerator, Henry Lightenberg.[219]

Augusta Dorothea Gerlach died on May 5, 1941 in Douglas County, South Dakota and she was buried in the St. John Lutheran Church Cemetery in Douglas County, South Dakota.

Ernest Gerlach Sr. died on May 17, 1941 in Douglas County, South Dakota and he was burin the St. John Lutheran Church Cemetery in Douglas County, South Dakota.

Tombstone for Ernest and Augusta Dorothea Gerlach located in the St. John Lutheran Church Cemetery In Douglas County, South Dakota[344]

Elisabeth Augusta Zirpel & Oscar Karl Gerlach Marriage & Family*

Elisabeth Augusta Zirpel, daughter of Johan and Augusta Anna Zirpel married Oscar Karl Gerlach, son of Ernest and Augusta Dorothea Gerlach, on February 14, 1922 in the Immanuel Lutheran Church in Douglas County, South Dakota.[220] They were married by Rev. Paul Hempel, the Lutheran minister.

Oscar Karl and Augusta Dorothea Gerlach had three children: a baby boy, Walter Herman and Bernice Elisabeth Gerlach.

Birth of Baby Boy Gerlach*

A baby boy, son of Oscar Karl and Elizabeth Augusta Gerlach was born on June 13, 1923. He died on June 16, 1923. The baby boy was buried in the St. John Lutheran Church Cemetery in Douglas County, South Dakota.

Oscar Karl Gerlach and Elisabeth Augusta Zirpel Wedding. Back row standing: Mathilda L. Zirpel, Edward Richard Zirpel, William Otto Zirpel, and Emma Martha Maria Zirpel. Front row sitting down: unknown flower girl, Oscar Karl Gerlach, Elisabeth Augusta Gerlach, and unknown flower girl. [345]

Oscar Karl and Elisabeth Augusta Gerlach. [346]

Tombstone for baby boy Gerlach is located in the
St. John Lutheran Church Cemetery in
Douglas County, South Dakota. [347]

Birth of
Walter Herman Gerlach*

Walter Herman Gerlach, son of Oscar Karl and Elisabeth Augusta Gerlach was born on February 24, 1926 in Douglas County, South Dakota at their home. He was christened on March 19, 1926 in the St. John Lutheran Church in Douglas County, South Dakota.

Walter Herman Gerlach was confirmed on April 27, 1941 at the Immanuel Lutheran Church in Douglas County, South Dakota.

Birth of
Bernice Elisabeth Gerlach*

Bernice Elisabeth Gerlach, daughter of Oscar Karl and Elisabeth Augusta Gerlach was born on June 29, 1935 in Douglas County, South Dakota at their home. She was christened on August 18, 1935 in the St. John Lutheran Church in Douglas County, South Dakota.

Bernice Elisabeth Gerlach was adopted.

Oscar Karl & Elisabeth Augusta Gerlach - The Later Years*

On April 18 & 19, 1930, Mrs. Ida Bertram,

the Census Enumerator, for the 1930 United States Census recorded Oscar Karl and Elisabeth Augusta Gerlach living on a farm in Washington Township, Douglas County, South Dakota with one son, Walter Herman Gerlach.[221] Walter Herman was four years old.

According to Walter Herman and Helen Louise Gerlach, Oscar Karl and Elisabeth Augusta Gerlach made their home in Washington Township in Douglas County, South Dakota, nine miles west and three quarters of a mile north of Dimock, South Dakota. There they had Hereford cattle, hogs, chickens, geese, as well as ducks. Walter had some sheep while he was still attending school.

Their old house in which the family lived in burned down on November 5, 1934. In the later part of 1934 and early part of 1935 that winter a new house was built.

New farm house built winter of 1934
and spring of 1935. [348]

Oscar Karl Gerlach Family. Back row standing: Walter Herman Gerlach. Front row sitting: Elisabeth Augusta, Bernice Elisabeth and Oscar Karl Gerlach[349]

On the 1940 United States Census taken on April 8, 1940 by the Census Enumerator, Henry Ligtenberg, Oscar Karl and Elisabeth Augusta Gerlach were still living Washington Township, Douglas County, South Dakota with two children: Walter Herman and Bernice Elisabeth Gerlach.[222] Oscar Karl main occupation was a farmer and their home value or Monthly rent was $1000. He worked over 52 hours a week in 1939.

Oscar Karl was forty years old and Elisabeth August was forty-two years old. Walter Herman Gerlach was fourteen years while Bernice Elisabeth Gerlach was only four years old.

Elisabeth Augusta and Oscar Karl Gerlach
40th Wedding Anniversary. [350]

Helen Louise Knott
& Her Family*

Helen Louise Knott's grandparents were Richard Wilson Knott and Ida M. Bronk.

Ida M. Bronk was born in December of 1854 in the state of New York according to the 1900 United States Census.

Richard Wilson Knott was born on September 26, 1849 in the state of Iowa.

Richard Wilson Knott married Ida M. Bronk On December 31, 1870 in Muscatine County, Iowa.[223]

On the 1880 United States Census taken by the Census Enumerator, James Hoon, on June 25, 1880 Richard Wilson and Ida M. Knott were living in Penn Township, Guthrie County, Iowa.[224] Richard Wilson Knott was register as a farmer and both his parents were born on Pennsylvania. On the report Richard Wilson and Ida M. had five children. They were Lewis J. eight years old, Howard was six years old, Alice H. was five years old, Arthur was two years old and Moody C. was two months old.

Clair Knott, son of Richard Wilson and Ida M. Knott was born on September 17, 1894 in Guthrie County, Iowa.

By June 6, 1900 the family of Richard Wilson Knott had moved to Jefferson Township in Adair County, Iowa according the Census Enumerator, M. J. Peters, for the 1900 United States Census.[225] On the report Richard Wilson and Ida M. had eight children living with them. They were Howard twenty-six years old, Arthur J. C. twenty-two years old, Moody C. was twenty years old, Carrie C. was seventeen years old, Edith E. was fifteen years old, Charles was thirteen years old, William R. was seven years old, and Helen Louise's father, Clair was five years old.

Richard Wilson Knott died on January 29, 1909 and he was buried in the El Reno Cemetery in Canadian County, Oklahoma.

Ida M Knott was listed as a widow on the 1910 United States Census taken by Census, Enumerator, C. L. Bell on April 22, 1910 in El Reno, Canadian County, Oklahoma with four children and one granddaughter.[226] They were Carrie twenty-seven years old, Charles twenty-three years old, William eighteen years old, Helen Louise's father, Clair was fifteen years old and granddaughter, Ruth Smith was one year old.

Clair Knott was living in El Reno, Canadian

County, Iowa according to the U.S. World War I Draft Registration Cards, 1917-1918 signed on June 5, 1917 by J. S. Campbell.[227] Clair was listed as single and twenty-two years old. He had blue eyes and brown hair.

On January15, 1920, Clair Knott was living in El Reno Ward 4, Canadian County, Oklahoma with his mother, Ida M. and his brother, Charles Knott according to the Census Enumerator, Mrs. Alice G. Comms on the 1920 United States Census.[228] Ida M. was listed as sixty-five years old and a widow. The children listed were Charles thirty-three years old and Clair twenty-four years old. There was also a granddaughter, Ruth Smith eleven years old on the report.

Clair Knott, son of Richard Wilson Knott and Ida M. Bronk, married Lydia Emilie Lichen sometime before 1930.

Lydia Emilie Lichen was born on September 16, 1898, location and parent's names are unknown

Clair and Lydia Emilie Knott were recorded living in Amarillo, Potter County, Texas according to the 1930 United States Census taken on April 12, 1930 by the Census Enumerator, Elizabeth Avery.[229] Clair was thirty-five years old and Lydia Emilie was thirty-two years old. Their son, William was one year old.

Helen Louise Knott, daughter of Clair and Lydia Emilie Knott was born on June 16, 1933 in Wilson, Lynn County, Texas.

Clair Knott and wife, Lydia Emilie were farming eight miles west of Slaton in Lubbock County, Texas with their children: William and Helen Knott according to the U.S. World War II Draft Registration Cards in 1942.[230] On this record, Clair was married. He had blue eyes and brown hair. He also had tattoos on both of his forearms according to G. Eurelolo on April 27, 1942 when the registration was filed in Lubbock County, Texas.

Clair Knott died on June 4, 1973 in Lubbock County, Texas and he was buried in the Englewood Cemetery located in Slaton, Lubbock County, Texas.[231] He had served in the U.S. Navy in World War I according to the inscription on his tombstone "Oklahoma 52 U.S. Navy WWI".

According to the tombstone located in the Englewood Cemetery in Slaton, Lubbock County, Texas where Clair Knott is buried his wife, Lydia Emilie Knott died on November 26, 1983.

Walter Herman Gerlach & Helen Louise Knott Marriage & Family*

Walter Herman went to country school for eight years. After that time, Walter started farming with his father, Oscar Karl.

In October of 1950, Walter Herman went into the United States Army, when the Korean War had started. Then Walter served in Texas for two years, during this time he met Helen Louise Knott. Walter left the service in October of 1952.

Walter Herman Gerlach U.S. Army picture. [351]

Helen Louise Knott and Walter Herman Gerlach Wedding Picture. [352]

Walter Herman and Helen Louise Gerlach
October 1952. [353]

Walter Herman Gerlach, son of Oscar Karl Gerlach and Elisabeth Augusta Zirpel, married Helen Louise Knott, daughter of Clair Knott and Lydia E. Lichen, on October 21, 1952 in the St. John Lutheran Church in Wilson, Lynn County, Texas.

Walter Herman and Helen Louise Gerlach left Texas and moved to South Dakota and started a farm together in 1953. They had some real good years.

They started milking cows in 1960. They had cattle "Herefords" and chickens until 1970. They also had Ayrshire cows for awhile. In May of 1977 they put up a new milking barn. In 1979, they changed to only Jersey cows.

Walter Herman and Helen Louise Gerlach had three children: Mildred Louise, Glen Gene and Susanne Helen Gerlach.

Birth of
Mildred Louise Gerlach*

Mildred Louise Gerlach, daughter of Walter Herman and Helen Louise Gerlach, was born on November 25, 1954 in the St. Benedicts Hospital in Parkston, Hutchinson County, South Dakota.

Birth of
Glen Gene Gerlach*

Glen Gene Gerlach, son of Walter Herman and Helen Louise Gerlach, was born on July 15, 1957 in the St. Benedicts Hospital in Parkston, Hutchinson County, South Dakota.

In 1975, Glen was working on the farm after he got out of school with his father, Walter.

Birth of
Suzanne Helen Gerlach*

Susanne Helen Gerlach, daughter of Walter Herman and Helen Louise Gerlach, was born on November 9, 1961 in the St. Benedicts Hospital in Parkston, Hutchinson County, South Dakota.

Iola M. Knutson
& Her Family*

Iola M. Knutson, daughter of Andrew O. and Clara O. Knutson was born on March 27, 1920 in South Dakota.

Iola M. Knutson and her family were recorded on the 1930 United States Census living in Woonsocket, Sanborn County, South Dakota on April 8, 1930 by the Census Enumerator, Birdie J. Kogel.[232] On the report, Andrew O. Knutson was thirty-eight years old and he was born in Iowa. His wife, Clara O. Knutson was forty years old and she was born on South Dakota. There were seven children listed on the census report and they was all born in South Dakota. Harold O. was sixteen years old, Iola M. was ten years old, Leonard S. was 8 years old, C. Burnette was six years old, Shirley M. was three years and four months old, Arles G. was two years and eight months old, and Marvin L. was nine months old.

Robert V. Goudy
& His Family*

Robert V. Goudy, son of George N. and Frieda Goudy, was born on December 30, 1914 in South Dakota.

On February 11, 1920, the Census Enumerator, Heida G. Haunpson, recorded the George N. Goudy family living in Oneida Township in Sanborn County, South Dakota on the 1920 United States Census.[233] Robert's father, George N. Goudy was born in Iowa and he was thirty-six years old, while Robert's mother, Frieda was born in South Dakota and she was thirty-two years old. There were five children listed. Frank was eleven years old, Clarence was nine years old, Albert was seven years old, Robert was five years old and Alice was two years and five months old.

By the 1930 United States Census taken on April 2, 1930 by the Census Enumerator, John R. Swanson the George N. Goudy family had moved to Floyd Township in Sanborn County, South Dakota.[234] George N. Goudy and his wife, Frieda as well as four children: Clarence, Albert W., Robert V. and Alice S. were listed.

Robert V. Goudy & Iola M. Knutson Marriage & Family*

Robert V. Goudy, son of George N. and Frieda Goudy was married to Iola M. Knutson, daughter of Andrew O. and Clara O. Knutson on January 4, 1936 by Clergyman, John Clayton, in Forestburg, Sanborn County, South Dakota.[235]

Robert V. and Iola M. Goudy were recorded on the 1940 United States Census living in Jackson Township in Sanborn County, South Dakota by the Census Enumerator, Harold C. Dudra.[236] Robert was listed as a farmer who rented their home. Robert was twenty-five years old and his wife, Iola M. was twenty years old. They had one child: Ila M. Goudy. She was three years old.

Gerald George Goudy, son of Robert V. and Iola M. Goudy was born on August 4, 1946 in South Dakota.

Robert V. Goudy died on June 8, 1984 in South Dakota and his was buried in the Mount Pleasant Cemetery in Artesian, Sanborn County, South Dakota.[237]

Iola M. Goudy died on February 21, 2001 in Mitchell, Davison County, South Dakota and she was buried by her husband, Robert in the Mount Pleasant Cemetery in Artesian, Sanborn County, South Dakota.[238]

Mildred Louise Gerlach & Gerald George "Hap" Goudy Marriage & Family*

Mildred Louise Gerlach, daughter of Walter Herman and Helen Louise Gerlach, married Gerald George "Hap" Goudy, on April 15, 1977 in the St. John Lutheran Church in Douglas County, South Dakota.

Gerald George "Hap" and Mildred Louise

Goudy had two children: Dawn Michelle and Jeffrey Scott Goudy.

Gerald George and Mildred Louise Goudy Wedding. Back row: Walter Hermann Gerlach, Helen Louise Gerlach, Mildred Louise Goudy, and Gerald George Goudy. Front row: Suzanne Helen Gerlach and Glenn Gene Gerlach. [354]

Birth of Dawn Michelle Goudy*

Dawn Michelle Goudy, daughter of Gerald George and Mildred Louise Goudy, was born on May 25, 1967 in the St. Joseph Hospital in Mitchell, Davison County, South Dakota.

Birth of Jeffery Scott Goudy*

Jeffery Scott Goudy, son of Gerald George and Mildred Louise Goudy, was born on born on April 30, 1979 in the St. Joseph Hospital in Mitchell, Davison County, South Dakota.

Gerald George & Mildred Louise Goudy - The Later Years*

Gerald George Goudy died on December 14, 2006 in the Huron Medical Center in Huron, Beadle County, South Dakota. He was buried in the Mount Pleasant Cemetery in Artesian, Sanborn County,. South Dakota.

Mildred Louise Goudy married Gary Mahony. The marriage ended in a divorce.

Jesse James Goudy, Mildred Louise Goudy and Sophia Ann Goudy.[355]

Mildred Louise Goudy worked in Alexandria as an office manager at the Hanson County Oil Producers which makes bio diesel fuel from vegetable oil waste.

Dawn Michelle Goudy & Chung-Hoon Baik Marriage & Family*

Dawn Michelle Goudy, daughter of Gerald George and Mildred Louise Goudy, married Chung-Hoon Baik on June 20, 1987 in the Walter Miller residence in Mitchell, Davison County, South Dakota.

Chung-Hoon and Dawn Michelle Baik had two children: Katie and Taylor Seung-han Baik.

Katie Baik was born in 1996.

Taylor Seung-han Baik was on August 14, 1999.

Jeffrey Scott Goudy & Kasey Larson & Family*

Jeffrey Scott Goudy and Kasey Larson had child: Sophia Ann Goudy. They were never married.

Sophia Ann Goudy was born on June 29, 2004. Sophia Ann lives part-time with her father, Jeffrey Scott and her mother, Kasey. They all live in Mitchell, Davison County, South Dakota.

Jeffrey Scott Goudy & Amy Rice & Family*

Jeffrey Scott Goudy and Amy Rice had one child: Jesse James Goudy. They were never mar-

ried.

Jesse James Goudy was born on March 7, 2008. Jessie James lives full-time with his father, Jeffrey Scott.

Jeffrey Scott works as the store manager at Taco Bell in Mitchell, South Dakota.

Jesse James Goudy, Jeffrey Scott Goudy and Sophia Ann Goudy. [356]

Suzanne Helen Gerlach & Glen Ray Dorzak Marriage *

When Suzanne Helen was about nineteen years old and out of school, she began working on the farm. She had milked and fed the calves, as well as fed the Hereford cows.

Suzanne Helen Gerlach, daughter of Walter Herman and Helen Louise Gerlach, married Glen Ray Dorzak on October 5, 1987 by the Justice of the Peace in Armour, Douglas County, South Dakota.

Glen Ray Dorzak was born on February 4, 1960.

In the year of 2000, Walter and Helen turned the farm over to Glen and Suzanne. They are doing all the farming now. They sold the milk cows in August of 2008.

They still have the Hereford cows.

Hilda Emma Gerlach & Her Family*

Hilda Emma Gerlach, daughter of Ernst

186

The Walter Gerlach farm on August3, 2010. [357]

Augusta Dorothea Kiunke, was born in 1906 in South.

Hilda Emma Gerlach's parents, Ernest and Augusta Dorothea Gerlach were recorded on the 1930 United States Census on April 18-19, 1930 by the Census Enumerator, Mrs. Ida Bertram, living in Washington Township, Douglas County, South Dakota.[239] On the census report, Ernest Gerlach had immigrated to the United States in 1883 from Germany. There were seven children listed on the report. Emil was twenty-two years old, Reinhold was twenty-one years old, Herbert was nineteen years old, Albert was seventeen years old, Hertha was sixteen years old, Eitel was fourteen years old and Martin Gerlach was twelve years old.

Both Ernest and Augusta Dorothea Gerlach died in 1941 in South Dakota. They were buried in the Immanuel Lutheran Church Cemetery located in Douglas County, South Dakota

Lawrence (Lorenz) Harold Bialas & His Family*

Fritz John Bialas, son of Herman and Martha Bialas was born around 1906 in South Dakota.

On April 25-26, 1910, Fritz John Bialas was recorded on the 1910 United States Census with his parents, Herman and Martha Bialas living in Berlin Township, Douglas County, South Dakota by the Census Enumerator, Walter L. Koehn.[240] The father, Herman was born in Germany and listed as thirty-five years old while the mother, Martha was born in South Dakota and she was twenty-seven years old. There were three children listed on report and they were born in South Dakota. Fritz John was four years old, Herman was two years old and Martha was one year and seven months old.

Herman Bialas died in 1912 and he was buried in the Immanuel Lutheran Church Cemetery in Douglas County, South Dakota.

After Herman's death, Martha Bialas was married to Adolph Metzger on February 15, 1914 in Douglas County, South Dakota by Pastor Hempel according to South Dakota Marriages, 1905-1949.

Adolph and Martha Metzger were recorded on the 1920 United States Census on January 20, 1920 by the Census Enumerator, Mrs. Carl Bertram living in Washington Township, Douglas County, South Dakota with eight children.[241] Five of children were from Martha's marriage to Herman Bialas. Fritz John was thirteen years old, Herman was twelve years old, Martha was eleven years old, Willie was nine years old, and Bertha was eight years old. Three of the children were from Martha's marriage to Adolph Metzger, who immigrated to the United States in 1913 from Germany. Ewald was three years old, Reinhart was one year and eleven months old and Ruth was nine months old.

On May 31, 1927 Fritz John Bialas, son of Herman and Martha Bialas, married Hilda Emma Gerlach, daughter of Ernest and Augusta Dorothea Gerlach in Armour, Douglas County, South Dakota.[242]

Fritz John and Hilda Emma Bialas were living in Washington Township, Douglas County, South Dakota on April 23, 1930 according to the Census Enumerator, Mrs. Ida Bertram for the 1930 United States Census.[243] There were two children listed on the report. Lorraine was two years old and Ivan was one year old.

Lawrence (Lorenz) Harold Bialas, son of Fritz John and Hilda Emma Bialas, was born on November 21, 1931 in Parkston, Hutchison County, South Dakota. He was confirmed on 1946 at the Immanuel Lutheran Church in Douglas County, South Dakota.

On the 1940 United States Census taken on April 7, 1940 by the Census Enumerator, Henry Lightenberg, the family of Fritz John and Hilda Emma Bialas were still living in Washington Township in Douglas County, South Dakota.[244] Fritz John was thirty-four years old and he completed the eight grade in school. And his wife, Hilda Emma was also thirty-four years old. There were seven children listed on the report. Lorraine was twelve years old, Ivan was eleven years old, Lawrence Harold was eight years old, Harvey was six years old, Floyd was five years old, Willard was three years old and Lambert Bialas was two years old. They rented their home and the farm. It was valued at $1,000.

Fritz John Bialas died in Parkston, Hutchison County, South Dakota in April of 1979. He was buried in the Immanuel Lutheran Church Cemetery in Douglas County, South Dakota.

Hilda Emma Bialas died in 2003 in South Dakota and she was buried by her husband, Fritz John in the Immanuel Lutheran Church Cemetery in Douglas County, South Dakota.

Fritz John and Hilda Emma Bialas tombstone located in the Immanuel Lutheran Church Cemetery in Douglas County, South Dakota. [358]

Bernice Elisabeth Gerlach & Lawrence Harold Bialas
Marriage & Family*

Bernice Elisabeth Gerlach, daughter of Oscar Karl and Elisabeth Augusta Gerlach, married Lawrence (Lorenz) Harold Bialas, son of Fritz John Bialas and Hilda Emma Gerlach, on October 21, 1954 in the St. John Lutheran Church in Douglas County, South Dakota.

Lawrence Harold and Bernice Elisabeth Bialas had five children: Michael Lawrence, Elizabeth Faye, May Dene, Diane Hilda, and Thomas Jason Bialas.

Birth of Michael Lawrence Bialas*

Michael Lawrence Bialas, son of Lawrence Harold and Bernice Elisabeth Bialas, was born on July 10, 1955 in Parkston, Hutchinson County, South Dakota. He was christened in 1955 in the Immanuel Lutheran Church in Douglas County, South Dakota.

Michael Lawrence Bialas was confirmed in 1970 at the Immanuel Lutheran Church in Douglas County, South Dakota.

Birth of Elizabeth Faye Bialas*

Elizabeth Faye Bialas, daughter of Lawrence Harold and Bernice Elisabeth Bialas, was born on October 4, 1956 in Parkston, Hutchinson County, South Dakota. She was christened in 1956 in the Immanuel Lutheran Church in Douglas County,

South Dakota.

Elizabeth Faye Bialas was confirmed in 1971 in the Immanuel Lutheran Church in Douglas County, South Dakota.

Birth of
May Dene Bialas*

May Dene Bialas, daughter of Lawrence Harold and Bernice Elisabeth Bialas, was born on June 3, 1959 in Parkston, Hutchinson County, South Dakota. She was christened in 1959 in the Immanuel Lutheran Church in Douglas County, South Dakota.

May Dene Bialas was confirmed in 1973 in the Immanuel Lutheran Church in Douglas County, South Dakota.

Birth of
Diane Hilda Bialas*

Diane Hilda Bialas, daughter of Lawrence Harold and Bernice Elisabeth Bialas, was born on October 9, 1963 in Parkston, Hutchinson County, South Dakota. She was christened in 1963 in the Immanuel Lutheran Church in Douglas County, South Dakota.

Diane Hilda Bialas was confirmed in 1977 in the Immanuel Lutheran Church in Douglas County, South Dakota.

Birth of
Thomas Jason Bialas*

Thomas Jason Bialas, son of Lawrence Harold and Bernice Elisabeth Bialas, was born on October 29, 1972 in Parkston, Hutchinson County, South Dakota. He was christened in 1972 in the Immanuel Lutheran Church in Douglas County, South Dakota.

Thomas Jason Bialas was confirmed but record of the date or location.

Michael Lawrence Bialas &
Carol Marlys Zirpel
Marriage & Family*

Michael Lawrence Bialas, son of Lawrence Harold Bialas and Bernice Elizabeth Gerlach, married Carol Marlys Zirpel on October 21, 1977 in the Immanuel Lutheran Church in Douglas County, South Dakota. The marriage ended in divorce on October 5, 1994.

Michael Lawrence and Carol Marlys Bialas had four children: Christen Carol, Matthew Michael, Emily Elizabeth and Mandy Marie Bialas.

Birth of
Christen Carol Bialas*

Christen Carol Bialas was born on November 26, 1980 in Sioux Falls, Minnehaha County, South Dakota.

She was christened in 1980 in the Immanuel Lutheran Church in Douglas County, South Dakota.

Birth of
Matthew Michael Bialas*

Matthew Michael Bialas was born on January 5, 1983 in Sioux Falls, Minnehaha County, South Dakota.

Birth of
Emily Elizabeth Bialas*

Emily Elizabeth Bialas was born on July 10, 1987 in Sioux Falls, Minnehaha County, South Dakota.

Birth of
Mandy Marie Bialas*

Mandy Marie Bialas was born on July 10, 1988 in Mitchell, Davison County, South Dakota.

Christen Carol Bialas &
Tim James Wermers Jr.
Marriage & Family*

Christen Carol Bialas married Tim James Wermers Jr. on September 22, 2001 in the Faith Lutheran Church in Parkston, Hutchinson County, South Dakota.

Tim James Jr. and Christen Carol Wermers have one child: Sophie Carol Wermers.

Sophie Carol Wermers was born on September 13, 2011.

Matthew Lawrence Bialas &
Danielle Wonch - Girl Friend*

In 2013, Matthew Michael Bialas had a special girl friend, Danielle Wonch.

Danielle Wonch was born on October 24, 1980.

Carol Marlys Bialas & Keith Allen Goehring Marriage*

On March 16, 2002, Carol Marlys Bialas married Keith A Goehring, son of Marvin and Shirley Goehring in the Faith Lutheran Church in Parkston, Hutchinson County, South Dakota. The ceremony was performed by Rev. Carl Rockrohr.

Carol Marlys & Keith Allen Goehring - The Later Years*

Carol Marlys Goehring had worked as a secretary for Lloyd Mahan, Toshiba and County Fair Mitchell, as well as Parkston Food Center in Parkston, South Dakota.

Keith Allen Goehring was an attorney in Parkston, South Dakota.

Carol Marlys Goehring died from cancer on October 31, 2007 at the Avera McKennan Hospital in Sioux Falls, Minnehaha County, South Dakota.

Her funeral services were held on November 2, 2007 at the Faith Lutheran Church in Parkston, Hutchinson County, South Dakota.

Her burial was in the Parkston Protestant Cemetery in Parkston, Hutchinson County, South Dakota.

Michael Joseph Hranicky & His Family*

Leonard Joseph Hranicky, son of Emil E. Hranicky and Emilee Wagner, was born on November 14, 1929 in Yorktown, DeWitt County, Texas.

Emil E. and wife, Emilie Hranicky as well as eight children were recorded on May 9-10, 1940 on the 1940 United States Census by the Census Enumerator, Rudolf H. Jaeger living in DeWitt County, Texas.[245] The family lived on Yorktown Davy Highway. Emil was forty-four years old and his wife, Emilie was forty-three years old. Emil was eighteen years old, Dorothy was sixteen years old, Lillian was fourteen years old, Emilia Mae was twelve years old, Leonard Joseph was ten years old, Ethel was eight years old, Joe Edward was six years old, and Annette was three years old.

Leonard Joseph Hranicky, son of Emil E. Hranicky and Emilie Wagner, married Patricia Marie Nolen on October 14, 1950 in Yorktown, DeWitt County, Texas.

Michael Joseph Hranicky, son of Leonard Joseph and Patricia Marie Hranicky, was born on December 13, 1966 in Calhoun County, Texas according the Texas Birth Index, 1903-1997.

Leonard Joseph Hranicky worked as a smelting supervisor with Alcoa in Rockdale, Texas for thirty-seven years.

Leonard Joseph Hranicky, of Rockdale, Texas since 1978 and formerly of Port Lavaca for twenty-eight years, died on June 12, 2007 in the Richards Memorial Hospital in Rockdale, Texas. A funeral mass service was held on June 16, 2007 at the St. Joseph's Catholic Church in Rockdale with the Rev. Edwin Kagoo officiating. He was buried in the Odd Fellows Cemetery in Rockdale, Miram County, Texas. The pallbearers were Tom Merka, Daniel Svrcek, Willie Barcak, Leo Dabey, Paul Leopold, Sr. and Phil Konarik.

He was preceded in death by his parents; two brothers, Emil and Joseph Hranicky; three sisters, Dorothy Dworaczyk. Lillian Brett, and Annette Hranicky.

Survivors included his wife, Patricia Hranicky of Rockdale, Texas; son, Michael Joseph Hranicky and wife, Elizabeth Faye of El Lago, Texas; two daughters, Phyllis Ann Hanson and husband, Steve of Midland, Texas and Dianne Marie Goodrich and husband, Mitch of Huston, Texas; brother, Benny Hranicky and wife, Phyllis of Port Lavaca, Texas; two sisters, Emilia Mae Cole and husband, Ed of Port Pierce, Florida and Ethel Turner of Port Lavaca, Texas; three grandchildren: Matthew Hanson, Peter Hanson and Ella Hranicky.

Elizabeth Faye Bialas & Michael Joseph Hranicky Marriage & Family*

Elizabeth Faye Bialas, daughter of Lawrence Harold and Bernice Elisabeth Bialas, married Michael Joseph Hranicky, son Leonard Joseph and Patricia Marie Hranicky, on February 25, 1995 in Nassau Bay, Harris County, Texas according to the Texas, Marriage Collection, 1914-1909, and 1966-2011.

Michael Joseph and Elizabeth Faye Hranicky have one child: Ella Marie Hranicky.

Birth of Ella Marie Hranicky*

Ella Marie Hranicky, daughter of Michael Joseph and Elizabeth Faye Hranicky, was born on

January 10, 1998.

May Dene Bialas & Todd Allen Juhnke
Marriage & Family*

May Dene Bialas, daughter of Lawrence Harold and Bernice Elisabeth Bialas, married Todd Allen Juhnke on June 25, 1982 in the Immanuel Lutheran Church in Douglas County, South Dakota.

Todd Allen Juhnke was born on March 19, 1959.

Todd Allen and May Dene Juhnke have three children: Evan Michael, Paige Justine, and Neal Patrick Juhnke.

Birth of Evan Michael Juhnke*

Evan Michael Juhnke, son of Todd Allen and May Dene Juhnke, was born on May 19, 1987.

Birth of Paige Justine Juhnke*

Paige Justine Juhnke, daughter of Todd Allen and May Dene Juhnke, was born on April 19, 1989.

Birth of Neal Patrick Juhnke*

Neal Patrick Juhnke, son of Todd Allen and May Dene Juhnke, was born on August 2, 2002.

Diane Hilda Bialas & Joel Hebrink
Marriage & Family*

Diane Hilda Bialas, daughter of Lawrence Harold and Bernice Elisabeth Bialas, married Joel Hebrink on July 10, 1986 in the Immanuel Lutheran Church in Douglas County, South Dakota.

Joel Hebrink was born on March 9, 1961.

Joel and Diane Hilda Hebrink have one child: Tony Hebrink.

Birth of Tony Hebrink*

Tony Hebrink, son of Joel and Diane Hilda Hebrink, was born on May 2, 1980.

Thomas Jason Bialas & Karen Ruth Westegaard
Marriage & Family*

Thomas Jason Bialas, son of Lawrence Harold and Bernice Elisabeth Bialas, married Karen Ruth Westgaard on April 18, 1998 in the Freeman Missionary Church in Freeman, Hutchinson County, South Dakota.

Karen Ruth Westgaard was born on January 6, 1973.

Thomas Jason and Karen Ruth Bialas have two children: Taryn Jo, Benjamin Owen and Theo Bjorn Bialas.

Birth of Taryn Jo Bialas*

Taryn Jo Bialas, daughter of Thomas Jason and Karen Ruth Bialas, was born on June 13, 2006.

Birth of Benjamin Owen Bialas*

Benjamin Owen Bialas, son of Thomas Jason and Karen Ruth Bialas, was born on May 26, 2010 in the Sanford Medical Center in Sioux Falls, Minnehaha County, South Dakota.

Birth of Theo Bjorn Bialas*

Theo Bjorn Bialas, son of Thomas Jason and Karen Ruth Bialas, was born on February 14, 2014 in the Avera McKennan Hospital in Sioux Falls, Minnehaha County, South Dakota.

Unfortunately, Theo Bjorn suffered from a heart condition which shorten his life. He died on February 15, 2014 in his mother's arms at the Avera McKennan Hospital in Sioux Falls, Minnehaha County, South Dakota.

Theo Bjorn Bialas was buried in the Graceland Children's Cemetery, Mitchell, Davison County, South Dakota.

CHAPTER 10

Birth of
Edward Richard Zirpel*

Edward Richard Zirpel, son of Johan and Augusta Zirpel, was born on September 1, 1899 in Douglas County, South Dakota and he was christened on October 15, 1899 in the St. John Lutheran Church in Douglas County, South Dakota.

Edward Richard Zirpel appeared with his parents, Johan and Augusta on 1900 United States Census in Berlin Township, now known as Washington Township, Douglas County, South Dakota. Information was recorded on June 21, 1900 by Census Enumerator, Henry Ruff.[246] There were six children on the report. Emma Bertha was seventeen years old. Wilhelm Otto was fourteen years old. Gottfried Johan was twelve years old. Elisabeth Augusta was twelve years old. Edward Richard was ten years old. Bertha Rosina was five years old.

Edward Richard Zirpel Confirmation [359]

On April 26, 1910, Edward Richard Zirpel was recorded with his parents, Johan and Augusta Zirpel on the 1910 United States Census taken by the Census Enumerator, Walter L. Koehn were living on the homestead located in Berlin or Washington Township in Douglas County, South Dakota.[247] There were only six children living at home on this report. There were Emma Bertha, Wilhelm Otto, Elisabeth Augusta, Gottfried Johan, Edward Richard and Bertha Rosina Zirpel.

Edward Richard Zirpel was confirmed on March 28, 1915 at the Immanuel Lutheran Church in Douglas County, South Dakota.

On September 12, 1918, Edward Richard Zirpel registered for the World War I Draft according to William Bertram in Douglas County, South Dakota.[248]

Left ti right: Edward Richard, Gottfried Johan, Wilhelm Otto and Robert Herman Zirpel. [360]

Matilda Louise Meinke
& Her Family*

It is believed that Johan Frederick Meinke, son of Johan Heinrich Meinke and Catharina Sophia Schwarz, was born on January 4, 1836 in Mecklenburg, Germany.[249]

Catharina Maria Elisabeth Scheper, daughter of John Scheper and Catharina Maria Baack, was born on July 25, 1837 in Mecklenburg, Germany.[250]

Johan Frederick Meinke married Catharina Marie Elisabeth Scheper in Germany.

Johan Frederick and Catharina Marie Elisabeth Meinke had a least three children in Germany. The children were John in 1863, Mary in 1868 and Frederick H. in 1871.

According to the 1900 United States Census taken in Mount Vernon, Davison County, South Dakota, the Meinke family immigrated to the

United States in 1872.

On June 11, 1880, the Census Enumerator, Harrison Sayles recorded the Meinke family living in Middletown Township, Dane County, Wisconsin on the 1880 United States Census.[251]

There were seven children listed on the census report. Three of the children: John, Mary and Frederick were born in Germany, while Bertha, Freda, Emil and Emma were born in Wisconsin. John was seventeen years old. Mary was twelve years old. Fredrick was nine years old. Bertha was seven years old. Freda was six years old. Emil was five years old and Emma was three years old.

Sometime after 1880 the Meinke family moved from Middle Township, Dane County Wisconsin to Mount Vernon in Davison County, South Dakota.

John Frederick Meinke died in 1894 in Mount Vernon, Davison County, South Dakota according to a Find A Grave Memorial #67711992. He was buried in the Mount Vernon Cemetery in Mount Vernon, Davison County, South Dakota.

Johan Frederick's wife, Catharina Marie Elisabeth Meinke was listed as a widow living in Mount Vernon, Davison County, South Dakota on June 11, 1900 on the 1900 United States Census taken by the Census Enumerator, H. W. Smith.[252]

Frederick was listed as a carpenter and twenty-eight years old, Emil was twenty-three years old and Otto was seventeen years old.

Catharina Marie Elisabeth Meinke died January 30, 1929 and she was buried in the Mount Vernon Cemetery, in Davison County, South Dakota with her husband, Johan Frederick according to a Find A Grave Memorial #67711992.

It is believed that Frederick H. Meinke, son of Johan Frederick Meinke and Catherine Marie Elisabeth Scheper, married Anna C. Schultz around 1902 in South Dakota. The actual date and location are not known.

Matilda Louise Meinke, daughter of Frederick H. Meinke and Anna C. Shultz, was born on January 20, 1904 in Hutchinson County, South Dakota.

On April 16, 1910, Frederick H. Meinke and his wife, Anna C. and five children were living in the Mount Vernon Ward 2, Davison County, South Dakota according to the Census Enumerator, George W. Lawrence on the 1910 United States Census.[253]

Frederick H. was thirty-seven years and his wife, Anna C. was twenty-five years old. According to the report, they both had been born in Germany. Frederick H. and Anna C. had five children listed on the report, Fred H., Matilda L., Sophia M., Viola E. and Hollis W. Meinke.

Fred H. was seven years old. Matilda Louise was six years old. Sophia M. was four years old. Viola E. was three years old. Hollis W. was one year and four months old.

All the children were born in South Dakota. The report said that Frederick immigrated to the United States about 1873.

Frederick H. and Anna C. Meinke must have died sometime after the 1910 United States Census, as there are no more records found for them. The actual dates of their death or location, and the location of where they are buried is unknown.

However, three children of Frederick H. and Anna C. Meinke, Matilda L., Sophia E., and Hollis W. were recorded on the 1920 United States Census living with their Uncle, Emil Meinke in Baker Township, Davison County, South Dakota on March 24, 1920 according to the Census Enumerator, Floyd R. Bowers.[254]

Matilda Louise was sixteen years, Sophia E. was fourteen years old and Hollis W. was eleven years old.

Emil was forty-three years old and his wife, Carolina was thirty-eight years old. Emil and Carolina Meinke had five children: John W., Edward E., Eric R, Irvin C., and Lorraine L., recorded on the census report.

John W. was sixteen years old. Edward E. was fifteen years old. Eric R. was thirteen years old. Irvin C. was twelve years old. Lorraine L. was seven years old.

Edward Richard Zirpel & Matilda Louise Meinke Marriage & Family*

Edward Richard Zirpel, son of Johan and Augusta Zirpel, married Matilda Louise Meinke, daughter of Frederick H. Meinke and Anna C. Shultz, on April 7, 1926 in Hillside, Douglas County, South Dakota by Rev. P. Tecklenburg, a Lutheran Minister.[255]

Edward Richard and Matilda Louise Zirpel had one child: Walter Robert Zirpel.

Matilda Louise Meinke &
Edward Richard Zirpel Wedding. [361]

Birth of
Walter Robert Zirpel*

Walter Robert Zirpel, son of Edward Richard and Matilda Louise Zirpel, was born on May 20, 1929 and he was christened on July 13, 1929 in the Immanuel Lutheran Church in Douglas County, South Dakota.

Walter Robert Zirpel. [362]

Walter Robert Zirpel. [363]

Walter Robert Zirpel was confirmed in 1943 at the Immanuel Lutheran Church in Douglas County, South Dakota.

Edward Richard and Matilda Louise Zirpel were recorded on the 1930 United States Census on April 16, 1930 by the Census Enumerator, Mrs. Ida Bertram living in Washington Township, Douglas County, South Dakota.[256] Edward Richard was listed as thirty years old and his wife, Matilda Louise was twenty-six years old. Their son, Walter Robert Zirpel was eleven month old.

The Edward Zirpel family had moved by 1940, they were recorded on the 1940 United States Census on April 30, 1940 by the Census Enumerator, Frank L. Patterson, living in Tobin Township, Davison County, South Dakota.[258] Edward Richard was forty years old and his wife, Matilda was thirty-six years old. Their son, Walter Robert was 10 years old and he had completed the 5th Grade in a Elementary School.

Edward Richard &
Matilda Louise Zirpel -
The Later Years*

Matilda Louise Zirpel died on July 5, 1944 in Hutchinson County, South Dakota. She was buried on July 9, 1944 in the Immanuel Lutheran Church Cemetery in Douglas County, South Dakota.

194

The large stone for Edward Richard and Matilda Louise Zirpel located in the Immanuel Lutheran Church Cemetery in Douglas County, South Dakota. [364]

The small stone for Matilda Louise Zirpel located In the Immanuel Lutheran Church Cemetery in Douglas County, South Dakota. [365]

Edward Richard Zirpel died on November 28, 1971 in Parkston, Hutchinson County, South Dakota and he was buried in the Immanuel Lutheran Church Cemetery, in Douglas County, South Dakota next to his wife, Matilda Zirpel.

The grave stone for Edward Richard Zirpel located In the Immanuel Lutheran Church Cemetery in Douglas County, South Dakota. [366]

Phyllis Maxine Cummings & Her Family*

Phyllis Maxine Cummings, daughter of Ray and Marie E. Cummings born on June 10, 1928 in South Dakota.

The Cummings family was recorded on the 1930 United States Census living in Fairview Township, Hanson County, South Dakota on April 8, 1930 for the 1930 United States Census according to the Census Enumerator, Mrs. Alma M. Scott.[258]

On the report, Ray Cummings was born in Iowa and he was twenty-eight years old. His wife, Marie E. Cummings was born in South Dakota and she was twenty-seven years old. Ray and Marie E. Cummings had four children: Darlene B., Francis R., Betty J., and Phyllis M. Cummings. Darlene B was eight years old. Francis R was six years old. Betty J. was four years and 5 months old. While Phyllis M. was eleven months old.

Walter Robert Zirpel & Phyllis Maxine Cummings Marriage & Family*

Phyllis Maxine Cummings and Walter Robert Zirpel Wedding. [367]

Phyllis Maxine Cummings, daughter of Ray and Marie E. Cummings, married Walter Robert Zirpel, son of Edward Richard and Matilda Louise Zirpel, on Sunday, October 19, 1947 in the

Lutheran parsonage at Luverne, Rock County, Minnesota with the Rev. John Mundahl officiating.

For her wedding the bride chose a white gown with a white shoulder veil. Her only jewelry was a strand of pearls, a gift of the bridegroom. She wore a corsage of pink roses.

Mrs. Albert Meier, sister of the bride, was the bridesmaid and wore a pink gown with a matching shoulder veil. Her corsage was of pink roses and white carnations.

Attending the bridegroom was Albert Meier.

After the ceremony a two-course dinner was served at the home of the bride's Aunt, Mrs. Kenneth Shade, in Luverne. There was a two–tiered wedding cake in the center of the table.

Walter Robert and Phyllis Maxine Zirpel made plans to have a home in Mitchell, Davison County, South Dakota, where the bridegroom had a business. Mrs. Zirpel was formerly employed in Mitchell, South Dakota.

Relatives and friends attending the wedding were Ray and Marie E. Cummings and family, Mr. and Mrs. Clifford Shade, Mr. and Mrs. Bill Hargens and family, all of Alexandria, South Dakota. Mr. & Mrs. Everett Letcher and family of Worthington, Minnesota, Mr. and Mrs. Kenneth Shade and son, Mr. and Mrs. Orville Iveland and daughter of Luverne, Minnesota; and Sharon, Karon, and Bobby Meier of Mitchell, South Dakota.

Walter Robert and Phyllis Maxine Zirpel had five children: Richard Lee, Barbara Kay, Kathrine Rae, Roger Wayne and Allen Dale Zirpel.

Their marriage ended in divorce.

Phyllis Maxine Zirpel married Wayne McHone on a unknown date and location.

Phyllis Maxine McHone died on August 12, 2000 in Sioux Fall, Minnehaha County, South Dakota. She was buried in Hills of Rest Memorial Park in Sioux Falls, Minnehaha County, South Dakota.

Birth of
Richard Lee Zirpel*

Richard Lee Zirpel, son of Walter Robert and Phyllis Maxine Zirpel, was born on April 13, 1948.

Birth of
Barbara Kay Zirpel*

Barbara Kay Zirpel, daughter of Walter Robert and Phyllis Maxine Zirpel, was born on August 14, 1952.

Birth of
Katherine Rae Zirpel*

Katherine Rae Zirpel, daughter of Walter Robert and Phyllis Maxine Zirpel, was born on February 7, 1959.

Walter Robert Zirpel Family.
Back row: Walter Robert, Richard Lee, and Phyllis M.
Middle row: Katherine Rae. Front row: Roger Wayne, Allen Dale and Barbara Kay Zirpel. [369]

Phyllis M. and Walter Robert Zirpel 1947. [368]

Birth of
Roger Wayne Zirpel*

Roger Wayne Zirpel, son of Walter Robert and Phyllis Maxine Zirpel, was born on April 4, 1960.

Birth of
Allen Dale Zirpel*

Allen Dale Zirpel, son of Walter Robert and Phyllis Maxine Zirpel, was born on January 17, 1963.

According to Barbara Kay Zirpel, her father, Walter Robert Zirpel built the first Hartford Speedway located in Hartford, South Dakota. She said that her brothers help their father, when he built the speedway from ground up. She said that it originally was a half mile track back then. It was very hard work to build the track.

According to Roger Wayne Zirpel the Hartford Speedway was that his father, Walter Robert, built was opened in 1976 on July 4th. The cars were backup all the way to Hartford which is 2.5 miles just to get in that night. Roger said that it was a heck of a sight.

Walter Robert Zirpel, Rosalene Gertrude Roth
And Clifford Edwin Roth. [370]

Walter Robert Zirpel &
Ruby Nell Davis Marriage*

Walter Robert Zirpel married Ruby Nell Davis on December 30, 1981 in Clark County, Nevada.[259]

Ruby Nell Davis was born on December 15, 1938.

Walter Robert &
Ruby Nell Zirpel -
The Later Years*

Walter Robert Zirpel lived in South Dakota, Nevada, and Arkansas.

Walter Robert Zirpel died on Wednesday, July 25, 2007 at the Forrest City Medical Center, in St. Francis County, Arkansas.

His funeral was held on July 28, 2007 at the Stevens Funeral Home and his burial was in Loughridge Cemetery in Colt St. Francis County, Arkansas.

He was survived by his wife, Ruby Nell Zirpel, Forrest City, Arkansas; along with three sons: Richard Zirpel of Mariette, California, Roger and Allen Zirpel of Sioux Falls, South Dakota; two daughters: Barbara Zirpel of Sioux Falls, South Dakota and Katherine LaRock of Plano, Texas; one step-daughter, Lynn Ross of Las Vegas, Nevada; 14 grandchildren and 11 great-grandchildren.

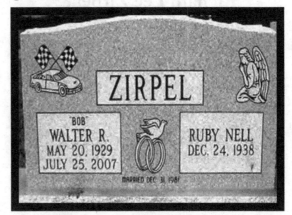

Walter Robert Zirpel grave located in the Loughridge Cemetery in Colt, St. Francis County, Arkansas. [371]

Richard Lee Zirpel &
Karanjo (Karen) Spears
Marriage & Family*

Richard Lee Zirpel, son of Walter Robert and Phyllis Maxine Zirpel, married Karonjo (Karen) Spears on July 10, April 1950.[260] The marriage ended in divorce.

Richard Lee and Karonjo (Karen) Zirpel had three children: Sarah D., Cortnee Brooke, and Meagan Leigh Zirpel.

Birth of
Sarah D. Zirpel*

Sarah D. Zirpel, daughter of Richard Lee and Karonjo (Karen) Zirpel, was born on July 10, 1974 in Orange County, California.[261]

197

Only eight days old, Sarah D. Zirpel died on July 18, 1974 in Orange County, California. No records of where she might be buried found.[262]

Birth of Cortnee Brooke Zirpel*

Cortnee Brooke Zirpel, daughter of Richard Lee and Karonjo (Karen) Zirpel, was born on December 30, 1975 in Orange County, California.[263]

Birth of Meagan Leigh Zirpel*

Meagan Leigh Zirpel, daughter of Richard Lee and Karonjo (Karen) Zirpel, was born on August 16, 1978 in Orange County, California.[264]

Richard Lee Zirpel & Diedra Maaz Marriage*

Richard Lee Zirpel married Diedra Maaz on April 27, 1986.

Cortnee Brooke Zirpel & Steve Todd Ingram Marriage & Family*

Cortnee Brooke Zirpel, daughter of Richard Lee and Karonjo (Karen) Zirpel, married Steven Tood Ingram on November 2, 2012 in Murrieta, California.

Steven Todd Ingram was born on April 15, 1966. He is from Riverside, California.

James Patrick Speeding, Cortnee Brooke Ingram's son, was born on August 27, 2005 from a different marriage.

Shawna Marie Ingram, Steve Todd Ingram's daughter was born on May 12, 1989 and Aylssa Marie Ingram, Steve Todd Ingram's daughter, was born on September 27, 2004 from a different marriage.

Dennis William John Baatz & His Family*

Both of Dennis William John Baatz's grandparents, Michael and Abbie Baatz, were born in Germany.

John Peter Baatz, Dennis William John Baatz's father was born on August 9, 1900 in Illinois.

On the 1910 United States Census on April 18, 1910 Michael and Abbie Baatz and their family were living in Sioux Township, Sioux County, Iowa according to the Census Enumerator, Albert J. Khumer.[265] John Peter was nine years old. Mattie was seven years old. Celia was five years old. George was three years old. Lena was eleven months old.

On January 12, 1920, the Census Enumerator, Ed J. Schmidt, recorded the Michael Baatz family living in Sioux Center, Sioux County, Iowa with nine children on the 1920 United States Census.[266]

The report stated that Michael was born in Luxemburg, Germany. Annie was twenty-one years old. John Peter was nineteen years old. Matt was seventeen years old. Celia was fourteen years old. Joe was twelve years old. Lena was ten years old. William was eight years old. Nettie was six years old. Albert was one year and two months old.

There was a Agnes Klein twenty-two years old listed on the report also.

Abbie Baatz, Michael Baatz's wife died between 1920 and 1930.

On the 1930 United States Census taken on April 14, 1930 by the Census Enumerator, Emmett R. Scanlan, Michael was listed as a widower living in Sioux Township, Sioux County, Iowa.[267]

Michael was fifty-seven years old and his birth year was about 1873. There were six children still living with him. John Peter was twenty-nine years old. Matt was twenty-seven years old. Joe was twenty-two years old.

On the 1940 United States Census taken on April 8, 1940, by the Census Enumerator, Mrs. Robert Jacobson, Michael Baatz was living with his son, William and his wife, Emma, in Sioux Township, Sioux County, Iowa.[268] William was twenty-eight years old and his wife, Emma was twenty-two years old.

John Peter Baatz, son of Michael and Abbie Baatz, married Loretta E. Schonhoff sometime during the 1930's possibly in Minnesota.

On April 12, 1940 for the 1940 United States Census, John Peter Baatz and his wife, Loretta were recorded by the Census Enumerator, H. H. Kiuper, living in Doon, Lyon County, Iowa with three children.[269]

The report stated that Loretta was born in North Dakota and she was thirty-one years old. Donald was born in Minnesota and he was seven years old.

Dennis William Baatz, son of John Peter Baatz and Loretta E. Schonhoff was born on April 1, 1946 in Rock County, Minnesota.[270]

John Peter Baatz was born on August 9, 1900 and he died on August 29, 1984. The same index said that Loretta E. Baatz was born May 2, 1908 and she died on January 16, 1991.

John Peter and Loretta E. Baatz are both buried in the Saint Mary's Cemetery located in Rock Valley, Sioux County, Iowa.[271]

Barbara Kay Zirpel & Dennis William John Baatz Marriage & Family*

Barbara Kay Zirpel, daughter of Walter Robert and Phyllis Maxine Zirpel, married Dennis William John Baatz, son of John Peter Baatz and Loretta E. Schonhoff, on August 23, 1969. Their marriage ended in divorce.

Dennis William John and Barbara Kay Baatz had four children: Lisa Kay, Laura Lynn, Robert John and Jonathan James Baatz.

Birth of Lisa Kay Baatz*

Lisa Kay Baatz, daughter of Dennis William John and Barbara Kay Baatz, was born on February 15, 1970 in Rock County, Minnesota.[272]

Birth of Laura Lynn Baatz*

Laura Lynn Baatz, daughter of Dennis William John and Barbara Kay Baatz, was born on July 3, 1971 in Rock County, Minnesota.[273]

Birth of Robert John Baatz*

Robert John Baatz, son of Dennis William John and Barbara Kay Baatz, was born on May 17, 1974 in Rock County, Minnesota.[274]

Birth of Jonathan James Baatz*

Jonathan James Baatz, son of Dennis William John and Barbara Kay Baatz, was born on January 7, 1977 in Rock County, Minnesota.[275]

Dennis William John Baatz died on August 6, 2008 and he was buried in the Saint Mary's

Cemetery in Rock Valley, Sioux County, Iowa where his parents were buried.

Dennis William John Baatz grave located in the Saint Mary's Cemetery in Rock Valley, Sioux County, Iowa. [372]

Barbara Kay Baatz & Dennis Peterson Marriage*

Barbara Kay Baatz married Dennis Peterson on September 19, 1987. The marriage ended in divorce.

Katherine Rae Zirpel & Brad LaRock Marriage & Family*

Katherine Rae Zirpel, daughter of Walter Robert and Phyllis Maxine Zirpel, married Brad LaRock on September 22, 1985. Their marriage ended in divorce

Brad LaRock was born on September 16, 1959.

Brad and Katherine Rae LaRock had one child: Brady LaRock.

Birth of Brady LaRock*

Brady LaRock, son of Brad and Katherine Rae LaRock , was born on September 19, 1989 in Las Vegas, Clark County, Nevada.

Brady LaRock & Stephanie Cutts Marriage & Family*

Brady LaRock, son of Brad and Katherine Rae LaRock, married Stephanie Cutts on November 1, 2014.

Stephanie Cutts was born on March 25, 1989

in Wylie, Collin County, Texas.

Brady and Stephanie LaRock have two children: Lucy Mae and Symphony Elizabeth LaRock.

Brady Stephanie, Lucy Mae, and
Symphony Elizabeth LaRock. [372]

Birth of
Lucy Mae LaRock*

Lucy Mae LaRock, daughter of Brady and Stephanie LaRock, were born on October 8, 2009.

Birth of
Symphony Elizabeth LaRock*

Symphony Elizabeth LaRock, daughter of Brady and Stephanie LaRock, was born on April 13, 2012 in Plano, Collin County, Texas.

Roger Wayne Zirpel &
Kim Dawn Thompson
Marriage & Family*

Roger Wayne Zirpel, son of Walter Robert and Phyllis M. Zirpel, married Kim Dawn Thompson.

Roger Wayne and Kim Dawn Zirpel have two children: Sarah Jo and Nicole Maria Zirpel.

Birth of
Sarah Jo Zirpel*

Sarah Jo, Kim Dawn, Roger Wayne and
Nicole Maria Zirpel. [373]

Sarah Jo Zirpel, daughter of Roger Wayne and Kim Dawn Zirpel was born on February 9, 1973 in Sioux Fall, South Dakota.

Birth of
Nicole Maria Zirpel*

Nicole Maria Zirpel, daughter of Roger Wayne and Kim Dawn Zirpel, was born on December 27, 1976 in Sioux Falls, South Dakota.

Allen Dale Zirpel &
Janet Lee Pritcher
Marriage & Family*

Allen Dale Zirpel, Walter Robert and Phyllis Maxine Zirpel, married Janet Lee Pritcher.

Janet Lee Pritcher was born on April 28, 1963 in Sioux Falls, Minnehaha County, South Dakota.

Allen Dale and Janet Lee Zirpel have two children: Zane Allen and Janay Lee Zirpel.

Birth of
Zane Allen Zirpel*

Zane Allen Zirpel, son of Allen Dale and Janet Lee Zirpel, was born on May 1, 2001 in Sioux Falls, Minnehaha County, South Dakota.

Birth of
Janay Lee Zirpel*

Janay Lee Zirpel, daughter of Allen Dale and Janet Lee Zirpel, was born on May 16, 2004 in Sioux Falls, Minnehaha County, South Dakota.

CHAPTER 11

Birth of Bertha Rosina Zirpel*

Bertha Rosina Zirpel, daughter of Johan and Augusta Zirpel, was born on September 14, 1904 in Douglas County, South Dakota and she was christened in 1904 in the St. John Lutheran Church in Douglas County, South Dakota.

On April 26, 1910, Bertha Rosina Zirpel was recorded with her parents, Johan and Augusta Zirpel on the 1910 United States Census taken by the Census Enumerator, Walter L. Koehn were living on the homestead located in Berlin or Washington Township in Douglas County, South Dakota. Johan Zirpel was twenty-seven years old and his wife Anna Augusta Zirpel was also twenty two years old. There were only six children living at home on this report. There were Emma Bertha, Wilhelm Otto, Elisabeth Augusta, Gottfried Johan, Edward Richard and Bertha Rosina Zirpel. Emma Bertha was seventeen years old. Wilhelm Otto was fourteen years old. Gottfried John and Elisabeth Augusta were twelve years old. Edward Richard was ten years old. Bertha Rosina was five years old.

Bertha Rosina Zirpel, the youngest daughter of Johan and Augusta Zirpel, gravestone located in the Immanuel Lutheran Church Cemetery in Douglas County, South Dakota. [375]

Johan & Anna Augusta Zirpel - Their Retirement Years*

The full view of Bertha Rosina Zirpel's grave. [374]

Unfortunately, Bertha Rosina Zirpel died on September 24, 1910 in Douglas County, South Dakota at the young age of six years old. She was buried in the Immanuel Lutheran Church Cemetery in Douglas County, South Dakota.

The third home of Johan and Augusta Zirpel is still in Parkston, South Dakota. [376]

When Johan and Augusta retired from the farm in Douglas County, South Dakota, they moved to Parkston, Hutchinson County, South Dakota. There Johan built his third home which was completed in 1921 and moved in to it in 1921.

The third home of Johan and Anna Augusta Zirpel was located on the corner of First Street and Teek Street in Parkston, South Dakota. On

April 2, 1930 the Census Enumerator, S. Mueller for the 1930 United States Census recorded Johan and Augusta living on First Street, in Parkston, Hutchinson County, South Dakota.[276]

Front view of John and Augusta Zirpel's home in 2000. [377]

The last known picture of Augusta and Johan Zirpel in 1929 [378]

The Passing of Anna Augusta Zirpel*

Anna Augusta Zirpel died on Wednesday, October 22, 1930 in her home in Parkston at the age of sixty-two years old.

During the last summer of Augusta's life she had some health problems. She improved some during the fall. Augusta and Johan had attended the dedication of the new St. John's Lutheran Church at Hillside in Douglas County, South Dakota on October 12, 1930. However, Immediately afterwards Augusta became seriously ill with the flu and liver complications. She passed away from her sickness.

Her funeral was held on Saturday, after noon at the Flensburg Lutheran Church in Douglas County, South Dakota. The service were conducted by Rev. Hempel and her burial was in the Immanuel Lutheran Church Cemetery in Douglas County, South Dakota.

She was survived by her husband, Johan; by four sons: Robert Herman, William Otto, Gottfried Johan, Edward Richard Zirpel who all lived west of Parkston, South Dakota; two daughters: Mrs. Elizabeth Augusta Gerlach of Hillside, South Dakota and Mrs. Emma Bertha Riecke of Blum Valley, South Dakota.

Besides twenty-one grandchildren mourn the death of their beloved grandmother, Anna Augusta Zirpel. She also left seven sisters and two brothers, three uncles and a step-mother.

Anna Augusta and Johan Zirpel gravestone Located in the Immanuel Lutheran Church Cemetery in Douglas County, South Dakota. [379]

The Passing of Johan Zirpel*

Johan Zirpel died on Saturday, January 16, 1937 in the home of William Otto Zirpel, northwest of Parkston, in Susquehanna Township in Hutchinson County, South Dakota at the age of seventy–eight years old.

According the death certificate, William G. Reib, M.D. of Parkston, South Dakota stated that

Johan and Augusta Zirpel home on October 25, 1930.
Gottfried Johan Zirpel, Edward Richard Zirpel, Gertrude Anna Zirpel, Matilda Louise Zirpel,
Emma Martha Maria Zirpel, William Otto Zirpel, Johan Zirpel, Robert Herman Zirpel,
Elisabeth Augusta Gerlach, Emma Bertha Riecke, Oscar Karl Gerlach, and George Peter Riecke,
The center photo is Anna Augusta Zirpel for her funeral, the last 2 people are unknown. [380]

Johan died from a influenza complicated with pneumonia and heart failure.

According to **THE PARKSTON AD-VANCE**, Parkston, South Dakota, Thursday, January 21, 1937. "Johan Zirpel, was one of the earliest settlers of Douglas County, and for a number of years a resident of Parkston, passed away at the home of his son, William Otto Zirpel, northwest of this city, Saturday afternoon, January 16, 1937, at the age of seventy-eight years old."

Johan had been healthy most of his life and he had been ill for only a week prior to his death. He began to feel ill on the Monday, January 11th. He had contracted a very hard cold, and was down in bed for only two days while it developed into pneumonia, and along with the heart failure caused his death. William said that his father,

Johan had been fully conscious until his peaceful and easy last hour came to a end. During his short illness Johan had been cared for by his son, William Otto Zirpel and his wife, Emma Martha Maria Zirpel.

The funeral service had been originally scheduled to be held at the home of his son, William Otto Zirpel the following Wednesday noon and also at the Flensburg Church in Douglas County, at two o'clock, with a service by Pastor Hempel.

However, there had been terribly large snow storm in the area which meant the funeral services were postponed. Due to all the blowing snow and snow block condition of the roads the funeral was postponed until Saturday in hopes of having better conditions.

Many of the roads were still blocked, on Saturday, they were able to get the funeral hearse and some cars to the county line. Many of the cars were unable to go any further than three miles west of Dimock, where they were met with horses and bob sleighs. With the bob sleighs Johan's body was carried to Hillside to the Flensburg Church where the services were held.

On account of the roads and weather conditions the attendance at the funeral was not very large, but it was much larger than expected, as all who had come with their teams.

The services were held at the Flensburg Lutheran Church. Rev. Hempel spoke on the text: Palms 90: 12 "So teach us to number our days that we may apply our hearts unto wisdom." A quartette also rendered an appropriate son. The interment was made at the Church Cemetery.

John Zirpel was born in November 2, 1858, in Steindorf, Silesia, Germany. His parent were John Zirpel and Johanna, Simonsek. Soon after his birth His parents, took Johan to Minken, where he was baptized and later confirmed in the Lutheran faith by Rev. Winkler.

At the age of fifteen Johan was apprenticed to learn the joiner's trade (Ischler handwerk). In 1882, at the age of twenty-four years, he left his homeland and came to America, where he homesteaded in the Hillside community in Douglas County, South Dakota.

One year later, on June 21, 1883, Johan was united in marriage to Anna Augusta Sperlich, by the Rev. Holter.

The young couple was forced to go through many hardships in the earlier days, but they built up good farms in the community, and his homestead place was in the Zirpel name for almost fifty five years.

To this union there were twelve children born. Five of the children died as babies or very young: a son, Johan Gottlieb Zirpel in 1889; twin daughters: Bertha Auguste and Emma Katharina Zirpel in 1890; a daughter, Bertha Rosina in 1893; another daughter, Bertha Rosina Zirpel in 1910; a daughter, Anna Emilie Heidner in 1912.

Johan Zirpel made two visits back to his homeland, Silesia, Germany, to visit his mother, Johanna Zirpel when she was sick.

In July of 1922, his younger sons took over the farming, while Johan and his wife, Anna Augusta Zirpel moved into Parkston and into their third home, a brick house which had built the year previous.

But only eight years later, on October 22, 1939, his faithful and loving wife, Anna Augusta, passed away, which was a great loss to him. Due to this, Johan's life was very lonely and he spent a lot of time with his son, William Otto, where he enjoyed playing with and being entertained by his twin grandsons, Martin Wilhelm and Melvin Otto Zirpel.

Those who preceded him in death were his parents, four brothers and three sisters, his wife and six children.

Those remaining to mourn his passing were six children: four sons – Robert Herman Zirpel, William Otto Zirpel, Gottfried Johan Zirpel and Edward Richard Zirpel; two daughters - Emma Bertha Riecke and Elisabeth Augusta Gerlach; three son-in-laws; four daughter-in-laws; two brothers in Germany and seven brother-in-laws in Germany, twenty-five grandchildren. Also a large number of relatives and descendants, old friends, who will remember him as a very helpful neighbor and friend, always ready to do his part for the community.

The Legacy Of
Johan and Augusta Zirpel Descendants*

There are over 1,372 known individuals, more than 522 families with more than 440 unique surnames in Johan and Anna Augusta Zirpel's family tree.

While Johan and Anna Augusta Zirpel were born in Germany, they made a courageous journey to the United States and followed their dream. The legacy of the family tree is scattered in over 261 locations, where the descendants were born, lived and died.

Here is a list of some known locations of the descendants and their families below.

1. Aberdeen, Brown County, South Dakota
2. Albuquerque, Bernalillo County, New Mexico
3. Alexandria, Hanson County, South Dakota
4. Alton, Madison County, Illinois
5. Ames, Story County, Iowa
6. Anoka, Anoka County, Minnesota
7. Appleton, Outagamie County, Wisconsin
8. Arapahoe County, Colorado
9. Armour, Douglas County, South Dakota

10. Augusta, Richmond County, Georgia
11. Aurora Center, Aurora County, South Dakota
12. Aurora, Arapahoe County, Colorado
13. Bakersfield, Kern County, California
14. Barton, Washington County, Wisconsin
15. Beadle County, South Dakota
16. Berlin or Washington Township, Douglas County, South Dakota
17. Berlin, Green Lake County, Wisconsin
18. Bernalillo County, New Mexico
19. Kaukauna, Outagamie County, Wisconsin
20. Bethesda, Montgomery County, Maryland
21. Omaha, Douglas County, Nebraska
22. Bismarck, Burleigh County, New York
23. Bleeker, Fulton, New York
24. Corsica, Douglas County, South Dakota
25. Blooming Valley, Douglas County, South Dakota
26. Bloomingdale, Jefferson County, Ohio
27. Bloomington, McLean County, Illinois
28. Blue Earth, Faribault County, Minnesota
29. Bon Homme County, South Dakota
30. Boxboro, Middlesex County, Massachusetts
31. Bozeman, Gallatin County, Montana
32. Brainerd, Crow Wing County, Minnesota
33. Brandon, Minnehaha County, South Dakota
34. Bridgeport, Fairfield County, Connecticut
35. Broadacre, Jefferson County, Ohio
36. Broken Arrow, Tulsa County, Oklahoma
37. Brookings County, South Dakota
38. Brookings, Brookings County, South Dakota
39. Brule County, South Dakota
40. Brunswick, Chariton County, Missouri
41. Burke, Gregory County, South Dakota
42. Calhoun County, Texas
43. California
44. Canova, Miner County, South Dakota
45. Canton, Lincoln County, South Dakota
46. Canton, Stark County, Ohio
47. Cascade, Sheboygan County, Wisconsin
48. Casper, Natrona County, Wyoming
49. Centennial, Arapahoe County, Colorado
50. Chamberlain, Brule County, South Dakota
51. Chambers County, Texas
52. Chambers, Holt County, Nebraska
53. Charleston County, Minnesota
54. Chicago, Cook County, Illinois
55. Lincoln, Lancaster County, Nebraska
56. Omaha, Douglas County, Nebraska
57. Clark County, Nevada
58. Clear Lake, Deuel County, South Dakota
59. Collier County, Florida
60. Colorado Springs, El Paso County, Colorado
61. Coon Rapids, Anoka County, Minnesota
61. Corsica, Douglas County, South Dakota
62. Cottonwood, Shasta County, California
63. Crow Lake, Jerauld County, South Dakota
64. Madison, Lake County, South Dakota
65. Davison County, South Dakota
66. Delmont, Douglas County, South Dakoa
67. Denver, Denver County, Colorado
68. Detroit Lakes, Becker County, Minnesota
69. Detroit, Wayne County, Michigan
70. Dimock, Hutchison County, South Dakota
71. Douglas County, Dakota Territory
72. Douglas County, South Dakota
73. Durbin, Cass County, North Dakota
74. Eagle Butte, Dewey County, South Dakota
75. Eatonton, Putnam County, Georgia
76. Canadian County, Oklahoma
77. Emery, Hanson County, South Dakota
78. Slaton, Lubbock County, Texas
79. Enid, Garfield County, Oklahoma
80. Epiphany, Miner County, South Dakota
81. Ethan, Minor County, South Dakota
82. Woonsocket, Sanborn County, South Dakota
83. Everett, Snohomish County, Washington
84. Fairmont, Martin County, Minnesota
85. Fairplay, Jefferson County, Ohio
86. Parkston, Hutchinson County, South Dakota
87. Fargo, Cass County, North Dakota
88. Farmington, Oakland County, Michigan
89. Spartanburg, Spartanburg County, South Carolina
90. Rio Rancho, Sandoval County, New Mexico
91. Platte, Charles Mix County, South Dakota
92. Mitchell, Davison County, South Dakota
93. Huron, Beadle County, South Dakota
94. Flandreau, Moody County, South Dakota
95. Glendale, California
96. Franklin County, New Mexico
97. Freeman, Hutchinson County, South Dakota
98. Fresno County, California
99. Tripp, Hutchinson County, South Dakota
100. Adams County, Wisconsin
101. San Diego, San Diego County, California
102. Garfield Township, Douglas County, South Dakota
103. Garretson, Minnehaha County, South Dakota
104. Gem Township, Brown County, South Dakota

105. German, Hutchinson County, South Dakota
106. Gillette, Campbell County, Wyoling
107. Grand Island, Hall County, Nebraska
108. Grand Rapids, Itasca County, Minnesota.
109. Grattan, Holt County, Nebraska
110. Green Valley, Oconto County, Wisconsin
111. Wolf Point, Roosevelt County, Montana
112. Gregory, Gregory County, South Dakota
113. Guthrie County, Iowa
114. Hall County, Georgia
115. Harrold, Hughes County, South Dakota
116. Hartford, Hartford County, Connecticut
117. Harford, Minnehaha County, South Dakota
118. Hawkinsville, Pulaski County, Georgia
119. Hawthorne, Los Angeles County, California
120. Helena, Lewis and Clark County, Montana
121. Hendricks, Lincoln County, Minnesota
122. Hennepin County, Minnesota
123. Hermann, Washington County, Nebraska
124. Hollywood, Los Angeles County, California
125. Milledgeville, Baldwin County, Georgia
126. Hopedale, Harrison County, Ohio
127. Horseshoe Bend, Boise County, Idaho
128. Howard, Miner County, South Dakota
129. Humboldt County, Iowa
130. Huntsville, Madison County, Alabama
131. Hutchinson County, South Dakota
132. Bertrand, Phelps County, Nebraska
133. Grand Island, Hall County, Nebraska
134. Santa Rosa, California
135. Irwinton, Wilkinson County, Georgia
136. Jasper, Pipestone County, Minnesota
137. Jefferson County, Ohio
138. Jerauld County, South Dakota
139. Kansas
140. Kaukauna, Outagamie, Wisconsin
141. Kaylor, Hutchinson County, South Dakota
142. Kingsbury County, South Dakota
143. La Crosse, La Crosse County, Wisconsin
144. Lake Andes, Charles Mix County, South Dakota
145. Lake County, South Dakota
146. Lane, Jerauld County, South Dakota
147. Las Vegas, Clark County, Nevada
148. Sioux City, Woodbury County, Iowa
149. Lemhi County, Idaho
150. Lincoln Township, Douglas County, South Dakota
151. Lincoln, Lancaster County, Nebraska
152. Livonia, Wayne County, Michigan
153. Los Angeles, Los Angeles County, California
154. Colt, St. Francis County, Arkansas
155. Lubbock, Lubbock County, Texas
156. Macon, Bibb County, Georgia
157. Luverne, Rock County, Minnesota
158. Lydon, Sheboygan County, Wisconsin
159. Lyon County, Minnesota
160. Madoning County, Ohio
161. Manteca, San Joaquin County, California
162. Marion, Turner County, South Dakota
163. Marshall, Lyon County, Minnesota
164. Brea, Orange County, California
165. Mentor, Lake County, Iowa
166. Mentor, Lake County, Ohio
167. Merced County, California
168. Miami, Dade County, Florida
169. Michigan
170. Miles City, Custer County, Montana
171. Miller, Hand County, South Dakota
172. Milwaukee County, Wisconsin
173. Miner County, South Dakota
174. Minneapolis, Hennepin County Minnesota
175. Minnehaha County, South Dakota
176. Mission, Todd County, South Dakota
177. Modesto, Stanislaus County, California
178. Monday, Hocking County, Ohio
179. Artesian, Sanborn County, South Dakota
180. Muscatine County, Iowa
181. Naples, Collier County, Florida
182. Nassau Bay, Harris County, Texas
183. Nebraska
184. Nashville, Davidson County, Tennesse
185. Neenah, Winnebago County, Wisconsin
186. Netherlands
187. New Mexico
188. New York
189. Nobles County, Minnesota
190. Norfolk County, Nebraska
191. North Carolina
192. North Dakota
193. O'Neil, Holt County, Nebraska
194. Oakdale, Stanislaus County, California
195. Rockdale, Milam County, Texas
196. Ohio
197. Okinawa, Japan
198. Omaha, Douglas County, Nebraska
199. Orange County, California
200. Painesville, Lake County, Ohio
201. Winter Park, Seminole County, Florida
202. Manteca, San Joaquin, California
203. Pender, Thurston County, Nebraska
204. Pennsylvania

205. Perham, Otter Tail County, Minnesota
206. Pickstown, Charles Mix County, South Dakota
207. Pierre, Hughes County, South Dakota
208. Pipestone, Pipestone County, Minnesota
209. Plankinton, Aurora County, South Dakota
210. Plano, Collin County, Texas
211. Platte, Charles Mix County, South Dakota
212. Poison, Lake County, Montana
213. Pope County, Minnesota
214. Portsmouth, Scioto County, Ohio
215. Bozeman, Gallatin County, Montana
216. Proctor, Lake County, Montana
217. Putnam County, Georgia
218. Rapid City, Pennington County, South Dakota
219. Reeds Mill, Jefferson County, Ohio
220. Reliance, Lyman County, South Dakota
221. Rio Rancho, Sandoval County, New Mexico
222. Fargo, North Dakota
223. Roberts County, South Dakota
224. Rochester, Monroe County, New York
225. Rock County, Minnesota
226. Rosebud County, Montana
227. Rockdale, Milam County, Texas
228. Rogue River, Jackson County, Oregon
229. Scotland, Bon Homme County, South Dakota
230. Saint Paul, Ramsey County, Minnesota
231. Salmon, Lemhi County, Idaho
232. San Diego, San Diego County, California
233. San Joaquin, Fresno County, California
234. San Jose, San Diego County, California
235. San Fe County, New Mexico
236. Saunders, Valley County, Nebraska
237. Savannah, Chatham County, Georgia
238. Scotland, Bon Homme County, South Dakota
239. Scott, Sheboygan County, Wisconsin
240. Seattle, Kitsap County, Washington
241. Shasta County, California
242. Sheboygan County, Wisconsin
243. Shiocton, Outagamie County, Wisconsin
244. Sioux Falls, Minnehaha County, South Dakota
239. Sisseton, Roberts County, South Dakota
240. Smithfield, Jefferson County, Ohio
241. Sonora, Tuolumne County, California
242. South Dakota
243. Springfield, Sangamon County, Illinois
244. St. Joseph, Buchanan County, Missouri
245. Enid, Garfield County, Oklahoma

246. Stanley County, South Dakota
247. Steubenville, Jefferson County, Ohio
248. Stickney, Aurora County, South Dakota
249. Stockton, San Diego County, California
250. Storrs, Tolland County, Connecticut
251. Stratton, Kit Carson County, Colorado
252. Taycheedah, Ford du Lac County, Wisconsin
253. Tennessee
254. Texas
255. Townsend, Broadway County, Montana
256. Trent, Moody County, South Dakota
257. Tuscarawas County, Ohio
258. Port Washington, Tuscarawas County, Ohio
259. Valentine, Cherry County, Nebraska
260. Valley Grove, Ohio County, West Virginia
261. Vermillion, Clay County, South Dakota
262. Perry, Dallas County, Iowa
263. Wagner, Charles Mix County, South Dakota
264. Wall Lake, Sac County, Iowa
265. Walnut, Pottawattamie County, Iowa
266. Watertown, Codington County, South Dakota
248. Watertown, Jefferson County, Wisconsin
249. Wathena, Doniphan County, Kansas
250. Wayne County, Michigan
251. Mingo Junction, Jefferson County, Ohio
252. West Alexander, Washington County, Pennsylvania
252. West Bend, Washington County, Wisconsin
253. Wheeling, Ohio County, West Virginia
254. Wichita, Sedgwick County, Kansas
255. Wisconsin
256. Wyandotte, Houghton County, Michigan
257. Wylie, Colin County, Texas
258. Wyoming, Colorado
259. Yale, Beadle County, South Dakota
260. Yankton, Yankton County, South Dakota
261. Yorktown, DeWitt County, Texas

ZIRPEL PHOTO ALBUM

Clara Elsie Riecke [382]

Back row: Albert Wilhelm Riecke, Erna Rosina (Schuh) Riecke, Clara Elsie Schrank, Kenneth August Schrank, George Gilbert Riecke Jr., Bernice (Vreugdenhil) Riecke, Sophia Alvina Elisabeth Semmler, Viola Alma Elizabeth Schuh, and Arnold Reuben Schuh. Next Row: George Peter Riecke, Emma Berth Riecke, Gloria Kaye Riecke, and Sheila Joan Schuh. Front Row: Larry Dean Schrank, Maylon Ray Schuh, Duane Arnold Schuh, Garland Kenneth Schrank, Barbara Lynn Schrank, Mavis Jean Riecke, Harvey Lee Schrank, and Janice Emma Schrank. [381]

The Riecke children [383]

Wilhelm Otto and Emma Martha Marie Zirpel Family.
Back Row: Malvin Otto, Wilma Norma, Waldemar Gotthelf, Margaret Maria, and Martin Wilhelm Zirpel.
Front row: Wilhelm Otto, Edna Emma and Emma Martha Maria Zirpel.[384]

Confirmation Class at the Immanuel Lutheran Church in Douglas County,
South Dakota in 1939. Back row: George Reimnitz, Wilma Norma Zirpel,
Ethel Neugebauer, Anita Reimnitz, Rev. Hempel and Gerhard Geidel.
Front row: Adela Schumacher, Irene Emma Gerlach, Waldemar Gotthelf Zirpel,
Wilbert Erich Zirpel, Eileen Sigmund and Francis Neugebauer.[385]

Confirmation Class at the Immanuel Lutheran Church in 1941.
Erwin Karl Zirpel, Lorraine Bialas, Agnes Geidel, Rev. Hempel, Nelda Geidel,
Lydia Reimnitz, and Norbert Neugebauer [386]

Immanuel Lutheran Church in Douglas County, South Dakota [387]

Viola Alma Elizabeth Riecke [389]

**Confirmation Class at the
Immanuel Lutheran Church in 1953.
Back row: Norbert Reichert,
Marjean Bartelt, Rev. Dewald,
Rosalene Gertrude Zirpel, Marie Schulz
and Sylvia Reichert. [388]**

Confirmation Class at the Immanuel Lutheran Church in 1943.
Back row: Herbert Geidel, Carola Koehn, Rev. Hempel, Lena Reimnitz, and
Walter Robert Zirpel, Front row: Norbert John Zirpel, Irma Geidel, Lillian Esther Moege,
Mildred Schumacher, Gladys Gerlach, and Ivan Bialas. [390]

Confirmation Class at the Immanuel Lutheran Church in 1958.
Back row: Rev. Eberhard. Middle row: Herbert Reimnitz, Mary Jane Gerlach,
Joyce Neugebauer, Sharon Ziebert and Wallace Schultz. Front row:
Mary Ellen Ruth Zirpel, Ruth Elaine Neugebauer, Doris Betram, and JoAnn Bialas [391]

Johan and Anna Augusta Zirpel had a sod house similar to this one. [392]

Bibliography

*Legacy Family Files owned by Mona Clydene Zirpel, Lane, South Dakota & St. John's Lutheran Church Records and Other family records.

1. Personal Knowledge of Erwin and Olinda Zirpel
2. Obituaries
3. Family Search U.S. Social Security Index Records.
4. South Dakota Marriage Records, 1905-1949.
5. Ancestry.com's Social Security Death Index Records.
6. Personal Knowledge of Lois Bialas.
7. Personal Knowledge of Melvin and Joan Frahm.
8. Personal Knowledge of Wilbert Zirpel Jr.
9. Personal Knowledge of Audrey May Zirpel.
10. Personal Knowledge of Mary Ellen Mettenbrink.
11. Personal Knowledge of Bryan Allen Zirpel.
12. Personal Knowledge of Victoria Lynn Miller Zirpel.
13. Personal Knowledge of Mary Ann Dammann.
14. Personal Knowledge of Elmer and Luella Zirpel.
15. Personal Knowledge of Norbert and Elaine Zirpel.
16. Personal Knowledge of Beverly Jean Pittman.
17. Personal Knowledge of Rodger Danner.
18. Personal Knowledge of Bonnie Schuh.
19. Personal Knowledge of Darlene Horst.
20. Personal Knowledge of Mildred Zirpel.
21. Personal Knowledge of Helen Gerlach.
22. Personal Knowledge of Karen Pooley.
23. Personal Knowledge of Harold and Virginia Zirpel.
24. Personal Knowledge of Tammy Semmler.
25. Personal Knowledge of Alma Bittiker.
26. Personal Knowledge of Dennis Bittiker.
27. Personal Knowledge of Karel Janis Amend.
28. Personal Knowledge of Kim Danner.
29. Personal Knowledge of Solomon and Mary Jo Semmler.
30. Personal Knowledge of Barbara Unland.
31. Personal Knowledge of Marlys Martha Moege.
32. Personal Knowledge of Edna Emma and Dennis Allen Stoebner
33. Personal Knowledge of Margaret Maria Bertram
34. Personal Knowledge of Eryn (Zirpel) Bowers
35. Personal Knowledge of Marvin Knock marvin@knock.com
36. Personal Knowledge of MaryAnn Dammann
37. Personal Knowledge of Melvin & Joan Frahm
38. Personal Knowledge of Rebecca Jean Stunes
39. Personal Knowledge of Rich Ludwig RBLudwig@aol.com
40. Personal Knowledge of Barbara Kay Zirpel.
41. Personal Knowledge of Roger Wayne Zirpel.
42. Personal Knowledge of Katherine Rae LaRock.
43. Personal Knowledge of Allen Dale Zirpel.
44. Personal Knowledge of Rosalene Gertrude Roth
45. Personal Knowledge of Margaret Lou Wendlandt.
46. Personal Knowledge of Karen Bekx.
47. Personal Knowledge of Kayla Proctor.
48. Personal Knowledge of Ruth Nelson.
49. Personal Knowledge of Cortnee Brooke Ingram

[1, 2, 3, 4, 5, 6, 7, 8,] Certification # - 943329—12.11 H-22364. © 1994, The Hall of Names Inc.

[9, 10,] Obituary, *The Parkston Advance*: Parkston, South Dakota, Thursday, February 4, 1937.

[11, 12,] Posted to the Ships List by Ted Finch - October 18, 1997.

[13] Copy of the 1st Paper for National Record were recorded in Volume 229, on page 187, in Davison County, South Dakota and owned by Mona Clydene Zirpel, Wessington Springs, South Dakota.

[14, 17,] DOUGLAS COUNTY HISTORY and Centennial Observances 1961. Stickney, SD: Argus Printers, P.25, History of Berlin Township by Mrs. William Zangle.

[15, 16,] Karolevitz, Robert L. (1983). *DOUGLAS COUNTY "THE LITTLE GIANT.* Freeman, South Dakota: Pine Hill Press. p.119.

[18,] Information from Sophia Goldammer, Karen Ludens, and Joan and Melvin Frahm, October 4, 2000.

[19, 20, 26, 30, 43,] Plat Map of Berlin Township, Douglas County, South Dakota, 1909 Atlas.

[21,] Year: 1920; Census Place: Washington, Douglas, South Dakota; Roll: T625_1719; Page:3B; Enumeration District: 80; 623.

[22,] Plat Map of Baker Township, Davison County, South Dakota, 1901 Atlas.

[23,] Plat Map of Mount Vernon Township, Davison County, South Dakota, 1901 Atlas.

[24,] Year: 1910; Census Place: Mount Vernon, Davison, South Dakota; Roll: T624_1470; Page: 8A; Enumeration District: 0133; Image: 382; FHL Number: 1375492.

[25] Year: 1930; Census Place: Mount Vernon, Davison, South Dakota; Roll:2221; Page: 3B; Enumeration District: 13; Image: 1033.0.

[27,] Year: 1910; Census Place: Berlin, Douglas, South Dakota; Roll: T624_1480; Page 1B; Enumeration District: 0169; Image: 63; FHL Number: 1375493.

[28,] Year: 1920; Census Place: Washington, Douglas, South Dakota; Roll: T625_1719; Page: 2B;

[29,] Year: 1930; Census Place: Washington, Douglas, South Dakota; Roll: 2222; Page: 4B; Enumeration District 17; Image: 939.0.

[31,] Year: 1910; Census Place: Berlin, Douglas, South Dakota; Roll: T624_1480; Page 5A; Enumeration District: 0169; Image: 70; FHL Number: 1375493.

[32,] Year: 1920; Census Place; Union, Davison, South Dakota; Roll: T625_1716; Page: 2B; Enumeration District: 64; Image: 856.

[33,] Year: 1930; Census Place; Cross Plains, Hutchinson, South Dakota; Roll: 2225; Page: 4B; Enumeration District: 3; Image: 30.0.

[35] Year: 1900; Census Place: Baker, Davison, South Dakota; Roll: T623_1548; Page:5A; Enumeration District: 109;

[36,] Year: 1910; Census Place: Baker, Davison, South Dakota; Roll: T624_1470; Page: 5A; Enumeration District: 0132; Image: 356; FHL Number: 1375492.

[37,] Year: 1920; Census Place: Baker, Davison, South Dakota; Roll: T625_1716; Page: 6A; Enumeration District: 64; Image: 863.

[39,] Year: 1910; Census Place: Baker, Davison, South Dakota; Roll: T624_1479; Page:5A; Enumeration District; 0132; Image:

[40,] Year: 1930; Census Place: Mount Vernon, Davison, South Dakota; Roll: 2221; Page: 3A; Enumeration District: 12; Image: 1022.0.

[34, 38, 41, 42,] Plat Map of Baker Township, Davison County, South Dakota, 1949 Atlas.

[44,] Year 1920; Census Place: Washington, Douglas, South Dakota; Roll: T625_1719; Page: 2B; Enumeration District: 80; Image: 621.

[45,] Year: 1930; Census Place: Washington, Douglas, South Dakota; Roll: 2222; Page: 2A; Enumeration District: 17; Image: 931.0.

[46,] Year: 1900; Census Place: Lincoln, Douglas, South Dakota; Roll: T623_1540; Page: 1B; Enumeration District: 136.

[47,] Year: 1910; Census Place: Baker, Davison, South Dakota; Roll: T624_1470; Page: 5A; Enumeration District: 0132; Image: 356; FHL Number: 1375492.

[48,] Year: 1920; Census Place: Baker, Davison, South Dakota; Roll: T625_1716; Page: 6A; Enumeration District: 64; Image 863.

[49,] Year: 1930 Census Place: Baker, Davison, South Dakota; Roll: 2221; Page: 2A; Enumeration District: 2; Image: 728.0.

[50,] Copy of a Final Receivers Receipt, Receivers Office Yankton Territory, August 26, 1887, Copy of Land Documents from Douglas County Courthouse, Armour, South Dakota.

[51, 52,] Copy of The Homesteader Land Patent Application Number 8492 with Certificate Number 4661, from Douglas County Courthouse, Armour, South Dakota.

[53, 54.] Copy of The Timber Culture Patent Application Number 4225 with Certificate Number 1071, from Douglas County Courthouse, Armour, South Dakota.

[55.] Year: 1880; Census Place: Green Valley, Shawano, Wisconsin; Roll: 1447; Page: 346B; Enumeration District: 152; FHL Microfilm 1255447.

[56.] Year: 1900; Census Place: Lincoln, Douglas, South Dakota; Roll: 1549; Page: 1A; Enumeration District: 136; FHL Microfilm: 124549.

[57.] Year: 1900; Census Place: Berlin, Douglas, South Dakota; Roll: 1549; Page 10A; Enumeration District: 137; FHL Microfilm: 1241549.

[58.] Copy of World War I Draft Registration Cards, 1917-1918. Registration State: South Dakota; Registration County: Douglas; Roll: 1877791. [database on-line]. Provo, UT, USA: Ancestry.com Operations Inc., 2005.

[59.] Year: 1920; Census Place: Lincoln, Douglas, South Dakota; Roll: T627_1719; Page 9A; Enumeration District: 80, Image 634.

[60, 64,] Ancestry.com. South Dakota Marriages, 1905-1949 [database on-line]. Provo, UT, USA: Ancestry.com Operations Inc., 2005.Original data: South Dakota Department of Health. South Dakota Marriage Index, 1905-1914 and South Dakota Marriage Certificates, 1905-1949. Pierre, SD, USA: South Dakota Department of Health.

[61,] Year: 1930; Census Place: Lincoln Township, Douglas County, South Dakota; Roll: 2222; Page: 3A; Enumeration District: 14; Image: 905.0; FHL Microfilm: 2341956.

[62,] Year: 1940; Census Place: Lincoln, Douglas, South Dakota; Roll: T627_3855; Page 3B; Enumeration District: 22-14.

[63,] Year: 1920; Census Place: Lincoln, Douglas, South Dakota; Roll: T625_1719; Page: 6B; Enumeration District: 80; Image: 629.

[65,] Year: 1920; Census Place: Tobin Township, Davison County, South Dakota; Supervisor's District number: 1; Enumeration District: 66; Sheet Number: 10B.

[66,] Year: 1930; Census Place: Tobin Township, Davison County, South Dakota; Supervisor's District Number: 5; Enumeration District Number: 11-17; Sheet Number: 5-B.

[67] Year: 1900; Census Place: Berlin Township, Douglas County, South Dakota; Roll: 1549; Page: 10A; Enumeration District: 137; FHL Microfilm: 124549.

[68] Year: 1910; Lincoln Township, Douglas County, South Dakota; Roll: T624_1480; Page: 6A; Enumeration District: 0169; Image: 72; FHL Microfilm: 1375493

[69,] Year: 1900; Place: Valley Township, Douglas County, South Dakota; Roll: 1549; Page: 5B; Enumeration District: 137; FHL Microfilm: 1241549.

[70,] Year: 1910; Census Place: Garfield Township, Douglas County, South Dakota; Roll: T624_1480; Page: 7B; Enumeration District: 0170; Image: 93; FHL microfilm: 137493.

[71, 73,] Year: 1920; Census Place: Lincoln Township, Douglas County, South Dakota; Roll: T625_1719; Page 7B; Enumeration District: 8-; Image 631.

[72,] Copy of World War I Draft Registration Cards, 1917-1918. Registration State: South Dakota; Registration County: Douglas; Roll: 1877791. [database on-line]. Provo, UT, USA: Ancestry.com Operations Inc., 2005.

[74,] Year: 1930; Census Place: Lincoln Township, Douglas County, South Dakota; Supervisor's District Number: 5; Enumeration District Number: 22-14.

[75,] Year: 1940; Census Place: Lincoln Township, Douglas County, South Dakota; Roll: T627_3855; Page: 1B; Enumeration District: 22-14.

[76,] Year: 1930; Census Place: Lake Flat Township, Pennington County, South Dakota; Roll: 2229; Page: 1B; Enumeration District: 12; Image: 649.0; FHL Microfilm: 2341963.

[77,] Census: 1940; Census Place: Flandreau, Moody County, South Dakota; Roll: T627_3865; Page: 9A; Enumeration District: 51-9.

[78,] Census: 1940; Census Place: Hersey Township, Nobles County, Minnesota; Roll: T627_1942; Page: 2B; Enumeration District: 53-12.

[79,] Ancestry.com. South Dakota Marriages, 1905-1949 [database on-line]. Provo, UT, USA: Ancestry.com Operations Inc., 2005.Original data: South Dakota Department of Health. South Dakota Marriage Index, 1905-1914 and South Dakota Marriage Certificates, 1905-1949. Pierre, SD, USA: South Dakota Department of Health.

[80] Year: 1920; Census Place: Township 143, Dunn County, North Dakota; Roll: T625_1333; Page: 7A; Enumeration District: 50; Image: 381.

[81,] Year: 1930; Census Place: Lincoln, Hamilton County, Iowa; Roll: 657; Page: 1A; Enumeration

District: 19; Image: 447.0; FHL Microfilm: 234392.

82, Year: 1940; Census Place: Lake Marshall, Lyon County, Minnesota; roll: T627_1934; Page:3A; Enumeration District: 42-13A.

83, Year: 1920; Census Place: Washington, Doniphan County, Kansas; Roll: T625_530; Page: 1B; Enumeration District: 46; Image: 743.

84 Year: 1930; Census Place: Lafayette, Clinton County, Missouri; Roll: 1183: Page: 4A; Enumeration District: 11; Image: 705.0; FHL Microfilm: 2340918.

85 Year: 1940; Census Place: Wathena, Doniphan County, Kansas; Roll: T627_1229; Page: 7B; Enumeration District: 22-14.

86 Year: 1930; Census Place: Winston-Salem, Forsyth County, North Carolina; Roll: 1690; Page: 26B; Enumeration District: 52; Image: 137.0; FHL Microfilm: 23341424.

87 Year: 1940; Census Place: Ogburn-East and Northeast Winston-Salem, Forsyth County, North Carolina; Roll: T627_2907; Page: 6A; Enumeration District: 34-17.

88, Year: 1930; Census Place: Lincoln Township, Douglas County, South Dakota; Roll: 2222; Page: 1A; Enumeration District: 14; Image: 901.0; FHL Microfilm: 2341956.

89, Year: 1940; Census Place: Lincoln Township, Douglas County, South Dakota; Roll: T627_3855; Page: 2B; Enumeration District: 22-14.

90, Ancestry.com. South Dakota Marriages, 1905-1949 [database on-line]. Provo, UT, USA: Ancestry.com Operations Inc., 2005.Original data: South Dakota Department of Health. South Dakota Marriage Index, 1905-1914 and South Dakota Marriage Certificates, 1905-1949. Pierre, SD, USA: South Dakota Department of Health.

91, Year: 1940; Census Place: Bailey, Lyman County, South Dakota; Roll: T627_3861; Page: 1A; Enumeration District: 43-3.

92, Staatarchive Hamburg; Volume: 373-7 I, VIII A 1 Band 048 B; Seite 561; Microfilm Number: K_1729. Staatarchive Hamburg. Passenger Lists, 1850-1934 [Database on-line], Provo, UT, USA: Ancestry.com Operations Inc., 2008. Original date: Staatsarchiv Hamburg, Bestand: 373-7 I, VIII (Auswanderungesamt I). Mikrofilmrollen K 1701– K 2008, S 17363 - S 17383, 13116 - 13183.

93, Staatarchive Hamburg; Volume: 373-7 I, VIII A 1 Band 132; Suite 1549; Microfilm Number: K_1775. Staatarchive Hamburg. Passenger Lists, 1850-1934 [Database on-line], Provo, UT, USA: Ancestry.com Operations Inc., 2008. Original date: Staatsarchiv Hamburg, Bestand: 373-7 I, VIII (Auswanderungesamt I). Mikrofilmrollen K 1701– K 2008, S 17363 - S 17383, 13116 - 13183.

94, Dictionary of American Navel Fighting Ships. Department of the Navy - Naval History and Heritage Command, 805 Kidder Breese SE, Washington Navy Yard, Washington DC 20374-5060.

95, 96, Copy of Deed Record, Douglas County Courthouse, Armour, Douglas County, South Dakota and Government records published before 1923 are Public Domain.

97, Year: 1900; Census Place: Berlin Township, Douglas County, South Dakota; Supervisor's District Number: 2; Enumeration District Number: 137; Sheet Number: 10; Page 40.

98, Year: 1910; Census Place: Berlin Township, Douglas County, South Dakota; Supervisor's District Number: 1; Enumeration District Number: 169; Sheet Number: 4; Page 7.

99, Year: 1920; Census Place: Lincoln Township, Douglas County, South Dakota; Supervisor's District Number: 1; Enumeration District Number: 80; Sheet Number: 7; Page: 14.

100, 101, Copy of Deed Record, Douglas County Courthouse, Armour, Douglas County, South Dakota and Government records published before 1923 are Public Domain.

102, Year: 1900; Census Place: Berlin Township, Douglas County, South Dakota; Roll: 1549; Page: 10A; Enumeration District: 137; FHL Microfilm: 124549.

103, Year: 1910; Census Place: Lincoln Township, Douglas County, South Dakota; Supervisor's District Number: 1; Enumeration District Number: 169; Sheet Number: 4; Page: 7.

104, Year: 1920; Census Place: Baker Township, Davison County, South Dakota; Roll: T625_1716; Page: 5A; Enumeration District: 64; Image: 861.

105, Year: 1930; Census Place: Baker Township, Davison County, South Dakota; Roll: 2221; Page: 1A; Enumeration District: 2; Image: 726.0; FHL Microfilm: 2341955.

106, Year: 1930; Census Place: Valley Township, Douglas County, South Dakota; Roll: 2222; Page: 3B; Enumeration District: 15; Image: 916.0 FHL Microfilm: 2341956.

107, Ancestry.com. South Dakota Marriages, 1905-1949 [database on-line]. Provo, UT, USA: Ancestry.com Operations Inc., 2005.Original data: South Dakota Department of Health. South Dakota Marriage Index, 1905-1914 and South Dakota Marriage Certificates, 1905-1949. Pierre, SD, USA: South Dakota Department of Health.

108, Year: 1940; Census Place: Washington Township, Douglas County, South Dakota; Roll: T627_3855; Page: 2A; Enumeration District: 22-17.

109, U.S. Directories, 1821-1989, Ancestry.com

110, Year: 1930; Census Place: Belmont, Douglas County, South Dakota; Roll: 2222; Page:1A; Enumeration District: 2; Image: 797.0; FHL Microfilm: 23411956.

111, Ancestry.com. South Dakota Marriages, 1905-1949 [database on-line]. Provo, UT, USA: Ancestry.com Operations Inc., 2005.Original data: South Dakota Department of Health. South Dakota Marriage Index, 1905-1914 and South Dakota Marriage Certificates, 1905-1949. Pierre, SD, USA: South Dakota Department of Health.

112 Year: 1940; Census Place: Rome Township, Davison County, South Dakota; Roll: T627_3853; Page: 5B; Enumeration District: 18-19.

113, U.S. Public Records Index, Volume 2, 1935-2001, Ancestry.com

114, Year: 1940; Census Place: Mitchell, Davison County, South Dakota; Roll: T627_3853; Page: 12A; Enumeration District: 18-7.

115, S Van Meir Family Tree owner: bikshelly on Ancestry.com

116, Year: 1930; Census Place: Garfield Township, Douglas County, South Dakota; Roll: 2222; Page: 2A; Enumeration District: 8; Image: 849.0; FHL microfilm: 2341956.

117, Year: 1940; Census Place: Garfield, Douglas County, South Dakota; Roll: T627_3855; Page: 2B; Enumeration District: 22-8.

118, Ancestry.com. South Dakota Marriages, 1905-1949 [database on-line]. Provo, UT, USA: Ancestry.com Operations Inc., 2005.Original data: South Dakota Department of Health. South Dakota Marriage Index, 1905-1914 and South Dakota Marriage Certificates, 1905-1949. Pierre, SD, USA: South Dakota Department of Health.

119, Year: 1930; Census Place: Joubert, Douglas County, South Dakota; Roll: 2222; Page: 4B; Enumeration District: 13; Image 898.0; FHL Microfilm: 2341956.

120, Year:1940; Census Place: Truro, Aurora County, South Dakota; Roll: T627_3847; Page: 2A; Enumeration District: 2-21.

121, Ancestry.com. South Dakota Marriages, 1905-1949 [database on-line]. Provo, UT, USA: Ancestry.com Operations Inc., 2005.Original data: South Dakota Department of Health. South Dakota Marriage Index, 1905-1914 and South Dakota Marriage Certificates, 1905-1949. Pierre, SD, USA: South Dakota Department of Health.

121, Year: 1900; Census Place: Berlin Township, Douglas County, South Dakota; Roll: 1549; Page: 10A; Enumeration District: 137; FHL Microfilm: 124549.

122, Year: 1910; Census Place: Lincoln Township, Douglas County, South Dakota; Supervisor's District Number: 1; Enumeration District Number: 169; Sheet Number: 4; Page: 7.

123, Copy of World War I Draft Registration Cards, 1917-1918. Registration State: South Dakota; Registration County: Douglas; Roll: 1877791. [database on-line]. Provo, UT, USA: Ancestry.com Operations Inc., 2005.

124, Ancestry.com. U.S. Department of Veterans Affairs BIRLS Death File, 1850-2010 [database on-line]. Provo, UT, USA: Ancestry.com Operations, Inc. 2011 Original data: Beneficiary Identification Records Locator Subsystem (BIRLS) Death File. Washington, D.S.: U.S. Department of Veterans Affairs.

125, Year: 1910; Census Place: Berlin Township, Douglas County, South Dakota; Roll: T624_1480; Page: 1A; Enumeration District: 0169; FHL Microfilm: 1375493.

126, Year: 1920; Census Place: Washington Township, Douglas County, South Dakota; Roll: T625_1719; Enumeration District: 80; Image: 620.

127, Year: 1930; Census Place: Washington Township, Douglas County, South Dakota; Roll: 2222; Page: 2A; Enumeration District: 17; Image: 931; FHL Microfilm: 2341956.

128, Year: 1930: Census Place: Susquehanna Township, Douglas County, South Dakota; Roll: 2225;   • Enumeration District: 23; Image: 244.0; FHL microfilm: 2341959.

129, Year:1940: Census Place: Susquehanna Township, Douglas County, South Dakota; Roll: T627_3858; Page: 4A; Enumeration District: 34-23.

130, Year: Census Place: Washington Township, Douglas County, South Dakota; Roll: 2222; Page: 2B; Enumeration District: 17; Image: 932; FHL Microfilm: 2341956.

131, Ancestry.com. South Dakota Marriages, 1905-1949 [database on-line]. Provo, UT, USA: Ancestry.com Operations Inc., 2005.Original data: South Dakota Department of Health. South Dakota Marriage Index, 1905-1914 and South Dakota Marriage Certificates, 1905-1949. Pierre, SD, USA: South Dakota Department of Health.

[132,] Year: 1930; Census Place: Tobin Township, Davison County, South Dakota; Roll: 2221; Page: 2A; Enumeration District: 17; Image: 1066.0; FHL microfilm: 2341955.

[133,] Year: 1940; Census Place: Tobin Township, Davison County, South Dakota; Roll: T627_3853; Page: 3A; Enumeration District: 18-20.

[134, 135,] Ancestry.com. South Dakota Marriages, 1905-1949 [database on-line]. Provo, UT, USA: Ancestry.com Operations Inc., 2005.Original data: South Dakota Department of Health. South Dakota Marriage Index, 1905-1914 and South Dakota Marriage Certificates, 1905-1949. Pierre, SD, USA: South Dakota Department of Health.

[135,] Ancestry.com. South Dakota Marriages, 1905-1949 [database on-line]. Provo, UT, USA: Ancestry.com Operations Inc., 2005.Original data: South Dakota Department of Health. South Dakota Marriage Index, 1905-1914 and South Dakota Marriage Certificates, 1905-1949. Pierre, SD, USA: South Dakota Department of Health.

[136,] Ancestry.com. South Dakota Marriages, 1905-1949 [database on-line]. Provo, UT, USA: Ancestry.com Operations Inc., 2005.Original data: South Dakota Department of Health. South Dakota Marriage Index, 1905-1914 and South Dakota Marriage Certificates, 1905-1949. Pierre, SD, USA: South Dakota Department of Health.

[137,] Year: 1940; Census Place: Kulm Township, Hutchinson County, South Dakota; Roll: T627_3858; Page: 4A; Enumeration District: 34-11.

[138,] Year: 1930; Census Place: Washington Township, Douglas County, South Dakota; Roll: 2222; Page: 1B; Enumeration District: 17; Image: 93.0; FHL Microfilm: 2341956.

[139,] Ancestry.com. South Dakota Marriages, 1905-1949 [database on-line]. Provo, UT, USA: Ancestry.com Operations Inc., 2005.Original data: South Dakota Department of Health. South Dakota Marriage Index, 1905-1914 and South Dakota Marriage Certificates, 1905-1949. Pierre, SD, USA: South Dakota Department of Health.

[140,,] Year: 1900; Census Place: Berlin Township, Douglas County, South Dakota; Roll: 1549; Page: 10A; Enumeration District: 137; FHL Microfilm: 124549.

[141,] Year: 1910; Census Place: Lincoln Township, Douglas County, South Dakota; Supervisor's District Number: 1; Enumeration District Number: 169; Sheet Number: 4; Page: 7.

[142,] Copy of World War I Draft Registration Cards, 1917-1918. Registration State: South Dakota; Registration County: Douglas; Roll: 1877791. [database on-line]. Provo, UT, USA: Ancestry.com Operations Inc., 2005.

[143,] Year: 1920; Census Place: Lincoln Township, Douglas County, South Dakota; Supervisor's District Number: 1; Enumeration District: 80; Sheet 7; Page 14.

[144,] Year: 1900; Census Place: Valley Township, Douglas County, South Dakota; Roll: 1549; Page: 8B; Enumeration District: 0137; FHL Microfilm: 1241549.

[145,] Year: 1910; Census Place: Berlin Township; Douglas County, South Dakota; Roll: T624_1480; Page: 2B; Enumeration District: 0169; FHK Microfilm: 1375493.

[146,] Year: 1920; Census Place: Washington Township, Douglas County, South Dakota; Roll: T625_1719; Page: 1A; Enumeration District: 80; Image: 618.

[147,] Year: 1930; Census Place: Washington, Douglas County, South Dakota; Roll: 2222; Page: 2B; Enumeration District: 17; Image: 932.0; FHL Microfilm: 2341956.

[148,] Year: 1900; Census Place: Lincoln Township, Douglas County, South Dakota; Supervisor's District Number: 2; Enumeration District Number: 136; Sheet Number: 2.

[149,] Year: 1910; Census Place: Valley Township, Douglas County, South Dakota; Roll: T624_1480; Page: 6B; Enumeration District: 0170; FHL Microfilm: 1375493.

[150,] Year: 1920; Census Place: Garfield Township, Douglas County, South Dakota; Roll: T625_1719; Page: 9A; Enumeration District: 84; Image: 708.

[151,] Year: 1930; Census Place: Parkston, Hutchinson County, South Dakota; Roll: 2225; Page: 14A; Enumeration District: 18; Image: 213.0; FHL Microfilm: 2341959.

[152,] Year: 1940; Census Place: Parkston, Hutchinson County, South Dakota; Roll: T627_3858; Page: 5B; Enumeration District: 34-18.

[153,] Ancestry.com. South Dakota Marriages, 1905-1949 [database on-line]. Provo, UT, USA: Ancestry.com Operations Inc., 2005.Original data: South Dakota Department of Health. South Dakota Marriage Index, 1905-1914 and South Dakota Marriage Certificates, 1905-1949. Pierre, SD, USA: South Dakota Department of Health.

[154,] Year: 1930; Census Place: Lincoln Township, Douglas County, South Dakota; Supervisor's District Number: 5; Enumeration District: 22-13; Sheet Number: 4A.

155, Year: 1940; Census Place: Lincoln Township, Douglas County, South Dakota; Roll: T627_3855; Page: 3A; Enumeration District: 22-14.

156, Ancestry.com. Web: Ohio, Find A Grave Index, 1787-2012 [database on-line]. Provo, UT, USA: Ancestry.com Operations, Inc., 2012.

157, Ancestry.com. Web: Ohio, Find A Grave Index, 1787-2012 [database on-line]. Provo, UT, USA: Ancestry.com Operations, Inc., 2012.

158, Year: 1930; Census Place: Bloomfield, Jefferson County, Ohio; Roll: 1825; Page 2B; Enumeration District: 55; Image: 515.0; FHL Microfilm: 2341559.

159, Year: 1940; Census Place: Bloomfield, Jefferson County, Ohio; Roll: T627_3092; Page 1B; Enumeration District: 41-74.

160, Ancestry.com. Web: Ohio, Find A Grave Index, 1787-2012 [database on-line]. Provo, UT, USA: Ancestry.com Operations, Inc., 2012.

161, Certificate: 034478; Volume: 31094.Ancestry.com and Ohio Department of Health. Ohio, Deaths, 1908-1932, 1938-2007 [database on-line]. Provo, UT, USA: Ancestry.com Operations Inc., 2010.Original data: Ohio. Division of Vital Statistics. Death Certificates and Index, December 20, 1908-December 31, 1953. State Archives Series 3094. Ohio Historical Society, Ohio. Ohio Department of Health. Index to Annual Deaths, 1958-2002. Ohio Department of Health, State Vital Statistics Unit, Columbus, OH, USA.

162, Ohio Department of Health; Columbus, Ohio; Ohio Divorce Index, 1962-1963, 1967-1971 and 1973-2007.

163, Ancestry.com. Web: Ohio, MOLO Obituary Index, 1811-2012 [database on-line]. Provo, UT, USA: Ancestry.com Operations, Inc., 2012.Original data: Obituary Index. North East Ohio Regional Library.

164, Ohio Department of Health; Columbus, Ohio; Ohio Marriage Index, 1970 and 1972-2007.

165, Certificate Number: 19487 in Volume Number: 3586. Ohio Department of Health; Columbus, Ohio; Ohio Divorce Index, 1962-1963, 1967-1971 and 1973-2007.

166, Certificate Number: 84453 in Volume Number: 9211Ohio Department of Health; Columbus, Ohio; Ohio Marriage Index, 1970 and 1972-2007.

167, Certificate: 400480; Volume: 00011.Ancestry.com and Ohio Department of Health. Ohio, Deaths, 1908-1932, 1938-2007 [database on-line]. Provo, UT, USA: Ancestry.com Operations Inc., 2010.Original data: Ohio. Division of Vital Statistics. Death Certificates and Index, December 20, 1908-December 31, 1953. State Archives Series 3094. Ohio Historical Society, Ohio. Ohio Department of Health. Index to Annual Deaths, 1958-2002. Ohio Department of Health, State Vital Statistics Unit, Columbus, OH, USA.

168, Ancestry.com. Ohio, Birth Index, 1908-1964 [database on-line]. Provo, UT, USA: Ancestry.com Operations, Inc., 2012.Original data: Ohio Birth Records. Columbus, Ohio: Ohio Vital Records Office.

169, Certificate Number: 82648 in Volume Number: 13968. Ohio Department of Health; Columbus, Ohio; Ohio Marriage Index, 1970 and 1972-2007.

170, Certificate Number: 21209 in Volume Number: 6658. Ohio Department of Health; Columbus, Ohio; Ohio Divorce Index, 1962-1963, 1967-1971 and 1973-2007.

171, Ancestry.com. Ohio, Birth Index, 1908-1964 [database on-line]. Provo, UT, USA: Ancestry.com Operations, Inc., 2012.Original data: Ohio Birth Records. Columbus, Ohio: Ohio Vital Records Office.

172, Certificate Number: 14891 in Volume Number: 14924. Ohio Department of Health; Columbus, Ohio; Ohio Marriage Index, 1970 and 1972-2007.

173, Certificate Number: 13061 in Volume Number: 7067. Ohio Department of Health; Columbus, Ohio; Ohio Divorce Index, 1962-1963, 1967-1971 and 1973-2007.

174, Certificate Number: 22723 in Volume Number: 15364. Ohio Department of Health; Columbus, Ohio; Ohio Marriage Index, 1970 and 1972-2007.

175, Certificate Number: 8190 in Volume Number: 18167. Ohio Department of Health; Columbus, Ohio; Ohio Marriage Index, 1970 and 1972-2007.

176, Certificate Number: 1650 in Volume Number: 15689. Ohio Department of Health; Columbus, Ohio; Ohio Marriage Index, 1970 and 1972-2007.

177, Year: 1930; Census Place: White Lake, Aurora County, South Dakota; Roll: 2217; Page: 1B; Enumeration District: 23; Image: 203.0; FHL Microfilm: 23411951.

178, Year: 1940; Census Place: White Lake, Aurora County, South Dakota; Roll: T627_3847; Enumeration District: 2-23.

179, Ancestry.com. South Dakota Marriages, 1905-1949 [database on-line]. Provo, UT, USA: Ancestry.com

Operations Inc., 2005.Original data: South Dakota Department of Health. South Dakota Marriage Index, 1905-1914 and South Dakota Marriage Certificates, 1905-1949. Pierre, SD, USA: South Dakota Department of Health.

180, Year: 1898; Arrival: New York, New York; Microfilm Serial: T715; Microfilm Roll: 18; Line: 12; Page Number: 153. Ancestry.com. New York, Passengers Lists, 1820-1957 [database on-line]. Provo, UT, USA: Ancestry.com Operations, Inc. 2010.

181 Year: 1900; Census Place: Lincoln Township, Douglas County, South Dakota; Roll: 1549; Page: 5A; Enumeration District: 0136; FHL Microfilm: 1241549.

182 Year: 1910; Census Place: Belmont Township, Douglas County, South Dakota; Roll: T624_1480; Page: 1A; Enumeration District: 0168; FHL Microfilm: 1375493.

183 Year: 1940; Census Place: Delmont, Belmont Township, Douglas County, South Dakota; Roll: T627_3855; Page:4A; Enumeration District: 22-6.

184 Year: 1920; Census Place: Independence Township, Douglas County, South Dakota; Roll: T625_1719; Page: 1B; Enumeration District: 81; Image: 637.

185 Year: 1930; Census Year: 1930; Census Place: Independence Township, Douglas County, South Dakota; Roll: 2222; Page 1B; Enumeration District: 11; Image: 874.0; FHL Microfilm: 2341956.

186 Year: 1940; Census Place: Independence Township, Douglas County, South Dakota; Roll: T627_3855; Page: 1A; Enumeration District: 22-11.

187 Scott E. Ehler, *The Parkston Advance*, Parkston, South Dakota, 1999.

188 Mary Gales Askren, *The Daily Republic*, Mitchell, South Dakota, Tuesday, March 27, 2001.

189 Year: 1900; Census Place: Township 96, Bon Homme County, South Dakota; Roll: 1546; Page: 1A; Enumeration District: 0029; FHL Microfilm: 1241546.

190, Ancestry.com. South Dakota Marriages, 1905-1949 [database on-line]. Provo, UT, USA: Ancestry.com Operations Inc., 2005.Original data: South Dakota Department of Health. South Dakota Marriage Index, 1905-1914 and South Dakota Marriage Certificates, 1905-1949. Pierre, SD, USA: South Dakota Department of Health.

191 Year: 1930; Census Place: German Township, Hutchinson County, South Dakota; Roll: 2225; Page: 1A; Enumeration District: 7; Image: 77.0; FHL Microfilm: 2341959.

192 Year: 1940; Census Place: German Township, Hutchinson County, South Dakota; Roll: T627_3858; Page: 5A; Enumeration District: 34-7.

193 Year: 1910; Census Place: Emanuel Precinct, Bon Homme County, South Dakota; Roll: T624_1475; Page: 4B; Enumeration District: 0034; FHL Microfilm: 1375488.

194 Year: 1920; Census Place: Emanuel Township, Bon Homme County, South Dakota; Roll: T625_1714; Page: 3A; Enumeration District: 12; Image:370.

195 Year: 1930; Census Place: Emanuel Township, Bon Homme County, South Dakota; Roll: 2217; Page: 2B; Enumeration District: 6; Image 288.0; FHL Microfilm: 2341951.

196 Year: 1940; Census Place: Emanuel Township, Bon Homme County, South Dakota; Roll: T627_3848; Page 2B; Enumeration District: 5-6.

197 Year: 1910: Census Place: Stickel Township, McPherson County, South Dakota: Roll: T624_1483; Page: 4A; Enumeration District: 0301; FHL Microfilm: 1375496.

198 Year: 1930; Census Place: Oak Hollow Township, Hutchinson County, South Dakota; Roll: 225; Page: 2B; Enumeration District: 16; Image: 176.0; FHL Microfilm: 2341959.

199 Year: 1940; Census Place: Oak Hollow Township, Hutchinson County, South Dakota; Roll: T627_3858; Page: 4B; Enumeration District 34-16.

200 Year: 1920; Census Place: Cross Plains Township, Hutchinson County, South Dakota; Roll: T625_1720; Page: 6A; Enumeration District: 96; Image: 979.

201 Year: 1920; Census Place: Rome Township, Hutchinson County, South Dakota; Roll: T625_1716; Page: 9B; Enumeration District: 66; Image: 902.

202 Ancestry.com. South Dakota Marriages, 1905-1949 [database on-line]. Provo, UT, USA: Ancestry.com Operations Inc., 2005.Original data: South Dakota Department of Health. South Dakota Marriage Index, 1905-1914 and South Dakota Marriage Certificates, 1905-1949. Pierre, SD, USA: South Dakota Department of Health.

203 Year: 1930; Census Place: Cross Plains Township, Hutchinson County, South Dakota; Roll: 2225; Page: 5B; Enumeration District: 3; Image: 32.0 FHL Microfilm: 2341959.

204 Year: 1940; Census Place: Cross Plains Township, Hutchinson County, South Dakota; Roll: T627_3858; Page: 6B; Enumeration District: 34-3.

[205] Year: 1940; Census Place: Wolf Creek Township, Hutchinson County, South Dakota; Roll: T627_3858; Page: 3A; Enumeration District: 34-28.

[206] Year: 1930; Census Place: Sharon Township, Hutchinson County, South Dakota; Roll: 2225; Page: 2A; Enumeration District: 20; Image: 223,0; FHL Microfilm: 2341959.

[207] Ancestry.com. South Dakota Marriages, 1905-1949 [database on-line]. Provo, UT, USA: Ancestry.com Operations Inc., 2005.Original data: South Dakota Department of Health. South Dakota Marriage Index, 1905-1914 and South Dakota Marriage Certificates, 1905-1949. Pierre, SD, USA: South Dakota Department of Health.

[208] Year: 1940: Census Place: Wittenberg Township, Hutchinson County, South Dakota: Roll: T627_3858; Page: 6B; Enumeration District: 34-27.

[209] Year: 1940; Census Place: Hasting Township, Adams County, Nebraska; Roll: T627_2235; Page: 20B; Enumeration District: 1-17A.

[210] Year: 1900; Census Place: Berlin Township, Douglas County, South Dakota; Roll: 1549; Page: 10A; Enumeration District: 137; FHL Microfilm: 124549.

[211] Year: 1910; Census Place: Lincoln Township, Douglas County, South Dakota; Supervisor's District Number: 1; Enumeration District Number: 169; Sheet Number: 4; Page: 7.

[212] Year: 1900; Census Place: Starr Township, Hutchinson County, South Dakota; Roll: 1550; Page: 4A; Enumeration District: 0186; FHL Microfilm: 1241550.

[213] Year: 1910; Census Place: Starr Township, Hutchinson County, South Dakota; Roll: T624_1482; Page: 2A; Enumeration District: 0234; FHL Microfilm: 137495.

[214] Year: 1900; Census Place: Valley Township, Douglas County, South Dakota; Roll: 1549; Page: 10A; Enumeration District: 0137; FHL Microfilm: 1241549.

[215] Year: 1910; Census Place: Berlin Township, Douglas County, South Dakota; Roll: T624_1480; Page: 4A; Enumeration District: 0169; FHL Microfilm: 1375493.

[216] Copy of World War I Draft Registration Cards, 1917-1918. Registration State: South Dakota; Registration County: Douglas; Roll: 1877791.[database on-line]. Provo, UT, USA: Ancestry.com Operations Inc., 2005.

[217] Year: 1920; Census Place: Washington Township, Douglas County, South Dakota; Roll: T625_1719; Page: 4B; Enumeration District: Image: 625.

[218] Year: 1930; Census Place: Washington Township, Douglas County, South Dakota; Enumeration District: 22-17; Sheet Number: 2A.

[219] Year: 1940; Census Place: Washington Township, Douglas County, South Dakota; Enumeration District: 22-17; Sheet Number: 1A.

[220] Ancestry.com. South Dakota Marriages, 1905-1949 [database on-line]. Provo, UT, USA: Ancestry.com Operations Inc., 2005.Original data: South Dakota Department of Health. South Dakota Marriage Index, 1905-1914 and South Dakota Marriage Certificates, 1905-1949. Pierre, SD, USA: South Dakota Department of Health.

[221] Year: 1930; Census Place: Washington Township, Douglas County, South Dakota; Roll: 2222; Page: 2B; Enumeration District: 17; Image: 932.0; FHL Microfilm: 2341956.

[222] Year: 1940; Census Place: Washington Township, Douglas County, South Dakota; Roll: T627_3855; Page: 4B; Enumeration District: 22-17.

[223] Dodd, Jordan, Liahona Research, comp.. Iowa Marriages, 1851-1900 [datebase on-line]. Provo, UT, USA. Ancestry.com Operation Inc. 2000.

[224] Year: 1880; Census Place: Penn Township, Guthrie County, Iowa; Roll: 342; FHL Film: 1254342; Page: 124A; Enumeration District: 078; Image: 0252.

[225] Year: 1900; Census Place: Jefferson Township, Adair County, Iowa; Roll: 415; Page: 3A; Enumeration District: 0012; FHL Microfilm: 1240415.

[226] Year: 1910; Census Year: El Reno, Canadian County, Iowa; Roll: T624_1246; Page: 10A; Enumeration District: 0090; FHL Microfilm: 1375259.

[227] Copy of World War I Draft Registration Cards, 1917-1918. Registration State: South Dakota; Registration County: Douglas; Roll: 1877791.[database on-line]. Provo, UT, USA: Ancestry.com Operations Inc., 2005.

[228] Year:1920; Census Place: El Reno Ward 4, Canadian County, Oklahoma; Roll: T625_1455; Page: 9B; Enumeration District: 92; Image: 781.

[229] Year: 1930; Census Place: Amarillo, Potter County, Texas; Roll: 2384; Page: 18A; Enumeration District: 5; Image: 209.0; FHL Microfilm: 2342118.

[230] Ancestry.com U.S. World War II Draft Registration Cards, 1942. United States Selective Service System,

Selective Service Registration Cards, World War II; Fourth Registration. Records of the Selective Service System, Record Group Number 147. National Archives and Records Administration.

[231] Texas, Death Certificates. 1903-1982. Provo, UT, USA. Ancestry.com Operations, 2013. Texas Department of State Health Services. Texas Death Certificates. 1903-1982.

[232] Year: 1930; Census Place: Woonsocket, Sanborn County, South Dakota; Roll: 2230; Page: 4A; Enumeration District: 0019; Image: 534.0; FHL Microfilm: 2341964.

[233] Year: 1920: Census Place: Oneida Township, Sanborn County, South Dakota; Roll: T625_1726; Page: 8A; Enumeration District: 223; Image: 485.

[234] Year: 1930; Census Place: Floyd Township, Sanborn County, South Dakota; Roll: 2230; Page: 1A; Enumeration District: 0007; Image: 418.0; FHL Microfilm: 2341964.

[235] Ancestry.com. South Dakota Marriages, 1905-1949 [database on-line]. Provo, UT, USA: Ancestry.com Operations Inc., 2005.Original data: South Dakota Department of Health. South Dakota Marriage Index, 1905-1914 and South Dakota Marriage Certificates, 1905-1949. Pierre, SD, USA: South Dakota Department of Health.

[236] Year: 1940; Census Place: Jackson Township, Sanborn County, South Dakota; Roll: T627_3867; Page 1A; Enumeration District: 56-8.

[237, 238,] Ancestry.com. *U.S., Find A Grave Index, 1700s-Current* [database on-line]. Provo, UT, USA: Ancestry.com Operations, Inc., 2012.

[239] Year: 1930; Census Place: Washington Township, Douglas County, South Dakota; Roll: 2222; Page: 2B; Enumeration District: 0017; Image: 932.0; FHL Microfilm: 2341956.

[240] Year: 1910; Census Place: Berlin Township, Douglas County, South Dakota; Roll: T624_1480; Page 4A; Enumeration District: 0169; FHL Microfilm: 1375493.

[241] Year: 1920; Census Place: Washington Township, Douglas County, South Dakota; Roll: T625_1719; Page: 3A; Enumeration District: 80; Image: 622;

[242] Ancestry.com. South Dakota Marriages, 1905-1949 [database on-line]. Provo, UT, USA: Ancestry.com Operations Inc., 2005.Original data: South Dakota Department of Health. South Dakota Marriage Index, 1905-1914 and South Dakota Marriage Certificates, 1905-1949. Pierre, SD, USA: South Dakota Department of Health.

[243] Year: 1930; Census Place: Washington Township, Douglas County, South Dakota; Roll: 2222; Page: 4B; Enumeration District: 0017; Image: 936.0; FHL Microfilm: 2341956.

[244] Year: 1940; Census Place: Washington Township, Douglas County, South Dakota; Roll: T627_3855; Page: 1B; Enumeration District: 22-17.

[245] Year: 1940; Census Place: DeWitt County, Texas, Roll: T627_4021; Page: 12A; Enumeration District: 62-11.

[246] Year: 1900; Census Place: Berlin Township, Douglas County, South Dakota; Roll: 1549;   Page: 10A; Enumeration District: 137; FHL Microfilm: 124549.

[247] Year: 1910; Census Place: Lincoln Township, Douglas County, South Dakota; Supervisor's   District Number: 1; Enumeration District Number: 169; Sheet Number: 4; Page: 7.

[248] Copy of World War I Draft Registration Cards, 1917-1918. Registration State: South Dakota; Registration County: Douglas; Roll: 1877791.[database on-line]. Provo, UT, USA: Ancestry.com Operations Inc., 2005.

[249, 250, 251,] Year: 1880; Census Place: Middletown Township, Dane County, Wisconsin; Roll: 1422; Family History Film: 1255422; Page: 229A; Enumeration District: 080.

[252,] Year: 1900; Census Place: Mount Vernon, Davison County, South Dakota; Roll: 1548; Page: 4B; Enumeration District: 0110; FHL Microfilm: 1241548.

[253] Year: 1910; Census Place: Mount Vernon Ward 2, Davison County, South Dakota; Roll: T624_1479; Page: 4A; Enumeration District: 0133, FHL Microfilm: 1375492.

[254] Year: 1920; Census Place: Baker Township, Davison County, South Dakota; Roll: T625_1716; Page: 7A; Enumeration District: 64: Image: 865.

[255] Ancestry.com. South Dakota Marriages, 1905-1949 [database on-line]. Provo, UT, USA: Ancestry.com Operations Inc., 2005.Original data: South Dakota Department of Health. South Dakota Marriage Index, 1905-1914 and South Dakota Marriage Certificates, 1905-1949. Pierre, SD, USA: South Dakota Department of Health.

[256] Year: 1930; Census Place: Washington Township, Douglas County, South Dakota; Roll: 2222; Page:2A; Enumeration District: 0017; Image: 931.0; FHL Microfilm: 2341956.

[257] Year: 1940; Tobin Township, Davison County, South Dakota; Roll: T627_3853; Page: 2A; Enumertion District: 18-20.

258 Year: 1930; Census Place: Fairview Township, Hanson County, South Dakota; Roll: 2224; Page: 3B; Enumeration District: 0005; Image: 491.0; FHL Microfilm: 2341958.

259 Nevada Marriage Index, 19562005. Provo, UT, USA. Ancestry.com Operations, 2007.

250 Ancestry.com. California Marriage Index, 1960-1985. Provo, UT, USA. Ancestry.com Operations, 2007. State of California. California Marriage Index, 1960-1985, Microfiche, Center for Health Statistics, California Department of Health Services, Sacramento, California.

261, 262, 263, 264, Ancestry.com. State of California. California Death Index, 1940-1997. Provo, UT, USA. Ancestry.com Operations, 2000. State of California. California Marriage Index, 1960-1997. Sacramento, California. California Department of Health Services, Center for Health Statistics.

262, 263, 264, Ancestry.com. California Birth Index, 1905-1995. Provo, UT, USA: Ancestry.com Operations Inc, 2005.Original data: State of California. California Birth Index, 1905-1995. Sacramento, CA, USA: State of California Department of Health Services, Center for Health Statistics.

265 Year: 1910; Census Place: Sioux Township, Sioux County, Iowa; Roll: T 624_423; Page: 4A; Enumeration District: 0156; FHL Microfilm: 1374436

266 Year: 1920; Census Place: Sioux Center, Sioux County, Iowa; Roll: T625_514; Page 1B; Enumeration District: 172; Image: 1031.

267 Year: 1930; Census Place: Sioux Township, Sioux County, Iowa; Roll: 683; Page: 3A; Enumeration District: 0034; Image: 367.0 Image: 367.0 FHL Microfilm: 2340418.

268 Year: 1940; Census Place: Sioux Township, Sioux County, Iowa; Roll: T627_1207; Page: 3B; Enumeration District: 84-34.

269 Year: 1940; Census Place: Doon, Lyon County, Iowa; Roll: T627_1179; Page: 4A; Enumeration District: 60-7.

270 Minnesota Department of Health, Minnesota Birth Index, 1935-2002. Provo, UT, USA, Ancestry.com Operations Inc. 2004.

271 Ancestry. Com. U.S. Find A Grave Index, 1600s-Current. Provo, UT, USA, Ancestry.com Operations Inc. 2012.

272, 273, 274, 275, Minnesota Department of Health, Minnesota Birth Index, 1935-2002. Provo, UT, USA, Ancestry.com Operations Inc. 2004.

276 Year: 1930; Census Place: Parkston, Hutchinson County, South Dakota; Roll: 2225; Page 1A; Enumeration District: 0018; Image: 187.0; FHL Microfilm: 2341959.

Photos

1883-1993 100th Anniversary St. John Lutheran Church. Stickney, SD: Stickney Argus. with written

permission from Glen Storm, Corsica, South [1], [2],

Photos Courtesy of Joan and Melvin Frahm, Neenah, Wisconsin with written permission [5], [6], [7], [8], [53],

Photos Courtesy of Norbert Zirpel, Parkston, South Dakota with written permission. [3], [10], [11], [12], 13], [14], [15], [16], [17], [18], [19], [380],

Photo Courtesy of Jim and Becky Zirpel, Burke, South Dakota with written permission. [20], [91], [92], [93], [94], [95], [96], [97],

Copy of Deed Record, Douglas County Courthouse, Armour, Douglas County, South Dakota and Government records published before 1923 are Public Domain.[42]

Copy of 1909-1910 Berlin Township Map, Douglas County Courthouse, Armour, Douglas County, South Dakota and Government records published before 1923 are Public Domain and a recreation by Mona Clydene Zirpel in 2013. [43]

Copy of 1909-1910 Lincoln Township Map, Douglas County Courthouse, Armour, Douglas County, South Dakota and Government records published before 1923 are Public Domain and a recreation by Mona Clydene Zirpel in 2013. [44]

Copy of Deed Record, Douglas County Courthouse, Armour, Douglas County, South Dakota and Government records published before 1923 are Public Domain. [48]

Photo Courtesy of Mona Clydene Zirpel, Wessington Springs, South Dakota. [9], [21], [22], [23], [28], [38], [41], [50], [85], [127], [167], [173],[175], [190], [200], [201], [202], [203], [204],[205], [209], [241], [269], [275], [279], [325], [326], [327], [337], [339], [343], [344], [347], [358], [364], [365], [366], [371], [372], [374], [375], [377], [379],

Photo Courtesy of Erwin & Olinda Zirpel, Parkston, South Dakota and given to Mona Clydene Zirpel, Lane, South Dakota after the deaths of Erwin & Olinda Zirpel by daughter-in-law, with written permission from Laurie Zirpel. Fort Worth, Texas. [21], [24], [25], [29], [46], [47], [49], [51], [82], [87], [138], [142], [143], [144], [145], [146], [147], [148], [149], [150], [152], [153], [154], [155], [158], [218], [219], [220], [221], [222]. [223], [224], [225], [226], [227], [228], [229], [230], [231], [232], [235], [236], [237], [238], [243], [244], [248], [250], [252], [253], [254], [256], [257], [258], [259], [260], [261], [262], [263], [266], [268], [283], [285], [286], [287], [290], [291], [292], [293], [302], [303], [304], [309], [310], [320], [321], [322], [324], [325], [328], [329], [330], [331], [335], [336], [338], [340], [342], [345], [359], [360], [361], [385], [386], [387], [388], [390], [391],

Photo Courtesy of Tammy Semmler, Gordon, Georgia and written permission. [25], [27], [30], [31],

Photo Courtesy of Bonnie Schuh, Mitchell, South Dakota. [32], [52], [53], [54], [55], [57], [59], [60], [63], [64], [65], [66], [67], [68], [69], [70], [71], [72], [73], [74], [75], [76], [77], [78], [79], [80], [81], [382], [383], [389],

Photo Courtesy of Dennis Bittiker, Meridian, Idaho. [25], [26, [27], [30],[31], [32], [34],

Photo Courtesy of Rodger Danner, Winchester, Ohio [31], [34], [35], [36],

Photo Courtesy of Karel Janis Amend, Hartford, South Dakota [33],

Photo Courtesy Barbara Unland, Naples, Florida [37], [40],

Photo Courtesy of Larry & Margaret Lou Wendlandt, Black River, Wisconsin [39],

Photo Courtesy of Laurie Zirpel, Fort Worth, Texas. [45],

Photo Courtesy of Charles Joseph Mentele, Canova, South Dakota with written permission. [58], [61], [62], [381],

Mildred Zirpel, Parkston, South Dakota. [83], [86], [88], [116], [117], [118], [119], [120], [121], [122], [123], [124], [133], [134],

Photo Courtesy of Darlene Horst, Gregory, South Dakota and written permission. [84], [88], [89], [90], [98], [99], [100], [101], [102], [103], [104], [105], [106], [107], [108], [109], [110], [111], [376], [378],

Photo Courtesy of Marlys Martha Moege, Parkston, South Dakota with written permission. [109], [110], [111], [112], [113], [114], 115], [125], [126], [128], [129], [130], [131], [132],

Photo Courtesy of Edna Emma and Dennis Allen Stoebner, Aberdeen, South Dakota with written permission [135], [136], [137], [384],

Certificate of Birth Records, Douglas County, South Dakota ,and Copies owned by Mary Ellen Mettenbrink, Sioux City, Iowa with written permission. [139], [140],

Photo Courtesy of Elmer and Luella Zirpel and Karen Bekx, Appleton, Wisconsin with written permission. [240],

Photo Courtesy of Gerald and Jan Wenzel, Parkston, South Dakota with written permission. [141],

Photo from Sanborn Weekly Journal, Thursday, August 16, 2007. Gerald W. Klass, Publisher and written permission [165]

Photo Courtesy of Marian Coleman Phillips, Winter Garden, Florida with written permission. [156], [157],

Photo Courtesy of Mary Ann Dammann, Woonsocket, South Dakota with written permission. [210], [211],

Photo Courtesy of Bryan Allen and Lisa Zirpel, Rio Rancho, New Mexico with written permission. [180], [182], [183], [184], [185], [186], [187], [188], [189], [212], [213], [215], [216], [217],

Photo Courtesy of Rebecca Stunes, Mitchell, South Dakota with written permission. [206], [207],

Photo Courtesy of Bryton Zirpel and Stephanie Nemec, Stratford, Connecticut with written permission. [214],

Photo Courtesy of Mary Gales Askren, *The Daily Republic* Mitchell, South Dakota, Tuesday, March 27, 2001 and Korrie Wenzel with written permission [234],

Photo Courtesy of Elizabeth Grosz, *The Parkston Advance*, Parkston, South Dakota, 1999 with written Permission. [233],

Photo Courtesy of Karen Ann Bekx, Little Chute, Wisconsin with written permission. [239], [240], [245], [246], [249], [251], [304],

Photo Courtesy of Richard and Renee Zirpel, Appleton, Wisconsin with written permission.[242], [245], [249],

Photo Courtesy of Rosalene and Clifford Roth, Huron, South Dakota and written permission. [247], [282], [284], [294], [295], [296], [297], [298], [299], [303], [305], [306], [307], [308], [311], [312], [313], [314], [315], [316], [317], [318], [319], [329], [341], [370],

Photo Courtesy of Kayla Proctor, St. Paul, Minnesota and written permission. [255], [264], [265], [267], [271], [272], [274], [276], [277], [278], [280],

Photo Courtesy of Mark and Lori Zirpel, Parkston, South Dakota and written permission. [288]

Photo Courtesy of Bruce Allen Zirpel, Elkhorn, Nebraska with written permission. [273]

Photo Courtesy of Eryn and Aaron Bowers, Manteca, California and written permission. [287]

Photo Courtesy of Douglas Zirpel, Manteca, California with written permission. [288]

Mary Ellen Ruth Mettenbrink, Sioux City, Iowa with written permission. [332], [333], [334],

Photo Courtesy of Ruth Nelson, Huron, South Dakota and photos originally owned by Audrey Zirpel with written permission [145], [151], [159], [160], [161], [162], [163], [164], [166], [168], [169], [170], [176], [177], [178], [179], [181], [208], [281],

Photo Courtesy of Ruth Nelson, Huron, South Dakota with written permission. [171], [172], [174],

Photo Courtesy of Bernice Bialas, Parkston, South Dakota with written permission. [346],

Photo Courtesy of Helen Gerlach, Dimock, South Dakota with written permission. Written permission from Jeffrey Scott Goudy.[348], [349], [350], [351],
[352], [353], [354], [355], [656], [357],

Photo Courtesy of Kathy LaRock, Piano, Texas and Barbara Kay Zirpel, Sioux Falls, South Dakota with their written permission. Written permission from Brady LaRock. [367], [368], [369], [368], [373],

Photo Courtesy of Roger Zirpel, Sioux Falls, South Dakota with his written permission. [362], [363], [374]

Photo Courtesy of Hazel Hernandez, Huron, South Dakota with her written permission. [392]

Index

Baumiller, Carol 163,
Baumiller, Christ Mrs. 106,
Baumiller, Reinhold Mrs. 106,
Baumiller, Inez 135, 136,
Baumiller, Ivan 149, 150,
Baumgart, Ernest 179,
Baumgart, Hedwig 179,
Baumgartner, Leo J. 15,
Bekx, Amanda Nicole [1995-]144, 146, 147,
Bekx, Jordon Johan [1991-]144, 146, 147,
Bekx, Karen Ann (Zirpel) [1960-]144, 146,
Bekx, Parker Logan [1997-]144, 146, 147,
Bekx, Peter 146,
Bekx, Peter Johan [1961-]144,
Bell, C. L. 183,
Bender, Lavon J. 149,
Bennett, Christine [1972-] 31,
Bennett, Mary Ellen 119,
Bernhard, Kim 137,
Bertera, Amanda Rose [1992-] 170, 171,
Bertera, Samantha Rae Bertera [1998-] 170, 171,
Berteram Stacy 168,
Bertera, Stacy Rae (Roth)[1976-] 170,
Bertera, William Anthony III [1970-] 170,
Bertram, Ally May [2003-] 99, 100,
Bertram, Carl Mrs. 8, 10, 13, 18, 21, 23, 28, 52, 72, 102,
    104, 179, 187,
Bertram, Doris 211,
Bertram, Doyle 173,
Bertram, Emma Nicole [2001-] 99, 100,
Bertram. Erin Lee [1975-] 98, 99,
Bertram. Ernest 15,
Bertram, Ernest William 98,
Bertram. Ernest William [1964-] 79, 99, 100,
Bertram, Ethan Lee [2005-] 99, 100,
Bertram, Ida Mrs. 10, 14, 15, 18, 24, 36, 72, 75, 96, 104,
    107, 179, 181, 187, 188, 194,
Bertram, Kari (Van Der Werff)[1977-] 99, 100,
Bertram, Marcia Leann [1957-] 98,
Bertram, Marie Diann [1960-] 98,
Bertram, Margaret 81,
Bertram, Margaret Maria [1937-] 75, 79, 98, 99, 100,
Bertram, Michelle (Thompson) [1972-] 79, 99, 100,
Bertram, Mira Susann [1969-] 98, 99,
Bertram, Noreen 142,
Bertram, Phyllis 173,
Bertram, Ryan William [1997-] 79, 99, 100,
Bertram, Sara Kate [2008-] 99,
Bertram, William 18, 23, 192,
Bertram, William John [1935-] 98, 99, 100,
Bertram, Viola 98,
Beutner, Eugene Wayne 115, 117,
Beutner, Audrey May [1925-2011] 114, 115,
Beutner, Gustave George 114, 115, 117,
Beutner, Ruth Minnie 115,
Beutner, True Gustave 115, 117,
Beutner, Viola Iva (Minor) 115, 117,
Bialas, Bernice Elisabeth (Gerlach) [1935-]188, 189,
    190, 191,
Bialas, Benjamin Owen [2012-] 191,
Bialas, Bertha 188,
Bialas, Chad 47,
Bialas, Carol Esther113,
Bialas, Carol Marlys (Zirpel) [1958-2007] 95, 96, 189,

Bialas, Christen Carol [1980-] 95, 189,
Bialas, Dewayne 173,
Bialas, Diane Hilda [1963-] 188, 189,
Bialas, Elizabeth Faye [1956-] 188, 189,
Bialas, Emily Elizabeth [1987-] 95, 96, 189,
Bialas, Floyd 188,
Bialas, Fritz John [1906-1979] 187, 188,
Bialas, Harvey 188,
Bialas, Herman 187, 188,
Bialas, Herman [1875-1912] 187, 188,
Bialas, Hilda Emma (Gerlach)[1906-2003] 188,
Bialas, Ivan 188, 211,
Bialas, Jeanette 173,
Bialas, Johan 4, 211,
Bialas, Johanna 71,
Bialas, Karen Ruth (Westgaard)[1973-] 191,
Bialas, Lambert 188,
Bialas, Lawrence 26,
Bialas, "Lorenz" Lawrence Harold [1931-] 95, 187,
    188, 189, 190, 191,
Bialas, Lena 80,
Bialas, Lois 67,
Bialas, Lorraine 188, 209,
Bialas, Mandy Marie [1988-] 95, 96, 189,
Bialas, Martha 187, 188,
Bialas, Martha ( ) 187,
Bialas, Matthew Michael [1983-] 95, 96, 189,
Bialas, May Dene [1959-] 188, 189, 191,
Bialas, Michael Lawrence [1955-] 95, 188, 189,
Bialas, Nikki 47,
Bialas, Taryn Jo [2006-] 191,
Bialas, Theo Bjorn [2014-2014] 191,
Bialas, Thomas Jason [1972-] 188, 189, 191,
Bialas, Willard 188,
Bialas, Willie 188,
Bich, Laurie 168,
Bies, Darlene 63,
Bietz, Betty 135, 136,
Bietz, Edwin 54, 106,
Bietz, Edwin Mrs.106,
Bietz, Laura D. 54,
Bietz, Mary Regina 53, 54,
Billard, Joshua Daniel Clay [1984-] 98, 100,
Billard, Stacy Sue (Meyer)[1985-] 100,
Billings, Steven S Rev. 146,
Bishoff, Pastor 4,
Bishoff, George A. Pastor 5,
Bishop, Alexis [2001-] 29,
Bishop, Angela Kaye (Sprecher) [1976-] 29,
Bishop, Jason B. [1976-] 29,
Bishop, Micala [1998-] 29,
Biteler, Beverly Jean (Sprecher)[1939-] 27, 28,
Biteler, Brekken Dean [2008-] 28,
Biteler, Brielle Christina [2003-] 28,
Biteler, Elmer E. [1937-] 27,
Biteler, Homer 27,
Biteler, Jamin Philip [2005-] 28,
Biteler, Josie Ann [2009-] 23,
Biteler, Kelly S. 28,
Biteler, Louisa A. (Parfay) [1974-] 28,
Biteler, Mae 27,
Biteler, Mae 27,
Biteler, Michael J. [1977-]27, 28,
Biteler, Pam 27,

Biteler, Philip [1970-] 27, 28,
Biteler, Roxann [1965-] 27, 28,
Biteler, Steven Christopher [1982-] 27, 28,
Biteler, Steven Eugene [1959-] 27, 28,
Biteler, Teresa 27,
Biteler, Vicki [1961-] 27, 28,
Bittiker, Agnes J. 32,
Bittiker, Alma Emma Elisabeth (Zirpel) [1920–]25, 26,
    32, 33,
Bittiker, Amber Ray [1972-] 33, 34,
Bittiker, Bertha May (Burright) 32,
Bittiker, Daisy M. 32,
Bittiker, David Robert [1977-] 33, 34,
Bittiker, Dennis Robert [1948-] 32, 33,
Bittiker, Dora B. 32,
Bittiker, Joseph Fredolin 32,
Bittiker, Janet Rae [1943-] 32, 33,
Bittiker, Lehman J. 32,
Bittiker, Marsha A. (Tuskey) [1951-] 33,
Bittiker, Margaret P. 32,
Bittiker, Mary L. 32,
Bittiker, Raymond F. [1916-2005] 25, 32, 33,
Bittiker, Tahnee Elizabeth [1976-] 33, 34,
Blackburn, Iva Lenore 110,
Blaha, Andrea Rae [1981-]170,
Blank, Barbara Jean [1962-]144,
Blaufuss, Rev. 149,
Blume, Lena Louise [1890-1968] 79, 80,
Boddicker, Lynn [1956-] 90,
Bocker, Velora 163,
Boelter, Vern 68,
Boetel, Dawn 168,
Bohr, Frank 6,
Borman, Donald W. 114,
Botts, Randy [1964-] 58,
Bowers, Aaron Michael [1981-] 161, 162,
Bowers, Eryn Elizabeth (Zirpel) [1981-]162, 163,
Bowers, Payton Aryn [2011-] 162,
Bowers, Floy Z. 11, 12, 14, 50,
Bowers, Floyd R. 193,
Bowman, Kourtney [1996-] 120,
Boyd, Frank A. 110,
Boyul, Michael J. 19,
Braiverman, Marc 55,
Braiverman, Marc Ross [1952-] 60,
Braiverman, Nola 55,
Braiverman, Nola Mae (Schuh) (Walinski) [1953-] 60,
Branick, Kevin 140,
Branson, Phyllis 65,
Braa, Dennis 42,
Braiverman, Marc 55,
Braiverman, Nola 55,
Bray, Amy Elizabeth (Semmler) [1975-] 38,
Bray, Austin Jeffrey [2009-] 38,
Bray, Jeffrey Philip 38,
Bray, Spencer Allen [2008-] 38,
Brett, Lillian 190,
Brink, Adam Leon [1976-] 86, 87,
Brink, Helena (Johnson) [1979-] 86,
Brink, Leon Arnold [1949-] 82, 86, 87, 88,
Brink, Logan Alexander [2003-] 86, 87,
Brink, Madison Rose [2001-] 86, 87,
Brink, Sallie Rose (Reimnitz) [1952-]81, 82, 86, 87, 88,
Brink, Stephanie Lynn[1979-] 86, 87,

Brinks, Cynthia Rose 167,
Brinks, John [1956-]167,
Bronk, Ida M.[1854-] 182, 183,
Brown, Ashley Nicole [1990-] 70,
Brown, Becky 43,
Brown, Brenda 68,
Brown, Brenda Lynn [1964-] 68,
Brown, C. H. 42, 43,
Brown, Kayla Marie [1993-1993] 70,
Brown, Kent 68,
Brown, Kent Eldon [1962-] 70,
Brown, R. E. 115,
Bruegel, Ernest Rev. 102, 103,
Buehner, Tobias Rev. 115,
Bueno, Mr. 122, 123,
Bueno, Mickayla Ann [2007-]122, 123,
Bundy, Adrienne Ty [2000-]122, 123,
Bundy, Justin [1973-]122,
Bundy, Roni Ann (Nelson) (Poage) [1979-] 122,
Burd, Megan Marie [1984-] 95,
Burke, Raymond W. 34,
Burright, Bertha May 32,
Burmeister, Alma Alvina Louise [1903-1978] 12,
Burmeister, Alvina Emma Martha [1905-1994] 12,
Burmeister, Edwin Otto Bernhardt [1908-1985] 12,
Burmeister, Ewald Wilhelm Harry [1911-2002] 12,
Burmeister, Emma Bertha (Sperlich)[1882-1977] 12,
Burmeister, Johann Hermann Leonardt [1902-1963] 12,
Burmeister, Otto [1872-1911] 12,
C
Campbell, Carol L. (Danner) (Kraft) [1956-] 35,
Campbell, Hollee Anita [1990-] 35,
Campbell, Jamie Elise [1987-] 35,
Campbelll, J. S. 182,
Campbell, Robert 35,
Carol 115,
Carr, Bernie 68,
Cerney, Chrissy (Kahler) 84,
Cerney, Caleb Wade [1994-] 84,
Cerney, Calla Ann [1995-] 84,
Cerney, Scott Wade [1971-] 84,
Cerney, Tanya 84,
Chivington, Patricia Ann 57,
Christiane 178,
Cihak, Shirley 154,
Clark, Freeman Edward [1913-1985] 127,
Clark, Karen J. [1957-] 40,
Clark, Richard 129,
Clark, Ramona Eileen (Stebbins) (Spear) [1929-1998]
    127,
Clayton, John Clergyman 185,
Cleveland, Grover President 15,
Cline, Lucille Louise 112,
Cole, Ed 190,
Cole, Emilia Mae 190,
Comms, Alice G. 182,
Cook, Guy W. 11, 12, 14,
Coolidge, Calvin Vice-President & President 28,
Coy, George L. 32,
Cresap, David J. [1947-] 112,
Cresap, Susanna Jo (Zirpel)(Pratt)[1948-1984] 112,
Cripps, Barbara 55,
Cripps, Kenneth 55,
Cripps, Ronald 55,

Heasley, Fern L. 69,
Heaton, Joyce 42,
Helbrink, Diane Hilda Bialas [1963-] 191,
Hebrink, Joel [1961-] 191,
Hebrink, Tony [1980-] 191,
Heidner, Anna Emilie (Zirpel)[1884-1912] 16, 17, 18, 204,
Heidner (Wermeister), Amalia Gladys Pauline [1906-2003] 18, 19,
Heidner, Arthur Benjamin 16,
Heidner, Bertha Emma [1912-1992] 17, 18, 19,
Heidner, Conrad Edward [1851-1930] 16, 17,
Heidner, Emilie Verla [1910-1910] 17, 19,
Heidner, Emma Emilie [1908-1908] 17, 19,
Heidner, George Julius [1884-1967] 16, 17, 18, 49,
Heidner, Gertrude Louise [1910-1910] 17, 19,
Heidner, Hannah (Klehn) [1859-1942] 16, 17,
Heidner, Hulda A. (Doering) 18,
Heidner, Infant daughter 56,
Heidner, Lillian Rosalie 16,
Heidner, Nelson Edward 16,
Heidner, Rosadie Georgina 16,
Heidzig, Kayle Dawn (Miller)[1986-] 66,
Heidzig, Jazmyne Marie 66,
Heidzig, Mr. 66,
Heiting, Ben 136,
Helgesen, Kenneth J. Rev. 26,
Hempel, Pastor 187,
Hempel, Rev. 202, 203, 204, 209, 211,
Hempel, Paul Rev. 73, 80, 180,
Hemprel, B. Rev. 48,
Henderson, H. 15, 16,
Henderson, Mary Ruth 127,
Herr, Lucille 150,
Herrick, Donald Mr. 137,
Herrick, Donald Mrs. 137,
Herring, Arlene Carol [1945-] 62,
Herring, Nicole 87,
Herring, William 62,
Hildeman, Irene 82,
Hildeman, Lodema 82,
Hildeman, Violet Ann 82,
Hildeward, S. H. 71,
Hill, Carla 63,
Hillie, Christina 18,
Hines, J. F. 135,
Hoes, Paul 117,
Hofer, Peter J. 148,
Hoffman, Anna Marie (Sperlich)[1876-1950] 10, 11,
Hoffman, Rosina 102,
Hoffmann, Alfred Bernhardt [1903-1977] 10,
Hoffmann, Amanda L. [1910-2005] 10,
Hoffmann, Bertha Louise [1897-1984] 10,
Hoffmann, Carl "Hermann" [1893-1963] 10,
Hoffmann, Carl "Wilhelm" [1894-1964] 10,
Hoffmann, Emil Karl [1902-1986] 10,
Hoffmann, Fred Edward "Fritz"[1900-1985] 10,
Hoffman, Ernest 56,
Hoffmann, Ernest Gottfried [1852-1913] 10, 11,
Hoffmann, Johann Gottfried "John" [1905-1992] 10,
Hoffmann, Leonhard Ehrich [1914-1967] 10,
Hoffmann, Otto Fredrich [1898-1985] 10,
Hoffman, Marie 49,
Hoffmann, Martha Annie Marie [1908-2002] 10,

Hoffmann, Wilhelmina E. [1896-1982] 10,
Holenzollerns 1,
Holce, Darlene 158,
Holce, Marvin 158,
Hollenback, Floyd 39,
Holter, Rev. 204,
Holter, Fred Pastor 4,
Holstein, Cory Lee [1986-] 69, 70,
Holstein, Dave 69,
Hoon, James 182,
Honstein, Georgian 68,
Honstein, Georgia Sue [1975-] 68, 69
Honstein, Gunther 70,
Honstein, Kimberly Sue 69, 70,
Honstein, Lisa Marie 69,
Horst, Codi [1995-] 83,
Horst, Darlene 84,
Horst, Darlene Marie [1945-] 79, 81, 82, 83, 84, 88,
Horst, Jack 82,
Horst, Richard William 82,
Horst, Robin Lee Ann [1962-1969] 82,
Horst, Roger 82,
Horst, Ronald William [1942-] 82, 83, 84, 88,
Horst, Steve 82,
Horst, Tanya Lee [1978-] 82, 83, 84,
Horst, Tracy Sue [1976-] 82, 83,
Horstman, Henry Jr. 47,
Houston, Kenneth H. C. Mowrey 83,
Howard, Curt 43,
Howard, Curtis Anthony [1979-] 39,
Howard, Eli Kenneth [2011-] 39,
Howard, Ethan Ray [2011-] 39,
Howard, Melissa Elizabeth (Semmler) (Smallwood) [1980-] 39,
Hoxsie, Angela Marie (Ryan) 119, 120,
Hoxsie, Ann [2005-] 119,
Hoxsie, Blake Harding [1996-]119,
Hoxsie, Charles 120,
Hoxsie, Darrell 119, 122,
Hoxsie Darrell H. 120,
Hoxsie, Darrell Harding [1949-2014] 118, 119, 120,
Hoxsie, Darrell (Ruby) Mrs. [1949-] 118,
Hoxsie, Daniel 119, 120,
Hoxsie Daniel Harding [1973-2014] 117, 118, 120,
Hoxsie, Delbert Harding 118,
Hoxsie, Doyle 119,
Hoxsie, Doyle Erich [1979-] 117, 118, 120,
Hoxsie, Jacob Daniel [2000-] 119,
Hoxsie, Renae Jean [1978-] 120, 118, 119,
Hoxsie, Rochelle Audrey [1972-]118,
Hoxsie, Ruby A. 118,
Hoxsie, Ruby Audrey (Zirpel) [1949-2010] 117, 118, 119, 120, 129,
Hoxsie, Shayla Daniela [2007-] 119,
Hoxsie, Zane [2003-] 119,
Hranicky, Annette 190,
Hranicky, Benny 190
Hranicky, Dorothy 190,
Hranicky, Ella 190,
Hranicky, Elizabeth Faye (Bialas) [1956-] 190,
Hranicky, Emil 190,
Hranicky, Emil E. 190,
Hranicky, Emilia Mae 190,
Hranicky, Emilee (Wagner) 190,

Hranicky, Ethel 190,
Hranicky, Joe Edward 190,
Hranicky, Joseph 190,
Hranicky, Leonard Joseph [1929-2007] 190,
Hranicky, Lillian 190,
Hranicky, Michael Joseph [1966-] 190,
Hranicky, Patricia Nolen 190,
Hranicky, Phyllis 190,
Hubbard, Jolinta [1952-] 40,
Huffman, Clark 137,
Huis, Kathy 131,
Hulbert, Scott Charles [1962-] 30,
Huntington, John 50,
Hurst, Linkhart 50,
Huseman, Aubrey Amelia 70,
Huseman, Brent 70,

I

Ibis, Amalia [1873-1972]164,
Ingram, Aylssa Marie [2004-] 198,
Ingram, Shawna Marie [1989-] 198,
Ingram, Steve Todd [1966-] 198,
Irwin, Kristi Kay [1969-] 93, 94,
Isaax, Clifford 52,
Iveland, Orville Mr. 196,
Iveland, Orville Mrs. 196,
Iverson, Carl Drake [1941-] 30,
Iverson, Courtney Rae [1984-] 30,
Iverson, Cory Dean [1961-] 30,
Iverson, Cynthia Rae (McBride) [1963-] 30,
Iverson, Julie Lynn [1964-] 30,
Iverson, Kyle Drake [1987-] 30,
Iverson, Opal (Drake) 30,
Iverson, Sylvia Martha (Anderson) [1940-] 30,
Iverson, Wallace 30,

J

Jacobson, Robert Mrs. 198,
Jäger, Dr. 35,
Jaeger, Rudolf H. 190,
Jatrielei, Maria 71,
Jamieson, G. H. 50,
Jenkins, Barbara [1950-] 38, 39,
Jerke, Christina 152,
Jeschke, Jodi 38,
Jeschke, Keaton Ryan [2006-] 38,
Jobbins, James 42, 43,
Johnson, Dinah Marie [2006-] 37,
Johnson, Helena [1979-] 87,
Johnson, H. W. 42, 43,
Johnson, Neida Marie (Schooler)[1974-] 37,
Johnson, Nora G. [2006-] 37,
Johnson, Robert William 37,
Jones, George 67,
Jones, Helen 67,
Jordon, Melinda [1975-] 120,
Jordon, Taylor [1993-] 120,
Jordon, Trenton [1994-] 120,
Jorgenson, Juliana D. [1828-1911] 26,
Jssenhusth, Franklin 73,
Juhnke, Evan Michael [1987-] 191,
Juhnke, Paige Justine [1989-] 191,
Juhnke, Todd Allen [1959-] 191,
Juhnke, May Dene Bialas [1959-] 191,
Juhnke, Neal Patrick [2002-] 191,
Jurgensen, Anna Catharina [1892-1965] 8, 9,

Jurgensen, Friedrich Wilhelm "William" [1894-1940] 8, 9,
Jurgensen, Johann Heinrich [1897-1943] 8, 9,
Jurgensen, Martha Wilhelmina [1890-1961] 8, 9,
Jurgensen, Anna Rosina (Sperlich)[1872-1921] 8, 9,
Jurgensen, Wilhelm H. [1985-1901] 8, 9,
Jurgensen, Wilhelmina Marie [1891-1905] 8,

K

Kafka, Branawen Schmidt [2000-] 69,
Kafka, Erik [1980-] 69,
Kafka, Natalie (Schmidt)[1975-] 69,
Kahler, Chrissy 84,
Kaiser Wilhelm I 2,
Kammerer, Gene Mrs. 137,
Karsällt, Julius von 35,
Kaubone, Hazel B. 27,
Kaufman, Deborah[1950-] 94,
Kaufman, Menno Mrs. 173,
Kemersine, G. L. 32,
Kennedy, Sarah Danielle [1985-] 87, 88,
Kerkeide, Laurie Jo [1969-]175, 176,
Kettner, David Rev. 83,
Khumer, Albert J. 198,
Kiemke, Margareta 22, 23,
Kiggins, Austin 69,
Kiggins, Autumn 69,
Kiggins, Brian Campbell [1991-] 69,
Kiggins, Jeanette Lillian [1972-] 69,
Kiggins, Jeremiah 69,
Kiggins, Julie [1994-] 69,
Kiggins, Mavis 68,
Kiggins, Mavis Jean [1947-] 68,
Kiggins, Michael Ray [1972-] 69,
Kiggins, Morgan 69,
Kiggins, Rhonda Jean 69,
Kiggins, Ronald 68,
Kiggins, Ronald J. [1941-] 69,
Kiggins, Ronald John 69,
Kiggins, Tamara 69,
Kiggins, Walter Allen [1970-] 69,
Kiggins, Walter L. 69,
Kimmons, Debra Jane 129,
Kimura, Mike 125,
Kimura, Virginia Rae (Zirpel)(Allen)[1973-]125,
King, Barbara Ann (Semmler) (Schooler) [1948-]37,
King, John Thomas [1978-] 37,
King, John William [1947-] 37,
Kiok, Daniel 16, 20,
Kirchhevel, Arnold 140, 141,
Kirchhevel, Arnold (Delores) Mrs.135,
Kirchhevel, Delores 140, 141,
Kirk, Rebecca L. (Pratt) (Milligan) [1965-] 113,
Kirk, Robert J. [1963-] 113,
Kiuper, H. H. 198,
Koda (a dog) 92,
Koehn, Carola 211,
Koehn, Walter L. 9, 11, 48, 55, 71, 102, 104, 178, 179, 187, 192, 201,
Kogel, Birdie J. 184,
Kogoo, Edwin Rev. 190,
Konarik;, Phil 190,
Konrad, Jamie Lyn [1993-] 98,
Konrad, Lance John [1970-] 97, 98,
Konrad, Lane John [1996-] 97, 98,

233

Reimnitz, Ann Marie [1967-] 84,
Reimnitz, Darlene Marie [1945-] 80, 82,
Reimnitz, Doris 85,
Reimnitz, Dorothy M. 80,
Reimnitz, Ethan Samuel [2009-] 88,
Reimnitz, George 81, 209,
Reimnitz, George A. 80,
Reimnitz, George R. 80,
Reimnitz, Herbert 211,
Reimnitz, John William [1963-] 80, 81, 82, 88, 89,
Reimnitz, Jordon Samuel [1983-] 87, 88,
Reimnitz, Judy 89,
Reimnitz, Judy Ellen [1950-] 80, 85,
Reimnitz, Kaitlin Anne 88, 89,
Reimnitz, Kevin John [1992-] 88, 89,
Reimnitz, Lacey Jean [1992-] 87,
Reimnitz, Larry Leonard [1947-] 79, 80, 81, 82, 84, 85,
    88,
Reimnitz, Lauryn Marie [2005-] 88,
Reimnitz, Lena 211,
Reimnitz, Lena Louise [1890-1968] 80,
Reimnitz, Leonard Gottlieb Adolf [1922-2003] 79, 80,
    81, 82, 85, 87, 88,
Reimnitz, Lindsey Marie [1984-] 87,
Reimnitz, Louis 81,
Reimnitz, Louis E. 80,
Reimnitz, Lydia 209,
Reimnitz, Lydia E. 80,
Reimnitz, Lynn Dianne [1941-] 82, 85, 88,
Reimnitz, Nancy Jean (Scholten) [1956-] 87, 88,
Reimnitz, Paul 81,
Reimnitz, Paul D. 80,
Reimnitz, Paul Robert [1890-1967] 79, 80,
Reimnitz, Robert L. 80,
Reimnitz, Sallie Rose [1952-] 80, 81, 88,
Reimnitz, Samuel Paul [1956-] 80, 81, 87, 88,
Reimnitz, Sarah Danielle (Kennedy) [1985-] 87, 88,
Reimnitz, Seth Cameron [1989-] 87,
Reimnitz, Stephanie Anne (Olsen) [1966-] 82, 88, 89,
Reimnitz, Trevor Allen [1994-] 88, 89,
Reimnitz, Wilma Norma (Zirpel) [1925-] 75,79, 80, 81,
    82, 85, 87, 88,
Reimpfer, Christian 50,
Reiner, Alice 150,
Reinhold, Rev. 105,
Renshaw, David Lee [1944-] 79, 85, 88,
Renshaw, Judy 84,
Renshaw, Judy Ellen (Reimnitz)[1950-] 79, 81, 82, 85,
    88,
Renshaw, Melinda Sue [1971– 1971] 85, 86,
Renshaw, Shannon 88,
Renshaw, Shannon Lee [1969-] 85,
Renshaw, Teresa Marie [1974-1974] 85, 86,
Renshaw, Travis Howard [1970-] 85, 86,
Rethel, U. 35,
Reuland, Charles H. 179
Reynolds, Andrea 62,
Rhode, Daniel 41,
Rhode, Maria 41,
Rice, Amy 186,
Riecke, Albert 26, 68,
Riecke, Albert Wilhelm [1916-1984] 49, 50, 51, 53, 208,
Riecke, Anna Catherine (Shottinger)[1853-1912] 20, 21,
    22,

Riecke, August 51,
Riecke, Bernice (Vreugdenhil) [1926-1996] 67, 68, 69,
    208,
Riecke, Bertha Rosina [1888-1968] 20, 21, 22,
Riecke, Brenda Lynn [1964-] 67,
Riecke, Carl August [1892-] 21, 22,
Riecke, Clara Elsie [1923-1987] 50, 51, 61,
Riecke, Doreen Faye [1953-] 67, 69,
Riecke, Elsie 55,
Riecke, Emma Bertha (Zirpel) [1893-1962] 20, 22, 48,
    49, 50, 51, 52, 53, 54, 61, 67, 72, 203, 204, 208,
Riecke, Emma Bertha Mrs. 202,
Riecke, Erna 55, 68,
Riecke, Erna Rosina [1950-] 53,
Riecke, Esther Frieda [1918-1920] 49, 50, 51, 68,
Riecke, George 22,
Riecke, George Gilbert [1928-2010] 50, 51, 68, 69, 208,
Riecke, George Peter [1886-1958] 21, 22, 25, 48, 49, 50,
    51, 52, 53, 54, 61, 67, 68, 72, 203, 208,
Riecke, Georgia Sue [1955-] 67, 69,
Riecke, Gloria Kaye [1945-] 67, 208,
Riecke, infant daughter 48,
Riecke, Johann Frederich [1822-1907] 26,
Riecke, John Fredrick [1883-] 20, 21,
Riecke, Juliana D. (Jorgenson) [1823-1911]20, 21,
Riecke, Margaret [1890-] 21,
Riecke, Martin 26,
Riecke, Mavis Jean [1947-] 67, 69, 208,
Riecke, Peter George [1853-1918] 21, 22, 25, 30, 48,
    51,
Riecke, Sophia Alvina Elisabeth [1914-1996] 49, 50, 51,
    52, 72,
Riecke, Viola Alma Elizabeth [1921-1987] 50, 51, 53,
    54, 210,
Riecke, William 51,
Riecke, William F. [1884-] 21, 22,
Roberts, Doris 124,
Roberts, D. P. 15,
Roberts, Laurie Rose [1953-] 124,
Roberts, Merle 124,
Rockrohr, Carl Rev. 99, 190,
Roe, Jason Gehn [1971-] 32,
Roe, Jennifer Marie (Anderson) (Rother) 32,
Roesler, August C. Pastor 129, 137,
Roheck, P. E. 52,
Rooney, John F. 30,
Ross, Lynn 197,
Ross, Robt. W. 15, 16,
Roth, Amalia (Ibis)[1873-1972] 164,
Roth, Arnold 165, 166,
Roth, Carol Ann [1963-]165,166,
Roth, Carla Jean [1961-1970]165, 166, 167, 168, 173,
Roth, Clifford 165,
Roth, Clifford E. 140, 157, 159,
Roth, Clifford Edwin [1937-]164, 165, 166, 168, 171,
    197,
Roth, Clifford Mr. 137,
Roth, Clifford Mrs. 137,
Roth, Clifford (Rosalene) Mrs. 118,
Roth, Cynthia Rose [1958-]165, 166, 171,
Roth, Darin Lee [1967-]165, 166, 167, 168, 171,
Roth, Elsie (Sedlezky)[1912-2006] 164, 165, 166, 168,
Roth, Gaylen Clifford [1960-] 114, 165, 166, 168, 171,
Roth, George 163, 164,